D0078759

Antony and Cleopatra

GARLAND SHAKESPEARE BIBLIOGRAPHIES
VOLUME 27
GARLAND REFERENCE LIBRARY OF THE HUMANITIES
VOLUME 1786

Garland Shakespeare Bibliographies

William Godshalk, *Series Editor*

Hamlet in the 1960s
compiled by Julia Dietrich

The Taming of the Shrew
compiled by Nancy Lenz Harvey

King John
compiled by Deborah T. Curren-Aquino

Henry IV, Parts 1 and 2
compiled by Catherine Gira and Adele Seeff

Antony and Cleopatra
compiled by Yashdip S. Bains

Antony and Cleopatra
An Annotated Bibliography

Yashdip S. Bains

Garland Publishing, Inc.
A member of the Taylor & Francis Group
New York and London
1998

Library of Congress Cataloging-in-Publication Data

Bains, Y. S.
Antony and Cleopatra : an annotated bibliography / by Yashdip S. Bains.
p. cm. — (Garland Shakespeare bibliographies ; v. 27) (Garland reference library of the humanities ; vol. 1786)
Includes index.
ISBN 0-8153-1474-4 (case : alk. paper)
1. Shakespeare, William, 1564–1616. Antony and Cleopatra—Bibliography. 2. Cleopatra, Queen of Egypt, d. 30 B.C.—In literature—Bibliography. 3. Antonius, Marcus, 83?–30 B.C.—In literature—Bibliography. 4. Egypt—In literature—Bibliography. 5. Rome—In literature—Bibliography. I. Title. II. Series: Garland Shakespeare bibliographies ; no. 27. III. Series: Garland reference library of the humanities ; vol. 1786.
Z8812.A68B35 1998
[PR2802]
016.8223'3—dc21 98-29860
CIP

Printed on acid-free, 250-year-life paper
Manufactured in the United States of America

Dedicated to the memory of

Hardial Bains
and
Margaret Jenckes

Contents

General Editor's Preface

In 1978 Lawrence Davidow, the Acquisitions Editor at Garland Publishing, invited me to edit a series of annotated bibliographies surveying Shakespeare scholarship published from 1940 until the present. Major contributions published before that period would also be included. We planned that each bibliography would be as comprehensive as possible, fully annotated, cross-referenced, and thoroughly indexed. Each would be divided into major sections that indicate the dominant critical and scholarly concerns of the play being discussed; these large divisions would be subdivided if such subdivision might be useful to the reader. The general format would thus have to remain flexible so that the form of each bibliography could reflect its contents. Although the authors would be presented with copies of our "Tentative Guidelines," we rejected a rigorous conformity to a style sheet in favor of humane, scholarly decisions based on individual perceptions and requirements. We desired a fairly uniform series of high quality, but we did not want to stifle creative initiative.

We emphasized that we wished complete surveys of current knowledge and critical opinion presented in such a way that the reader could retrieve that information rapidly and easily. To help the reader sift through large quantities of material, each bibliography would contain an Introduction that would trace briefly the history of recent criticism and research, as well as indicate new areas to be explored, if such areas had become apparent during the author's work on the project. Finally, the Introduction would make clear any special decisions made or procedures followed by the author in compiling and ordering his or her bibliography.

These were our plans, which now come to fruition in the individual bibliographies of the plays. We wish to thank all those who made this series possible, especially Ralph Carlson, Pam Chergotis, and Julia Johnson. Perhaps, however, our greatest thanks must go to the authors themselves, who, during the frequent meetings of the Garland Shakespeare Authors, came to act as a board of editors. Many of the most difficult questions confronting the series were raised and answered at those meetings. And, of course, we must acknowledge with thanks the hard work that went into the compiling, reading, and writing done by our authors.

W.L. Godshalk

Introduction

The terms of Shakespearean studies have generally been determined by the literary, intellectual and social climate of any period. One might speak of a Neoclassical Shakespeare, a Romantic, a Victorian, and so on. The concerns of one age become irrelevant and redundant in another. *Antony and Cleopatra* has aroused strong reactions among scholars because of its unconventional structure and the moral nature of its principal characters. It has also appealed to many admirers of Shakespeare's imitation of nature.

In 1664, Margaret Cavendish emphasized how Shakespeare "had been transformed into every one of those persons he hath described." Nahum Tate described Shakespeare as "a most diligent spy upon Nature" who "traced her through her darkest recesses." Nicholas Rowe and Charles Gildon, who were the first ones to object to the plot and the large number of scenes and geographical range of *Antony and Cleopatra*, acknowledged that what compensated for this "carelessness" were "the manners of his characters" which are "proper to the persons represented." Some of their contemporaries characterized the play as "the hasty production of a true Dramatick Genius." John Upton even found a link between Antony's "Asiatic manner of speaking" and the playwright's "own temper."

Since the late seventeenth century, scholars have investigated Shakespeare's use of his sources in classical literature. Gerard Langbaine was the first to name Shakespeare's sources in Plutarch and Appian, and Charles Gildon also commented on the playwright's reliance on Plutarch. The comparisons between the finished play and Shakespeare's sources have focused on his dramatic transformation of the prosaic writing into a magnificent poetic play.

One of the prominent features of the critical response to *Antony and Cleopatra* up to the 1920s has been the qualified praise, an unwillingness to admit it to the greats of tragedy, and a strained effort to speak in its favor. Samuel Johnson, Samuel Taylor Coleridge, and A.C. Bradley represent a consensus of opinion that everyone has to contend with. Some of the staunch supporters of the play try to avoid their questions by dismissing them as inconsequential. The same hesitation can be found in the play's standing in stage history. Most directors treat it as a problem because of its loose and unwieldy structure and the large number of characters. This attitude of scholars and directors has changed since the 1920s, when critics have presented coherent studies of the play in opposition to Johnson, Coleridge and Bradley.

Shakespeare's disregard of classical unities and mixture of genres offended Samuel Johnson and others in the eighteenth century. Johnson stresses that Shakespeare had constructed a rambling plot "without any art of connection or care of disposition." But he also states how "this play keeps curiosity always busy, and the passions always interested." Still, it was Dryden's classically sound version which dominated the stage well into the nineteenth century. This indicates that there have been two Shakespeares since the Restoration and the eighteenth century—one for the reading public and one for the audiences.

The characters of Antony and Cleopatra have divided critics on the basis of moral issues. Dr. Johnson did not like the "low" feminine arts "which distinguish Cleopatra." But Thomas Davies found a nobility of spirit in Cleopatra and commended her manner of death which raised her in his esteem. George Steevens recommended to his contemporary women Cleopatra's "variety of accomplishments" which would make them attractive to men. These irreconcilable views interested most writers in the nineteenth century.

The terms of discourse changed in the romantic period when critics began to stress the organic unity of the plot and an ambiguous unfolding of events and the difficulty of passing judgment on the lovers. Despite his dislike for the play's rambling structure, Schlegel was fascinated by Cleopatra's "seductive charms" and by "the splendour" of Antony's actions: "As they die for each other, we forgive them for having lived for each other." Coleridge commended it for its "happy valiancy of style" and singled it out as perhaps "the most wonderful" of all his plays and "a formidable rival" of the four great tragedies. Hazlitt labelled it as "the finest of his historical plays, that is, of those in which he made poetry the organ of history." But neither Coleridge nor Hazlitt would endorse it without reservations.

As the nineteenth century progressed, Cleopatra became a troublesome figure to some and admirable to others. Augustine Skottowe identifies Cleopatra's "licentiousness" as "the link which binds her to the heart of Antony." Anna Brownell Jameson is attracted to Cleopatra because in her "all anomalous shapes and impossible and wild combinations of form are woven together in regular confusion and harmonious discord," which makes her "the living woman herself, when she existed upon this earth." Cleopatra's contradictions made her human and worthy of sympathy. But these contradictory qualities are also the source of audiences' ambivalence towards the play and its main characters. As Hartley Coleridge summed it up, "perhaps both Antony and Cleopatra are too heroic to be pitied for weakness, and too viciously foolish to be admired for their heroism."

There is disagreement among critics about the general themes of the play. For G.G. Gervinus, the play is about the impossibility of reconciling the world of politics with that of sensuality. Hiram Corson calls it Shakespeare's "grandest production," with "the moral interest predominating over the historical or political." Harley Granville-Barker argues that the play's theme is "the wider ruin" in the Roman world brought about by Antony's personal downfall. E.K. Chambers considers that the play's main idea is "passion as the ruin of greatness." The argument goes that if Shakespeare had wanted his audience to pass a favorable judgment on Antony and Cleopatra, he would have delineated the lovers as noble superhuman figures, and no questions would be asked about their moral guilt or innocence.

Antony's warmth and vigor counterbalance his sin of self-indulgence. From this perspective, the play may be a moralistic warning against intemperance and dissipation. Edward Dowden says that the spirit of the play is "essentially severe." William Winter postulates that "mortal delight in mortal love" is doomed. Antony is a man of only "seeming greatness and seeming nobleness." John Heraud, on the other hand, elevates Antony and Cleopatra to the stature of superhuman figures who are "the very deities of love." For A.C. Swinburne, Shakespeare has created in Cleopatra "the perfect and the everlasting woman."

Bernard Shaw fueled the debate about Cleopatra's character at the turn of the century by insisting that she is a whore and not a tragic figure; her change of personality in the fifth act of the play is totally unconvincing. Bradley emphasized "her spirit of fire and air" which "makes her wonderful and sovereign." Cleopatra emerges as a tragic figure only after Antony's death and undergoes a transformation. R.H. Case takes up the question of Cleopatra's suicide and suggests that "something apparently stronger than her love for Antony yet, perhaps, connected with it—her royal determination to endure no bonds nor ignominy—seems to transform Cleopatra after his death and to allow that passion to gain depth and dignity under powerful shelter." L.L. Schücking developed a theory of two Cleopatras in the play, but H.H. Furness, E.E. Stoll, Derek Traversi and others have defended the consistency of Shakespeare's characterization.

Early twentieth-century critics have disagreed as much over Antony's character as over that of Cleopatra. Bernard Shaw "can't feel any sympathy with Antony after he runs away disgracefully from the battle of Actium because Cleopatra did." Shaw dislikes Shakespeare's portrayal of love because, "after giving a faithful picture of the soldier broken down by debauchery, and the typical wanton in whose arms such men perish, Shakespeare finally strains all his huge command of rhetoric and stage pathos to give a theatrical sublimity to the wretched end of the business, and to persuade foolish spectators that the world was well lost by the twain." Bradley, however, treats Antony both as a strumpet's fool and as a tragic figure.

Writing in the tradition of Samuel Johnson and Samuel Taylor Coleridge, A.C. Bradley reiterated the aesthetic limitations of the play and excluded it from the the group of the great four tragedies. He justified his decision by saying that *Antony and Cleopatra* does not meet his criteria for tragedy; "the tragic emotions are stirred in the fullest possible measure only when such beauty or nobility of character is displayed as commands unreserved admiration or love; or when, in default of this, the forces which move the agents, and the conflict which results from these forces, attain a terrifying and overwhelming power." This play does not have anything "terrible or piteous"; for a tragedy, "it is not painful."

Critical opinion began to turn in favor of *Antony and Cleopatra* gradually with the perceptive analyses of Granville-Barker, G. Wilson Knight, and Derek Traversi, who addressed afresh the questions of plot, theme, and language. Their studies have led to the work of Julian Markels, Janet Adelman, and J. Leeds Barroll, to mention a few of the prominent scholars. The most notable trend in the interpretation of this play is the displacement of traditional criticism by the exponents of theory. The movement from Bradley's character studies to critical theory encompasses the twentieth century.

Granville-Barker challenged Bradley by conceding that this play "may lack the spiritual intimacy of *Hamlet*, the mysterious power of *Macbeth*, the nobilities of *Othello*, may reach neither to the heights nor depths of *King Lear*; but it has a magnificence and a magic all its own, and Shakespeare's eye swept no wider horizon." He comments in detail on the fluid and seamless nature of the plot. He points out that Shakespeare "neither takes nor uses his material haphazardly. If, with one dramatic aim, he frees himself from ties of place, with another he creates for himself ties of time." Granville-Barker brings out Shakespeare's realistic touches. "From wantonness, trickery and folly," Shakespeare seeks to raise Cleopatra "to a noble end. But, even in doing it, he shirks no jot of the truth about her."

G. Wilson Knight begins by identifying the unifying symbols and poetry of the play. In this play "our whole vision is condensed, crystallized in these single delineations of our two protagonists, both strongly idealized, ablaze with impossible beauty or infinite in majesty and power." Shakespeare blends the finite and the infinite, and so also "element everywhere blended, mated, with element, sun with earth or water with air, giving birth to the 'strange serpent' of Nile, or the strange forms of 'hail', 'snow', or evanescent and multiform cloud." Knight examines the imagery and figurative language to explore different themes: "first, the theme of imperial magnificence, the imperial power and warrior-honour Antony sacrifices for love; second, the more physical and sensuous love-themes and love-imagery in dialogue and suggestion; third, the natural and elemental symbolisms, in their suggestion of the mating of elements, and also, in their varying from the material to the ethereal, reflecting and blending with our love-theme; and, finally, the more spiritual and transcendental elements in this love-theme itself." Knight exposed the limitations of Bradley's preoccupation with character and pointed out the profundity of the playwright's insights in the play.

Traversi asks if *Antony and Cleopatra* is "a tragedy of lyrical inspiration, justifying love by presenting it as triumphant over death," or if it is "rather a remorseless exposure of human frailties, a presentation of spiritual possibilities dissipated through a senseless surrender to passion." He sees these points "less as contradictory than complementary aspects of unified artistic creation." According to Traversi, "Rottenness becomes the ground for fertility, opulence becomes royalty, infatuation turns into transcendent passion, all by means of an organic process which ignores none of its own earlier stages, which, while never denying the validity of the realistic estimates of the situations which accompany it to the last, integrates these in the more ample unity of its creative process." Bradley and many of his predecessors would have been shocked by this approach.

In recent years, scholars have moved beyond moralistic evaluations of Antony and Cleopatra and elaborated the nature of their experience in love. Reuben A. Brower takes a highly rational view of the two: "In Antony nobility is seen in its most complete form, at times glorified by love, at times debased by it, or defeated by a failure of the self. In Cleopatra love rises to nobility, and though Antony's failure is not brushed over, her vision and death renew our certainty of his greatness, and beyond that our certainty that greatness, though inherently tragic, is attainable." Similarly, S.L. Bethell recognizes in Cleopatra "a paradoxical figure in whom seemingly opposite qualities are fused, and her role as a symbolic representation of immortal love and beauty." John Dover Wilson underlines the pertinence of their experience for the audiences: "There is an ennoblement and a purification through suffering: an ennoblement for the tragic protagonists; a purification for us the spectators who share in their suffering vicariously and in their triumphant reconciliation." Donald A. Stauffer feels that Shakespeare "takes the classical tragic theme—the conflict between love and duty—and treats it romantically."

Critics have also recognized the grandeur of Antony and Cleopatra's passion for one another and wondered whether or not Shakespeare portrays the protagonists' love as transcendent over worldly considerations. Arthur Quiller-Couch saw in Antony and Cleopatra two "transcendent" figures who are "great as the gods are great." John Middleton Murry gives a biblical reading of some of the scenes by comparing Antony and his attendants with Christ and His disciples at the Last Supper.

A large number of studies have altered the direction of analysis from the Victorian or Bradleyan firmness about character and morality and brought out the paradoxical and other aspects of the play. Julian Markels, Janet Adelman, and J. Leeds Barroll will suffice as three examples of new directions in the reading of *Antony and Cleopatra.* Markels argues that the play forces the audience to hold "poised in our minds two morally contradictory actions" that "transform all moral actions into postures which become not false poses but the protean forms of life." Shakespeare "has made us amoral, in order to produce at last an imaginative experience of omniscience to accompany the experience of timelessness." Markels reveals the limitations of the moral outlook of the many critics who saw everything in either/or terms. He accepts Antony's transcendence as absolute and unqualified in his refusal to choose between "public and private values."

Janet Adelman exposes the one-sidedness of much criticism when she asks a question about which one to believe: "Critics who wish Antony and Cleopatra to fit Shakespeare's normal tragic mold (if they can decide what it is) will tend to stress the primacy of character and action; those who wish to assimilate the play to the romances will stress the claims of the poetry." This play is "essentially a tragic experience embedded in a comic structure": "In that sense it is as treacherous and painful as life itself: each of us has moments in which we experience our lives with a tragic concentration and intensity; but each of us must know that these moments can equally well be experienced as comic, if seen from the perspective of the varying shore." This play is a paradox, which is based on the skepticism of the post-war years. Adelman shows the discrepancy between poetry and romantic events heightened by paradox and hyperbole.

Barroll situates Shakespeare and this play in the western tradition of tragedy. He argues that "the world of the tragic vision requires the presence of embracing ordinances. These natural or supernatural imperatives are crucial, for they are the efforts of dramatic art to make man's world something more than meaningless. If we just obeyed such cosmic Laws, tragedy argues, then perhaps life could avoid disaster." The tragic view is the "warp and woof of Western civilization with its continually urgent need to explain catastrophe and sudden death as part of some sane scheme of existence."

Barroll makes a distinction between major and minor characters. "Those figures who have been called 'minor'—the Eroses—have no personality, while the 'major' figures are conceived as imitated personalities." Barroll proposes that "some kind of rule prohibits us from thinking of Eros as a person with complex motives," and Caesar also falls into this category. Shakespeare "had to shape his imagining of human beings according to the rigorous demands of an art composed only in part of a psychological and philosophical tradition concerning the nature of man. The other part demanded the creation of fictive lives in human beings standing on a stage."

Another prominent change in post-war interpretations has been effected by the gradual shift from Practical Criticism and American New Criticism to the concerns of critical theory. Unlike the New Critics, who studied literature as a universe in itself, the advocates of theory have stressed the recognition of ideology as a formative influence in literary judgment. No reader is so "self-contained" that he or she can derive eternal truths from a time-bound text. Literary works like *Antony and Cleopatra* cannot be revered as containers of universal truths about the human condition, which can be tapped at any time to replenish the sagging spirit. *Antony and Cleopatra* does not contain a single meaning which can be mined and packaged for the reader who wants to learn the truths about love and politics lying at its heart. The advocates of theory want to make the reader conscious of his ideology and its role in the production and dissemination of literature. Similarly, they try to examine the play in the context of different social and individual conflicts in Tudor and twentieth-century Englands. There is a direct connection between an awareness of one's ideology and the determinants of one's readings.

It is not possible to give here a comprehensive view of the changes in criticism wrought by theory, but a few examples of the studies of *Antony and Cleopatra* in the context of ideology and criticism illustrate their perceptiveness as well as controversial nature. Shakespeare cannot be detached from history, nor can the reader of his plays. Terry Eagleton has underlined this point: "What we judge in the plays as relevant, what we actually see, is shaped by what we see in our own culture, in ourselves." Hence he says that *Antony and Cleopatra* "explores one response to the problem of reconciling authentic and responsible living, a response in which one aspect of the dilemma is taken, chosen, and lived to the full tragic affirmation." This gives the reader "a new insight into the depth of authentic life which has to be part of any attempt to make this life responsible, to put it back within society." A play exists in a specific context of time and means something to the audiences in that climate of ideology.

Linda Fitz deals more polemically with a view to display the sexist angle of men who masquerade as "universal" human beings in search of "truth." Plays like *Antony and Cleopatra* have been absorbed by men to suit their patriarchal needs. In fact, "male critics feel personally threatened by Cleopatra and what she represents to them." Male critics say that "Cleopatra cannot be understood," which is related to their "notion that women in general are impossible for men to understand."

A play about love cannot be understood as one about universal love and desire. Several critics have raised crucial questions about differences between man and woman, between male and female psyches, and their impact on the pursuit of power in history. There is no consensus among scholars about these issues, but they are drawing attention to the need for re-examining the texts. Barbara Vincent contends that Cleopatra is the "prime desirer in the play" who generates a heroic identity for Antony and also a world "which encompasses tragedy and is only made the loftier for it, which grows the more by reaping." This play, according to Vincent, embodies a theory which "could be characterised as comic because desire plays a greater role in creating the reality of the play than allegiance to an objectively realistic vision."

Marilyn French may be cited here as one who postulates some essential and irreducible difference between male and female and who defines tragedy as the result of a conflict between the two. Cleopatra became "the outlaw feminine principle"; she challenged the authority of Rome which had expected its women like Octavia to be models of the "in-law feminine principle." This awareness affects one's traditional response to the play.

Jonathan Dollimore has broadened the definition of desire and pointed out that desire, "far from transcending the power relations which structure relations which structure this society, is wholly in-formed by them." The contradictions at the heart of Jacobean culture have influenced the playwright, and the questions of power are a formative influence on the reader in the twentieth century. Dollimore explains an "aspect of the contradiction which defines Antony: his sexuality is informed by the very power relations which he, ambivalently, is prepared to sacrifice for sexual freedom; correspondingly, the heroic *virtus* which he wants to reaffirm in and through Cleopatra is in fact almost entirely a function of the power structure which he, again ambivalently, is prepared to sacrifice for her."

Ania Loomba has studied the same text with the relationships between race, gender and patriarchy on her mind. "Roman patriarchy demonises Cleopatra by defining her world as private (Antony is no longer a serious general by entering it); as female (Egypt robs Antony and his soldiers of their manhood); and as barbaric (Antony is now a slave of gypsies)." She discusses the play as "a narrative of masculinity and imperialism" in which there is "a politics of sublimation rather than a transcendence of politics."

Jyotsna Singh has suggested another line of enquiry by discussing the links between femininity and theatricality which, "as embodied in Cleopatra, function specifically both to reveal and to subvert the existing ideology of order by which traditional sexual and social hierarchies were held in place." She argues that "no identity is fixed and immutable, and that agents of representation on the Renaissance public stage could freely take on identities that transgress boundaries of gender and hierarchy."

Like its critical history, the stage history of *Antony and Cleopatra* has been full of attempts to tame Shakespeare and to present him to the public either in the classical garb made for him by Dryden or in a sequence cut and pasted together by a director according to his own conception of the play's theme and characters. Versions of Dryden and Shakespeare dominated the stage from Restoration to the middle of the nineteenth century. The directorial versions of the play have been the bill of fare since Samuel Phelps's attempts to restore Shakespeare's text. Instead of mixing Dryden and Shakespeare, Phelps and his successors have created their own versions freely. For this reason, directorial concepts of the play reflect the shifting social and political values of the nineteenth and twentieth centuries. In this sense, directors generally mount "politically correct" and socially acceptable scenes.

On the basis of a comparative analysis of performances by Helen Faucit, Mrs. Siddons, Isabella Glyn, Mrs. Cora Potter, Sarah Bernhardt, Lillie Langtry and Fannie Davenport, Doris Adler has suggested that "the nature and attributes of Cleopatra are associated in the communal mind or imagination with a particular physical configuration and a particular mode of dress. An audience in a particular time knows how Cleopatra must look and accepts only those realized images that match that knowledge." Hence a successful rendering of Cleopatra is a "mysterious and irrational act of discovering that the audience knows must be there, but only recognizes when it appears." The same is true of the stage images of Antony or the scenic designs of Rome and Egypt and the luxuries of Cleopatra's court. This process of transformation can be substantiated from contemporary reviews of productions.

Most scholars agree that *Antony and Cleopatra* was written about 1606-1607, and its text in the Folio does not present any serious problems. I am least satisfied with the section entitled "Editions," because many of the single-volume editions are difficult to find. "The Stage History" in my bibliography does not claim to be thorough. Full coverage of theatrical biographies and autobiographies, productions and reviews would be so large that it would be impractical, but the main lines of the play's history are clear. The list of "Major Productions" gives some idea of the notable English and American stagings of the past century or so. "Films," "Television," and "Music" sections are not exhaustive because this play has been infrequently treated by movie producers and composers. I have included only those studies of films, television and music which discuss the play. "Translations" are listed, mainly of single-volume editions, without annotation. "Teaching Aids" is a list of materials that are useful for the teaching of this play. I have not seen or heard most of the items included. In recent years there has been an increase in electronic and other media for the improvement of teaching, and these materials are so extensive that they deserve to be covered separately. "The Index" is limited to names of authors, editors, directors, actors and composers.

This bibliography covers scholarship and criticism of *Antony and Cleopatra* from 1940 to 1995. Some of the significant items before 1940 and after 1995 have also been included. My primary bibliographical sources are the annual listings in *Shakespeare Quarterly*, *PMLA* and *Shakespeare Jahrbuch*. I have deliberately mentioned some of the studies of *Antony and Cleopatra* in Japanese because a great deal of work is being done on Shakespeare in Japan.

I am grateful to Bill Godshalk, Nancy Harvey and Eric Sams for their advice in dealing with various problems. I thank for their assistance the staff of the University of Cincinnati Libraries, Dr. Susan Brock and the Shakespeare Institute Library of the University of Birmingham, The Folger Shakespeare Library, The British Library, and University of Toronto Robarts Library. Gary Cox has given me technical help in using the software. The pre-press section of New

Concept, Toronto, has formatted my manuscript. I am most grateful to my wife, Norma Jenckes, whose encouragement and support have enabled me to complete my study.

Yashdip S. Bains
University of Cincinnati
October 9, 1997

Antony and Cleopatra

Criticism

1 Brathwait, Richard. *The English Gentleman*. 1631. Reprinted in *Shakespeare: Antony and Cleopatra*. Ed. John Russell Brown. A Casebook. London: Macmillan, 1968, p.25.

The relationship between Cleopatra and Mark Antony "promised to itself as much secure freedom as fading fancy could tender; yet the last scene closed all those comic passages with a tragic conclusion."

2 Cavendish, Margaret. "Letter CXXIII." *CCXI Sociable Letters*. 1664. Reprinted in *Shakespeare Criticism. A Selection: 1623-1840*. Ed. D. Nichol Smith. World's Classics. London: Oxford UP, 1916, pp. 13-15.

Cavendish praises Shakespeare for having "expressed in his plays all sorts of persons, as one would think he had been transformed into every one of those persons he hath described." She mentions Antony and Cleopatra as two examples of this quality.

3 Dryden, John. *All for Love*. 1678. *Four Tragedies*. Ed. L.A. Beaurline and Fredson Bowers. Chicago: U of Chicago P, 1967, pp. 190-279.

Playwrights after Shakespeare have sought to delineate "the excellency of the moral. For the chief persons represented were famous patterns of unlawful love; and their end accordingly was unfortunate."

4 Tate, Nahum. "To Edward Tayler." *The Loyal General*. London: Henry Bonwicke, 1680. 12, 59 pp.

Shakespeare "never touches on a Roman story, but the persons, the passages, the manners, the circumstances, the ceremonies, all are Roman." In his Antony can be found "all the defects and excellencies of his mind, a soldier, a reveller, amorous, sometimes rash, sometimes considerate, with all the various emotions of his mind." Shakespeare "was a most diligent spy upon Nature, trac'd her through her darkest recesses, pictur'd her in her just proportion and colours; in which variety 'tis impossible that all shou'd be equally pleasant, 'tis sufficient that all be proper."

5 Rowe, Nicholas. *Some Account of the Life of William Shakespeare*. 1709. Augustan Reprint Society No. 17. Los Angeles: Augustan Reprint Society, 1948. xl pp.

Most of Shakespeare's historical plays "comprehend a great length of time, and very different and distinct places;" the scenes in his *Antony and Cleopatra* cover a large territory between Rome and Egypt. But "in recompence for his carelessness in this point, when he comes to another part of the drama, the manners of his characters, in acting or speaking what is proper for them, and fit to be shown by the poet, he may be generally justified, and in very many places greatly commended."

6 Gildon, Charles. "Remarks on the Plays of Shakespear: The Argument of Antony and Cleopatra." *The Works of Mr. William Shakespear*. Ed. Nicholas Rowe. 9 vols. London, 1714, IX, 364-67.

Shakespeare covers too wide an area in the play, "seldom a line allow'd for a Passage to so great a distance." *Antony and Cleopatra* "is full of Scenes strangely broken, many of which exceed not ten Lines."

7 Upton, John. *Critical Observations on Shakespeare*. 1746. Reprint. New York: AMS, 1973. 346 pp.

Upton identifies "the Asiatic manner of speaking" in Antony, "which much resembled his own temper, being ambitious, unequal, and very rodomontage."

8 *An Examen of the New Comedy, call'd The Suspicious Husband*. London: J. Roberts, 1747.

Dryden "observed the unities in *All for Love*, but Shakespeare's play is natural without them." Shakespeare's is "the hasty Production of a true Dramatick Genius."

9 Johnson, Samuel. "*Antony and Cleopatra*." 1765. *Selections from Johnson on Shakespeare*. Ed. Bertrand H. Bronson with Jean M. O'Meara. New Haven and London: Yale UP, 1986, pp. 287-98.

While the play "keeps curiosity busy and the passions always interested," Johnson felt that "[t]he continual hurry of action, the variety of incidents, and the quick succession of one personage to another, call the mind forward without intermission from the first Act to the last." The play derives its "power of delighting" "principally from the frequent changes of the scene; for, except the feminine arts, some of which are too low, which distinguish Cleopatra, no character is very strongly discriminated."

Trying to capture the events of history, Shakespeare constructed a rambling plot "without any art of connection or care of disposition."

10 Davies, Thomas. *Dramatic Miscellanies: Consisting of Critical Observations on Several Plays of Shakespeare*. 2 vols. 1783. Reprint. New York: AMS, 1973, II, 333-70.

In comparison with other plays about Antony and Cleopatra, Shakespeare's deals with passions. It "represents more of action, character, and manners, than May's *Cleopatra* or Dryden's *All for Love*."

11 Schlegel, August W. von. *A Course of Lectures on Dramatic Arts and Literature*. Trans. John Black. 2 vols. 1815. Reprint. New York: AMS, 1965. 535 pp.

Antony "is Hercules in the chains of Omphale, drawn from the fabulous heroic ages in history, and invested with the Roman costume. The seductive arts of Cleopatra are in no respect veiled over; she is an ambiguous being made up of royal pride, female vanity, luxury, inconstancy, and true attachment."

"Although the mutual passion of herself and Antony is without moral dignity," it "still excites our sympathy as an insurmountable fascination:—they seem formed for each other, and Cleopatra is as remarkable for her seductive charms as Antony for the splendour of his deeds. As they die for each other, we forgive them for having lived for each other."

12 Coleridge, Samuel Taylor. *The Literary Remains of Samuel Taylor Coleridge*. Ed. H.N. Coleridge. London: William Pickering, 1836. *Coleridge's Shakespeare Criticism*. Ed. Thomas Middleton Raysor. 2 vols. Cambridge, MA: Harvard UP, 1930, I, 85-89.

"The highest praise or rather form of praise" Coleridge could bestow on this play "is the doubt which perusal always occasions in me, whether it is not in all exhibitions of a giant power in its strength and vigor of maturity, a formidable rival of the *Macbeth*, *Lear*, *Othello* and *Hamlet*. *Feliciter audax* is the motto for its style comparatively with his other works, even as it is the general motto of all his works compared with those of other poets. Be it remembered too, that this happy valiancy of style is but the representative and result of all the material excellencies so exprest."

Cleopatra's characterization is "profound" in "that the sense of criminality in her passion is lessened by our insight into its depth and energy, at the very moment that we cannot but perceive that the passion itself springs out of the habitual craving of a licentious nature, and that it is supported and reinforced by voluntary stimulus and sought-for associations, instead of blossoming out of spontaneous emotion."

Coleridge also called this play "the most wonderful" of "all perhaps" of his plays, for there are "scarcely any in which he has followed history more minutely, and yet few even of his own in which he impresses the notion of giant strength so much, perhaps none in which he impresses it more strongly."

13 Goethe, J.W. von. "Shakespeare und kein Ende." 1815. "Shakespeare ad Infinitum." Trans. Randolph S. Bourne. *Shakespeare in Europe*. Ed. Oswald Le Winter. Meridian Books.

Cleveland and New York: World Publishing Co., 1963, pp. 57-69.

Goethe thought that "it would be hard to find a poet each of whose works was more thoroughly pervaded by a definite and effective idea than his [Shakespeare's]." *Antony and Cleopatra* expresses the idea that "pleasure and action are ever incompatible." In reading Shakespeare, one would always discover "new cause for astonishment and admiration."

14 Hazlitt, William. *Characters of Shakespeare's Plays.* London: C. H. Reynell for R. Hunter, 1817. *The Complete Works*. Ed. P. P. Howe. Centenary Edition. 21 vols. London: Dent, 1930, IV, 228-32

Antony and Cleopatra is "the finest of his historical plays, that is, of those in which he made poetry the organ of history, and assumed a certain tone of character and sentiment, in conformity to known facts, instead of trusting to his observation of general nature or to the unlimited indulgence of his own fancy."

Antony's scene with Eros is the most overwhelming: "The splendour of the imagery, the semblance of reality, the lofty range of picturesque objects hanging over the world, their evanescent nature, the total uncertainty of what is left behind, are just like the mouldering schemes of human greatness."

15 Skottowe, Augustine. *The Life of Shakespeare.* 2 vols. London: Longman, 1824, II, 231-44.

"The licentiousness of Cleopatra," according to Skottowe, "is the link which binds her to the heart of Antony; dissolute and voluptuous himself, her depravity is congenial to his nature: that which others would have revolted from, is to him a spell."

Shakespeare's "adherence to his authority is minute, and he bestowed little pains in the adaptation of the history to the purposes of the drama, beyond an ingenious, and frequently elegant, metrical arrangement of the humble prose of Sir Thomas North."

16 Jameson, Anna Brownell. "Cleopatra." *Characteristics of Women, Moral, Poetical and Historical.* London, 1832. Reprint. New York: AMS, 1967, pp. 252-88.

"Great crimes, springing from high passions, grafted on high qualities, are the legitimate source of tragic poetry," says Jameson. "But to make the extreme of littleness produce an effect like grandeur—to make the excess of frailty produce an effect like power—to heap up together all that is most unsubstantial, frivolous, vain, contemptible, and variable, till the worthlessness be lost in the magnitude, and a sense of the sublime spring from the very elements of littleness,—to do this, belonged only to Shakspere, that worker of miracles. Cleopatra is a brilliant antithesis, a compound of contradictions, of all that we most hate, with what we most admire."

Shakespeare's Cleopatra, for Jameson, "is like one of those graceful and fantastic pieces of antique Arabesque, in which all anomalous shapes and impossible and wild combinations of form are woven together in regular confusion and harmonious discord: and such, we have reason to believe, was the living woman herself, when she existed upon this earth."

17 Heine, Heinrich. *Shakespeares Madchen und Frauen.* 1839. Trans. Ida Benecke. *Heine on Shakespeare: A Translation of his Notes on Shakespeare's Heroines.* London: Constable, 1895. 189 pp.

Shakespeare's Cleopatra is a woman who "loves and betrays at the same time." It is wrong to think that "women cease to love us when they betray us." Women "do but follow their nature; and even if they have no desire to empty the forbidden cup to the dregs, they would often like to take a sip, must touch the cup's edge with their lips at least, in order to taste what poison is like."

18 Courtenay, Thomas Peregrine. *Commentaries on the Historical Plays of Shakespeare.* 2 vols. London: Colburn, 1840, II, 264-75.

Antony's fascination with Cleopatra and its impact upon Roman and Egyptian events "furnish a definite and interesting plot: and Cleopatra's part is executed with consummate skill."

19 Birch, W.J. *An Inquiry into the Philosophy and Religion of Shakespeare*. London: C. Mitchell, 1848. Reprint. New York: AMS, 1972, pp. 464-78.

Birch does not find any evidence of Christian afterlife in this play: "It is given as a hope, not as a belief; not arising from religion, not exactly from the love of life in oneself; it was a sense of existence which only in the conscious reciprocity of each other's love transported them beyond this world." "This play illustrates the principle that the omnipotence of the passions (in this case that of love) can annihilate all expectation or anxiety concerning death or futurity." Antony, "in his love, excludes all idea of, or room for, religion."

20 Knight, Charles. *Studies of Shakespeare's: Forming a Companion Volume to Every Edition of the Text*. London: C. Knight, 1849. Reprint. New York: AMS, 1971. 560 pp.

Antony and Cleopatra "pours such a flood of noonday splendour upon our senses, that we cannot gaze upon it steadily."

21 "Shakespeare's Character of Cleopatra." *Fraser's Magazine* (London) 40 (Sept. 1849): 277-91.

Posterity has judged Antony and Cleopatra kindly because of their deaths: "The disasters which befell them—their sudden precipitation from the height of power and worldly felicity to distress, physical pain, and death—appear to expiate the follies, even the crimes, of which had both been guilty; and as we aid in dismissing them from the scene, our pity for human frailty, and the calamities it entails, mitigates our indignation."

Shakespeare "has not, to our mind, succeeded in unriddling the historical Cleopatra to us. He describes her as exercising an irresistible influence over men's minds, but fails to account for the power which he bestows upon her."

22 Coleridge, Hartley. *Essays and Marginalia.* Ed. Derwent Coleridge. 2 vols. London: Moxon, 1851, II, 183-84.

Not many plays excel *Antony and Cleopatra* for poetry and character, and it is full of "deep and grand pathos," but "perhaps both Antony and Cleopatra are too heroic to be pitied for weakness, and too viciously foolish to be admired for their heroism." Shakespeare has made unlawful love most interesting, but "the interest, though not dangerous, is not perfectly agreeable."

23 Bathurst, Charles. "Antony and Cleopatra." *Remarks on . . . Shakespeare's Versification.* London: Parker, 1857, pp. 130-34.

Antony and Cleopatra "is carelessly written, with no attempt at dignity, considering what great personages are introduced; but with a great deal of nature, spirit, and knowledge of character, in very many parts, and with several most beautiful passages of poetry and imagination; as, for instance, the dream of Cleopatra." Shakespeare "represents [Antony] as, what he certainly was not, a man of the most noble and high spirit, capable at times, notwithstanding the luxury he afterwards fell into, of a thoroughly soldier-like life, and full of kind and generous feelings."

24 Lloyd, William Watkiss. *Essays on the Life and Plays Shakespeare.* London: Whittingham, 1858, n.p.

This is a reprint of the introductory essays Lloyd had contributed to Singer's edition of 1856. The unity of the play depends on the contrast between Antony and Octavius, who "are displayed with unmatched vivacity and force, and if the catastrophe neither touches deeply with awe nor melts us with pity, it comes on through a series of events so linked with the causation of disposition, temperament, and motive that we are engaged and interested to the last."

Antony's passion for Cleopatra "is too obviously spurious to command our sympathy, but at least it is passion; it is in its way sympathetic, and so far unselfish." The play "reads with unchecked freshness, as though it flowed with quickest facility from his pen, at the same time that every line is charged with the maturest autumn of his ripened mind. Luxuriant as the execution is, it is so governed by appropriateness, that I doubt whether any of Shakespeare's plays can be more justly entitled correct, in the technical sense than Antony and Cleopatra—whether from any other a single line could less easily be struck out without apparent injury and loss."

25 Clarke, Charles Cowden. *Shakespeare-Characters; Chiefly Those Subordinate*. London: Smith, Elder, 1863, pp. 213-42.

This play represents "the stage of Cleopatra's voluptuous and reckless career; and this point in the world's history Shakespeare has touched with his magician's wand, and the characters start into light, life, and identity." Shakespeare has made Cleopatra "appear, speak, move, breathe, and live again before us: he has caused us to behold her in all that marked individuality, in those minute betrayals of character, which only either personal knowledge or Shakespeare's page enables us to witness." Cleopatra is a paradoxical figure: "Diversified, yet complete; inconsistent, yet in keeping; whimsical, yet direct of purpose; replete with jarring elements, yet in perfect consonance with itself."

26 Gervinus, G.G. *Shakespeare Commentaries*. Trans. F.E. Bunnet. 2 vols. London: Smith Elder, 1863, II, 353-86.

Gervinus complains about plot structure: "A wanton multiplicity of incidents and personages pass before our eyes; political and warlike occurrences run parallel with the most intimate affairs of domestic life and of the affections: the interest is fettered to the passion of a single pair, and yet the scene of it is the wide world from Parthia to Cape Misenum. For the historical character this is indeed highly expressive and striking, but it does no little damage to the dramatic clearness." By these "too numerous and discordant interruptions," Shakespeare has damaged the psychological continuity "which is necessary to the development of such a remarkable connection of the innermost soul as that between Antony and Cleopatra."

27 Harting, James E. *The Ornithology of Shakespeare*. 1864. Reprint. London: Unwin Brothers, 1978. 321 pp.

This is a sketch of Shakespeare's general knowledge of natural history and field sports and his references to birds. In Antony and Cleopatra, Shakespeare refers to eagles, cocks, quails, cuckoos, swans, kites, mallards, doves and other birds.

28 Heraud, John A. *Shakespeare: His Inner Life as Intimate in His Works.* London: Maxwell, 1865, pp. 374-87.

Shakespeare was identifying "himself with two mortals at the height of fortune, who, in a species of heroic madness, had conceived themselves to be in the position of Divine Powers, exempt from all laws except that of their own wills." Antony and Cleopatra "absolutely transcend all relative conventions, all possible forms of manners. They consciously acknowledge, and therefore transgress, no law. They live in an ideal region, far above the reach of a moral code, and justify their acts on the warranty of their own nature."

29 Keightley, Thomas. *The Shakespeare-Expositor: An Aid To the Perfect Understanding of Shakespeare's Plays.* London: J. Russell Smith, 1867. Reprint. New York: AMS, 1973, pp. 310-21.

Keightley provides explanatory notes on difficult passages from the play.

30 Hudson, H.N. *Shakespeare: His Life, Art, and Characters. With an Historical Sketch of the Origin and Growth of the Drama in England.* 2 vols. Boston: Ginn, 1872, II, 358-87. Reprint. Boston: Ginn, 1880, II, 388-417.

Hudson does not find any moral or immoral quality in the actions of Antony and Cleopatra. Through the comments of Enobarbus, Shakespeare "keeps up a secret understanding with us, all the while inwardly sporting himself with his characters, and laughing at them, yet at the same time gravely humouring their extravagances and clothing them with his most cunning style."

Cleopatra is "an inexhaustible magazine of coquetry: yet all along in her practice of this, and even in part as the motive and inspirer of it, there mingles a true and strong attachment, and a warm and just admiration of those qualities which ennoble the manly character."

Lying helpless under Egypt's spell, Antony rises to perform some noble deeds; "yet these appear rather as the spasms of a dying manhood than the natural and healthy beatings of its heart." Hudson praises the play for its compact dramatic structure "insomuch that it seems impossible to change either the form or order of them without impairing their mutual intelligence."

31 Taine, Hippolyte A. *History of English Literature.* Trans. H. Van Laun. 4 vols. 1880. Reprint. New York: Ungar, 1965, II, 104-23.

Cleopatra is someone who "holds Antony in the whirlwind of her devices and caprices, who fascinates and kills, who scatters to the winds the lives of men as a handful of desert dust, the fatal Eastern sorceress who sports with love and death, impetuous, irresistible, child of air and fire, whose life is but a tempest, whose thought, ever barbed and broken, is like the crackling of lightning flash." If Shakespeare had "framed a psychology, he would have said, with Esquirol: Man is a nervous machine, governed by a mood, disposed to hallucinations, carried away by unbridled passions, essentially unreasoning, a mixture of animal and poet, having instead of mind rapture, instead of virtue sensibility, imagination for prompter and guide, and led at random, by the most determinate and complex circumstances, to sorrow, crime, madness, and death."

32 Dowden, Edward. *Shakespeare: A Critical Study of His Mind and Work.* 3rd. edition. 1875. Reprint. New York: Barnes & Noble, 1967. 434 pp.

The characters of Antony and Cleopatra "insinuate themselves through the senses, trouble the blood, ensnare the imagination, invade our whole being like colour or like music. The figures dilate to proportions greater than human, and are seen through a golden haze of sensuous splendour."

33 Delius, Nicolaus. "On Shakespeare's Use of Narration in His Dramas. Part II." *New Shakespeare Society's Transactions*, Ser. 1, no. 4 (1875-76): 332-45.

Shakespeare used the epic element in this play because he had to recount and relate "what could not be exhibited in additional scenes; decorative detail-painting had to supply the deficiencies of the stage, prevailing even at Shakspere's later period."

34 Wilkes, George. "*Antony and Cleopatra.*" *Shakespeare, from an American Point of View*. New York: Appleton, 1877, pp. 359-62.

Wilkes opposes the Baconian theory of authorship; he considers Cleopatra and Cressida "as the only two completed female portraitures that Shakespeare ever drew. They were not portraitures from the cold and studied pen of Bacon, but such only as could have sprung from the singular experience of a man of Shakespeare's life and nature."

35 Stapfer, Paul. *Shakespeare and Classical Antiquity*. Trans. Emily J. Carey. London: Routledge & Kegan Paul, 1880. Reprint. New York: Franklin, 1970, pp. 379-416.

"Notwithstanding all its poetry and all its magnificent glow and colour," Stapfer argues that this play "is the weakest of the three Roman tragedies. Its principal fault is its diffuseness."Antony is "forgetful of all his duties as a Roman citizen, as a politician and a soldier, and as one of the heads of the government, and wholly given up to the fascinations of a woman." But even in "this state of bondage," Antony retains his "aesthetic sense of morality, which enabled him to comprehend and to love, and even wish to imitate, what is beautiful or honourable—never forsakes him, and it is the struggle between his higher and lower instincts that makes him a true tragic hero."

36 Swinburne, Algernon Charles. *A Study of Shakespeare*. London: Chatto & Windus, 1880. 309 pp.

For Swinburne, "Shakespeare has elsewhere given us in ideal incarnation the perfect mother, the perfect wife, the perfect wife, the perfect daughter, the perfect mistress, or the the perfect maiden: here only once for all he has given us the perfect and the everlasting woman."

37 Canning, Albert S.G. *Thoughts on Shakespeare's Historical Plays*. London: Allen, 1884, pp. 12-30.

The whole play "is engrossed with Roman characters and politics, while Cleopatra's evident policy is to please her Roman sovereigns, and to study and imitate what she herself calls 'the high Roman fashion' in everything."

38 Corson, Hiram. *An Introduction to the Study of Shakespeare*. Boston: Heath, 1889, pp. 252-315.

This play is Shakespeare's "grandest production," a tragedy, "the moral interest predominating over the historical or political." The historical forms "a background against which individualities are exhibited." One of Shakespeare's great achievements is "to unite moral proportion with a more or less unrestrained play of the passions."

Corson sums up "the dramatic situation: a man of extraordinary possibilities, altogether of colossal but unsymmetrical proportions, brought under the sway of a fascinating woman—fascinating in a sensuous direction—with all possible adventitious aids to her intrinsic fascination; but to induce a vigorous resistance to this sway under which he is brought, and to save him from becoming helpless victim of her magic, the greatest possible demands are made upon his asserting his nobler self—demands which, if met, would enable him 'to walk the earth with dominion,' though wanting in the civic genius of his colleague in the triumvirate, Octavius."

In his treatment of "passion-fated" love, the spectators "are nowhere brought into a sympathetic relationship with the moral obliquity of either Antony or Cleopatra. We are protected by the moral spirit with which the dramatist works, from any perversion of the moral judgment."

39 Sampson, Martin Wright. "An Examination of the Metre of 'Antony and Cleopatra'." *Shakespeariana* (New York) 6 (May 1889): 227-36.

Sampson discovers "a freedom in the management of blank verse in *Antony and Cleopatra* that is not found in the earlier plays." He believes that "the deviations from strict metre are intentional; even more, warrantable; in many cases adding to the strength of the verse." The "irregularities render the verse rugged, but thereby make it stronger and more suited to the subject."

40 Winter, William. *Old Shrines and Ivy.* Edinburgh: Douglas; New York: Macmillan, 1892, pp. 219-23.

This play is about the fall of a demigod: "The language glows with a prodigal emotion and towers to a superb height of eloquence." "While the pageant endures it endures in diamond light, and when it fades and crumbles the change is instantaneous to darkness and death."

41 Lewes, Louis. *The Women of Shakespeare.* Trans. Helen Zimmern. London: Hodder, 1894, pp. 254-58.

Cleopatra "embodies the extent to which Rome had grown corrupt even in the person of her best men." Antony "meets her in her full-blown maturity of beauty, as the experienced priestess of exuberant sensual enjoyment, in which refined coquetry, wild passion, and great sense of beauty are united to produce a lasting ever-new impression." Her behavior toward Antony "is deliberately planned. She is playing a part, but she is, nevertheless, filled with a passionate love."

42 Boas, Frederick Samuel. *Shakespeare and His Predecessors.* London: Murray, 1896. Reprint. London: Gordian P, 1925, pp. 473-84.

Boas finds something eternal about the passion of Antony and Cleopatra, "cloying for the moment in its voluptuous fullness, carries at its heart the secret of an eternal unrest. The palace of pleasure in which they have lain at east melts into a cloud-land castle, drifting and dissolving for ever before a chill night-wind."

43 Brandes, Georg. *William Shakespeare. A Critical Study*. Trans. William Archer and Diana White. 2 vols. London: William Heinemann, 1898, II, 142-51.

Shakespeare felt himself attracted by Cleopatra in a personal way. Cleopatra "poisons slowly, half-involuntarily, and in wholly feminine fashion, the faculty of rule, the generalship, the courage, the greatness of Antony, ruler of half the world—and her, Cleopatra, he, Shakespeare, knew." Shakespeare knew her "as we all know her, the woman of women, quintessentiated Eve, or rather Eve and the serpent in one." He wrote this play when "he was a maturer man, a gentleman, a landed proprietor and tithe-farmer, but in him still lived the artist-Bohemian, fitted to mate with the gipsy queen."

44 Sherman, Lucius A. *What Is Shakespeare? An Introduction to the Great Plays*. New York: Macmillan, 1901, 315-18. Reprint. Folcroft, PA: Folcroft Library Editions, 1973.

Cleopatra's tragedy is greater than that of Antony's, "for Antony had never lived selfishly or ignobly." The play "is a study in character consequences, and makes for righteousness more potently than a thousand sermons."

45 Moulton, Richard G. *The Moral System of Shakespeare: A Popular Illustration of Fiction as the Experimental Side of Philosophy*. New York: Macmillan, 1903. 381 pp.

Cleopatra "is not a woman, but a bundle of all womanly qualities tied together by the string of pure caprice." Instead of being a woman or a human soul, Cleopatra is "a 'great fairy,' an enchantress; it is her 'magic' that has ruined Antony." The play presents a conflict between the public and private lives of Antony: "Antony conjoining himself with Caesar is the life rising to public duty; Antony inclining to Cleopatra is the life falling to private passion."

46 Root, Robert K. *Classical Mythology in Shakespeare*. Yale Studies in English 19. New Haven: Yale UP, 1903. 134 pp.

Shakespeare makes thirty-nine allusions to classical mythology in this play—Jove six times, Mars three times, Venus three times, Cupid, Mercury, and Bacchus one each. The play contains 5 examples of nature-myth, six of Ovidian myth, 4 of Troy, and 2 of Lethe.

47 Bradley, A.C. "*Antony and Cleopatra*." *Oxford Lectures on Poetry*. London: Macmillan, 1909, pp. 279-305.

"In any Shakespearean tragedy," according to Bradley, "we watch some elect spirit colliding, partly through its error and defect, with a superhuman power which bears it down; and yet we feel that this spirit, even in the error and defect, rises by its greatness into ideal union with the power than overwhelms it. In some tragedies the latter feeling is relatively weak." In *Antony and Cleopatra* "it is unusually strong; stronger, with some readers at least, than the fear and grief and pity with which they contemplate the tragic error and the advance of doom." Antony and Cleopatra do not gainthe audience's admiration: "With all our admiration and sympathy for the lovers we do not wish them to gain the world. It is better for the world's sake, and not less for their own, that they should fail and die."

This play does not meet Bradley's criteria for tragedy: ". . . the tragic emotions are stirred in the fullest possible measure only when such beauty or nobility of character is displayed as commands unreserved admiration or love; or when, in default of this, the forces which move the agents, and the conflict which results from these forces, attain a terrifying and overwhelming power." In comparison with *Hamlet*, *Othello*, *Macbeth* and *Lear*, *Antony and Cleopatra* lacks in substance; it is defective in structure and does not have anything "terrible or piteous." For a tragedy, "it is not painful."

48 Grindon, Rosa Leo. *A Woman's Study of Antony and Cleopatra*. Manchester: Sherratt and Hughes, 1909. 75 pp.

Grindon "could not claim 'majesty' for this play if the great characters had left us without coming into touch with the reality of things; and if we would get to know them thoroughly we shall have to stretch out our own minds indeed." Rome,

Athens and Alexandria are the play's three centers. The play "opens in all sensuous delights; it closes in darkness and death." Grindon considers it "one of the plays wherein Shakespeare gives us failure in a high nature on the one hand and the success of a low nature on the other. And he leaves us with hope and expectation that the failure will not be eternal, while the low success will never rise beyond itself."

49 Harris, Frank. *The Man Shakespeare and His Tragic Life Story.* London: Palmer, 1909, pp. 304-29.

Antony and Cleopatra provides "the finest possible example of the strife between Shakespeare's yielding poetic temperament and the severity of his intellect." Shakespeare treats Antony "as a sort of superb *alter ego*, and yet his intellectual fairness is so extraordinary that it compelled him to create a character who should uphold the truth even against his heart's favourite." "The finest work of Shakespeare's maturity," in this play "his passion for Mary Fitton finds supreme example—expression."

50 Strindberg, August. "Antony and Cleopatra." *Open Letters to the Intimate Theatre.* Trans. Walter Johnson. Seattle and London: U of Washington P, 1909, pp. 267-78.

Shakespeare characterizes Cleopatra "by having her always speak in fury, slapping the people about her (exactly as Queen Elizabeth did), kicking servants out, swearing, and cursing (exactly as Queen Elizabeth did)." *Antony and Cleopatra* "is heavy, because one has to know thirty-four characters and their family trees."

51 Theobald, William. *The Classical Element in the Shakespeare Plays.* London: Robert Banks, 1909. 408 pp.

Theobald, a Baconian, tries to "adduce some passages from the plays to prove the author's acquaintance with the Greek and Latin and classical usages, and showing how hopeless is the task when once we come seriously to correlate the man of Stratford, as portrayed by history, with the reputed works of the same subjected to careful criticism."

52 MacCallum, M.W. "*Antony and Cleopatra.*"*Shakespeare's Roman Plays and Their Background.* London: Macmillan, 1910, pp. 300-453. Reprint. With a Foreword by T.J.B. Spencer. London: Macmillan, 1967.

This play occupies a distinctive position among Shakespeare's tragedies and histories: "On the one hand there is no play that springs more spontaneously out of the heart of its author, and into which he has breathed a larger portion of his inspiration; and on the other there is none that is more purely historical, so that in this respect it is comparable among the Roman dramas to *Richard II* in the English series." Shakespeare felt an affinity with Antony because of his own age.

Shakespeare does not borrow much from Plutarch. His "literal indebtedness is for the most part confined to the exploitation here and there of a few short phrases or sentences, generally of a not very distinctive character." Shakespeare's Antony is much more heroic than that of Plutarch: "He is still, though fallen, the Antony who at Caesar's death could alter the course of history; a dissolute intriguer no doubt, but a man of genius, a man of enthusiasms, one who is equal or all but equal to the highest occasion the world can present, and who, if he fails owning to the lack of steadfast principle and virile will that results from voluptuous indulgence and unscrupulous practisings, yet remains fascinating and magnificent even in his ruin. And by means of this transfiguration, Shakespeare is able to lend absorbing interest to his delineation of this gifted, complex, and faulty soul, and to rouse the deepest sympathy for his fate."

Antony's love appears as infatuation: "Part Siren, part Fury, that in truth is precisely who Plutarch would personify the love of Antony: and yet it is just this love that makes him memorable. Seductive and destructive in its obvious manifestations, nevertheless for the great reason that it was so engrossing and sincere, it reveals and unfolds a nobility and depth in his character, of which we should otherwise never have believed him capable." In the course of the play, Antony "seems to become bolder, grander, more magnanimous, as the fuel is cut off from his inward fire and it burns and wastes in its own heat."

Cleopatra "is all life and movement, and never the same, so that we are dazzled and bewildered, and too dizzy to measure her by any fixed standard." Cleopatra's "artifices are successful, because they are the means made use of by a heart that is deeply engaged; and it is no paradox to say that they are evidence of her sincerity." Antony and Cleopatra's love "is genuine and intense; and if it leads to shame as well as to glory, this is to be explained, apart from the circumstances of the time, apart from the characters of the lovers, in the nature of the variety to which it belongs." Their affinity "may mean sympathy with what is deepest and highest in us, our aspiration after the ideal, our bent towards perfection; or it may mean sympathy with our whole nature and with all our feelings and tendencies, alike with those that are high and with those that are low." The two are "alike in their emotionalism, their impressibility, their quick wits, their love of splendour, their genial power, their intellectual scope, their zest for everything."

This play, for MacCallum, is a personal tragedy and a love poem, and Antony and Cleopatra, "with all their errors, are lovers and partake of beauty, which we cannot say of the arid respectability of Octavius. It is well and right that they should perish as they do: but so perishing they have made their full atonement; and we can rejoice that they have at once triumphed over their victor, and left our admiration for them free."

53 Robertson, J.G. "Shakespeare on the Continent." *Cambridge History of English Literature*. Cambridge: Cambridge UP, 1910, V, 315-43.

Robertson outlines the impact of Shakespeare's work on the stage and on writing in Germany, France, Italy, and other countries to the end of the nineteenth century.

54 Harris, Frank. *The Women of Shakespeare*. London: Methuen, 1911, pp. 196-216.

Harris contends, without providing any evidence,that Shakespeare modeled his Cleopatra on his mistress, Mary Fitton, "who came to be maid of honour to Queen Elizabeth as a girl of sixteen in 1596": "In this picture of Cleopatra we have by far the finest and most complex portrait of Shakespearean mistress; we even learn some new physical features from it; she was tall with a high forehead and oval rather than round face."

55 Masefield, John. *William Shakespeare*. London: Williams & Norgate, 1911; New York: Holt, 1911, pp. 202-07.

In this "most noble" play, Shakespeare "applies to a great subject his constant idea, that tragedy springs from the treachery caused by some obsession." Cleopatra "is the only Shakespearean woman who dies heroically upon the stage. Her death scene is not the greatest, nor the most terrible, but it is the most beautiful scene in all the tragedies." Antony "is drunken to destruction with a woman like a raging thirst."

56 Collison-Morley, Lacy. *Shakespeare in Italy*. 1916. Reprint. New York: B. Blom, 1967. 180 pp.

This review of Shakespeare's influence, translations, and performances from the sixteenth to the nineteenth century includes a number of references to *Antony and Cleopatra*.

57 Gray, Henry David. "Antony's Amazing 'I Will to Egypt'." *Modern Philology* 15.1 (May 1917): 43-52.

The Soothsayer scene makes the audience feel "a certain paltriness" in Antony's effort to free himself from Cleopatra. This means that the scene is "out of place," and Shakespeare had probably placed it at the end of Act II. This would make Antony "a fit hero for a lofty tragedy."

58 Croce, Bendetto. *Ariosto, Shakespeare and Corneille*. Trans. Douglas Ainslee. London: Allen & Unwin, 1920, pp. 241-66.

Antony and Cleopatra belongs in a class of tragedies in which "the will, instead of holding the passions in control—making its footstool of them—allows itself to be dominated by them in their onrush." The play "is composed of the violent sense of pleasure, in its power to bind and to dominate, coupled with a shudder at its abject effects of dissolution and of death." This kind of tragedy is "morally a low form," because "it is simple and elementary in its roughness, such would manifest itself in a soldier like Antony, the bloody, quarrelsome, pleasure-seeking, crapulous Antony."

59 Quiller-Couch, Arthur. "Antony and Cleopatra." *Studies in Literature. Second Series*. Cambridge: Cambridge UP, 1922, pp. 168-205.

This play is to be placed "among the very greatest, and in some ways the most wonderful of Shakespeare's triumphs." Its theme is: "Love the invincible destroyer—destroying the world for itself—itself, too, at the last: Love voluptuous, savage, perfidious, true to itself though rooted in dishonour, extreme, wild, divine, merciless as a panther on its prey." In his language, Shakespeare "never touches a generalisation but he must visualise it and force us to see it thus in concrete images," and in his descriptions "he shades us off into a thought."

60 Schücking, Levin L. *Character Problems in Shakespeare's Plays*. London: Harrap, 1922. Reprint. Gloucester, MA: Smith, 1959. 270 pp.

Shakespeare's Cleopatra does not have any culture; she is vulgar. Shakespeare delineates her as "an intelligent, passionate, astute, heartless, essentially vulgar, and profoundly immoral creature, but by no means a remarkable or 'nobly planned' woman." This courtesan, "who now is inwardly as well as outwardly a queen, has but little in common with the harlot of the first part." This signifies an inconsistency in her character. Schücking explains the disparity by suggesting that Shakespeare composed this play by the "single-scene" method, not a sign of "a careful mental digestion and welding together of the materials found in the original source." Shakespeare also "may become dependent on the historical fact to an extent which seriously imperils the dramatic sense of the play."

61 Winchester, Caleb Thomas. "Antony and Cleopatra." *An Old Castle and Other Essays*. New York: Macmillan, 1922, pp. 64-90.

This play "is not merely based on Plutarch's Life of Mark Antony, but it follows Plutarch so closely that it might almost be called a poetic paraphrase." It "is not the tragedy of thought but the tragedy of passion," and it has "an eastern opulence and prodigality in its sensuous imagery, an intensity and desperation in its passion, under which language fairly seems to strain and sway." As the tragedy comes to a close, "who can turn away without feeling that this human life of ours is too high a thing to be wasted upon pleasures however splendid, and that swift upon the heels of our proudest transgressions walk the stern-eyed retributions of offended law."

62 Mathew, Frank. *An Image of Shakespeare.* New York: Moffat, Yard, 1923. 452 pp. Reprint. New York: Haskell House, 1972.

Mathew discovers the right order of Shakespeare's plays and poems which "would show us an image of him as he was altered by a natural growth and it would help us to value the stories about his private affairs." He believes that Shakespeare "was exhausted for a time by the agonies of Lear and Othello and turned to quieter work" in *Antony and Cleopatra.* Shakespeare "ennobled Plutarch's haughty Antonius and made his wild Cleopatra the greatest picture of a passionate woman." Unlike Plutarch, "he made Antony's disastrous surrender to Cleopatra exalt him to a greater nobility."

63 Mackenzie, Agnes Mure. *The Women in Shakespeare's Plays.* London: Heinemann, 1924, pp. 367-404.

Mackenzie considers Cleopatra to be "a woman who is neither chaste, nor brave, nor wise, nor even very beautiful, ruins no passionate youth but a great soldier-prince who is one of the three men that rule an empire, makes him false to his ruling, false to the men who trust him, false to the fair and honourable wife he marries to get free from her, and brings him down at last to a huddled squalid clumsy sort of death, with kingdoms crashing into war over her worthlessness: and the end for both is a sense that their destinies have soared out of the dust like royal flames."

64 Chambers, E. K. "*Antony and Cleopatra.*" *Shakespeare: A Survey.* London: Sidgwick & Jackson, 1925, pp. 249-57.

This is a reprint of Chambers's introduction to his single-volume edition in the Red Letter Shakespeare series (London:

Blackie, 1905). Dealing with the themes of chivalry and love in this play, Shakespeare seeks "to strip the mask of worship from the spectre of egoism, and to indict passion as the ruin of greatness, magnificent and devastating as Attila and his Huns." Antony "rejects nothing and will drink to the full of every cup that life proffers." Shakespeare does not "belittle passion:" "Tragedy lies in the incompatibility and clash of greatness, and love that is to be the scourge of the world, even if it is rooted in sensuality, must possess the attributes of majesty."

65 Haines, Charles Moline. *Shakespeare in France; Criticism: Voltaire to Victor Hugo*. London: Oxford UP, for the Shakespeare Association, 1925. 170 pp.

Haines's thesis is: "For a hundred years he was unknown; for a hundred years he was despised; for a hundred years he was adored." Haines narrates the fierce controversies over Shakespeare in France, with special attention to Voltaire and Victor Hugo.

66 Tolman, Albert H. "The Fifth Act of 'Antony and Cleopatra'." *Falstaff and other Shakespearean Topics*. New York: Macmillan, 1925, pp. 161-68.

Shakespeare "deliberately sought to intensify and idealize the mutual devotion of the princely lovers, Antony and Cleopatra."

67 Simpson, Lucie. "Shakespeare's Cleopatra." *Fortnightly Review* 129 (March 1928): 332-42. Reprint. *The Secondary Heroes of Shakespeare and Other Essays*. London: Kingswood P, [1950], pp. 27-37.

In Cleopatra Shakespeare expressed "the qualities of all his women—the wit and perversity of a Beatrice, the freshness of a Rosalind, Cressida's duplicity, Imogen's pervasive charm, the sweet womanliness of Hermione, the tragic fire of Constance, and the swift and melting sympathy of Cordelia." Consequently, "Cleopatra is not only the greatest of his heroines but the culmination of feminine characterisation in all literature."

68 Stoll, E.E. "Cleopatra." *Modern Language Review* 23 (1928): 145-63. Reprinted in *Poets and Playwrights*. Minneapolis: U of Minnesota P, 1930, pp. 1-30 pp.

Shakespeare observes decorum in his characterization of Cleopatra as consistent in her inconsistency, as one who "changes as a vivacious, amorous, designing woman changes, not so as to lose her identity, like Proteus." Shakespeare "makes the lovers jealous and suspicious, and yet glorifies them with poetry and elicits our sympathy. This is not a contradiction save as it is a contradiction in life (as we have seen) and as it must be (still more) in art."

69 Gerwig, George William. *Shakespeare's Cleopatra: Shakespearian Story of Passion*. Shakespeare's Ideals of Womanhood series. East Aurora, NY: Roycroft Shops, 1929. 28 pp.

According to Gerwig, "Mark Antony's was really a great nature, one capable under proper conditions, of rendering the world a great service. But Cleopatra drags him down along with her in the ruins of honor and of manhood." The play enacts a "spectacle of a human soul in its contest with temptation."

70 Wilson, John Dover, ed. *Six Tragedies of Shakespeare: An Introduction for the Plain Man*. Workers Educational Association Outlines. London: Longmans, Green, 1929, pp. 56-64.

Shakespeare presented Antony and Cleopatra "without illusion; he saw their sordidness, their self-indulgence and their meanness—and he makes us see it too. Yet in the end he lifts them on to the plane of high tragedy and gives them some of his very finest poetry."

71 Grindon, Rosa E. "*Antony and Cleopatra*." *Shakespeare and His Plays from a Woman's Point of View*. Manchester: The Policy-Holder Journal Company, 1930, pp. 3-12.

This play "is majestically grand in its setting, but it is even more majestically grand in the personages with which it deals." Octavia had safeguarded Antony's interest, but, after his separation from her, "he struck straight across the Mediterranean to Egypt." Cleopatra's departure from Antony "was a woman's sudden fright for herself, and she never stayed to think of anyone else." Antony and Cleopatra are united at the end, and "it is impossible for us not to identify ourselves with their sorrow, if not with their joy."

72 Mackail, J.W. *The Approach to Shakespeare.* Oxford: Clarendon P, 1930, pp. 89-91.

This "is the tragedy not of the Roman world, but of Antony and Cleopatra: and of both of them equally." Here, "neither single name gives the central tone to the drama; Antony does not exist for the sake of Cleopatra (as one might put it), nor does Cleopatra exist for the sake of Antony: they are two immense and in a sense equivalent forces which never coalesce, and the interaction between them is the drama."

73 Spurgeon, Caroline F.E. *Leading Motives in the Imagery of Shakespeare's Tragedies.* Shakespeare Association Papers No. 15. London: Oxford UP, 1930, pp. 41-45. Reprint. *Shakespeare's Imagery and What It Tells Us.* Cambridge: Cambridge U P, 1935.

This play contains "images of the world, the firmament, the ocean and vastness generally."

74 Knight, G. Wilson. *The Imperial Theme.* London: Oxford UP, 1931, pp. 199-350.

Knight identifies two unifying symbols at the play's "core" when he says that "our whole vision is condensed, crystallized in these single delineations of our two protagonists, both strongly idealized, ablaze with impossible beauty or infinite in majesty and power." Shakespeare blends the finite and the infinite, and so also "is element everywhere blended, mated, with element, sun with earth or water with air, giving birth to the 'strange serpent' of Nile, or the strange forms of 'hail', 'snow', or evanescent and multiform cloud." This is "throughout a life-vision, a mating of essence with essence."

Knight analyses the imagery and figurative language to explore different themes: "first, the theme of imperial magnificence, the imperial power and warrior-honour Antony sacrifices for love; second, the more physical and sensuous love-themes and love-imagery in dialogue and suggestion; third, the natural and elemental symbolisms, in their suggestion of the mating of elements, and also, in their varying ascent from the material to the ethereal, reflecting and blending with our love-theme; and, finally, the more spiritual and transcendental elements in this love-theme itself." Antony and Cleopatra find life in their deaths: "This is the high metaphysic of love which melts life and death into a final oneness; which reality is indeed no pulseless abstraction, but rather blends its single design and petalled excellence from all life and all death, all imperial splendour and sensuous delight, all strange and ethereal forms, all elements and heavenly starts; all that is natural, human, divine; all brilliance and all glory."

Knight points out that this play "is fired by an intenser realism than play from *Hamlet* to *Timon*." "By synchronizing death, the most absolute of all negations, with the positive aspect of live, love," he says, "we are left with a sense of peace and happiness, an apprehension of pure immortality." There is an antagonism between the masculine and the feminine, between war or empire and love. Knight concludes: "*Antony and Cleopatra* is a dramatic microcosm of human, and other, life viewed from within the altitudes of conscious Divinity; that we have here our most perfect statement of the real; that, whereas the sombre plays are aspects of 'appearance,' in *Antony and Cleopatra* we touch the Absolute."

Knight compares *Antony and Cleopatra* with *Macbeth*, both of which "are clearly dominated by a woman." Lady Macbeth and Cleopatra "each possess a unique power and vitality which is irresistible and, in both, expressly feminine: their mastery is twined with their femininity." The two men are similar in their strengths and weaknesses: "They fail in warriorship and practical affairs in proportion as they absorb and are absorbed by the more spiritual forces embodied in their women."

75 Murry, John Middleton. "North's Plutarch." *Countries of the Mind.* Second Series. Oxford: Oxford UP, 1931, pp. 78-96.

Tracing the influence of North's Plutarch on Shakespeare, Murry argues that "through Plutarch he saw an heroic Rome: a mode of life wherein some chosen men seemed to stand for a moment co-equal with Destiny—a giant world." In *Antony and Cleopatra*, Shakespeare "used North's language because he had none better."

76 Knight, G. Wilson. *The Shakespearian Tempest*. London: Oxford UP, 1932. 332 pp.

In this play, "the turbulence of mortality's warring is ever subdued to a new and strange harmony, and tempests are now enclosed in music, so that there is no direct tempest symbolism, but instead the single fine supernatural effect of unearthly music." The peculiar quality of this work "is well shown by the absence here of tempests."

77 Draper, John W. "The Realism of Shakespeare's Roman Plays." *Studies in Philology* 30 (1933): 225-42.

Draper argues that *Antony and Cleopatra,* "with its carefulness of detail, would seem to be the best criterion of Shakespeare's classical learning; but, even here, it is broad rather than deep, and scattered rather than full or systematic; and apparently he made no effort to supplement such knowledge as he had. Indeed, a greater knowledge would have helped him little; for the use of it would merely have been a stumbling block to many of his audiences; and classical dramatic structure, running counter to the strongly intrenched conventions of Elizabethan stagecraft, had already its nemesis in the plays of Jonson."

78 Shaw, George Bernard. "The Tragedy of Infatuation." *Prefaces by Bernard Shaw*. London: Constable, 1934, pp. 716-17.

Shakespeare's *Antony and Cleopatra* "must needs be as intolerable to the true Puritan as it is vaguely distressing to the ordinary healthy citizen, because, after giving a faithful picture of the soldier broken down by debauchery, and the typical wanton in whose arms such men perish, Shakespeare finally strains all his huge command of rhetoric and stage pathos to give a theatrical sublimity to the wretched end of the business, and to persuade foolish spectators that the world was well lost by the twain."

79 Strachan, L.R.M. "The Spelling 'Anthony'." *Notes and Queries* 167 (1934): 85-86.

In the fourteenth century, "the *h* was erroneously inserted in 'author', and doubtless about the same time or a little later, say in the fifteenth century it crept into 'Anthony'."

80 Sprague, Arthur C. *Shakespeare and the Audience: A Study in the Technique of Exposition*. Cambridge, MA: Harvard UP; London: Oxford UP, 1935, pp. 217-23.

Enobarbus is "intensely interesting in himself—a fine example of the way Shakespeare can wipe out the distinction between major and minor characters. That first Jacobean audience found him, one may suppose, a bit enigmatic at the outset."

81 Leavis, F.R. "*Antony and Cleopatra* and *All for Love*: A Critical Exercise." *Scrutiny* 5.2 (1936): 158-69.

Shakespeare is superior to Dryden in his use of metaphors and in his tone and movement: "These too exhibit Shakespeare's marvellous power of realization, of making language create and enact instead of merely saying and relating."

82 Murry, J. Middleton. *Shakespeare*. London: Jonathan Cape,1936, pp. 352-379; New York: Harcourt, Brace, 1936, pp. 294-318.

The real theme of Shakespeare play is that "Royalty and loyalty, then, go hand in hand; and the man who is loyal, by his loyalty, becomes royal." Shakespeare's "prodigious art consists first and foremost in convincing us of Antony's royalty" and "the great motion of the drama derives from that." "What I am driving at is the power of poetry, as it was used by Shakespeare in this play. The ultimate and enduring structure of the play is in the poetry. Its life, its inward progression, derive from the response of poetry to poetry."

83 Muir, Kenneth, and Sean O'Loughlin. *The Voyage to Illyria: A New Study of Shakespeare*. London: Methuen, 1937, pp. 209-12.

Shakespeare achieved three objectives in this play. "Metrically, it exhibits a new freedom, a certain royal carelessness, born perhaps of even greater fluency of inspiration. Psychologically, it reflects, at last, a satisfactory synthesis of the desires and the affections. Metaphysically, it is a poem of the conquest of death by love. It is certain that Shakespeare was able to write the play because he had solved the sex-problem of his own life."

84 Ridley, Maurice R. *Shakespeare's Plays: A Commentary.* London: 1937; New York: Dutton, 1938, pp. 186-94.

Shakespeare "neglects the unities, and hurries us about in space and time (bringing in, for example, stray captains from Syria) so that we feel the surge of great events, and Antony's greatness among them, as determined things hold their way to destiny. And the greater, even in this historical sense, that Antony can be made, the greater, by a natural, if illogical, process, do we feel to be the woman who enslaves him; and, moving further round the same circle, the greater that Cleopatra becomes the less do we experience either wonder or distress at Antony's subjugation."

85 Cadoux, Arthur Temple. *Shakespearean Selves: An Essay in Ethics*. London: Epworth, 1938, pp. 84-92.

Antony "sacrificed to Cleopatra as a plaything what need not have been sacrificed, had he seen her as more than a plaything. And only through the sacrifice does he learn what she really is to him."

86 Fripp, Edgar I. *Shakespeare: Man and Artist.* 2 vols. London: Oxford UP, 1938, II, 673-85.

Antony "is not like Dryden's hero, in his adaptation of the play, *All for Love*, a weak profligate, but the most attractive and, after Brutus, the greatest man of his time. Nor is Cleopatra a common wanton. Were she that, she would have no power over Antony. She is a brilliant and splendid creature, with mental as well as physical gifts, and as tragic in her fate as her lover in his."

87 Menon, C. Narayana. *Shakespeare Criticism: An Essay in Synthesis*. London: Oxford UP, 1938. 238 pp.

Shakespeare "had to show us Antony acting and talking as the slave of his charmer, and to make it clear at the same time that there is within Antony, hidden regret and shame." Antony "is never without regrets. When intoxicated by the company of Cleopatra, he must forget a portion of himself in revels; when in Pompey's gallery after re-establishing himself in power, he must steep his Lethe with wine." Hence "the inner history of Antony has three sections; conscious struggle against the fascination, unconscious obedience, and final resignation to it. This is true of all tragic passion."

88 Rosenblatt, Louise M. *Literature as Exploration*. New York: Appleton-Century, 1938. 340 pp. 4th ed. New York: Modern Language Association, 1983. 303 pp.

In classroom discussions, students indicate that "although morally some of Cleopatra's actions merit condemnation, she possesses great vitality, the ability to feel and act on a grand scale." Students can gain an understanding "from living through the fugue of emotions that the play presents, to their resolution in those noble last scenes."

89 Tillyard, E.M.W. *Shakespeare's Last Plays*. London: Chatto & Windus, 1938. 85 pp.

This is "a transitional play." Shakespeare "no longer seeks to unify, rather he seeks to emphasise by juxtaposition those worlds which once he had ventured to arrange." This "is neither the tragedy nor the triumph of the pair of lovers, it is both simultaneously though on different planes of reality."

90 Traversi, D. A. *An Approach to Shakespeare*. London: Paladin P, 1938. Reprint. "Antony and Cleopatra." *An Approach to Shakespeare*. 2nd. ed., revised and enlarged. Garden City, NY: Doubleday Anchor Books, 1956, pp. 235-61.

Is *Antony and Cleopatra* "a tragedy of lyrical inspiration, justifying love by presenting it as triumphant over death, or is it rather a remorseless exposure of human frailties, a presentation of spiritual possibilities dissipated through a senseless surrender to passion?" Traversi sees these points "less as contradictory than complementary aspects of a unified artistic creation." According to Traversi, "Rottenness becomes the ground for fertility, opulence becomes royalty, infatuation turns into transcendent passion, all by means of an organic process which ignores none of its own earlier stages, which, while never denying the validity of the realistic estimates of the situation which accompany it to the last, integrates these in the more ample unity of its creative process."

The poetic quality of the play redeems the disintegration of Antony and Cleopatra's situation: "The emotions of Antony and Cleopatra, like their weaknesses, are built upon 'dungy earth,' upon 'Nilus' slime,' and so upon time which these elements by their nature imply; but, just as earth and slime are quickened into fire and air, while retaining their sensible qualities as constituent parts of the final experience, so time itself, in which this tragedy of waste and vanity was nurtured, becomes simultaneously a necessary element in the creation of 'immortality'."

91 Alexander, Peter. *Shakespeare's Life and Art*. London: James Nisbet, 1939. 247 pp.

In his brief assessment of this play, Alexander argues that "the story of Antony and Cleopatra can show its most dramatic aspect only against the world-wide background Shakespeare chose for its setting. For the solitude to which their passion brings them cannot be made more absolute than by the fierce society in which they must play out their part."

92 McKerrow, Ronald B. *Prolegomena for the Oxford Shakespeare: A Study in Editorial Method*. Oxford: Oxford UP, 1939. 110 pp.

McKerrow does not discuss textual problems in this play, but he explains his general principles. His objective is "to discuss the formation of the text itself." This "generally involves the choice of one of the early editions and the reproduction of this save where it appears to be wrong; secondly, the exactitude with which it is desirable to follow the chosen edition and the value of other editions than the one selected in supporting or emending the readings of this."

93 Van Doren, Mark. "*Antony and Cleopatra*." *Shakespeare*. New York: Holt, 1939, pp. 230-243. Reprinted in *Shakespeare: Modern Essays in Criticism*. Ed. Leonard F. Dean. Galaxy Books. New York: Oxford UP, 1961, pp. 345-59.

Shakespeare has broken the action "into as many as forty-two scenes; our attention is constantly shifted from one to another portion of the single scene which is the earth. And so with the speech, the characteristic unit of which is almost breathlessly short. There are no rolls of rhetoric, no attempts to loop the universe with language. This universe is too large to be rendered in anything but fragments, too much alive in its own right to care for extended compliment and discourse."

94 Lyman, Dean B. "Janus in Alexandria: A Discussion of 'Antony and Cleopatra'." *Sewanee Review* 48 (1940): 86-104.

This is a high tragedy because of "the splendid pageantry of the drama, its piercing love-theme, its gigantic classes of tramping armies, its portrayal of the tortured courage of a soul drawn this way and that as Fate snatches at a heard-won divinity."

95 Phillips, J.E., Jr. *The State in Shakespeare's Greek and Roman Plays*. Columbia University Studies in English and Comparative Literature No. 149. New York: Columbia UP, 1940. Reprint. New York: Octagon, 1972, pp. 188-205.

In *Antony and Cleopatra*, "secondary as the political theme is in importance, we witness the inevitable restoration of monarchy in the process of elimination which singles out the one man naturally qualified to exercise supreme authority in a political society." "Each step in Antony's downward course from political power is explicitly linked with his infatuation for Cleopatra and its effect on his character as a leader of men."

96 Spencer, Hazelton. *The Art and Life of William Shakespeare*. New York: Harcourt, Brace, 1940, pp. 341-46. Reprint. London: Bell, 1948.

Antony and Cleopatra "are too well known to be ideal tragic figures; they resist the symbolizing tendency of all serious and poetic drama." In Shakespeare "she is that identical dusky Egyptian (as he supposed her to be), and none other. He holds us with a tale of a grand passion, told powerfully and with a good deal of sympathy, which does not obscure the dramatist's judgment that Antony has made a mess of his life. But the play is half pageant." Antony comes nearer to that sublimation than Cleopatra does, except in her dying speech; but it is chiefly her play, and, however Shakespeare adorns and vivifies her, she always remains the celebrated historical figure. That is what keeps this tragedy below the plane on which the great four move."

97 Cairns, Huntington, Allan Tate, and Mark van Doren. *Invitation to Learning*. New York: Random House, 1941, pp. 198-212. Reprint. New York: New Home Library, 1942.

Joseph Wood Krutch, Cairns, Tate and van Doren emphasize Shakespeare's new concept of the hero and heroine: "For Antony and Cleopatra are represented in the maturity of their loves, and as there is nothing simple about their feelings so there is nothing elementary about the story which their speeches tell." The two "are beyond romantic illusion; they have been everywhere and seen everything; and each knows that the other is not to be trusted." They "are infinitely changeable and perennially fascinating; and they have the honor to inhabit Shakespeare's most sophisticated play."

98 Spencer, Theodore. "*Antony and Cleopatra*." *Shakespeare and the Nature of Man*. The Lowell Lectures 1942. New York: Macmillan, 1943, pp. 162-76.

In *Antony and Cleopatra* "there is no awareness, on the part of any character, that what happens is unnatural; nothing is hideous or monstrous, like the real lust of Gertrude, the apparent lust of Desdemona, the cruelty of Goneril and Regan, or the criminality of Macbeth. The geographical reach of the Roman empire may be vast, and Antony's warm gold share of it may fall into the dry manipulating hands of Caesar; the passion of Antony and Cleopatra may destroy them—but that, we feel, is how things happen. It is not unjust; it is how things are. Shakespeare's final vision of man, though still under a tragic guise, is already in sight."

99 Webster, Margaret. *Shakespeare without Tears.* With an introduction by John Mason Brown. London: Whittlesey House, 1942. 319 pp.

Every speech in this play "reveals the speaker and furthers the play's design." Antony's disintegration is inevitable and "implicit in the play's very first lines." The play has "no dark corners, no unguessed terrors; light informs the play with reason; there are causes and effects, and they lie in character itself, and character in action."

100 Cecil, Lord David. *Antony and Cleopatra.* W. P. Ker Memorial Lecture No. 4, Glasgow University Publications vol. 58 (1943). Reprinted in *Poets and Story-tellers.* New York: Macmillan, 1949, pp. 1-24..

This play is "the most virtuosic of all his [Shakespeare's] performances; that in which, arrived as he was at the full maturity of his superb technical accomplishment, he stretches the capacities of his form to the most daring limits." Antony "is so besotted with Cleopatra that he cannot give her up; and he deludes himself into thinking that he can somehow manage to have her and political power at once." Antony and Cleopatra are not ideal figures, but "the figures of both are resplendent with romance." Shakespeare "states all the facts. And his conclusion seems to be that it is impossible to be certain in our judgment of Antony's conduct."

101 Wallerstein, Ruth. "Dryden and the Analysis of Shakespeare's Techniques." *Review of English Studies* 19 (1943): 165-85.

In her assessment of Dryden's imitation of Shakespeare in *All for Love*, Wallerstein argues: "By the sheer study of Shakespeare's passions and language, Dryden carried himself into a much larger world than any in which he had earlier lived." Dryden "freed and brought into play his real observation of human nature" and learned "to unite the rhythms of normal speech with the formal measures of verse as only he and Shakespeare can."

102 Bethell, S. L. *Shakespeare and the Popular Dramatic Tradition*. London and New York: Staples, 1944, pp. 116-32.

Bethell draws attention to the play's "Brobdingnagian imagery: objects of tremendous size and power are constantly utilised to illustrate some quality of character or situation." The playwright applies "the same colossal imagery—the world, the heavenly bodies, the gods, etc.—to the theme of empire and the theme of love." The two themes are "conflicting alternatives" for Antony to choose in pursuing the good life. Shakespeare is exploring "the bases of the good life" and "finds them in the affections, and the affections as rooted deep in the sensual nature." Cleopatra is Antony's "good, and not his evil genius, rescuing him from an undue preoccupation with the world, which is a snare and a delusion." Purged of selfishness, Antony and Cleopatra are united in death.

103 Kirschbaum, Leo. "Shakespeare's Cleopatra." *Shakespeare Association Bulletin* 19 (1944): 161-171. Reprinted in *Character and Characterization in Shakespeare*. Waynebook No. 4. Detroit: Wayne State UP, 1962, pp. 99-110.

Shakespeare uses "iterative imagery" to show that Cleopatra is a harlot. Even in her suicide, she remains a courtesan—"avid of love, impatient, jealous of rivals, quick-tempered, voluptuous, feline, thinking in sheerly female terms." Antony and Cleopatra are voluptuaries, and "she almost escapes moral judgment—but not quite."

104 Brooks, Cleanth, and Robert B. Heilman, eds. "Questions on *Antony and Cleopatra*." *Understanding Drama: Twelve Plays*. New York: Holt, Rinehart & Winston, 1945, pp. 673-74.

This is a set of questions, for the benefit of college students, about problems of imagery in the play.

105 Griffiths, G. S. "*Antony and Cleopatra*." *Essays and Studies* 31 (1945): 34-67.

Treating Cleopatra as a Dionysian figure, Griffiths argues that "the play exists much more than any other of Shakespeare's in its ecstatic moments, its pure sensations, its gusts of sheer passion: pride, jealousy, remorse, anger, above all love, absolute sole lord of Life and Death, presented with rapturous lyrical energy."

106 Horne, Herman Harrell. *Shakespeare's Philosophy of Love*. Raleigh, NC: Edwards & Broughton, 1945, pp. 145-53.

Portraying "the personal and political effects of a wanton love," Shakespeare suggests that "When love is not love, it is the caricature of itself, as in Antony's passion, however devoted, and Cleopatra's bargaining, however clever."

107 Jenkin, Bernard. "*Antony and Cleopatra*: Some Suggestions on the Monument Scenes." *Review of English Studies* 21 (1945): 1-14.

The Folio text contains two versions of the beginning of the Monument scene "in a confused form." In the first version, "Cleopatra was on the inner stage as 'Lockt in her Monument'." The second version, "in which Antony is hoisted up at the back of the Monument instead of at the front, in no way precludes the use of the inner stage as the inside of the Monument."

108 Sewell, Arthur. "Time and Place in Shakespeare's Plays." *Studies in Philology* 42 (1945): 205-24.

The major rhythms of *Antony and Cleopatra* and other plays are "the product of fruitful interplay between stage time, the time of the plot, and ideal time. It is in ideal that the play takes its outward form; but this form takes something of its structure, too, from the disposition of stage time and the representation of the time of the plot."

109 Taylor, George Coffin. "Shakespeare's Use of the Idea of the Beast in Man." *Studies in Philology* 42 (1945): 530-43.

Shakespeare uses "the beast idea in *Antony and Cleopatra*, where sensuality and lust are expanded" to a great extent.

110 Draper, John W. "Speech-Tempo and Humor in Shakespeare's Antony." *Bulletin of the Institute for the History of Medicine* (Baltimore) 20 (1946): 426-32.

This is an analysis of Antony's language.

111 Granville-Barker, Harley. "Cleopatra." *Prefaces to Shakespeare.* 2 vols. Princeton: Princeton UP, 1946. Reprint. London: Batsford, 1958, pp. I, 367-458.

Granville-Barker concedes that this play "may lack the spiritual intimacy of *Hamlet*, the mysterious power of *Macbeth*, the nobilities of *Othello,* may reach neither to the heights nor depths of *King Lear*; but it has a magnificence and a magic all its own, and Shakespeare's eyes swept no wider horizon." The opposition between Rome and Egypt "braces the whole body of the play, even as conflict between character and character will sustain each scene." Granville-Barker gives a detailed analysis of the play's structure, the questions of act-division and scene, staging, costumes, music and verse, and the characters of Antony, Cleopatra, Octavia, Octavius Caesar, Enobarbus, Pompey, Lepidus and the rest. Shakespeare "neither takes nor uses his material haphazardly. If, with one dramatic aim, he frees himself from ties of place, with another he creates for himself ties of time."

Since a boy actor could not show Cleopatra's charm, Shakespeare used "his magic of words" to display it. He has endowed her with "wit, coquetry, perception, subtlety, imagination, inconsequence." This "passionate woman has a child's desires and a child's fears, an animal's wary distrust; balance of judgment none, one would say." She is "quick, jealous, imperious, mischievous, malicious, flagrant, subtle; but a delicate creature, too, and the light, glib verse seems to set her on tiptoe."

112 Seaton, Ethel. "*Antony and Cleopatra* and *The Book of Revelation.*" *Review of English Studies* 22 (1946): 219-24.

Seaton has identified parallels between passages in *Antony and Cleopatra* and *The Book of Revelation.* Antony and Cleopatra "themselves undergo a purification of their passion;

and it may well have been brought about by their creator's self-submission to the poetry and the mystery of the Book of Revelation."

113 Camden, Carroll. "Elizabethan Chiromancy." *Modern Language Notes* 62 (1947): 1-7.

The Soothsayer does not believe that Iras is chaste; she probably "has on her hand a cross which touches the life of life at its upper corner, for this, as John ab Indgine writes, 'signifieth a libidinous and an unshamefac'd woman'."

114 Cook, Albert. "Shakespeare's *Antony and Cleopatra*, V.ii.338-341." *Explicator* 6 (1947): Item 9.

Air and fire "are metaphorical for the soul which will rise to Antony when the asp has stung Cleopatra dead; earth and water, for the body which will be interred in the ground ('baser life')."

115 Ellis, Oliver C. de C. "A Discussion of *Antony and Cleopatra*." *Cleopatra in the Tide of Time*. London: Poetry Lovers' Fellowship Publication, 1947, pp. 146-60.

Labelling it "rather a pageant than a play" and "the apotheosis of the chronicle-play," Ellis considers it "a study of greatness in decline: not of greatness not swiftly overthrown as in Lear, but of greatness cunningly sapped."

116 Miriam Joseph, Sister. *Shakespeare's Use of the Arts of Language*. Columbia University Studies in English and Comparative Literature 165. New York: Columbia UP, 1947. 423 pp.

Miriam Joseph argues, "first, that Shakespeare's development of his subject matter and his mode of expression in his plays and poems are characteristic of his time; secondly, that he utilized every resource of thought and language known to his time; thirdly, that his genius, outrunning precept even while conforming to it, transcends that of his contemporaries and belongs to all time." She cites numerous passages from *Antony and Cleopatra* as examples of Shakespeare's use of language.

117 Ransom, John Crowe. "On Shakespeare's Language." *Sewanee Review* 55 (1947): 181-98.

Ransom analyzes "Shakespeare's way of compounding latinical elements with his native English" and discusses Antony's conversation with Eros about Cleopatra robbing him of his substance.

118 Reyher, Paul. "Antony and Cleopatra." *Essay sur les Idées dans L'Oeuvre de Shakespeare.* Bibliothèque des Langues Modernes 1. Paris: Didier, 1947, pp. 527-546.

Reyher treats it primarily as a grand tragedy of the love and passion of two older persons.

119 Craig, Hardin. *An Interpretation of Shakespeare.* New York: Dryden P, 1948, pp. 267-81.

Shakespeare does not stress "the passion of love alone, but the great issues of character and conduct that arise out of the heart." Hence the play is "the tragedy of the fallen man. He stagggers to his end. Cleopatra has her colossal part in ruining him, bringing on his downfall."

120 Price, Hereward T. "Mirror-Scenes in Shakespeare." *Joseph Quincy Adams Memorial Studies.* Ed. James G. McManaway. Washington, DC: Folger Shakespeare Library, 1948, pp. 101-13.

Some of the scenes like 2.7, 3.1, and 4.3 perform "the function of enforcing a contrast of character in action." In 4.3, for example, Shakespeare "invents a special symbol in a special scene in order to represent the actions of the gods."

121 Sitwell, Edith. *A Notebook on William Shakespeare.* London: Macmillan, 1948. Reprint. Boston: Beacon Paperback, 1961, pp. 136-43.

Sitwell considers the play "as one of the greatest miracles of sound that has ever come into this world": "Kings drunken with time, with wine, with the noonday light, nod to each other across a universe of light over which Antony reigns, like the Sun from Cleopatra, the 'day of the world', takes her light."

122 Wilson, Elkin Calhoun. "Shakespeare's Enobarbus." *Joseph Quincy Adams Memorial Studies*. Ed. James G. McManaway et al. Washington, DC: Folger Shakespeare Library, 1948, pp. 391-408.

Enobarbus, "like Lear's Fool, is Shakespeare's translation of the chorus of Renaissance neo-classical drama into dramatic character." The Fool and Enobarbus "live in that elusive borderland between pure comedy and high tragedy." They "smile wryly at the absurdity of the proud passions that strut around them, baldly tell truth about things as they are, and speak for sanity in the midst of madness and infatuation. But both are mere mortals, living quite in earnest amid the follies they behold, and overwhelmed by the disasters bred by the ill-starred masters they serve."

123 Wimsatt, W.K., Jr. "Poetry and Morals." *Thought* 23 (1948): 281-99. Reprinted in *The Verbal Icon*. Lexington, KY: U P of Kentucky, 1954, pp. 85-100.

Wimsatt reconciles poetry and morals by arguing that "the poetic splendor of this play, and in particular of its concluding scenes, is something which exists in closest juncture with the acts of suicide and with the whole glorified story of passion." The values of poetry depend on morality. "Even though, or rather because, the play pleads for certain evil choices, it presents these choices in all their mature interest and capacity to arouse human sympathy." In this play Shakespeare "imitates or presents the reasons for sin, a mature and richly human state of sin."

124 Bacon, Wallace A. "The Suicide of Antony in *Antony and Cleopatra*, Act IV, Scene xiv." *Shakespeare Association Bulletin* 24 (1949): 193-202.

Bacon argues against the interpretation that Antony sends Eros away so that he may be alone to kill himself and then lacks courage to do so.

125 Brown, Ivor. *Shakespeare*. London: Collins, 1949; Garden City, NY: Doubleday, 1949, 185-99.

Brown analyzes the play "as a salute to love which tolerates no mitigation, to a lavishness and a luxury which count the world well lost if love be satisfied."

126 Danby, John Francis. "The Shakespearean Dialectic: An Aspect of *Antony and Cleopatra*." *Scrutiny* 16 (1949): 196-213. Reprinted in *Poets on Fortune's Hill*. London: Faber & Faber, 1952, pp. 128-51.

Shakespeare possessed the capacity for renewal in each phase of his development. The play can be understood best in terms of the movies: "There is more cinematic movement, more panning, tracking, and playing with the camera, more mixing of shots than in any other of Shakespeare's tragedies." There is also the ambiguity "which invests everything in Egypt equally with all things in Rome. Yet this ambiguity is central to Shakespeare's experience in the play. If it is wrong to see the 'mutual pair' as a strumpet and her fool, it is also wrong to see them as a Phoenix and a Turtle."

In *Antony and Cleopatra* "Shakespeare needs the opposites that merge, unite, and fall apart. They enable him to handle the reality he is writing about—the vast containing opposites of Rome and Egypt, the World and the Flesh." Caesarism may stand for "the World" and Cleopatra for "flesh," "There is no suggestion that the dichotomy is resolvable: unless we are willing to take the delusions of either party as a resolution, the 'universal peace' of Caesar, the Egypt-beyond-the-grave of Antony and Cleopatra in their autotoxic exaltations before they kill themselves."

This play is "Shakespeare's study of Mars and Venus—the presiding deities of Baroque society, painted for us again and again on the canvasses of his time. It shows us Virtue, the root of the heroic in man, turned merely into *virtu*, the warrior's art, and both of them ensnared in the world, very force entangling itself with strength. It depicts the 'man of men' soldiering for a cynical Rome or whoring on furlough in a reckless Egypt. It is the tragedy of the destruction of man, the creative spirit, in perverse war and insensate love—the two complementary and opposed halves of a discreating society."

127 Knights, L.C. "On the Tragedy of *Antony and Cleopatra.*" *Scrutiny* 16 (1949): 318-23.

Disagreeing with John F. Danby, Knights asserts that, in this play, "the sense of potentiality in life's untutored energies is pushed to its limit, and Shakespeare gives the maximum weight to an experience that is finally 'placed.' If we do not feel both the vitality and the sham vitality, both the variety and the monotony, both the impulse towards life and the impulse towards death, we are missing the full experience of the play."

128 Schwalb, Harry M. "Shakespeare's *Antony and Cleopatra* I,ii,1-5." *Explicator* 7 (1948/49): Item 53.

Schwalb finds ironic foreshadowing of Charmian's coming death in Alexas' description of her husband-to-be.

129 Stauffer, Donald A. *Shakespeare's World of Images:The Development of His Moral Ideas.* New York: Norton, 1949. 393 pp.

In *Antony and Cleopatra*, Shakespeare "dares to defend the illicit passion that set the halves of the world at war and destroyed its possessors." He does it by taking four steps: "he must demonstrate that 'reason' is mistaken; he must belittle or blacken the cause of empire; he must make passion larger than the world; and he must spiritualize and ennoble an historical liaison until it appears as the true quality of love." Enobarbus "serves as the moral microcosm for the play."

130 Stewart, J.I.M. "Professor Schücking's Fatal Cleopatra." *Character and Motive in Shakespeare.* London and New York: Longmans, Green, 1949, pp. 64-78.

Opposing Schücking's criticism that the play is full of inconsistencies, Stewart argues that "the neglect of minor consistencies and correspondences is simply a function of concentration upon a whole which has been apprehended with unusual urgency in that mysterious world, beyond common consciousness, in which the artist's creations live." Proposing that the idea of human nature is conditioned "by the system of proprieties operative in the culture to which we belong," Stewart suggests that Schücking's opinion of Cleopatra is tainted by his own culture. Stewart's "impression of truth in the fable results not from an illusion which the poetry creates but from an actual correlation between high dramatic poetry and insight into substantial human nature."

131 Berkeley, David. "Antony, Cleopatra, and Proculeius." *Notes and Queries* 195 (1950): 534-35.

Antony's advice to Cleopatra concerning Proculeius was proven treacherous by events.

132 Farnham, Willard. "*Antony and Cleopatra*." *Shakespeare's Tragic Frontier*. Berkeley: U of California P, 1950, pp. 139-205.

"Unlike the heroes of the middle tragic world those of the last tragic world are deeply flawed," according to Farnham. These plays reach a "tragic frontier" at which truth "is discovered in paradox." This "was a spirit that could extend sympathy to the sinner or the faulty character in a mood far more complex than that of medieval charity, for it could represent serious shortcomings as apparently inseparable from the heroic greatness for which it had sympathy, yet without letting its sympathy minimize the shortcomings." Antony and Cleopatra's "paradox is that by being voluptuaries, for which they may be scorned, they are led to have certain qualities for which they may be respected." "Seeing tragedy more and more as a product of flaw in character," Shakespeare "sees less and less of mystery in its causation." At last, "Shakespeare's growing interest in the paradox he has discovered in deeply flawed yet noble character becomes very distinctly his sustaining interest in the writing of tragedy."

133 McManaway, James G. "Recent Studies in Shakespeare's Chronology." *Shakespeare Survey* 3 (1950): 22-33.

There is no reason to change the date accepted by E.K. Chambers for the composition of *Antony and Cleopatra* in 1606-7.

134 Pogson, Beryl. *In the East My Pleasure Lies: An Esoteric Interpretation of Some Plays of Shakespeare*. London: Stuart & Richards, 1950. Reprint. New York: Haskell House, 1974, pp.107-16.

The union of the lovers represents "Transcendental Love, which was enacted in the outer world of history, and later on the European stage, as an ideal to which Man could aspire."

135 Waith, Eugene M. "Manhood and Valor in Two Shakespearean Tragedies." *ELH: Journal of English Literary History* 17 (1950): 262-73.

Waith examines the "complex relationship of valor to manhood in *Macbeth* and in *Antony and Cleopatra*."

136 Watkins, W.B.C. *Shakespeare and Spenser*. Princeton: Princeton UP, 1950, pp. 24-35.

In *Antony and Cleopatra* Shakespeare delineates a kind of love "in which for the first time since *Venus and Adonis* we find characters and situations closely approximating the *Amores* of Ovid." Antony and Cleopatra's romantic "reaches heights of spiritual intensity by including rather than excluding even the grossly physical." "Without passion the spiritual is cold, merely intellectual, sterile," Watkins stresses that Antony and Cleopatra's love "has become obsessive disease, for love like theirs can exist only by denying this world and creating a romantic paradise 'where souls do couch on flowers,' eternally consuming each other rather than consummating something of greater importance than either."

137 Chute, Marchette. *An Introduction to Shakespeare*. New York: E.P. Dutton, 1951. 123 pp.

Shakespeare presents Antony as "a great man and great soldier who is wrecking himself for love as Othello did for jealousy and Macbeth for ambition." Cleopatra is "a wanton and a coward, unreasonable and jealous and violent."

138 Clemen, W.H. "*Antony and Cleopatra.*" *The Development of Shakespeare's Imagery*. London: Methuen,1951, pp. 159-67. Reprint. New York: Hill & Wang, 1962.

Shakespeare's imagery, "which at first glance seems only to create the atmosphere of the play, actually affects more than this. It is symbolically related to the characters, serves their self-interpretation and the expression of their feelings."

139 Crane, Milton. "Antony and Cleopatra." *Shakespeare's Prose*. Chicago: U of Chicago P, 1951, pp. 177-81.

Shakespeare uses prose in this play "for purely dramatic reasons." The use of prose "is restricted by the enormously flexible and varied quality of the verse," and "the fluidity of the play makes of verse and prose a single medium, at once infinitely delicate and powerful."

140 Goddard, Harold C. "Antony and Cleopatra." *The Meaning of Shakespeare*. Chicago: U of Chicago P, 1951, pp. 570-94.

This play represents the finest achievement of Shakespeare's genius: "Here history, comedy, and tragedy are chemically combined; here the scope of the drama is world-wide; here sprawling and recalcitrant material is integrated with a constructive art that only many rereadings permit one to appreciate; here all the important characters of a huge cast are distinctly individualized, the central figures ranking among Shakespeare's masterpieces; here the humor is so inherent that we do not think of it and could not conceivably speak of it as comic relief; here the poetry of the highest order remains continually in keeping with the immense variety of scene and subject; here, finally, a conclusion that borrows touches from the death scenes of Romeo and Juliet, Hamlet, Othello, and King Lear blends them into what is in some respects the most complex, sustained, and magnificent piece of musical orchestration to be found anywhere in Shakespeare."

In spite of these qualities, this play cannot compete with the four great tragedies because "Antony and Cleopatra, compared with Shakespeare's other heroes and heroines, even the Macbeths, are a pair soiled and stained by long submersion in the world." The specific effect of the play depends on this submersion. Love "has usually lost some of its pristine quality when it appears late or in natures already tarnished with carnality, but its miraculousness may on that account be actually enhanced." Anyone frustrated in love will turn to the pursuit of power, and Shakespeare fuses love and power in *Antony and Cleopatra*. He "certainly is saying that there is something in life in comparison with which battles and empires are of no account."

141 Harrison, G.B. "*Antony and Cleopatra*." *Shakespeare's Tragedies*. London: Routledge & Kegan Paul, 1951, pp. 203-26.

This play "is not deep tragedy but rather a comment on history." It "is a genial play in which all, no matter what frailties and errors they commit, are shown at their best in failure." The play "is gorgeous, with the loveliest word-music, but it never reaches down to the depths of emotion." The reason is that the story "is not by any standard essentially tragic, for a man who throws his wealth into the lap of a harlot and then kills himself is no tragic hero; his death is not heroic, but the final degradation."

142 Kyd, Thomas [pseud.]. "Comic Card Game." *American Scholar* 20 (1951): 325-33.

This is a parody of the methods of the "new critics" through an analysis of *Antony and Cleopatra*.

143 Entry deleted.

144 Sewell, Arthur. *Character and Society in Shakespeare*. Oxford: Clarendon P, 1951, pp. 122-26.

According to Sewell, "Action and volition are determined within the play not primarily by psychological motivation, but by those conflicting moral addresses to the universe which go to fashion the presiding vision." Antony and Cleopatra "do not lead us beyond themselves. We see them in the universe and somehow or other within that universe we have to subdue them; to that universe they must, though in death, be reconciled." Hence the two "make no discovery and they experience no transformation of vision." The spectators may feel pity for them but not any compassion.

145 Walker, Roy. "The Northern Star: An Essay on the Roman Plays." *Shakespeare Quarterly* 2 (1951): 287-93.

Walker traces Shakespeare's "idea of Rome" through *Antony and Cleopatra* and other plays. This play "shows the fatal quarrel of the victorious triumvirate, the beginnings of imperial disintegration, the downfall of two of the triple pillars, and the final restoration of Octavius as Caesar."

146 Wentersdorf, Karl. "Shakespearean Chronology and the Metrical Tests." *Shakespeare-Studien: Festschrift für Heinrich Mutschmann*. Ed. Walther Fischer and Karl Wentersdorf. Marburg: 1951, pp. 161-93.

Metrical tests are "a reliable confirmation of the dating assigned to the plays for which there is no definite evidence." There is no reason to disagree with E.K. Chambers about the dating of *Antony and Cleopatra* in 1606-7.

147 Evans, B. Ifor. *The Language of Shakespeare's Plays*. London: Methuen, 1952, pp. 191-200. 3rd. ed. London: Methuen, 1964, pp. 191-97.

"Though it has not the supreme poetic identity of theme and poetry of *Macbeth*, or the unmatched originality of the storm scenes of *King Lear*," Evans points out, "it has beauty, splendour and brilliance, unparalleled elsewhere, and the whole great variety of the theme, and its scenes, geographically so widely stretched, are somehow brought together by the individual *personality* of the language." Yet, Evans also finds that "there is not the spiritual depth, and, ultimately, not the originality. Hamlet, Macbeth, and Lear are driven on by something outside possible control, while Antony is a study of the decay of will, which for moments is arrested, and could conceivably be controlled."

148 Halliday, F.E. *A Shakespeare Companion, 1550-1950*. London: Duckworth, 1952. 742 pp. Rev. ed. *A Shakespeare Companion, 1564-1964*. New York: Schocken Books, 1965. 569 pp.

This is a comprehensive handbook to Shakespeare's life and works, his plays and characters, companies and theaters, and other playwrights. There are numerous articles about *Antony and Cleopatra.*

149 Helton, Tinsley. "The Concept of Women's Honor in Jacobean Drama." *Dissertation Abstracts* 12 (1952): 795A. (Minnesota).

Heywood, Chapman and Shakespeare modified and questioned the traditional ideal of chastity. Cleopatra, "although she violates all the Elizabethan precepts, is wholly dispensed from moral judgment."

150 Nicoll, Allardyce. *Shakespeare.* Home Study Books. London: Methuen, 1952. 181 pp.

The language of this play "is vibrant with a nervous tension and a peculiar facility of phrase the like of which can only with difficulty be paralleled elsewhere." But the play "hardly leaves us with the overwhelming emotion which enwraps our minds in the other." Antony and Cleopatra, "conceived in essentially non-heroic terms, are encased in a heroism of words which do not integrate with the action itself."

151 Ogburn, Dorothy, and Charlton Ogburn. *This Star of England: "William Shake-speare," Man of the Renaissance.* New York: Coward-McCann, 1952. 1297 pp.

The Ogburns believe that Edward de Vere, seventeenth Earl of Oxford, wrote this play in 1579-80, when his "star shone at the zenith." In their opinion, the play "was drastically revised more than once, and while the Egyptian Queen was partially Anne Vavasor in the first version, to Oxford's Antony, she was in the last all Elizabeth, with the great drama becoming an epic of Lord Oxford's relationship with the Queen."

152 Weilgart, Wolfgang J. *Shakespeare's Psychognostic: Character Evolution and Transformation.* Tokyo: Hokuseido P, 1952. Reprint. New York: AMS, 1972. 276 pp.

Psychognosis "is an intuitive, creative, contemplative, universal knowledge of the human mind, and its insights hold true in the systems of every generation." All the characters in this play "desire either love or power, and the lovers, especially Antony, vacillate between both." Antony "is softened into an Egyptian, while Cleopatra rises to his former dignity of a Roman."

153 Berkeley, David S. "The Crux of *Antony and Cleopatra*."*Bulletin of the State U of Oklahoma A& M College:* Arts & Sciences Studies, Humanistic Ser. No. 4, 50 No. 2 (1953): 1-13.

Not seen.

154 Brown, Huntington. "Enter the Shakespearean Tragic Hero." *Essays in Criticism* 3 (1953): 285-302.

What sets Antony apart from other Shakespearean heroes is "the wavering of the active man between love and glory, and a measure of understandable doubt in the inner man as to which ideal is the right one."

155 Fluchère, Henri. *Shakespeare*. Trans. Guy Hamilton. London: Longmans, Green, 1953. 272 pp.

This play indicates that "the Shakespearian planet has emerged from the darkness of shadow and entered the light. Cosmic images abound in it, effortlessly studding the terrestrial universe and conferring upon it celestial dimensions and prestige." Cleopatra's death "is one of the greatest moments in the drama of the whole world," and Shakespeare "has recovered his calm of spirit."

156 Jepson, Laura. *Ethical Aspects of Tragedy: A Comparison of Certain Tragedies by Aeschylus, Sophocles, Euripides, Seneca and Shakespeare*. 1953. Reprint. New York: AMS, 1971. 130 pp.

Romantic irony lies in the ambiguous resolution of *Antony and Cleopatra*;; Shakespeare does not assert a well-defined attitude towards his characters. He "neither glorifies nor condemns the illicit love of his protagonists" which "are a law unto themselves." Antony is "a man caught between two powerful forces, between the extremes of emotion on the one hand and reason on the other—and unable to pursue a safe course between them." In a world "in which the forces of right and wrong are neutral, Cleopatra, like Dionysus, is a principle which, though it destroys, is yet exalted in the ambiguity of romantic irony."

157 Pearce, T.M. "Shakespeare's *Antony and Cleopatra*, V.ii.243-359." *Explicator* 12 (Dec. 1953): Item 17.

It seems most likely that the "pretty worm of Nilus" was one of the Sand Vipers, Cerastes, which the Clown brings in his basket.

158 Spalding, K.J. *The Philosophy of Shakespeare*. Oxford: George Ronald, 1953. 191 pp.

Shakespeare can be compared with a scientist who looks at the chaos of the world around him and seeks "some rational remedy for its irrationalities." In this play, he presented "the fall of a man and the rise of a woman." "Whether with or without their intention, men are influences which, like sunshine or plague, may spread freely about them health or sickness, good or evil." Antony is one such man.

159 Wheelwright, Philip. "Philosophy of the Threshold." *Sewanee Review* 61 (1953): 56-75.

Wheelwright defines the Threshold as an imaginative procedure "to create a fresh relationship between two or more images" and the Melting Pot as one "to see a general idea in and through the particular images drawn from the real world"; then he analyzes aspects of the death scene "standing in effective tension with the idea of lurking deadliness."

160 Whitaker, Virgil K. *Shakespeare's Use of Learning: An Inquiry into the Growth of His Mind and Art*. San Marino: Huntington Library, 1953. 366 pp.

In his brief discussion, Whitaker argues that in *Antony and Cleopatra* Shakespeare has "much less concern to work out the dramatic action and to explain it in terms that are fundamentally philosophic." The play shows "a slight failure of creative energy," because Shakespeare "merely dramatizes successive episodes in his source as he did in the early chronicles."

161 Aboul-Enein, A. M. "Cleopatra in French and English Drama from Jodelle to Shakespeare." Ph.D. Thesis, Trinity College, Dublin, 1953.

Abstract not available.

162 Eckhoff, Lorentz. *Shakespeare: Spokesman of the Third Estate.* Trans. R.I. Christophersen. Oslo Studies in English 3. Oslo: Akademisk forlag, 1954; Oxford: Basil Blackwell, 1954, pp. 57-65.

Antony and Cleopatra throw away everything "because they lose sight of everything but their love." The author finds the two figures so admirable that "we almost forget to be appalled at their fate; we hardly hear the advice which Shakespeare, in muffled tones, whispers in our ears."

163 Halliday, F.E. *The Poetry of Shakespeare's Plays.* London: Duckworth; Cambridge, MA: Robert Bentley, 1954, pp. 161-66.

The language in the play "is kneaded into a sculptor's medium, a plastic substance to be modelled into forms of any shape or size."

164 Henderson, Archibald, Jr. "Family of Mercutio." *Dissertation Abstracts* 14 (1954): 1395A (Columbia).

Enobarbus is one of the mockers who "warns his master against love in a temper much like that of the symposium mockers."

165 Pearson, Norman Holmes. "Antony and Cleopatra." *Shakespeare: Of an Age and for All Time.* Ed. Charles T. Prouty. The Yale Shakespeare Festival Lectures. [Hamden, CT:] Shoe String Press, 1954, pp. 123-47.

For Pearson, "It was the amalgamation of seeming contraries of heart and mind that counted in the end to fill the lacks in each alone, and make a mutual pair. This was a twain to make a union firm; and they had learned to read what words contain, and what they spoke."

166 Schanzer, Ernest. "A Plot-Chain in 'Antony and Cleopatra'." *Notes and Queries* ns 1 (1954): 379-80.

Schanzer sees the same chain of events in *Antony and Cleopatra*, III.iv.15ff and *King John*, III.i.331ff. This means that "the habit of association, which exerted such a powerful influence on Shakespeare's method of composition, could extend beyond his choice of words to the very plotting of the play itself."

167 Aldus, Paul J. "Analogical Probability in Shakespeare's Plays." *Shakespeare Quarterly* 6 (1955): 397-414.

Aldus analyses the scene of the drunken brawl on board Pompey's ship and scenes from *Julius Caesar* and *Henry IV, Part 1*, which "serve the function of establishing probability for later important actions or sequences of actions, or of producing significant retrospects, or sometimes of doing both."

168 Beauchamp, Virginia Walcott. "Dramatic Treatment of Antony and Cleopatra in the Sixteenth and Seventeenth Centuries: Variations of Dramatic Form upon a Single Theme." Diss. Chicago, 1956. *Index to American Doctoral Dissertations 1955/56*, p. 139.

Abstract not available.

169 Berkeley, David S. "On Oversimplifying Antony." *College English* 17 (1955): 96-99.

Since Antony's character can be read in opposite ways, "the play takes on more shadowy outlines and becomes a richer, more subtle, more dramatic, and more human drama worthy of more critical esteem than it has generally won."

170 Cunningham, Dolora G. "The Characterization of Shakespeare's Cleopatra." *Shakespeare Quarterly* 6 (1955): 9-17.

Cleopatra's final decision "is complicated by the fact that in the end she has to choose between life as she has lived it and the final change of death." She has "to choose between sin and virtue, this world and eternity. It is, therefore, the traditional scheme of Christian ethics which provides the standards of realism for judging the character of Cleopatra and the entire dramatic action."

171 Gerstner-Hirzel, Arthur. "Stagecraft and Poetry." *Shakespeare Jahrbuch* (Weimar) 91 (1955): 196-211.

This study deals with "gestures implied in Shakespeare's lines." *Antony and Cleopatra* has thirty-four gestures per thousand lines.

172 Knights, L. C. "*King Lear* and the Great Tragedies." *The Pelican Guide to English Literature*. Ed. Boris Ford. Harmondsworth: Penguin, 1955, II, 228-256. Revised and Expanded ed. London: Penguin, 1982, II, 327-56.

In this play, Shakespeare "embodies different and apparently irreconcilable evaluations of the central experience." He "evokes the passion of the lovers with the greatest possible intensity, and invests it with the maximum of positive significance. But, more realist than some of his critics, he makes it impossible for us not to question the nature and conditions of that very energy that the lovers release in each other."

173 MacLure, Millar. "Shakespeare and the Lonely Dragon." *University of Toronto Quarterly* 24 (1955-1956): 109-20.

Thomas More and Shakespeare considered politics "as a great play, the world of affairs a great stage whereon moved great persons." Shakespeare "has shown us in the conflict of Antony and Caesar the inevitable failure of the self-deluding hero in the arena of practical politics." Caesar "has taken care that he should be vindicated before the tribunal of history, while Antony couches on immortal flowers with Cleopatra."

174 Nathan, Norman. "*Antony and Cleopatra,* IV.vii.6-10." *Notes and Queries* ns 2 (1955): 293-94.

Scarus is implying that "he has the nine lives proverbially accredited to a cat."

175 Russell, Bertrand. "The Psychoanalyst's Nightmare." *Nightmares of Eminent Persons*. New York: Simon and Schuster, 1955, pp. 17-28.

Antony meets Dr. Bombasticus, a psychoanalyst, at the time of the Battle of Actium. Dr. Bombasticus "explained to me the workings of my unconscious, and I soon perceived, under his influence, that Cleopatra had not the charms with which I had invested her, and that my love for her was only a fantasy-passion." Antony "regretted that public duty compelled me to put Cleopatra to death, for only so could my reconciliation with Octavia and her brother be solid." Later on, Dr. Bombasticus is found in hell for killing the souls of his clients.

176 Speaight, Robert. "*Antony and Cleopatra.*" *Nature in Shakespearian Tragedy*. London: Hollis & Carter, 1955, pp. 122-49.

In this play "is the end of contradiction and division; and the crucifying dialectic of human nature is resolved, not in terms of psychology or philosophy, but by the sheer, superabundant power of the poetic image; not in terms of religious dogma, but in the triumph, beyond all reason or analysis, of a transcendent humanism." This "is the most dazzling, even if it is not the most profound, of Shakespeare's visions, and it would never quite come to him again. Through it he asserts, without either moral censure or romantic compromise, his belief in the resurrection of the flesh." The dimensions of the play "are not temporal but eternal; not local but spatial." The drama "is inherent in the poetry; the poetry is not a decoration of the drama." Shakespeare's task here "is to construct a hypostasis which at one moment shall seem to be compounded of mere dross and at another of purest gold; a hypostasis where the dross shall be miraculously transformed."

177 Bush, Geoffrey. *Shakespeare and the Natural Condition.* Cambridge, MA: Harvard UP, 1956. 135 pp.

In Shakespeare's last plays, "*Antony and Cleopatra* and the four romances, we approach most nearly to meanings that suggest allegory and a single reality." There is "a contract frequently drawn in the last plays between natural fact and human art; and it is nature that is the superior." *Antony and Cleopatra* is "set in Shakespeare's southern world; and the goodness of nature is stated with confidence and wonder." In this play, "the visions of comedy and tragedy merge."

178 Daiches, David. "Guilt and Justice in Shakespeare." *Literary Essays.* Edinburgh and London: Oliver & Boyd, 1956, pp. 1-25.

This play "is—among many other things—the story of a tawdry sensual love raised to tragic heights by sheer poetry." Antony "in the end surrenders wholly to his passions and loses the political world to young Octavius Caesar, the man whose fortunes he had earlier saved. *There*, perhaps, is Shakespeare's ideal practical man, Octavius Caesar, shrewd, cool-headed, altogether a cold fish." Cleopatra "is shrewish, hysterical, sadistic, dishonest and cowardly, as well as beautiful, queenly and heroic."

179 Donno, Elizabeth Story. "Cleopatra Again." *Shakespeare Quarterly* 7 (1956): 227-33.

Traditional Christian interpretations do not illuminate Cleopatra's death. An explicit Christian reading can be imposed on the play "only by a wrenching of the poetic and dramatic context."

180 Harrison, Thomas P. "Shakespeare and Marlowe's *Dido,Queen of Carthage.*" *Texas Studies in English* 35 (1956): 57-63.

Marlowe's play "anticipates *Antony and Cleopatra* in the famous Cydnus passage and in the management of neoclassical situations involving the protagonists."

181 Hayashi, Shigeko. "Antony and Cleopatra." *Studies in English and American Literature* (Christian Women's University, Tokyo) 4.1 (1956). In Japanese.

This is a discussion of characters from women's viewpoint.

182 Jorgensen, Paul A. *Shakespeare's Military World*. Berkeley: U of California P, 1956. 345 pp.

There is no detailed discussion of the wars in this play, but this study makes about ten references to it.

183 Nosworthy, James M. "Symbol and Character in *Antony and Cleopatra*." *Shakespeare Newsletter* 6 (1956): 4.

In Shakespeare's tragic period, "the image of the world or earth was generally a symbol of the sublime, but in *Antony and Cleopatra* it hardened into a purely terrestrial image."

184 Stempel, Daniel. "The Transmigration of the Crocodile." *Shakespeare Quarterly* 7 (1956): 59-72.

Stempel rejects the romantic idea of Cleopatra's femininity and considers the play as a satire rather than a tragedy, in which Shakespeare has adopted the Elizabethan misogynic notion of woman's degrading influence on man. Antony "is one of the contenders for the rule of an empire," and "the morbid disease which has destroyed him must be removed completely as a source of danger to the state."

185 Stirling, Brents. "The nobleness of life." *Unity in Shakespearian Tragedy: The Interplay of Theme and Character*. New York: Columbia UP, 1956, pp. 157-92.

Shakespeare did not "see life truly and think about it romantically," and "there is no meretricious sublimity cast even over the ending of *Antony and Cleopatra*. Instead, it is engagingly satirical throughout, but it remains great tragedy because the satire is combined effectively with other qualities." *Antony and Cleopatra* "asserts human dignity, value, because it confronts defeat with a superb expression of ironical truth. As the audience joins in the confrontation and expression, it perceives events not in the manner of Antony or Cleopatra but of Shakespeare." In this satirical tragedy, the playwright "offered protagonists who combine impressive qualities with an artless and self-conscious claim to the 'nobleness of life', which is satirized almost to the end."

186 Stull, Joseph S. "Cleopatra's Magnanimity: The Dismissal of the Messenger." *Shakespeare Quarterly* 7 (1956): 73-78.

Stull rejects a literal reading of III.v.132-36 and proposes a more noble interpretation of both Antony's and Cleopatra's role in it.

187 Barnet, Sylvan. "Recognition and Reversal in *Antony and Cleopatra*." *Shakespeare Quarterly* 8 (1957): 331-34.

Barnet explains the relevance of Aristotle's terms to *Antony and Cleopatra*. The deaths of the two principals are "preceded by a recognition (anagnorisis), or transition from ignorance to knowledge, which produces a reversal (peripeteia), or unexpected action."

188 Barroll, John Leeds III. "Shakespeare and Roman History." *Dissertation Abstracts 17* (1957): 626-27A (Princeton).

Barroll approaches *Antony and Cleopatra* and *Julius Caesar* in terms of Renaissance attitudes towards the relevant episodes in Roman history. In this play, "the failure of the lovers to gain what the Christians regarded as the fourth monarchy is suggested to be a reflection of God's disqualification of the couple in favor of Augustus."

189 Bowling, Lawrence E. "Duality in the Minor Characters in *Antony and Cleopatra*." *College English* 18 (January 1957): 251-55.

The theme of unity and duality "is worked out in terms of four important minor characters: Pompey, Lepidus, Octavia, and Enobarbus. Each of these characters occupies a more or less intermediate position between Antony and Caesar, each attempts to pursue dual interests, and each fails because of this duality."

190 Bowman, Thomas D. "Antony and the 'lass unparallel'd'." *Shakespeare Newsletter* 7.6 (Dec. 1957): 47.

In 4.4 Shakespeare begins to stress Cleopatra's "latent nobility of character." This scene represents "the turning point in Cleopatra's character development, the genesis of the audience's moral sympathy toward her, and a significant preparation for her ultimate preference of death to living dishonor."

191 Brown, Ivor. "Cleopatra." *Dark Ladies*. London: Collins, 1957, pp. 160-252.

In this literary biography of Cleopatra VII, Shakespeare's heroine is mentioned occasionally "as one of his most superb creations and the vehicle of incomparable poetry."

192 Charney, Maurice. "Shakespeare's Antony: A Study of Image Themes." *Studies in Philology* 54 (1957): 149-61.

The symbolic conflict between the values of Egypt and Rome "is deeply rooted in the imagery of the play, especially in the themes of sword and armor, vertical dimension, and dissolution."

193 Dickey, Franklin. *Not Wisely But Too Well: Shakespeare's Love Tragedies*. San Marino, CA: Huntington Library, 1957. 205 pp.

After reviewing the classical views of the lovers, the medieval tradition, and the work of the French Senecans, Dickey argues that "there is nothing niggardly about the world that Shakespeare has built for his peerless amorists to win and lose." Shakespeare is neither ascetic nor snobbish in his treatment. "Yet this golden world is tarnished; Shakespeare is always shifting his viewpoint so that each magnificent wayward gesture is countered either by a glimpse of its futility or by a sober estimate of its cost both to the lovers and to the universe." The play leaves the audience feeling that "the most magnificent love affair the world has ever known blazed like a fire in the night and like a great fire left sad ashes in the morning." The scale and size of the sensuality and luxury of the play shock the audience by a paradox: "The contemptus mundi which other playwrights preach in vain follows upon our awe at the sight of the most glittering world conceivable lying in ruins."

194 Mahood, M. M. *Shakespeare's Wordplay.* London: Methuen, 1957. 192 pp.

In her analysis of wordplay, Mahood uses of number of examples form *Antony and Cleopatra.*

195 Schanzer, Ernest. "Daniel's Revision of his *Cleopatra.*" *Review of English Studies* ns 8 (1957): 375-81.

In his revision of *Cleopatra*, Daniel was not influenced by his visit to a performance of Shakespeare's play, because "most of the additions supposed to be inspired by Shakespeare's play are far more closely paralleled in Antonius."

196 Spencer, T.J.B. "Shakespeare and the Elizabethan Romans." *Shakespeare Survey* 10 (1957): 27-38.

Shakespeare's plays have been influential "in creating the English notions of the ancient Romans," and his Romans have been very similar to his own contemporaries. From his plays people have learned "how clocks strike in ancient Rome" and "how Cleopatra has lace in her stays and plays at billiards."

197 Warner, Alan. "A Note on *Antony and Cleopatra.*" *English* 11 (1957): 139-44.

Shakespeare is dramatizing "a variation of a theme that is deeply rooted in myth and legend, the ruin of the strong man by his sexual weakness."

198 Webster, Margaret. *Shakespeare Today.* London: Dent, 1957. 318 pp.

In this play, Shakespeare's intellect "is at work on the problems of high tragedy compressed into the dramatic form which his stage demanded, and he produces what is perhaps his most impressive piece of theater craftsmanship in the tragic vein." Shakespeare "is free of the over-elaborate and decorated writing of his middle period; his verse is more flexible and more subtly adapted to the rhythms of speech than ever before."

199 Wilson, Harold S. "*Antony and Cleopatra.*" *On the Design of Shakespearian Tragedy.* Toronto: U of Toronto P, 1957, pp. 159-82.

This play "is a vision of love which glorifies man and woman, so that with all their faults of ambition and deceit, sensuality and careless pride, they yet rise to a tragic dignity, a tragic reconciliation and serenity, compared with which the dreams of earthly empire shrink almost into insignificance.; ultimately, their love is everything, or all that matters, to them and to us." Shakespeare "gives the form, by the most skilful selection, abridgement, apportioning of emphasis, until a pattern of action emerges that is wholly Shakespeare's, wherein we see causes and consequences of which Plutarch never dreamed and experience the pathos of the conflict, and the tragic purification of that pathos, under the spell of some of Shakespeare's greatest poetry." This play "ends in serenity, not with pain but with grandeur." It is made of materials like "the passions, the imperfections, the griefs and sufferings of humanity, but these limitations are countered by some heroic action or example that reconciles us to the spectacle of human frailty." The audiences watch "an ennoblement and a purification through suffering: an ennoblement for the tragic protagonists; a purification for us the spectators who share in their suffering vicariously and in their triumphant reconciliation."

200 Barroll, J. Leeds. "Antony and Pleasure," *Journal of English and Germanic Philology* 57 (1958): 708-20.

In this play, Shakespeare continues "to portray the individual as responsible, by some failure of reasoning or by some moral weakness, for his own tragedy." Antony "dies unreclaimed and deluded, in the lap of his fatal lure, his head swimming with self-deceptive thought. Yet his stature is sufficient to motivate even Cleopatra's actions in Act V, which in its constant allusion to Antony renders tribute to his essential greatness."

201 Barroll, J. Leeds. "Enobarbus' Description of Cleopatra." *Texas Studies in English* 37 (1958): 61-78.

Antony's love for Cleopatra "is almost a symbol of his proneness to the kind of life he leads in the play, a life for which Cleopatra is not always to blame." Antony's action is, "in principle, a surrender to *Voluptas* itself."

202 Barroll, J. Leeds. "Scarrus and the Scarred Soldier." *Huntington Library Quarterly* 22 (1958-59): 31-39.

"Scarrus" and the scarred soldier appear to be one character in the consistency of their role, appearance on stage, and diction. They may have been played by one actor, with quick changes in appearance.

203 Hulme, Hilda M. "The Spoken Language and the Dramatic Text: Some Notes on the Interpretation of Shakespeare's Language." *Shakespeare Quarterly* 9 (1958): 379-86.

Hulme tries "to show some of the ways by which we can test out, and perhaps increase, our sensitivity to the spoken language of a past age." She analyses 2.7.5 to suggest that the passage offers no difficulty if "we suppose that, with the words 'drink alms-drink' the servant is merely changing the known idiom 'drunk as a beggar,' getting his laugh by delaying recognition of a current phrase."

204 Jenkins, Raymond. "The Tragic Hero of Aristotle and Shakespeare." *Renaissance Papers 1958-60*. Ed. George Walton Williams. Durham: Southern Renaissance Conference, 1961, pp. 29-35.

The defects and virtues of the heroes of *Antony and Cleopatra* and other tragedies "are inseparable," and their flaws are intertwined with everything that is admirable." Antony "is so transfigured by the deaths of Eros, Enobarbus, and Cleopatra that he becomes a king in the realms of the spirit." The "greatness of soul" enables these heroes "to face calamity and death with heroic fortitude, that quality of moral nobility which is the chief trait of Aristotle's ideal man."

205 Knight, G. Wilson. *The Sovereign Flower*. London: Methuen, 1958. 324 pp.

In brief discussions of this play, Knight argues that "Antony is a mighty oak of a man, a vast strength uprooted, and crashes in magnificent and rebounding echoes of poetry." Shakespeare handles names in a subtle manner, "an inevitable part of his creative method, of-a-piece with the rest."

206 Markels, Julian. "The Public and Private Worlds of Shakespeare's Roman Plays." *Dissertation Abstracts* 18 (1958): 221-22A (Minnesota).

See item 426.

207 Norman, Arthur M.Z. "Daniel's *Tragedy of Cleopatra* and *Antony and Cleopatra*." *Shakespeare Quarterly* 9 (1958): 11-18.

The assumption that Daniel's play was "a possible secondary influence" on Shakespeare's play "provides an explanation of Shakespeare's daring use of two climaxes and of his conception of Cleopatra as the embodiment of a love transcending worldly obligations."

208 Purcell, J.M. "*A. & C.*, I.i.42-43." *Notes and Queries* ns. 5 (1958): 187-88.

At the back of Cleopatra's speech are certain proverbs of Shakespeare's day which will help to interpret her words.

209 Siegel, Paul N. "Foreshadowings of Cleopatra's Death." *Notes and Queries* ns 5 (1958): 386-87.

Siegel calls attention to the foreshadowings of Cleopatra's death in the text.

210 Smith, Constance I. "A Further Note on *Antony and_Cleopatra*, I.i.42-43." *Notes and Queries* ns 5 (1958): 371.

In these lines Shakespeare "has indicated the whole drama of a man who, in the supreme crisis, failed to be himself, failed his own integrity."

211 Soellner, Rolf. "The Four Primary Passions: A Renaissance Theory Reflected in the Works of Shakespeare." *Studies in Philology* 55 (1958): 549-67.

In *Antony and Cleopatra* and other plays, Shakespeare may have followed the Stoic theory that "all emotions originate from a judgment on whether an act or event occurring in the present or in the future is good or evil." This "results in a mental disturbance which falls into one of four classes: pleasure, pain, desire, or fear." Also, Shakespeare associated the four passions with the fourfold order of things."

212 Soellner, Rolf. "The Madness of Hercules and the Elizabethans." *Comparative Literature* 10 (1958): 309-24.

As a soldier and general, Mark Antony resembles Hercules; he also "emulates his ancestor's passionate outbreaks."

213 Spencer, Benjamin T. "*Antony and Cleopatra* and the Paradoxical Metaphor." *Shakespeare Quarterly* 9 (1958): 373-78.

Spencer analyses Shakespeare's use of a "paradoxical metaphor," which "involves the sense of bafflement and surprise, the inherent contradiction, and the unexpected reality beneath appearance which are associated with paradox."

214 Thomas, Mary Olive. "The Repetitions in Antony's Death Scene." *Shakespeare Quarterly* 9 (1958): 153-57.

Thomas argues in favour of "the present order of lines as the order of composition" and considers "the repetitions as Shakespeare's employment of rhetorical figures, *epimone*, for example at a time when he wishes to heighten effect and evoke compassion." She accepts interpolation by Shakespeare as an explanation rather than cutting by another hand.

215 Wright, Austin. "*Antony and Cleopatra.*" *Shakespeare: Lectures on Five Plays*. Carnegie Studies in English 4. Pittsburgh: Carnegie Institute of Technology, 1958, pp. 37-51.

This play "is permeated by a vast sadness, and yet it is a noble and inspiring work, one that fills us with pity for the weakness of man and admiration for his heroism, and holds us spellbound by the beauty of its poetry. Shakespeare "exhibits in lurid color Cleopatra's moral amnesia." "Yet at the end she flinches not for a moment, and by a final act of courage is transformed from a treacherous strumpet into a dignified heroine."

216 Bandel, Betty. "Cleopatra's Creator." *Shakespeare Newsletter* 9.6; 10.1 (Dec. 1959-Feb.1960): 10.

This is an argument for the constancy of Cleopatra's love for Antony, even if Shakespeare has made her "far less queenly than even Plutarch's Cleopatra." Shakespeare's men and women may know that "the world is not well lost for love," but, still, his women "bring the world down about their ears."

217 Behrens, Ralph. "Cleopatra Exonerated." *Shakespeare Newsletter* 9 (Nov. 1959): 37.

There is "no real evidence that Cleopatra's love for Antony ever wavered."

218 Bonjour, Adrien. "L'Anticipation Tragique dans les Scènes Initiales d'*Antoine et Cléopâtre*." *Etudes de Lettres* (U. de Lausanne) Ser. 2.2 (1959): 134-46.

Not seen.

219 Charney, Maurice. "Shakespeare's Style in *Julius Caesar* and *Antony and Cleopatra*." *ELH: Journal of English Literary History* 26 (1959): 355-67.

These two plays "offer an illustrative contrast between a carefully limited and controlled 'Roman' style, functioning within a defined framework of order and disorder, and a hyperbolical and expansive 'Egyptian' style which expresses the deep conflict between the world of Egypt and Rome."

220 Hotson, Leslie. *Shakespeare's Wooden O*. London: Chatto & Windus, 1959. 335 pp.

Arguing that the traditional method of production on the Elizabethan stage was "in the round," Hotson suggests that in the final two acts of this play, Shakespeare used "both sides of the Egyptian queen's famous monument." All the action involving Cleopatra took place in "the upper room of the monument."

221 Hubbell, Lindley W. "Antony and Cleopatra." *Lectures on Shakespeare*. Tokyo: Nan'un-do, 1959. Reprint. New York: AMS P, 1972, 132-45.

This play is "unequalled" for its opulence. Shakespeare has "lavished more of his genius on Marc Antony than on any other of his characters." His Cleopatra is "an infinitely subtle study of a woman, vain, perverse, sluttish, who, in adversity and facing destruction, becomes 'fire and air'."

222 Knights, L.C. *Some Shakespearean Themes*. London: Chatto & Windus, 1959. 183 pp.

The themes of *Antony and Cleopatra* and *Coriolanus* are "complementary in obvious but interesting ways, sexual passion being by its nature personal and subjective, though never merely a matter of individual feeling, the impulse towards authority and command necessarily manifesting itself in a wide social field, though both its origin and effects belong to the realm of personal life." Shakespeare "evokes the passion of the lovers with the greatest possible intensity, and invests it with the maximum of positive significance," but through his "moral realism" he also urges us "to question the nature and conditions of that very energy that the lovers release in each other."

The imagery of feasting and food and drink underlines "the element of repetition and monotony in a passion which, centring on itself, is self-consuming, leading ultimately to what Antony himself, in a most pregnant phrase, names as 'heart of loss'." Shakespeare has pushed to its limits "the sense of potentiality in life's untutored energies," and this makes the play "so sombre in its realism, so little comforting to the romantic imagination."

223 Lloyd, Michael. "The Roman Tongue." *Shakespeare Quarterly* 10 (1959): 461-68.

Rome, not Egypt, reveals itself as degenerate, hypocritical, selfish, loveless, and callous. Romans are known in the play for their "display not merely of the self-seeking but of the insensitiveness and incomprehension that lie behind the Roman tongue."

224 Lombardo, Agostino. "Le immagini dell'acua in *Antony and Cleopatra*." *English Miscellany* 10 (1959): 107-33.

This is an analysis of water imagery in the play.

225 McFarland, Thomas. "Antony and Octavius." *Yale Review* 48 (Winter 59): 204-28. Reprinted in *Tragic Meanings in Shakespeare*. New York: Random House, 1966, pp. 92-126.

Love and the world form the two opposites in *Antony and Cleopatra:* "Love is being; the world, non-being. We see the world degenerate from its moral ascendancy at the first of the play, and as the world becomes stumbling and uncertain, the at first stumbling and uncertain love of Antony and Cleopatra soars into fire and air. The empire becomes a self-seeking rabble; the whore becomes Cleopatra." Antony "relinquishes the world to Octavius, and is rewarded by paradise. Love, as total reality, rejects the world. There is no conflict."

226 Quayle, Calvin K. "Humor in Tragedy." *Dissertation Abstracts* 19 (1959): 2687A (Minnesota).

This study examines "the use made of humorous material to demonstrate or establish character personalities and character relationships" in *Antony and Cleopatra* and other plays.

227 Stein, Arnold. "The Image of Antony: Lyric and Tragic Imagination." *Kenyon Review* 21 (1959): 586-606. Reprinted in *Essays in Shakespearean Criticism*. Ed. James L. Calderwood and Harold E. Toliver. Englewood Cliffs, NJ: Prentice-Hall, 1970, pp. 560-75.

Stein explains Antony's images of himself in public life, expressed "not directly in soul-searching, but indirectly in imaginative gestures that project the self he has in his mind's eye." Other characters qualify and modify the public image. What "proves the tragic truth finally is not so much the world and its unattractive material concerns (or the countering effects of Enobarbus and Dolabella), but the follies of the protagonists and their central illusion of greatness, their checkered dream of 'nobleness of life' that cannot destroy the dream."

228 Walker, Roy. "Shakes v Shaw." *Shavian* (London) Feb. 1959: 7-9.

Walker compares the moral structures of Shakespeare's *Antony and Cleopatra* and Shaw's *Caesar and Cleopatra.*

229 Baker, Donald C. "The Purging of Cleopatra." *Shakespeare Newsletter* 10 (1960): 9.

"The clown in effect purges the baser elements of the language of the play as Cleopatra purges herself and leaves her other elements 'to baser life'."

230 Boughton, Charles Roy. "Production Problems in the Pivotal Scenes in Six of Shakespeare's Tragedies." *Dissertation Abstracts* 21 (1960): 3190A (Northwestern).

In his analysis of *Antony and Cleopatra* and five other tragedies, Boughton "stresses the forces that seem to animate and shape the development of the plot, as well as other aspects of the script important to problems that arise in the staging of the pivotal scene."

231 Draper, John W. "Subjective Conflict in Shakespearean Tragedy." *Neuphilologische Mitteilungen* 61 (1960): 214-21.

Shakespeare builds his tragedies like *Antony and Cleopatra* on conflict originating with the protagonist.

232 Ellis-Fermor, Una. "The Nature of Plot in Drama." *Essays and Studies* 13 (1960): 65-81.

In this play, "the magnitude of the issues, the grandeur of the chief characters, the multiplicity of figures and events witness to the vastness of its design and the cosmic imagery leads the imagination on to a universe beyond, into which the immediate world of the play seems limitlessly extended." The dramatic function of the perspective is to convey "the sense at once of vastness, of coherence and of significance."

233 Grill, Cynthia. "Antony, Cleopatra, and Proculeius." *Notes and Queries* ns 7 (1960): 191.

When Antony learns that Octavius has reached Toryne, "all his deeds and decisions are doomed to ignominious failure, and this is symbolized at the end by his bungled suicide and his erroneous advice to Cleopatra."

234 Lombardo, Agostino. "Ritratto di Enobarbo." *English Miscellany* 11 (1960): 33-58.

Enobarbus performs different roles in the play—as "fool" or ironic commentator, prophet, "chorus," artist, "fucille" in Henry James' sense, and soldier and confidant. He is rational and farseeing but subject to similar desires, and he serves as a foil to Antony.

235 Marsh, D.R.C. "The Conflict of Love and Responsibility in *Antony and Cleopatra.*" *Theoria* (U of Natal) 15 (1960): 1-27.

To care for someone outside oneself is to live. This play is neither romantic nor anti-romantic.

236 McGinn, Donald J. "Cleopatra Immolation Scene." *Essays in Literary History Presented to J. Milton French.* Ed. Rudolf Kirk and C.F. Main. New Brunswick, NJ: Rutgers UP, 1960. 57-80.

McGinn takes a middle road between Bradley's condemnation and Dover Wilson's praise of this play. "Certainly at the end of the play Shakespeare implies that Cleopatra is transformed into a nobler person than she earlier appears. Nevertheless she does not immediately, nor even entirely, cast off her sensuality; indeed, only her knowledge of the shame awaiting her in Rome forces her to rise above her natural fear of pain and death. Yet her eventual triumph is another vindication of Shakespeare's conviction expressed in *Hamlet* and *King Lear* that human nature may be purified through suffering."

237 Mendel, Sydney. "Hamletian Man." *Arizona Quarterly* 16 (1960): 221-236.

In Max Plowman's terms, Shakespeare's evolution from *Hamlet* to *Antony and Cleopatra* is one from painful Self-consciousness to liberating Consciousness.

238 Mills, Laurens J. "Cleopatra's Tragedy." *Shakespeare_Quarterly* 11 (1960): 147-62.

This "play presents the tragedy of Antony and then the tragedy of Cleopatra." Cleopatra's "tragedy is inherent in her equivocality, in her utter self-interest, and in her complete ignorance of the existence of an unselfish love apart from the physical." It is "pathetic and tragic that a beginning of anything other than sensual self-interest comes when there is neither the opportunity not the time for growth to ensue."

239 Moriya, Sasaburo. "*Gubijinso* to *Hamuretto* to *Antoni to Kureopatora*." *Journal of Literature and Linguistics* (Toyama U) 9 (1960). In Japanese.

Not seen.

240 Nakamura, Mutsuo. "A Historical Study on the Criticism of Shakespeare's *Antony and Cleopatra*." *Journal of the Faculty of Textile and Sericulture* (Shinsu University), Ser. D, Arts & Sciences No. 3.25 (1960): 1-70.

This monograph surveys earlier and recent criticism of the play under the categories of "character," "historical," "aesthetical," and "multiconscious."

241 O'Connor, Frank [O'Donovan, Michael]. "*Antony and Cleopatra*." *Shakespeare's Progress*. New York and Cleveland: World Publishing Company, 1960, pp. 170-75.

Shakespeare may have intended this play as satire, but "in the process [he] fell in love with Cleopatra himself, and by playing upon the antithesis in himself succeeded in transforming her into a universal figure like Shylock or Falstaff." For O'Connor, "the only rule for any production of *Antony and Cleopatra* is to look after the comedy and let the tragedy look after itself—as it will."

242 Ribner, Irving. "The Final Paradox: Antony and Cleopatra and Coriolanus." *Patterns in Shakespearian Tragedy*. London: Methuen, 1960, pp. 168-201.

Shakespearean tragedy "translates a moral vision into dramatic form, and thus it is a way of knowing." Shakespeare presents two plays in one: "For four acts it is a portrait of a great man's self-destruction through devotion to a sin which is itself heroic and magnificent. In the fifth act it is a portrait of a great queen's awareness of sinful lust, her casting it off, and her dedication of herself instead to a love to which her death is a sacrifice in expiation for former sin. The final feeling of the audience is not one of sordidness; rather it is one of the grandeur and nobility of triumphant love. But what triumph Antony and Cleopatra may achieve is in defiance of the Christian moral order, and that we should emotionally share in this sense of triumph while we perceive that it is rooted in sin is a reflection of the paradox which this play in its totality embodies." This play "is a powerful and moving experience, but in its intellectual statement it confirms only a paradox: that in a sinful path to destruction there may be a heroic grandeur which assures the sinner a kind of triumph in spite of all, that the public spirit of an Octavius and the private morality of an Octavia may seem small and insignificant in the light of such heroic destruction, and that the great world and its moral order may at times seem scarcely worth the preservation."

243 Rosen, William. "Antony and Cleopatra." *Shakespeare and the Craft of Tragedy*. Cambridge, MA: Harvard UP, 1960, pp. 104-60.

This play is baffling to critics, "for while we have, as in other Shakespearian plays, a clash of two worlds, the two worlds are so corrupt—as in *Troilus and Cressida*—that one is not morally superior to the other." Antony is divided between two ideals—the soldier's ideal and the desire to return to public life and the "private emotion, the all-consuming passion for Cleopatra." The plot presents "Antony's endeavor to escape the domination of Cleopatra so that he might regain his glory and once again be the most noble of men." But he can achieve nobility only in death. In dealing with the world, "Antony undergoes no change or development; no new possibilities are opened to him, and through him, to the community which is the audience." Similarly, Cleopatra does not change identity either.

244 Salerno, Nicholas A. "Shakespeare and Arnold's 'Dover Beach'." *Shakespeare Quarterly* 11 (1960): 495-96.

Arnold may have been influenced by *Antony and Cleopatra* 4.15.8-11 in his poem.

245 Schanzer, Ernest. "Three Notes on *Antony and Cleopatra*." *Notes and Queries* ns 7 (1960): 20-22.

The first note on I.i.36-40 suggests that there should be no punctuation mark after "thus:" Antony "is saying that the nobleness of life is to do thus provided such a peerless pair of lovers as they can do it." The second note explains the sources of the names like Scarus, Demetrius, Philo and others. The third note explicates III.x.10, meaning "just as it refers to a particular nag, Cleopatra, so it refers to a particular ribaud horse, Antony."

246 Schanzer, Ernest. "*Antony and Cleopatra* and *The Legend of Good Women*." *Notes and Queries* ns 7 (1960): 335-36.

Editors are not justified "in explaining Shakespeare's allusions to Ptolemy as referring either to the older or to the younger of Cleopatra's brothers, for it is unlikely that he knew much more about the matter than what he found in Chaucer's lines: that Cleopatra was a widow and that her deceased husband was called Ptolemy."

247 Sisson, Charles J. "The Roman Plays." *The Living Shakespeare*. Ed. Robert Gittings. London: Heinemann, 1960.

Cleopatra "is the Hamlet among Shakespeare's women characters, the most complex, incomparably the greatest in stature, and the most diversely interpreted," because "she alone among Shakespeare's women dominates a whole play, which rises and falls with her presence or absence." Shakespeare "has triumphed over Rome and the Roman thought, in the assertion of the things of the spirit which are more eternal than the Eternal City." Antony "finds honour in truth to himself, not to Rome, in this fulfilment of two noble souls." This is "romantic tragedy in its full stature."

248 Styan, J.L. *The Elements of Drama*. Cambridge: Cambridge UP, 1960. 306 pp.

Styan includes close analyses of several passages from Shakespeare, especially *Antony and Cleopatra*.

249 Watson, Curtis Brown. *Shakespeare and the Renaissance Concept of Honor*. Princeton: Princeton UP, 1960. 471 pp.

Characters like Hamlet, Lear, Antony and Macbeth "do not seem to be guided primarily by the law. They obey the dictates of their own conscience and when they fail to adhere to their own ideals, they tend to remake themselves." Even when a tragic hero "gives way to vice, the primary ethical criterion involved is his innate sense of honor and shame." Antony and Cleopatra "is almost a study in shame. From the very beginning of the play, Antony's former reputation as a great Roman general, as austere and disciplined as any of the great military leaders of Spartan Greece, is contrasted with his present decline into an epicurean, pleasure-loving wastrel who cannot break away from Cleopatra's bewitching snares." In spite of his numerous shortcomings, "Antony is constantly concerned to uphold his honor, and when he fails to live up to his own ideal of what he should be a sense of shame immediately seizes him." Shakespeare's portrayal of Cleopatra "in the early scenes of the play is intended to make her the epitome of feminine infidelity." In the final act, she is "a woman of the greatest tragic dignity."

250 Bryant, J.A., Jr. "*Antony and Cleopatra*." *Hippolyta's View: Some Christian Aspects of Shakespeare's Plays*. Lexington: U of Kentucky P, 1961, pp. 173-91.

From the Christian perspective, Antony and Cleopatra are "two people whose selfless expenditure of themselves enabled them to achieve an image of humanity greater than themselves and greater than the Caesar who, in a worldly sense, triumphed over them." That image "embodies the distinctively Christian ideal of humanity as a collection of uniquely valuable individual human beings wholly committed to the expenditure of themselves in love—and, if need be, sacrifice—for one another." Antony and Cleopatra cannot save themselves through this expenditure just as Caesar cannot save himself through commonsense and morality, but the understanding Antony and Cleopatra "achieve by it is more than enough to make their play a tragedy. The great irony is not that Antony and Cleopatra fail to see the full significance of the role they play, but that Caesar, who has the easily recognizable virtues of order and propriety on his side, fails to see any of the real significance of it at all."

251 Charney, Maurice. *Shakespeare's Roman Plays: The Function of Imagery in the Drama*. Cambridge: Harvard UP, 1961. 250 pp.

Charney analyzes three image themes which illustrate "the tragic conflict between the values of Egypt and Rome: sword and armor, vertical dimension, and dissolution." The tragedy is "also reflected in images of lowness and height and in a very characteristic imagery of dissolution." Antony "abandons the Roman style and values of Octavius Caesar—they are public, political, and objective as in *Julius Caesar*—and enters into the Egyptian style and values of Cleopatra." Shakespeare's typical figure is hyperbole, "the reaching-out of the imagination for superlatives," which is suitable for the spaciousness and scope of the play's subject matter.

252 Couchman, Gordon W. "*Antony and Cleopatra* and the Subjective Convention." *PMLA: Publications of the Modern Language Association* 76 (1961): 420-25.

By paying scant attention to Shakespeare's delineation of the moral decadence of the Roman world in *Antony and Cleopatra*, Bernard Shaw "reveals how completely his anti-romantic enthusiasms could blind him to an example of realism that was under his very nose."

253 Fergusson, Francis. "*Antony and Cleopatra*." Laurel Shakespeare. 1961, pp. 7-17. Reprinted in "*Antony and Cleopatra*." *Shakespeare: The Pattern in His Carpet*. New York: 1970, pp. 249-57.

Shakespeare "makes all the motivation of the play to center around that passion, which like a dream or the flickering light from a fire, dominates the Mediterranean world while the story lasts. So he gives the play the unity of action that poetic drama requires."

254 Frye, Dean Carson. "Choral Commentary in Shakespearean Tragedy." *Dissertation Abstracts* 22 (1961): 1997A (Wisconsin-Madison).

In *Antony and Cleopatra*, "the force of the choral judgments upon the hero and heroine depends upon how completely the audience accepts the political ideal of Rome, upon the extent to which its participation in Antony's story is created by action, character and poetry, and upon its reaction to the attitudes that lie behind and are expressed by these judgments."

255 Goldberg, S.L. "The Tragedy of the Imagination: A Reading of *Antony and Cleopatra*." *Melbourne Critical Review* (University of Melbourne) 4 (1961): 41-64.

Shakespeare's "pivotal insight" in this play is "that every mode of life necessarily loses even as it gains. The art encompasses them all, juxtaposes them in mutual criticism, but in the end it leaves the emergent 'questions' open."

256 Holloway, John. "Antony and Cleopatra." *The Story of the Night: Studies in Shakespeare's Major Tragedies*. Lincoln: U of Nebraska P, 1961, pp. 99-120.

Shakespeare delineates Antony and Cleopatra in terms of "their intense and exuberant physical energy; and it seems to be part of his sense of the whole situation, that exuberance of this order actually issues, in its turn, from sexuality itself in the full tide of its fulfilment." He "sees both the central characters as impelled into conduct which is sometimes exalted and sometimes abject . . .; and he also sees both as partially divested of the trappings of greatness, because their essential being as humans, their innermost condition of 'unaccommodated man', begins in calamity to transpire." At the time of her death, Cleopatra is a hunted creature, "because only just behind the stage spectacle of the queen of Egypt in all her glory, is the sense of an outcast from society—gipsy, felon, whatever it may be—baited as the victim of the common people." Death, a recurrent motif, "is the ordeal of the great and alienated who are pursued by life until they are sacrificed." Shakespeare's tragedies "*ritualize reality,*" and "they embed the essential movement of that ritual in life's common fabric."

257 Hyman, Stanley Edgar. "English Neo-Classicism." *Poetry and Criticism: Four Revolutions in Literary Taste*. New York: Atheneum, 1961, pp. 39-55.

Hyman concentrates primarily "on the images of Egypt and Rome, Egypt becomes a cluster of richness, fertility, excess represented by Cleopatra, and Rome something poor, barren, and miserly, represented by Octavius, with Antony then naturally choosing Egypt."

258 Khanna, Urmila. "Antony and Cleopatra." "The Isolation of the Tragic Hero: A Study of Shakespeare's Concept and Practice." Ph.D. Thesis, U of Birmingham, 1961.

Khanna analyzes Antony's isolation and his personal values. Antony reveals his heroic nature when he has rejected his Roman world. His isolation from his social and political milieu falls into three stages. In the first, up to Act 3, Scene 4, he attempts to retain his political position in Rome. The second is initiated in Act 3, Scene 5, when his return to Cleopatra is announced. Only at the battle of Actium does he accept that his sword must obey affection. This final surrender to his love for Cleopatra and the rejection of all other ambitions is expressed in his farewell to his soldiers.

259 Lerner, Laurence. "Tragedy: Religious and Humanist." *Review of English Literature* 2.4 (1961): 28-37.

This play is a tragedy of Triumph, not of disintegration. "Lear and Cleopatra are alike examples of human greatness in defeat: Lear great in the charity he has learned through suffering, Cleopatra marble-constant in the proud gesture of her poetry." Lear "dies asserting the Christian virtues, Cleopatra the pagan." Cleopatra "is the best that man can do without grace, and her limitations are the limitations of the natural man."

260 McCutchion, David. "Creation and Contrivance: Dryden's Adaptation of *Antony and Cleopatra* Set Against the Background of His Age." *Jadavpur Journal of Comparative Literature* March 1961: 46-64.

Not seen.

261 Muir, Kenneth. "The Imagery of *Antony and Cleopatra.*" *Kwartnalnik neofilologiczny* (Warsaw) 8 (1961): 249-264. Reprint. "The High Roman Fashion." *Shakespeare the Professional and Related Studies.* London: Heinemann, 1973, pp. 158-70.

The imagery of the world and heavenly bodies, eating, bodily movement, and melting is related to nobility, the goods, serpents' poison, kinship, and fortune. This indicates that Antony "is at once ruined and ennobled by his passion while Cleopatra's frailty is sublimated into this same passion." The ambiguity of imagery may mean that Shakespeare "presented the facts about the situation and left the members of his audience to draw their own conclusions."

262 Muir, Kenneth. "*Antony and Cleopatra*, III.xiii.73-8." *Notes and Queries* ns 8 (1961): 142.

"Rhythm and sense would be improved" if lines 76-77 were amended to ". . . there to kneele,/Till, from his . . .".

263 Nakamura, Mutsuo. "An Appreciation of 'Antony and Cleopatra' Mainly from the Standpoint of Its Three Principal Themes." *Journal of the Faculty of Textile Science and Technology* (Shinsu U), Series D, Arts No. 4. 28 (1961): 117-37. In Japanese.

Not seen.

264 Sen Gupta, Subodh C. *The Whirligig of Time: The Problem of Duration in Shakespeare's Plays*. Calcutta: Orient Longmans, 1961. 201 pp.

The author's intention is "to show how the temporal or durational sequence is interwoven into the dramatic movement, and, in his greater play, Shakespeare steps out of Time and projects pure Duration in which Time is transcended." Time reflects only the surface, but Duration shows the inner reality. There are indications of passage of time, but "they are more or less like facade behind which lies true dramatic duration reflected in the continuous development of characters" of Antony and Cleopatra. "This development is portrayed through a ceaseless succession in which one stage slides into another and a sense of duration is produced by the emergence and decline of human personality."

265 Troy, William. "'Antony and Cleopatra': The Poetic Vision." *Antony and Cleopatra*. Ed. C.J. Sisson. Laurel Shakespeare. New York: Dell, 1961, pp. 21-31.

Troy interprets this play as a "tragedy of the soul in space, of the soul struggling in a universe of illimitable space of which it is only a limited and self-limiting fragment."

266 Bonjour, Adrien. "From Shakespeare's Venus to Cleopatra's Cupids." *Shakespeare Survey* 15 (1962): 73-80.

Shakespeare's vision of Cleopatra's barge can be traced back to *Venus and Adonis*. Shakespeare's "phraseology and images anticipated in his salad days of *Venus and Adonis* the luscious mellow maturity of *Antony and Cleopatra*."

267 Daiches, David. "Imagery and Meaning in *Antony and Cleopatra*." *English Studies* 53 (1962): 343-58.

Shakespeare used the player image to construct "a moral universe out of non-moral materials" and stressed the different roles a man can play and the relationship of these roles to the player's true identity. After playing a variety of "roles," Antony unites in his suicide both warrior and lover, and Cleopatra "brings together in her death in a great vindication the varied meanings of her histrionic career and temperament."

268 Harrier, Richard C. "Cleopatra's End." *Shakespeare Quarterly* 13 (1962): 63-65.

Antony and Cleopatra V.ii.70-110 establishes the spirit in which Cleopatra commits suicide: "The loss—not of herself and her kingdom—but of Antony strikes her fully for the first time." Antony's suicide "places Cleopatra where she can feel the reality of Antony's ideal and his heavenly reality."

269 Hulme, Hilda M. *Explorations in Shakespeare's Language: Some Problems of Lexical Meaning in the Dramatic Text.* London: Longman, 1962. 351 pp.

Hulme comments on about six passages from this play. In 4.12.21, she suggests that the verb "pannelled" combines two meanings: the noun "panel" in the sense of a prostitute and "panele" meaning sugar.

270 Lever, J.W. "Venus and the Second Chance." *Shakespeare Survey* 15 (1962): 81-88.

Shakespeare explicated the Venus and Adonis myth in this play. "Chaos is an illusion; the Boar and Caesar are not fortune, but fortune's knaves. And Venus and Adonis, fallen and risen as Cleopatra and her Antony, live to triumph in the kingdom of the second chance."

271 Lloyd, Michael. "Antony and the Game of Chance." *Journal of English and Germanic Philology* 61 (1962): 548-54.

Lloyd evaluates the imagery of the sea and the games of chance which require a combination of skill and chance. Fortune in this play is "the reward of the man whose own initiative in 'sea peril' is timely."

272 Lyons, Clifford. "Stage Imagery in Shakespeare's Plays." *Essays on Shakespeare and Elizabethan Drama in Honor of Hardin*

Craig. Ed. Richard Hosley. Columbia: U of Missouri P, 1962, pp. 261-74.

Stage imagery can be defined as "all that the spectators see on the stage, together with all that they hear other than the spoken lines—music and sound effects." There are a number of stage-like images like Antony's sword. Some of the characters adopt "a reiterated manner of address in words and bodily attitude" and assume "a humble, penitent, submissive attitude." In all the plays, "stage imagery has important implications of meaning and delight for the reader as well as for the hearer-observer-participant in the theater; for it is a functional part of that total 'image' which is the play."

273 McManaway, James G. "Notes on Act V of *Antony and Cleopatra*." *Shakespeare Studies* (Japan) 1 (1962): 1-5.

A comparison of the final scene of this play with Anouilh's *The Lark* suggests that Shakespeare wants the audience to leave the theater with a vision of the Cleopatra for whom Antony gave up half the world.

274 Matthews, Honor M.V. *Character and Symbol in Shakespeare's Plays*. Cambridge: Cambridge UP, 1962. 211 pp.

Shakespeare "not only places a man's public and private lives in explicit conflict but finally uses the events of his private, not his public, life to express the play's essential values." Antony and Cleopatra's personal loyalties "are the ultimate values, though even the two lovers discovered their true nature very slowly." The pattern in this play is "formed by the concepts of sin, judgment and redemption." Shakespeare finally achieved a synthesis in the romances where he "is able to accept the positive goodness of each generation and to allow both old and young to share the moment of peace which his imagination achieves for them."

275 Miyauchi, Bunshichi. "Cleopatra." *Buka Hokoju* (Kagoshima U) 11 (1962): 153-76. In Japanese.

Not seen.

276 Righter, Anne. *Shakespeare and the Idea of the Play*. London: Chatto and Windus, 1962. Reprint. Penguin Shakespeare Library 1. Harmondsworth: Penguin, 1968. 224 pp.

Righter cites this play as one of the tragedies in which Shakespeare shows "the tendency to insult the theatre." In *Antony and Cleopatra* "the play metaphor continues to express emptiness and deceit. Cleopatra infuriates her lover by insisting that his protestations of faith are merely those of an actor."

277 Schwartz, Elias. "The Shackling of Accidents: *Antony and Cleopatra*." *College English* 23.7 (April 1962): 550-58.

This study deals with the play's movement from Philo's initial viewpoint to its radically contrasting terminal vision. Antony's "exploitation of Cleopatra and his imperial ambitions do not fundamentally conflict with each other; they both stem from the egoistic drive toward possession and dominance." "For just as there is a shackling of accidents in love, so there is a bolting up of change in death." In the last scenes of the play, "we believe for the moment that there is a forever and forever in love."

278 Scott, William I.D. *Shakespeare's Melancholics*. London: Mills & Boon, 1962. 192 pp.

The Antony of this play is quite different from that of Julius Caesar. Antony's "intuitive orientation has given way to sensation. He lives for the appetite of the day, with little foreboding of the future; but the basic type is still extraverted."

279 Waith, Eugene M. "*Antony and Cleopatra*." *The Herculean Hero in Marlowe, Chapman, Shakespeare and Dryden*. London: Chatto & Windus, 1962, pp. 113-21.

Antony possesses a number of Herculean traits like sensual indulgence, magnanimity and self-immolation, and His most Herculean trait, "through its sheer intensity," is rage. This play is more episodic than any other Shakespeare, and it "ranges like *Tamburlaine* over vast areas and achieves the effect of the sort of magnitude which we normally associate with epic."

280 Williams, George Walton "Shakespeare's *Antony and Cleopatra*, III,xiii,26." *Explicator* 20 (May 1962): Item 79.

"Gay comparisons" should be emended to "gay caparisons," because Shakespeare "invariably uses 'gay' to modify nouns of clothing."

281 Yagi, Tsuyoshi. "*Antony and Cleopatra*." *Eigo Eibungaku Ronshu* (Seinan Gakuin U) 2.2 (1962): 119-38. In Japanese.

Not seen.

282 Brittain, Kilbee Cormack. *The Sin of Despair in English Renaissance Literature. Dissertation Abstracts* 24 (1963): 281A. (UCLA)

Brittain examines sources for "Christian concern about despair, and English medieval and Renaissance literary presentations of despair showing secular application of religious tradition." In *Antony and Cleopatra*, Roman despair is "secular," but it has "theological colors."

283 Brockbank, J.P. "Shakespeare and the Fashion of These Times." *Shakespeare Survey* 16 (1963): 30-41.

Readers in each generation interpret a play in light of their "current of relevant perceptions" which limit them in their awareness of the sense of plays like *Antony and Cleopatra*.

284 Cowser, Robert G. "The Use of *Salad Days* in *Antony and Cleopatra*." *Word Study* February 1963: 8.

Cleopatra's metaphor implies youth and inexperience—cold, green appetizers before the feast itself.

285 Datta, Amaresh. "Towards New Tragic Values." *Shakespeare's Tragic Vision and Art*. Allahabad: Kitab Mahal, 1963, pp. 160-78.

This play "reveals a Shakespeare who can not only accept things as they are, but also discover a pattern in them." Since "he was deeply conscious of the spiritual nature of human life, he could also go beyond the dogmas of religion and yet see divine glory in human love and passion. There is consequently a greater freedom in the use of apocalyptic images, for Shakespeare now can extend their meaning and is not forced to accept only their formal religious significance."

286 Harbage, Alfred. *William Shakespeare: A Reader's Guide.* New York: Noonday, 1963. 498 pp.

This play "is not a tragedy of the same order as *Hamlet, Othello, Macbeth* and *King Lear.*" It "is secular and documentary, rather than religious and allegorical." "This absence of human attractiveness in the characters, and the unrelieved somberness of tone have prevented the play from being a favorite with readers and playgoers despite its vital theme and its stylistic excellence."

287 Hawkes, Terence, and Michael Quinn. "Two Points of View on *Antony and Cleopatra.*" *The Anglo-Welsh Review* (Pembroke Dock, Wales) 13 (1963): 7-11.

"Ambiguity extends through every aspect of the play," says Hawkes, and this makes readers' responses ambiguous and complex. But, for Quinn, *Antony and Cleopatra* is not ambiguous but complex, and its theme is: "What is the price of love and how does one learn to pay it?"

288 Ishida, Higashi. "Concerning Antony and Cleopatra." *Osaka Literary Review* 2 (Summer 1963): 1-9. In Japanese.

Ishada examines *Antony and Cleopatra*'s symbolic imagery in relating setting to character and theme.

289 Longo, Joseph Anthony. "Shakespeare's 'Dark Period' Reviewed in the Light of Mid-Twentieth Century Criticism." *Dissertation Abstracts* 24 (1963): 2892A (Rutgers).

Shakespeare anticipates *Antony and Cleopatra* in his *Macbeth*: "The disordered world of *Macbeth* prepares for the paradoxes of *Antony and Cleopatra* with its antagonism between the moral and the sensual." The playwright presents love from "from a dual perspective: a distrust of the flesh and a release in the flesh."

290 MacMullan, Katherine Vance. "Death Imagery in *Antony and Cleopatra*." *Shakespeare Quarterly* 14 (1963): 399-410.

Shakespeare "employs death imagery skillfully to depict aspects of weakness, bravado, and destructiveness through character and action but culminating in a display of nobility in the presence of death infused with a sense of the immortal nature of passion." The imagery of death "accompanies Antony's tragic passion and decline, demonstrating with forceful irony the strengthening of his attachment to Cleopatra and the weakening of his judgment in the command of practical affairs."

291 Purdom, C.B. *What Happens in Shakespeare: A New Interpretation.* London: John Baker, 1963, pp. 166-70.

Purdom praises the play for its splendor, and he considers it Antony's play, "he being the protagonist and the vision his." But he finds it difficult to "sympathize with Anthony, because of excessive love and great failure as a soldier." Hence he finds it "a little displeasing."

292 Quennell, Peter. *Shakespeare, the Poet and His Background.* London: Weidenfeld & Nicolson, 1963, pp. 288-94.

Quennell praises the main characters because they "share our ordinary human appetites and failings."

293 Schanzer, Ernest. "*Antony and Cleopatra.*" *The Problem Plays of Shakespeare: A Study of* Julius Caesar, Measure for Measure, Antony and Cleopatra. London: Routledge & Kegan Paul, 1963, pp. 132-83.

Schanzer stresses that the structural pattern in *Antony and Cleopatra* "consists (*a*) of a series of contrasts between Rome and Egypt; and (*b*) of a series of parallels between Antony and Cleopatra." Shakespeare also uses two analogues: "that of the choice of Hercules between Pleasure and Virtue, and that of the kindred choice of Aeneas between Dido and the fulfilment of his divine mission." This play "contains both a De Casibus tragedy in the medieval manner and a tragedy of hubris and "até in the manner of the Greeks." The main focus of the tragic experience is "a sense of disillusion with that person or object, of desertion or betrayal by it." The play provides "enough of a sense of wonder, of exultation, and delight to make our emotional experience resemble more closely that at the end of *The Winter's Tale* than that at the end of *Othello* or *Lear*."

294 Shibata, Toshihiko. "An Essay on *Antony and Cleopatra*—a Negative Creation." *Essays* 16 (1963): 30-42. In Japanese.

Not seen.

295 Shirley, Frances A. *Shakespeare's Use of Off-Stage Sounds*. Lincoln: U of Nebraska P, 1963. 258 pp.

This study refers to some of the scenes from *Antony and Cleopatra*.

296 Spencer, T.J.B. *William Shakespeare: The Roman Plays*. Bibliographical Series of Supplements to "British Book News on Writers and Their Work" No. 157. Gen. Ed. Geoffrey Bullough. London: Longmans, Green, for the British Council, 1963. 60 pp.

In *Antony and Cleopatra*, Shakespeare "concentrates the dramatic attention upon the relation between the two characters, without losing his hold on the imperial background in which the two find their fate." The play's main theme "is the conflict in Antony, who is repeatedly confronted with a choice between his love for Cleopatra and his loyalty to the political and moral dignity of Rome."

297 Thomas, Mary Olive. "Cleopatra and the 'Mortal Wretch'." *Shakespeare Jahrbuch* (Heidelberg) 99 (1963): 174-83.

The serpent represents "a possible reminder of the classical Nourishing Earth, the mediaeval Lust, and the Renaissance Charity," and Shakespeare's idea is that "human love, paradoxically compounded of *concupiscentia* and *caritas*, is the source both of life and its value."

298 Traversi, Derek. "*Antony and Cleopatra*." *Shakespeare: The Roman Plays*. London: Hollis & Carter, 1963, pp. 79-206.

This is an expanded version of Traversi's 1938 and 1956 analyses of the play, the latest containing an extensive commentary on the action of the play. "As a chronicle play, the marvellously fluent presentation of historical events carries with it a balanced estimate of the hero's political stature; as a tragedy, it relates the story of his downfall to the desire, at least as old as some of the Sonnets, to see in the ecstasies of love a manifestation of spiritual value." "The rich and revealing interplay of these two themes, political and 'metaphysical' respectively, constitutes the glory of the play and makes it one of the culminating achievements of Shakespeare's genius." Antony and Cleopatra "are led to a public disaster which reflects the degradation which their perverse choices have imposed, but, once freed from this degradation by the very completeness of the ruin which they have brought upon themselves, they achieve by contrast with death a measure of fulfilment which, illusory it may be on the plane of daily living, implies while it lasts some measure of spiritual value." Traversi argues: "The balancing of the generosity which Antony's folly has at times implied against Caesar's mixture of competence, public vocation, and successful manners; the gradual ascent of the love imagery, in its very progress towards failure and self-destruction, from earth and 'slime' to 'fire and air'; the corresponding ascent of Cleopatra herself, provoked by circumstance, from sensual frivolity to the tragic affirmation of the only 'nobility' left to her; all these are parts of one great process which has needed death to complete it."

299 Lerner, Laurence, ed. "*Antony and Cleopatra*." *Shakespeare's Tragedies: an Anthology of Criticism*. Harmondsworth: Penguin, 1963, pp. 225-45.

This volume reprints excerpts from the following items: Granville-Barker, Middleton Murry, and Wimsatt.

300 Ahern, Matthew Joseph, Jr. "The Roman History Play, 1585-1640: A Study Indicating How Plays Dealing with Roman History Reflect Changing Political and Social Attitudes in England during This Period." *Dissertation Abstracts* 24 (1964): 3319A (Tulane).

This analysis of the Roman history plays, written in English between 1585 and 1640, shows that the "political and social attitude of the playwrights and, one must assume, the audience changed from optimism about the future of England in 1585 to pessimism in the Caroline period."

301 Alexander, Peter. *Shakespeare.* London: Oxford UP, 1964, pp. 238-41.

The theme is "the tension between the contrary instincts in the character of the protagonist," who "loved Cleopatra, that for her he left even the ranks in which he had been proud to fight, and that it was not weakness and mere dotage that made him her victim; for the force and power of the passion that destroyed him is itself the evidence of the strength that gives his fate its tragic interest."

302 Alexander, Peter. "*Antony and Cleopatra.*" *Introductions to Shakespeare.* New York: Norton, 1964, pp. 168-70.

This play should not be judged by standards of the realistic stage, because Shakespeare's theater "allowed of the same fluidity that is found in reading." Rome and Egypt "stand for two different and indeed opposite views of life." Antony "does not bear himself as one broken down by debauchery and incapable of anything more than lechery in idleness; he turns to Cleopatra not in his decay but at the very time when he has vindicated his position as one of the rulers of the world."

303 Arthos, John. *The Art of Shakespeare.* London: Bowes, 1964, pp. 53-67.

Since Antony and Cleopatra have an excess of imagination, they can "deny morality, and although they pay the obvious price in the loss of power and discretion, like the gods they think themselves they escape the tragic judgment." In this play "the game has been played out and Shakespeare commences what will provide still other forms for drama in the romances, where instead of men approaching the gods, the gods come to them."

304 Berkeley, David S. "On Desentimentalizing Antony." *Notes and Queries* 11 (1964): 138-42.

Antony's "attitude toward Cleopatra is one of love-hate." His final intentions, especially in recommending Proculeius, are ambiguously "past finding out."

305 Blakiston, J.M.G. "The Three Nook'd World." *Times Literary Supplement* 17 September 1964: 868.

In *Antony and Cleopatra* IV.vi.6 Shakespeare may refer to the triple-sectoring of medieval world maps.

306 Bonjour, Adrien. "Shakespeare and the Toil of Grace." *Shakespeare 1564-1964: Collection of Modern Essays by Various Hands.* Ed. Edward A. Bloom. Providence, RI: Brown UP, 1964, pp. 88-94.

Opposing Bethell's claim that "Shakespeare is applying theological categories" to Cleopatra's character, this study argues that "despite the raptures of theologians who would turn it into a hymn to the resurrection of the body, the end of *Antony and Cleopatra* is, and remains, a tragedy."

307 Bowers, Fredson T. "Shakespeare's Art: The Point of View." *Literary Views: Critical and Historical Essays*. Carroll Camden, ed. Chicago: U of Chicago P, 1964, pp. 45-58.

Shakespeare uses the touchstone character (Enobarbus) "to illuminate another by word of mouth, or by the example of parallelism and contrast." He uses plot "as a means of enforcing the dramatist's point of view." Act 3, Scene 7 "represents the climax, or crisis, since in this scene the fatal decision was reached to fight from weakness rather than from strength." "When made for faulty motives, as the result of a tragic flaw in character that affects the power of choice, the motivation is everything, the action is morally determinated, and on it hinges the tragedy." Acting in reverse, therefore, "Cleopatra repeats Antony's error in allowing her passion, or desires, to overcome her reason, thereby to assume command in a project for which she was not fitted, and finally to turn female coward when her hubris falters." Shakespeare "uses extraordinary methods to manipulate the audience's point of view."

308 Bowling, Lawrence Edward. "Antony's Internal Disunity." *Studies in English Literature, 1500-1900* 4 (1964): 239-46.

Antony suffered a tragedy on account of the conflict of love and honor. After bodily defeat, he achieved "that spiritual unity which made his tragedy a triumph."

309 Bullough, Geoffrey. "The Uses of History." *Shakespeare's World.* Ed. James Sutherland and Joel Hurstfield. London: Arnold, 1964, pp. 96-115.

Shakespeare tried "to conceive the tragedy of Antony and Cleopatra not as the chill and moral spectacle seen by the Countess of Pembroke and other classicists in their versions, but as a passionate conflict between duty and pleasure set forth through the Rome-Egypt antithesis." In this play, "the poetry makes us suspend our ethical standards and accept and rejoice in behavior which sets law, duty, morality at defiance, as we share in a fever and a passion which are not only of the flesh but of the spirit."

310 Burke, Kenneth. "Shakespearean Persuasion." *Antioch Review* 24 (1964): 19-36.

Shakespeare uses rhetoric to manipulate his audience so that they respond to *Antony and Cleopatra* as a play that "glorifies romantic love in terms of politics," with love "in essence an Empire."

311 Coghill, Nevill. *Shakespeare's Professional Skills*. Cambridge: Cambridge UP, 1964. 224 pp.

In his analysis of the juxtaposition of scenes, Coghill stresses that "the doubled sense of Eros is borne in upon us by reiteration." The "simplicity of love in Eros has been contrasted with the devious twists in the Serpent of old Nile: once more we have been shown her shot-silk of love and treachery."

312 Dyson, H.V.D. "This Mortal Coil—II: Shakespeare and Life in Death." *The Listener* 16 April 1964: 637, 639.

As his imagination matured, in *Antony and Cleopatra* and the romances, Shakespeare changed death from "an intrusive goblin" to "bare non-existence" to "a terror in a dream" to "a song, a vehicle of self-offering, an object of contemplation."

313 Eliot, T.S. "*Hamlet*." *Elizabethan Essays*. New York: Haskell House, 1964, pp. 55-63.

Eliot contends that "*Coriolanus* may not be as 'interesting' as *Hamlet*, but it is, with *Antony and Cleopatra*, Shakespeare's most assured artistic success."

314 Faber, Melvyn Donald. "Suicide in Shakespeare". *Dissertation Abstracts* 24 (1964): 4697A (UCLA).

Shakespeare arouses positive and negative emotions about suicides at the end of his tragedies. Experiencing an emotional conflict, the spectator "is both attracted and repelled: he experiences catharsis." This formula accounts for the diversely motivated suicides in *Antony and Cleopatra* and other plays.

315 Foakes, R.A. "Vision and Reality in *Antony and Cleopatra*." *Durham University Journal* 25 (1964): 66-76.

Antony and Cleopatra should be admired, not judged morally: "The power of their love lies precisely in the way it could transform them, for each other, at the right moments, into god and goddess," giving them a "touch of divinity transcending ordinary mortals."

316 Foakes, R.A. "Shakespeare's Later Tragedies." *Shakespeare 1564-1964: A Collection of Modern Essays by Various Hands*. Ed. Edward A. Bloom. Providence, RI: Brown UP, 1964, pp. 95-109.

Marston's early play signals "a new consciousness, a new spirit in the drama, one connected with the vogue for satire in the late 1590's, with the new comedy of humors, and with the first recorded use of the word 'parody' in English, in Ben Jonson's

Every Man in his Humour." When Shakespeare "turned, after *Macbeth*, to new tragic themes, in *Timon of Athens*, *Coriolanus*, and *Antony and Cleopatra*, it may be that he was, in his way, catching up with a new fashion on the stage." In these plays, all values "are relative, and Octavia's chastity is not a standard against which to measure Cleopatra's lechery. They show us men and women as they are rather than as they might be, engaged with one another in a world in which good and evil cannot be separated out, but are inextricably mixed."

317 Frost, David L. "*Antony and Cleopatra*—All for Love; or the World Ill-Lost?" *Topic* (Washington and Jefferson College), 7 (1964): 33-44.

The double meanings of the Clown in *Antony and Cleopatra* V.ii clarify what is already known: "sensual passion divorced from reality brings soft self-deceit and death."

318 Grace, William J. *Approaching Shakespeare*. New York and London: Basic Books, 1964, pp. 114-23.

Grace analyzes the tensions "between the passionate private world and the public world of legal order, war, and politics." Since Shakespeare believed in "the established moral pattern of tragedy," his hero has "to pay for his violation of decorum, of convention."

319 Heilman, Robert B. "From Mine Own Knowledge: A Theme in the Late Tragedies." *Centennial Review* (Michigan State) 8 (1964): 17-38.

Antony and Cleopatra depicts "the decay of conscience in passion" in "a world where all vital powers conspire against self-knowledge."

320 Holland, Norman N. "Antony and Cleopatra." *The Shakespearean Imagination*. New York: Macmillan, 1964, pp. 261-83.

Assigning this play to the last phase of Shakespeare's writing, Holland finds that "fragmentation" and "the disintegration of the body" have "suddenly become heroic, triumphant, practically comic." The play's atmosphere "is expansive, sunny, casual. Food and sexuality have become signs of health." This and other last plays celebrate life. In *Antony and Cleopatra* "we most clearly see the transition toward the late romances: the tragedy of two sharply contrasted worlds, the hard, competitive one of Rome, the other, lush, liquid, of Alexandria." The tension between these two worlds generates tragedy.

321 Howarth, Robert G. *A Pot of Gillyflowers: Studies and Notes.* Cape Town: by the author, 1964. Mimeographed. 110 pp.

These are notes on the unique elusiveness of *Antony and Cleopatra.*

322 Kaula, David. "The Time Sense of *Antony and Cleopatra.*" *Shakespeare Quarterly* 15 (1964): 211-23. Reprinted in *Essays in Shakespearean Criticism.* Ed. James L. Calderwood and Harold E. Toliver. Englewood Cliffs, NJ: Prentice-Hall, 1970, pp. 576-90.

This play "shows the intimate relationship the sense of time bears to the basic contours of the dramatic action, and its significance as one of the principal media through which the characters reveal their governing attitudes and thereby locate themselves within the moral universe of the play." In her readiness to "play till doomsday," Cleopatra "asserts the supremacy of being over becoming, and illuminates the meaning of one of the key Shakespearean terms: 'ripeness'."

323 Kott, Jan. "Let Rome in Tiber Melt." *Shakespeare Our Contemporary.* Trans. Boleslaw Taborski. New York: Doubleday, 1964, pp. 125-32.

Antony and Cleopatra "is a tragedy about the smallness of the world." This world "is small, because to master it, chance, or a helping hand, or a skillful blow will do." Heaven and earth are too small for love: "When Antony and Cleopatra kill themselves, the tragedy is over, but history and the world go on existing." The great ones have died, and Octavius lives to rule the flat world.

324 Lerner, Laurence. "Love and Gossip: or, How Moral is Literature?" *Essays in Criticism* 14 (1964): 126-47.

Focusing on Cleopatra in Act V, this is a dialogue of conflicting critical approaches.

325 Mills, Laurens J. *The Tragedies of Shakespeare's* Antony and Cleopatra. Bloomington: Indiana UP, 1964. 66 pp.

This play "presents first the tragedy of Antony and then the tragedy of Cleopatra, with each tragedy giving significance to the other and increasing its poignancy and thereby providing a unified tragic effect to the play as a whole." Antony "possessed man's virtues: courage, courtesy, generosity, liberality, magnanimity, forgiveness, the ability to think logically, firmness when at his best, humanity." But he did not have "the firmness to repel the fascination of a charmer 'in the East,' whatever he included in the word 'East'." Cleopatra's tragedy "is inherent in her equivocality, in her utter self-interest, and in her complete ignorance of the existence of an unselfish love apart from the physical." Cleopatra's tragedy "gains poignancy through contrast to Antony's as his gains pathos through contrast to hers."

326 Nandy, Dipak. "The Realism of *Antony and Cleopatra*." *Shakespeare in a Changing World*. Ed. Arnold Kettle. New York: International Publishers, 1964, pp. 172-194.

Shakespeare explores the nature and value of Antony and Cleopatra's relationship: "The contrast is between the condition of Egypt, whose heart and core is Cleopatra, and the condition of Rome, embodied and personified in Octavius Caesar. These are the twin poles between which the action works out. Antony's career is a discovery, I want to suggest, of his true bearings in relation to these poles. Enobarbus's career is a confirmation of this discovery. Cleopatra's career, especially the events of the last act, is a revelation of the full implications of her relationship with Antony."

327 Nelson, Conny Edwin. "The Tragedy of Power in Racine and Shakespeare." *Dissertation Abstracts* 25 (1964): 2985-86A (Washington).

This study considers the "dramatic function of rank, power, and politics" in Shakespeare and Racine. In *Antony and Cleopatra*, *Coriolanus*, Racine's *Brittanicus* and other plays, "power and politics are seen as essential determinants of character and the play's tragic structure."

328 Nowottny, Winifred. "Shakespeare's Tragedies." *Shakespeare's World: Centenary Essays*. Ed. James Sutherland. New York: St. Martin's P, 1964, pp. 48-78.

This play, "in its daring, its opulence and its sweep, may seem to stand apart from the other tragedies of Shakespeare. Yet there is one respect in which it develops from, and best expresses, the whole tragic energy of Shakespeare, namely, in its compassion—by which I mean that emotion we feel when we are made to experience, simultaneously, the suffering and the majesty of humanity."

329 Orrell, John Overton. "The Repeated Scene: A Study of Female Parallelism in Elizabethan Tragedy." *Dissertation Abstracts* 31 (1970): 2933A (Toronto).

This study of *Antony and Cleopatra* and other plays explains how "the meaningful use of repeated action urges on conclusions which profoundly affect our understanding of the whole."

330 Proser, Matthew N. "The Heroic Image in Five Shakespearean Tragedies." *Dissertation Abstracts* 24 (1964): 4683A. (Washington)

Proser analyzes the role of "the hero's self-image in precipitating his tragedy" in *Julius Caesar*, *Macbeth*, *Othello*, *Coriolanus*, and *Antony and Cleopatra*. Antony's "attempts to reclaim his self-image as the world's 'foremost man' and Cleopatra's 'transformation' at the play's conclusion are pitted against realistic and satirical perspectives" in the play.

331 Roddman, Philip. "André Gide on Shakespeare." *Shakespeare Encomium* 81 (1964): 71-89.

This is a transcript of Gide's lecture on *Antony and Cleopatra*, *Hamlet* and the Sonnets, as broadcast in 1946.

332 Sam'an, Angel. "Shakspir wa Shakhsiyyat Cleopatra." *Al-Masrah* (Cairo) April 1964: 55-59.

In Cleopatra there is a contradiction between her role as woman and as queen, and this accounts for her great vitality.

333 Shipley, Joseph T. *Antony and Cleopatra: a scene by scene analysis with critical commentary*. Study Master. New York: American R.D.M., 1964. 70 pp.

This is a study guide for students.

334 Smith, J. Oates. "The Alchemy of *Antony and Cleopatra*." *Bucknell Review* 12 (1964): 37-50.

In *Antony and Cleopatra*, Shakespeare translates prosaic reality into something rich and strange through his poetry. The defeat of reality "goes unmourned."

335 Smith, Sheila M. "'This great solemnity': A Study of the Presentation of Death in *Antony and Cleopatra*." *English Studies* 45 (1964): 163-176.

After exploring the "complexities, contrarieties and conflicting forces of life" in *Antony and Cleopatra*, Shakespeare "finally stills them and transcends them in an acceptable and exhilarating presentation of death."

336 Stirling, Brents. "Cleopatra's Scene with Seleucus: Plutarch, Daniel, and Shakespeare." *Shakespeare Quarterly* 15 (1964): 299-311.

The Seleucus episode is a culmination of a repeated "dialectic of resolution and back-sliding, selflessness and vanity." It is the last and "most critical of the scenes that 'test' Cleopatra." Even the spectators cannot recognize her victory until after Caesar's departure.

337 Stroup, Thomas B. "The Structure of *Antony and Cleopatra.*" *Shakespeare Quarterly* 15 (1964): 289-98.

Antony and Cleopatra "belongs to Polonius's 'tragicall-historical' kind; and though this kind may employ a Senecan device, style, or character here and there, it takes its shape chiefly from the later morality play, its direct ancestor." The play shows that "the actions of a man, especially a public man, affect all men," and its unity is based "on the unity of the universe."

338 Sutherland, James. "The Moving Pattern of Shakespeare's Thought." *Papers, Mainly Shakespearean.* Ed. G.I. Duthie. Aberdeen U Studies 147. Edinburgh: Oliver & Boyd, 1964, pp. 10-20.

"A moving pattern" refers to Shakespeare's "ability to shape long speeches, passages, and even whole scenes in a continuously developing movement." In 5.2.71ff of this play, the presence of Eros in one scene and that of Dolabella in the other enables Shakespeare "to give to thought and feeling the shapely movement that increases their poignancy, and that makes us realize the spiritual point of no return that both Antony and Cleopatra have reached."

339 Takei, Naoe. "Between Consciousness and Existence, a tragedy of Antony and Cleopatra." *Mejiro Gakuen Joshi Tandai Kenkyu Kiyo* 1 (1964): 221-33. In Japanese.

The protagonists were torn between "heavenly race" and limited human conditions.

340 Taylor, Marion A. "'Not Know Me Yet?'" *Ball State Teachers College Forum* 5 (1964): 63-66.

"Throughout the play" Cleopatra "is the same woman, any woman high or low who finds herself in love with a man who belongs to another woman."

341 Wain, John. "*Antony and Cleopatra.*" *The Living World of Shakespeare: A Playgoer's Guide.* London: Macmillan, 1964, pp. 129-41.

Romans give up their discipline in Egypt. "Once the emissary of a civilization drops the conspicuous habits of that civilization, and begins to adopt those of the people he governs, his authority declines." Antony is submerged by the barbaric attraction of Cleopatra's world. "Like water, she is unbiddable and unstable; immediately finds her own level; wins every battle not by fighting but by absorbing the strength of the assailant." This "is not 'tragedy', nor is it 'love poetry', as either is ordinarily understood. It is the working of the richest and most delicate imagination in all literature, utterly absorbed in its own concerns."

342 W[hitney], C[ynthia] K[olb]. "The War in *Antony and Cleopatra.*" *Literature and Psychology* (New York) 13 (1964): 63-66.

The basic antagonism of war has its source in the conflicting demands within individual psyches.This tragedy consists of "the ill timings of events and feelings." The war takes place at several levels, external and internal. "It is natural for a man [like Antony] to desire eternal uninterrupted union with the mother goddess. But man is forcibly separated from his identity with the nurturing mother by his own span."

343 Barroll, J. Leeds. "The Chronology of Shakespeare's Jacobean Plays and the Dating of *Antony and Cleopatra.*" *Essays on Shakespeare*. Ed. Gordon Ross Smith. University Park: Pennsylvania State UP, 1965, pp. 115-62.

Antony and Cleopatra may have been performed "in the last six days of December, 1606, or the first two weeks of January, 1607, or at some time even prior to all of these dates."

344 Berry, Francis. *The Shakespeare Inset: Word and Picture*. London: Routledge & Kegan Paul, 1965, pp. 45-52.

An "Inset," according to Berry, is an episode "where the imagined spectacle is at odds with the actual spectacle." Berry discusses Enobarbus' account of the lovers' first meeting in *Antony and Cleopatra*, II.2, as the only instance of an Expository Inset which must "narrate a single main event that took place previous to events shown on the stage."

345 Caputi, Anthony. "Shakespeare's *Antony and Cleopatra*: Tragedy without Terror." *Shakespeare Quarterly* 16 (1965): 183-91.

Antony and Cleopatra have chosen to live by embracing "the possible with perpetual enthusiasm." Finally, "they must lose it all, for the tragic fact that men are always insecure is as true for their world as for any other." However, "Shakespeare's emphasis on the grandeur of the attempt and the sadness of the loss leaves no room for terror."

346 Doran, Madeleine. "'High Events as These': The Language of Hyperbole in *Antony and Cleopatra.*" *Queen's Quarterly* 72 (1965): 26-51. Reprinted in *Shakespeare's Dramatic Language.* Madison: U of Wisconsin P, 1976, pp. 154-81.

The rhetorical type of hyperbole reflects the alternatives of Antony's choice—the world of power and the world of love.

347 Draper, John W. "'Hybris' in Shakespeare's Tragic Heroes." *Etudes Anglaises* 18 (1965): 228-34.

This play has little to do with pride. "Antony deserts Rome for Alexandria because of passion, not pride; and Cleopatra, certainly not through pride, plays her traitorous part Actium. Pride may well be the motive for her final suicide; but Antony's subservience to a 'gypsy's lust' is certainly in a noble Roman no matter of pride."

348 Draper, John W. "Shattered Personality in Shakespeare's Antony." *Psychiatric Quarterly* 39 (1965): 448-56.

Draper argues that "Plutarch has obligated the playwright to set aside accepted medical theory, and depict advancing years as turning the soldier into the sybarite; and such a change implies a protracted tension in which native ideals and obvious good sense give way by degrees to overwhelming passion."

349 Herbert, T. Walter. "A Study of Meaning in *Antony and Cleopatra.*" *All These to Teach: Essays in Honor of C.A. Robertson.* Ed. Robert A. Bryan, Alton C. Morris, A.A.

Murphee, and Aubrey L. Williams. Gainesville: U of Florida P, 1965, pp. 47-66.

This play "has a meaning for us proportional to our knowledge of history and our own time if we perceive it as a microcosm alluding to the great world Shakespeare lived in and the great world we live in." After commenting on its setting, poetry, action, and characterization, Herbert concludes that "it is a tragedy of tremendous figures: an Antony whose legs bestride the ocean and a Cleopatra whose body servant could call her 'O Eastern Star'."

350 Hope, Alec Derwent. "All for Love, or Comedy as Tragedy." *The Cave and the Spring: Essays on Poetry*. Adelaide: Rigby, 1965. Reprint. Chicago: U of Chicago P, 1970, pp. 144-63.

This is "a play based on a genuinely tragic opposition of values to be decided by a choice having the seriousness of a public action of the utmost moment." Shakespeare "presents us with a picture of things as they are. We can draw our own moral conclusions from the events. But for Dryden, it is the business of the playwright to put the moral into the play, to show virtue rewarded and vice punished." Hence Dryden's is an inferior play.

351 Horowitz, David. "New Heaven and New Earth." *Shakespeare: An Existential View*. New York: Hill & Wang, 1965, pp. 40-70.

Horowitz argues that "a tension between imagination and reality underpins the tragedy of the imperial lovers Antony and Cleopatra, a couple who realize in their beings something like the fullness of human potential. It is this very fullness, moreover, that brings them to crisis. For too rich a realization is its own dissolution." The tensions which "beset their relation" are tensions "of worlds and of faith," "archetypal tensions of love," and "their development and resolution is the motive force of the tragedy."

352 Jorgensen, Paul A. "Antony and the Protesting Soldiers: A Renaissance Tradition for the Structure of *Antony and Cleopatra*." *Essays on Shakespeare*. Ed. Gordon R. Smith. University Park: Pennsylvania State UP, 1965, pp. 163-81.

For the structure of the opening acts of this play, Shakespeare appears to have relied on "Elizabethan plays which depict the struggle, internal and external, of the conqueror impeded by love." It was "dramatic pattern which not only was ready-made for his subject but had proved itself both successful and necessary on the stage." Some of the "ideas for the stress created by the repeated rebuke from the soldiers came from the convention which placed them in opposition to a seductress, whether or not she was Venus."

353 Knoepflmacher, U.C. "'O rare for Strether!' *Antony and Cleopatra* and *The Ambassadors*." *Nineteenth-Century Fiction* 19 (March 1965): 333-44.

The confrontation scene in Chapter 33 of *The Ambassadors* "is the culmination of a carefully constructed sequence, begun early in the novel, which depicts Strether's progressive abstraction of Chad's mistress into Shakespeare's Cleopatra, an abstraction made even more ironic by his resulting, unconsciously wishful, self-portrayal as the Antony of his imagined queen."

354 Long, John H. "*Antony and Cleopatra*: A Double Critical Reversal." *Renaissance Papers 1964*. Ed. S.K. Heninger, Jr., et al. Durham: Southern Renaissasnce Conference, 1965, pp. 28-34.

The musical portions of the drinking party aboard Pompey's galley (2.7) are indebted to Plutarch, but music beneath the stage at Antony's departure (3.3) differs markedly in intention from Plutarch.

355 Matinuddin, Abu Rushd. "Shakespeare and the East." *Homage to Shakespeare*. Ed. Syed Sajjad Husain. Dacca: Dacca UP, 1965, pp. 29-39.

Not seen.

356 Noel, J. "Shakespeare's Roman Plays." *Revue des Langues Vivantes* 31 (1965): 186-89.

Troy analyzes this as a Roman play.

357 Palmer, Roderick. "Treatments of 'Antony and Cleopatra'." *CEA Critic* 27 (Jan. 1965): 8-9.

Palmer compares this play with that of Dryden.

358 Proser, Matthew N. "*Antony and Cleopatra*:The Heroic Image." *The Heroic Image in Five Shakespearean Tragedies*. Princeton: Princeton UP, 1965, pp. 171-235.

The triumph in this play "lies not in its forcing us to dismiss the claims of a Caesar, or even those of Cleopatra, strumpet; it lies in the establishment of a realm of its own, the realm, for lack of another word, of the imagination—a force which, in spite of its apparent dissociation from reality, from the prosaic, nevertheless can manage to live with the prosaic and remain a fertilizing catalyst in the spirit of man." Shakespeare's final position in the play is "that of accepting all of life with its insoluble contradictions and complexities." The final order here "is 'natural' to the extent that politics and self-interest are embraced by dependable cycles of time and change; it is 'aesthetic' to the degree that art is capable of embracing nature, of redefining it, and giving it transcendence."

359 Roerecke, Edith M. "Baroque Aspects of *Antony and Cleopatra*." *Essays on Shakespeare*. Ed. Gordon Ross Smith. University Park, PA: Pennsylvania State UP, 1965, pp. 182-95.

Following Wylie Sypher's definition that "the baroque is style of plenitude, capable of absorbing, and robustly transforming to grandeur, every sort of realism," Roerecke argues that *Antony and Cleopatra* has all these elements. Shakespeare "immerses us in the panorama of the ancient world where we, as spectators, are hurriedly shifted back and forth between Egypt, the land of fruitfulness and decay, and Rome, the land or honor and treachery; where, when we are in Egypt, our thoughts are turned to Rome, when in Rome, our senses are pulled back to Egypt; and where the vastness of the setting (constantly reinforced by the imagery) promises us, finally, that beyond this huge world there lies yet another."

360 Schwartz, Elias. "The Idea of the Person and Shakespearian Tragedy." *Shakespeare Quarterly* 16 (1965): 39-47.

This play "is about human love and human persons, and the supreme good in such a contest is the realization that thee lovers achieve in bestowing their all on each other."

361 Seng, Peter J. "Shakespearean Hymn-Parody?" *Renaissance News* 18 (1965): 4-6.

The song, "Come thou monarch of the vine" (II.vii), duplicates the meter and rhyme scheme of a Latin Pentecostal hymn.

362 Siegel, Aaron Howard. "The Dramatic Function of Comic Elements in Three Shakespearean Love Tragedies." *Dissertation Abstracts* 26 (1965): 2193A (Southern California).

In *Antony and Cleopatra*, Shakespeare "follows his sources in presenting the lovers in a partially satirical light." The play's theme "is duality, and the lovers are presented as both heroic and foolish, dignified and comic."

363 Toliver, Harold E. "Shakespeare and the Abyss of Time." *Journal of English and Germanic Philology* 64 (1965): 234-54.

Toliver places this play "among Shakespeare's last comedies" because of Cleopatra's talk and "the life-in-death that it creates enable lovers to achieve a timeless world beyond Caesar." Cleopatra "discovers timelessness within time," "'eternity' in 'lips and eyes'," and "creates a self-contained, self-evaluated world."

364 Traci, Philip J. "The Love Play of *Antony and Cleopatra*: A Critical Study of Shakespeare's Play." *Dissertation Abstracts* 26 (1965): 1030A (Duke).

Shakespeare "dramatizes questions of love" in *Antony and Cleopatra*. The play "leaves us provoked to think of the many unanswered paradoxes of love, rather than merely purged of emotion."

365 Viswanathan, K. "Shakespeare in Telugu Translation." *Andhra University Quatercentenary Souvenir*. Waltair: The English Association, College of Arts. 1965.

This critical review of translations of *Antony and Cleopatra* and other plays into Telegu between 1874 and 1962 concludes that they are "a disservice to Shakespeare."

366 Whitaker, Virgil K. "The World Opposed: *Antony and Cleopatra* and *Coriolanus*." *The Mirror up to Nature*. San Marino, CA: Huntington Library, 1965, pp. 276-310.

In these two plays, "Nature and God have disappeared; so has the hero's desire for another and better way of life. He is still the center of a sweeping tragedy." This "vision of man's life as part of a larger order had given meaning to all Shakespeare's earlier tragedies." This vision does not inform *Antony and Cleopatra*, and "the metaphysic apparently lost its fascination. When the special vision and the creative energy that had produced the great tragedies faded, he retreated from all time into his own age." Hence, this play "is a tale of true but sullied love that sprawls over half the Roman world and through innumerable episodes."

367 Yamada, Yutaka. "*Antony and Cleopatra*—Paradoxical Value of Nobleness." *Prelude* 8 (1965): 28-39. In Japanese.

Not seen.

368 Bose, Amalendu. "The barge she sat in." *Calcutta Essays on Shakespeare*. Ed. A. Bose. Calcutta: Calcutta UP, 1966, pp. 81-97.

Not seen.

369 Green, J.T. "Shakespearean Women Contrasts: Cleopatra, Cordelia and Isabella." *Fort Hare Papers* (Fort Hare U, South Africa) 3, 5 (1966): 17-23.

Cleopatra "is all life and movement" and "satisfies Antony's whole being"; Cordelia "belongs to another world"; and Isabella "is egocentric in her fearful regard for her own purity."

370 Hunter, G.K. "The Last Tragic Heroes." *Later Shakespeare, Stratford-upon-Avon Studies* 8 (1966): 10-28.

Hunter examines *Antony and Cleopatra*, *Timon of Athens*, *Macbeth* and *Coriolanus* as "in some sense plays of exile." They present "a more complex psychological exile from social normality." Antony and Cleopatra's "is an exile from a world that we never see in the play, which existed splendidly in the past and will never be recovered again." The play gives an idea of "the abandonment of the good ordinariness of a life lived among compromises, or the loss of a sense of reverence for the unknown in destiny, a sense of submission to the immanence of higher powers."

371 Izaguirre, Ester de. "El Tema de la Muerte en Cinco Tragedias de Shakespeare." *La Prensa* (Buenos Aires) 11 Sept. 1966.

These are a series of reflections on themes in *Antony and Cleopatra* and other plays.

372 Lings, Martin. "*Antony and Cleopatra*." *Shakespeare in the Light of Sacred Art*. London: Allen & Unwin, 1966, pp. 77-94.

Antony and Cleopatra have "a double aspect, according to whether the play be considered as the story of Antony or the story of Cleopatra. If Cleopatra be taken as the more central figure, then it is she who represents the soul, while Antony, apotheosized after his death, symbolizes the Spirit, whereas for Antony as Everyman, the Spirit is symbolized by the Queen of Egypt."

373 Lothian, John Maule, comp. *Shakespeare's Characters; a Book of Characters from Shakespeare*. New York: Barnes & Noble, 1966. 271 pp.

Shakespeare many character sketches in his plays, and some of them were so well-known that the more conventional character writers imitated them. Cited here from *Antony and Cleopatra* are characters like "a captain transformed," "a woman infinite," "a man born lucky," and "an incomparable emperor."

374 Mason, H.A. "*Antony and Cleopatra*: Angelic Strength—Organic Weakness?" *Cambridge Quarterly* 1 (1966): 209-236.

See item 488.

375 Mason, H.A. "Telling versus Showing." *Cambridge Quarterly* 1 (1966): 330-354.

See item 488.

376 Milward, Peter. "Shakespeare and Theology." *Essays in Criticism* 16 (1966): 118-22.

In the Roman plays, "Christian allusions would constitute an obvious anachronism; yet certain ideas and images are carried over into them from previous History plays and the tragedies, where they have their natural Christian setting."

377 Nelson, C.E. "*Antony and Cleopatra* and the Triumph of Rome." *University Review* (Kansas City, MO) 32 (1966): 199-203.

The theme of power determines the power structure of the love story; the love affair does not contain seeds of its own destruction.

378 Ornstein, Robert. "The Ethic of the Imagination: Love and Art in *Antony and Cleopatra*." *Later Shakespeare, Stratford-upon-Avon Studies* 8 (1966): 31-46.

Rome and Egypt "are eternal aspects of human experience and form a dichotomy as elemental as that of male and female." Rome is associated with swords, armour, and war; Egypt with "uniting the artifices of sexual temptation to the naturalness of fecundity and to the processes of growth and decay which depend on sun, wind, and water."

The "tension between image and plot" leads again and again to paradox. The "patterns of imagery insist that Egypt is a Circean land of Mandragora and lotus-eaters, where sensuality breeds forgetfulness of Rome and duty. But the action shows us that it is Cleopatra, the Serpent of the Old Nile, not Antony, who would hear the Roman messengers; and it is Cleopatra, not Octavia, who demands her place in the war by Antony's side."

Shakespeare "can accept a world of mutability in *Antony and Cleopatra*, as in the tragedies and the late romances, because it offers the possibility of renewing change, in later generations, and in the heart of a Lear, an Antony, or a Leontes." The security of this play and of the late romances "is founded on the paradox of tragic art, which depicts immeasurable loss and yet preserves forever that which the artist supremely values."

379 Perret, Marion. "Shakespeare's Use of Messengers in *Antony and Cleopatra*." *Drama Survey* (Minneapolis) 5 (1966): 67-72.

The messengers in this play perform various roles like "uniting Rome and Egypt, creating our sense of space and time, indicating prestige and power, and revealing character."

380 Rabkin, Norman. "*Coriolanus*: The Tragedy of Politics." *Shakespeare Quarterly* 17 (1966): 195-212.

Like *Coriolanus*, *Antony and Cleopatra* offers no hope "about the possibilities of heroism and self-fulfillment in this world, in which the hero's passion, self-destructive as it is, leads him to a better world than political reality can provide—and to death."

381 Shapiro, Stephen A. "The Varying Shore of the World: Ambivalence in *Antony and Cleopatra*." *Modern Language Quarterly* 27 (1966): 18-32.

The ambiguity of this play "is 'integrative' and serves to present us with an image of our ambiguous world." The play's "meaning does not inhere in the sage words of any single character, in its conflict between the lyric dream and the world of fact, and in our ambivalent response to Cleopatra's death and Caesar's life."

382 Shaw, J. "Cleopatra and Seleucus." *Review of English Literature* (Leeds) 7 (1966): 79-86.

The Seleucus episode (V.ii.133-78) reveals a bit of play-acting on Cleopatra's part; the passage shows artificiality of sentiment, language, and rhythm.

383 Smith, Marion Bodwell. "No Midway: The Structure of Duality in *Antony and Cleopatra*." *Dualities in Shakespeare*. Toronto: U of Toronto P, 1966, pp. 189-214.

This play "presents a conflict of opposed views of the good which is predominantly a worldly good, a conflict in which the one suffers a partial defeat in victory and the other a partial victory in defeat. For in defeat one aspect of worldliness is transcendentalized." Its theme is "the impossibility of maintaining the wholeness of life in the circumstances in which its characters are placed." The contrary forces "profess to seek a reconciliation but fail to find any permanently satisfactory resolution of their conflicts."

384 Waddington, Raymond B. "*Antony and Cleopatra*: 'What Venus Did with Mars'." *Shakespeare Studies* 2 (1966): 210-27.

Antony and Cleopatra "is a romance which is designed to evoke primarily the mythical and cosmological affair of Mars and Venus, rather than the unrelated characters of Hercules and Isis—though the latter are subsumed typologically by Mars and Venus."

385 Adams, Martha L. "The Greek Romance and William Shakespeare." *Studies in English* (Mississippi) 9 (1967): 43-52.

Adams cites Heliodorus's *Aethiopica* and *Clitophon and Leucippe* to suggest that "the love which surmounts massive obstacles of birth and politics and defies death is the concept which vitalizes the Greek romance" and that Shakespeare uses this concept in *Antony and Cleopatra*.

386 Blissett, William. "Dramatic Irony in *Antony and Cleopatra*." *Shakespeare Quarterly* 18 (1967): 151-66.

This play is full of dramatic ironies from beginning to end, in its expository passages, characters, scenes, and scriptural and classical references.

387 Bowers, Fredson. "Death in Victory: Shakespeare's Tragic Reconciliations." *Studies in Honor of DeWitt T. Starnes*. Ed. Thomas P. Harrison. Austin: U of Texas P, 1967, pp. 53-75.

Antony "has not truly altered, as Cleopatra is to alter or as Hamlet or Lear alters, as a result of learning from his tragic error, and thereby willing himself not to repeat it." Antony is one of the characters "who enter the catastrophe without having having digested and understood the nature of their past tragic error in the climax although recognizing its fact." Shakespeare "prepares the audience, whether it is experiencing the clarification in company with the character or whether, ironically, its knowledge is well in advance of the understanding reached by the protagonist."

388 Burge, Barbara June. "'Nature erring from itself.' Identity in Shakespeare's Tragedies: A Study of the Use of 'I am not what I am' and Its Related Variations in the Delineation of Character." *Dissertation Abstracts* 27 (1967): 4216-4217A (Pittsburgh).

A character's identity depends on his or her being what he or she says. Antony is "remaining what he is but meeting destruction in attempting to reconcile the two sides of his nature to the two worlds in which he lives."

389 Cutts, John P. "Charmian's 'Excellent Fortune'." *American Notes and Queries* 5, 10 (1967): 148-49.

By referring to three kings in I.ii.25-30, Shakespeare is not being "profane in his use of the scriptural analogy; it is yet another means of emphasizing the world-shattering significance of the events he describes."

390 Demizu, Shunzo. *Shakespeare's Tragedy*. Tokyo: Apollon P, 1967. 197 pp. In Japanese.

Not seen.

391 Eagleton, Terence. "*Antony and Cleopatra*." *Shakespeare and Society: Critical Essays in Shakespearean Drama*. London: Chatto & Windus; New York: Schocken, 1967, pp. 122-29.

Antony and Cleopatra "explores one response to the problem of reconciling authentic and responsible living, a response in which one aspect of the dilemma is taken, chosen, and lived to the full tragic affirmation." This gives us "a new insight into the depth of authentic life which will have to be part of any attempt to make this life responsible, to put it back within society."

392 Eskin, Stanley G. "Politics in Shakespeare's Plays." *Bucknell Review* 15 (1967): 47-64.

This play has "an almost mystical culmination at the end," because Shakespeare had expanded Egyptian values "into a romantic commitment."

393 Frye, Northrop. *Fools of Time: Studies in Shakespearean Tragedy*. Toronto: U of Toronto P, 1967, pp. 70-74.

Antony and Cleopatra "is the definitive tragedy of passion, and in it the ironic and heroic themes, the day world of history and the night world of passion, expand into natural forces of cosmological proportions." This is "not a morality play, and Egypt is not hell: it is rather the night side of nature, passionate, cruel, superstitious, barbaric, dissolute, what you will, but not to be identified with its vices, any more than Rome can be identified with its virtues."

394 Fujii, Takeo. "A New Heaven Is Antony and Cleopatra." *Kansai Gaikokugo University Kenkyu Ronshu* 12 (1967): 17-36.

This is an analysis of the human maturity of characters through their speeches.

395 Jones, William M. "Protestant Zeal in the Personality of Shakespeare's Mark Antony." *McNeese Review* (McNeese State College, Louisiana) 18 (1967): 73-85.

"The most obvious characteristic of Antony's zeal is his physical indulgence," sometimes aided "by a healthy enthusiasm." This is a realistic, not a satiric, portrait.

396 Josephs, Lois. "Shakespeare and a Coleridgean Synthesis: Cleopatra, Leontes, and Falstaff." *Shakespeare Quarterly* 18 (1967): 17-21.

In the simple line, "Husband I come" (V.ii.286), "we see the synthesis of all diversities in the character of Cleopatra; she embodies universal love for which she struggles, sometimes teasing, sometimes devilish, sometimes heroic."

397 Knight, G. Wilson. *Shakespeare and Religion*. London: Routledge, 1967. 374 pp.

In his comments on *Antony and Cleopatra*, Knight argues that it signals the change "to the mystical dramas, in which Shakespeare blends tragedy with romance to make art-forms different from either." In the last two acts of this play, "all the threads of obstinate questionings, fears, passions and aspirations of the earlier great plays are caught up into those supreme moments where love and death—the two most recurrent of Shakespeare's problems—are harmonized into one spiritual reality and shown to be mutually relevant and explanatory."

398 Krook, Dorothea. "Tragic and Heroic in Shakespeare's *Antony and Cleopatra*." *Scripta Hierosolymitana* 19. (1967): 231-61. Reprinted in *Elements of Tragedy*. New Haven: Yale UP, 1969, pp. 184-229.

Antony and Cleopatra presents a heroic view of life defined by Aristotelian *megalopsuchia* or magnanimity, a quality which includes pride, passion for honor, and courage: "It is a different species of drama, remarkably interesting in itself, which is represented in Shakespeare's work only by this play and *Coriolanus*, and at this level of artistic accomplishment probably occurs nowhere else in European literature." Krook calls "it heroic drama, using the term 'heroic' in a sense patently different from that in which is commonly applied to Restoration tragedy or French neoclassic tragedy, and in a way which clearly distinguishes the heroic from the tragic yet shows them to be closely connected."

399 Labriola, Albert C. "An Organization and Analysis of the Post-Variorum Criticism of *Antony and Cleopatra.*" *Dissertation Abstracts* 27 (1967): 3430A (Virginia).

This study "orders the amorphous body of post-Variorum criticism of the play into the several approaches or critical methods that twentieth-century critics have used in understanding the play."

400 Lee, Kyung-Shik. "*Antony and Cleopatra.*" *English Language and Literature* (Seoul) 23 (Autumn 1967): 20-35.

Not seen.

401 Maxwell, J.C. "'Rebel Powers': Shakespeare and Daniel." *Notes and Queries* 212 (1967): 139.

Shakespeare may have taken the expression, "rebel powers," from Daniel's play.

402 Mendilow, A.A., and Alice Shalvi. "The World Well Lost: *Antony and Cleopatra.*" *The World and Art of Shakespeare.* Jerusalem: Israel Universities P, 1967, pp. 233-43.

A prominent feature of the play "is the highly ambivalent way in which the initial act of shame is presented, so that throughout almost the whole of the play we are in a state of indecision as to what attitude we are intended to adopt towards the royal lovers and their life of sensual, adulterous pleasure." In this work, "to fulfil oneself in love is seen as the greatest object in life. This is less self-centred than it sounds, since Shakespeare shows us that finding this self-fulfilment necessarily involves giving satisfaction and fulfilment to another person as well." This tragedy is one of the few "which as a hero and a heroine of equal stature, who, *jointly*, serve as the major protagonist of the dramatic action."

403 Ness, Verna Marlene. "Some Aspects of Renaissance English Tragedy." *Dissertation Abstracts* 29 (1967): 235A (Washington).

Antony and Cleopatra and some of the other tragedies answer the question,'Why does the protagonist fall?' "with choric commentary on the idea of a fatal blemish." This shows that "lines in specific plays point clearly to the existence of the concept as an integral part of the tragedy."

404 Nevo, Ruth. "The Masque of Greatness." *Shakespeare Studies* 3 [1967] (1968): 111-28.

This play stands between Roman tragedies and romances. "It shares a pivotal ambiguity with its two companion tragedies of the Roman world: it is indeed an ambiguity inherent in a representation of Rome in the mind of a Renaissance Christian. With the later romances, on the other, it shares its preoccupation with the theme of the life and power of the imagination, the solving and saving truths of the imagination." The theatre-metaphor of the masque in the final act "sets these elements into an illuminating relationship."

405 Piper, H.W. "Shakespeare's *Antony and Cleopatra*." *Explicator* 26 (1967): Item 10.

This note explains Cleopatra's longing for immortality and the significance of her robe and crown.

406 Rabkin, Norman. *Shakespeare and the Common Understanding*. New York: Free P, 1967. 267 pp.

Rabkin applies to Shakespeare the concept of "complementarity" developed by Niels Bohr and nuclear physicists; it is an approach to experience in which "radically opposed and equally total commitments to the meaning of life coexist in single harmonious vision." Shakespeare's "perhaps intuitive, certainly habitual understanding of the truth as in some sense complementary and of poetry as the proper vehicle for the conveyance of that sense of the truth is a constant in his work." "As the last of Shakespeare's studies of romantic love," *Antony and Cleopatra* "bases its complementarity as much on its author's late vision of the political world and of tragedy as it does on his previous understanding of love." "[A]s a simultaneously exultant and despairing dramatization of the unresolvable dialectic between values that claim us equally and of the necessary tragedy of choice," *Antony and Cleopatra* "is a paradigm of Shakespeare's art."

407 Sewall, Richard B. "Ahab's Quenchless Feud: The Tragic Vision in Shakespeare and Melville." *Comparative Drama* 1. 3 (1967): 207-18.

Each one of the "monumental people" in Shakespeare and Melville "has looked into the abyss—of his own nature and the world's." In this play, "there is at times the silly, at times the obscene, at times the deadly corruption of the Roman world."

408 Shibata, Toshihiko. "A Short View of *Antony and Cleopatra*." *The Rising Generation* 113 [6] (1967): 376-77. In Japanese.

Not seen.

409 Spencer, Lois. "The Antony Perspective." *London Review* 2 (1967): 20-29.

Not seen.

410 Stamm, Rudolf. "The Transmutation of Source Material." *The Shaping Powers at Work: Fifteen Essays on Poetic Transmutation*. Heidelberg: Winter, 1967, pp. 74-84.

The comparison between this play and its source illuminates Shakespeare's "methods as a dramatic and theatrical artist as well as on the ways of his actors and the functions of his stage"; it "renders us particularly sensitive to all those features in it that characterize it as a text intended for stage performance."

411 Styan, J.L. *Shakespeare's Stagecraft*. Cambridge: Cambridge UP, 1967. 244 pp.

Styan uses different passages from this play to illustrate various points about staging and acting. For example, the costumes reminded "the spectator constantly of the play's seesaw issues when the formal Roman soldiery is visually opposed to the colourful Egyptians."

412 Usherwood, Stephen. "Antony and Cleopatra." *Shakespeare: Play by Play*. London: Phoenix House, 1967, pp. 80-82.

This is a summary of the play "in a pagan and oriental setting." Illustrations are by Raymond Piper.

413 Vaish, Y.N. "*Antony and Cleopatra*." *The Modern Review* (Calcutta) 120, 3 (Sept. 1967): 183-90.

Not seen.

414 Brown, John Russell, ed. *Antony and Cleopatra: A Casebook*. London: Macmillan, 1968. 224 pp.

This collection of essays reprints, in whole or in part, the following items found in this bibliography: Dryden, Johnson, Schlegel, Coleridge, Hazlitt, Mrs Jameson, Charles Bathurst, Edward Dowden, A.C. Swinburne, Georg Brandes, Bradley, Granville-Barker, Murry, Goddard, Dickey, Charney, Knights, Holloway, Mason.

415 Burckhardt, Sigurd. *Shakespeare's Meanings*. Princeton, NJ: Princeton UP, 1968. 317 pp.

The characters in this play seek "to forswear the absolutes, to surrender with open eyes to falsehood and thus to gain sovereignty and truth." But there is no truth or sovereignty at the end. Still, "the play leaves us, like no other play by Shakespeare, with a sense of triumph that asks for no compensations beyond it. These lovers, though dead, are no 'poor sacrifices' but victors."

416 Coppedge, Walter Raleigh. "Shakespeare's Oaths and Imprecations." *Dissertation Abstracts* 28 (1968): 2643A (Indiana).

Oaths and imprecations reveal dramatic themes as they "indicate the mutual idolatry of Romeo and Juliet, the seemingly perdurable yet arbitrary love of the quartet in the Athenian wood, Desdemona's trust and innocence, and Cleopatra's association with Isis and Antony's with Hercules (the opposed themes of love and duty)."

417 Eastman, Arthur M. *A Short History of Shakespearean Criticism*. New York: Random House, 1968. 418 pp.

Eastman cites various critical opinions about *Antony and Cleopatra* from the seventeenth century to the twentieth, and he focuses especially on Granville-Barker's preface to this play: "Granville-Barker does what Coleridge does, but for an acting audience, first, and with a feeling for theater that Coleridge does not have." Granville-Barker, "as no one else in the history of Shakespearean criticism, helps us to a sense of the stage actuality of a Shakespearean play."

418 Fitch, Robert E. "No Greater Crack?" *Shakespeare Quarterly* 19 (1968): 3-17.

In this play, "it is the show, not the people in it, that grips us most powerfully." The play does not engage the spectator intimately. What creates a psychic distance between the audience and the action is "the conflict between Pleasure and Power" and "the staging on a World which is coldly geopolitical and presided over by a capricious Fortune rather than warmed by the impulses of Nature or made significant by the visitations of the Gods."

419 Frantz, David O. "Concepts of Concupiscence in English Renaissance Literature." *Dissertation Abstracts* 30 (1968): 1133A (Pennsylvania).

This is an analysis of *Antony and Cleopatra* in the context of the Renaissance concept of concupiscence, which means "excessive sexual appetite, concupiscence the vice, physical and psychological lust."

420 Frost, David L. "The Clarity of "Antony and Cleopatra'." *The School of Shakespeare: The Influence of Shakespeare on English Drama 1600-1642*. Cambridge: Cambridge UP, 1968, pp. 136-45.

This play "is remarkable for its imaginative recreation of the pagan Roman ethos."In his last scenes, Shakespeare "exposes the nature and consequences of that passion, and resolves what had once seemed ambiguities of theme and characterisation." The final tableau "should strike us as shockingly unnatural, a perversion of normal fertility and maternal instinct." Like other Renaissance historians, Shakespeare is "recreating but also judging the past."

421 Gardner, C.O. "Themes of Manhood in Five Shakespeare Tragedies: Some Notes on *Othello, King Lear, Macbeth, Antony and Cleopatra* and *Coriolanus*." *Theoria* (U of Natal) 30 (1968): 19-43.

Not seen.

422 Haines, Charles. *William Shakespeare and His Plays*. London and New York: Watts, 1968. 181 pp.

This play presents "the most colorful spectacle of any of Shakespeare's plays," "the most exquisite lines of poetry," and "the truth of the role that love between a man and a woman can play in life."

423 Iwamoto, Fujio. "*Antony and Cleopatra*: The World of Cleopatra." *Miyagi Kyoiku University Bulletin* (1968): 99-129. In Japanese.

Not seen.

424 Lyons, Charles R. "The Serpent, the Sun and 'Nilus Slime': A Focal Point for the Ambiguity of Shakespeare's *Antony and Cleopatra*." *Rivista di Letterature Moderne e Comparate* (Firenze) 21 (1968): 13-34.

The importance of apocalyptic imagery is that it characterizes the death of the lovers with its evocation of celestial union together with demonic imagery which has also been used to project the quality of their love. Basic ambiguity seems to be focused in a series of images relating to the annual flooding of the River Nile.

425 Madden, J.L. "Peacock, Tennyson and Cleopatra." *Notes and Queries* ns 15 (1968): 416-17.

Madden explains Tennyson's use of *Antony and Cleopatra* I.v as a source for his portrait of Cleopatra in his "A Dream of Fair Women."

426 Markels, Julian. *The Pillar of the World: Antony and Cleopatra in Shakespeare's Development*. Columbus: Ohio State UP, 1968. 191 pp.

Markels argues that the play forces the audience to hold "poised in our minds two morally contradictory actions" so that "we transform all moral actions into postures which become not false poses but the protean forms of life." Shakespeare "has made us amoral, in order to produce at last an imaginative experience of omniscience to accompany the experience of timelessness."

According to Markels, "Mark Antony is disciplined in the distinctive vision of the play, wherein he is challenged either to choose between the opposed values represented by Cleopatra and Octavius or not to choose between them; and that instead of choosing, he resolves the conflict by striving equally toward both values and rhythmically making each one a measure and condition of the other." Thus, Antony grows larger in manhood until he can encompass both Rome and Egypt, affirming the values that both have taught him until both are fulfilled." Antony's death "comes, as Cleopatra's does later, not as dissolution but as transcendence, a sign of his having approached as close to immortality as a poet may dare to imagine by becoming everything that it was in him to be." Markels analyzes Shakespeare's concern with the conflict of public and private values in the cycle of history plays from *Richard II* to *Henry V*, to *Julius Caesar*, and to *Hamlet* and *King Lear*.

Markels accepts Antony's transcendence as absolute and unqualified in his refusal to choose between "public and private values." Antony's achievement lies in finally reconciling the Roman and the Egyptian experience. Antony combines the two sets of values and thus achieves "that heady vision in which his public and private lives are necessary conditions for each other." Learning something from him, Cleopatra "gives up her one-sided effort to bend the public world to her narrow purposes, and by her loyalty to him confirms Antony's achieved balance of public and private values." *Antony and Cleopatra* "encompasses both the naturalism of death in *King Lear* and the symbolism of reconciliation in *The Tempest*. That is why, in this play alone among Shakespeare's works, death itself is exuberant."

Antony feels lost, "for his society offers him no room, no comfort, no coherent emblems of conduct marked upon its pillars." When the ambiguities and instabilities of his experience "have thrown him back upon his innermost self, he finds the power to generate that visible shape in which, if he must, he becomes his flaw." "In that graceful shape" Antony "achieves for himself, and bequeaths to Cleopatra, a joyous exuberance, which transfigures death itself." Antony's "world has forced him to find himself; in rising to his occasion and becoming the generous author of himself, he nurtures and transcends his world."

427 Mendel, Sydney. "Shakespeare and D.H. Lawrence: Two Portraits of the Hero." *Wascana Review* 3.2 (1968): 49-60.

This is "an attempt to show that Lawrence's development from *Sons and Lovers* to *Lady Chatterley's Lover* is . . . similar to Shakespeare's development from *Hamlet* to *Antony and Cleopatra*." This development goes from a rebellious son figure to an identification with an older man in conflict with a younger man.

428 Morgan, Margery M. "'Your Crown's Awry': *Antony and Cleopatra* in the Comic Tradition." *Komos* (Monash University) 1 (1968): 128-39.

Morgan stresses the function of the comic elements of farce, bawdy language, parody, mockery, comic mixture of metaphors, quibbles and mock deaths in *Antony and Cleopatra*.

429 Morris, Helen. "Shakespeare and Durer's Apocalypse." *Shakespeare Studies* 4 (1968): 252-62.

Durer's woodcuts of Apocalypse, published in 1498 and 1511, may have inspired various passages in this play. For example, there is a dolphin in Durer, "in the sea at the feet of Durer's great angel, among ships and swans, there swims an unmistakable dolphin."

430 Morris, Helen. *Antony and Cleopatra.* Notes on English Literature 25. Oxford: Blackwell, 1968.

This is a guide for school and college students.

431 Entry deleted.

432 Pandurangan, Prema. "Shakespeare's Enobarbus." *Aryan Path* (Bombay) May 1968: 227-30.

This is a study of Enobarbus' role as soldier, chorus, humorist, and poet.

433 Quinones, Ricardo Joseph. "Time in Dante and Shakespeare." *Symposium* 22 (1968): 261-84.

According to the concept of "augmentative time," the "possibility of resisting emulative nature is open to those who would exercise a virtuous control of experience." In *Antony and Cleopatra* Shakespeare expresses "man's desire for continuance" in a grand manner.

434 Rice, Julian C. "Renaissance Perspectives on *Antony and Cleopatra*: A Study of Themes, Sources, and Elizabethan Skepticism." *Dissertation Abstracts* 29 (1968): 1877A (UCLA).

Dealing with the concerns of human identity and the tragic as well as comic dominance of folly, Rice treats *Antony and Cleopatra* "as a mature dramatic statement of the skepticism and naturalism implicit in Shakespeare's early poetry."

435 Riehle, Wolfgang. "Antonius und Kleopatra." *Shakespeare-Kommentar zu den Dramen, Sonnetten, Epen und Kleineren Dichtungen.* Ed. Werner Habicht, Dieter Mehl, et al. Introd. by Wolfgang Clemen. Munich: Winkler, 1968, 143-46.

Not seen.

436 Riemer, A.P. *A Reading of Shakespeare's* Antony and Cleopatra. Sydney: Sydney UP; London: Methuen, 1968. 119 pp.

Plutarch did not consider Antony and Cleopatra from a single fixed point of view; hence Shakespeare's hero is not a moral *exemplum* but a complex human being with contradictory attitudes. Instead of imposing any metaphysical values on his characters, Shakespeare allows them to establish themselves in their myriad aspects. The play does not have a tragic resolution. Antony and Cleopatra aspire for but never reach perfection. This play "examines and questions the tragic implications of its material" and "is, perhaps, the first iconoclastic play in English."

In his review of criticism, Riemer outlines two approaches: "*Antony and Cleopatra* can be read as the fall of a great general, betrayed in his dotage by a treacherous strumpet, or else it can be viewed as a celebration of transcendental love." Disagreeing with these traditions, Riemer proposes that the play exists "on the human, social and political level; it has no religious or metaphysical overtones, and its protagonists are presented only in relation to the temporal world in which they live. In such circumstances, tragedy is impossible." "It is in this lack of fixity in his protagonists that Shakespeare discovers his most poignant statement about the central relationship in the play." The final resolution "is no longer wholly meaningful because in this play we do not have the metaphysical world of tragedy: it is the process itself, the state of flux that provides the central vision of the play."

437 Simmons, Joseph L. "The Moral Environment in Shakespeare's Roman Plays." *Dissertation Abstracts* 28 (1968): 3157A (Virginia).

The stress in the Roman tragedies "is not on the inner spiritual life as such but on man's actions within the state." In *Antony and Cleopatra*, "love is invested with its Neoplatonic possibilities of transcendence, but the lovers can never escape the 'dung' to reach 'new heaven, new earth'."

438 Sipe, Dorothy L. *Shakespeare's Metrics*. Yale Studies in English 167. New Haven: Yale UP, 1968. xviii, 266 pp.

Sipe has "investigated Shakespeare's metrical or unmetrical use of syllabic variants such as *quite* vs. *quittance* and *requite*" and uses many examples from *Antony and Cleopatra.*

439 Stampfer, Judah. "*Antony and Cleopatra*." *The Tragic Engagement: A Study of Shakespeare's Classical Tragedies*. New York: 1968, pp. 217-81.

Stampfer comments on "the range and structure of its gray area, the participation of its cosmos in the dramatic action, its texture, surfaces, types of energy and movement." In this play, "the entire tissue of society is in the process of losing its tense exuberance, its kick of health," and it "presents a wrangle of tempestuous living in the workaday world, grotesque, funny at times, impossible to maintain, impossible to break off, a marriage out of wedlock which somehow works."

440 Ueno, Yoshiko Y. "*Antony and Cleopatra*—The Last Phase of Shakespearean Tragedy." *Shakespeare Studies* (U. of Tokyo) 6 (1968): 1-36. In Japanese.

Antony experiences an unheroic death. Cleopatra never finds spiritual development: "she is essentially a comic character who is given a splendiferous finale."

441 Vickers, Brian. *The Artistry of Shakespeare's Prose*. London: Methuen; New York: Barnes & Noble, 1968. 452 pp.

Vickers argues that, in the Renaissance, "prose is the vehicle of an inferior class" and that "prose is used for those below dignity and seriousness." He analyzes the scene with the Soothsayer and the use of prose by Enobarbus and the Clown.

442 Williamson, Marilyn L. "Fortune in *Antony and Cleopatra*." *Journal of English and Germanic Philology* 67 (1968): 423-29.

Shakespeare stresses the external world of Roman business and Egyptian pleasure by frequently using the word "fortune" and images of fortune. It is not a tragedy of character, as such.

443 Adams, Martha Lou Latimer. "The Origins of the Concept of Romantic Love as It Appears in the Plays of William

Shakespeare." *Dissertation Abstracts* 29 (1969): 3968A (Mississippi).

Most of the action in *Romeo and Juliet* and *Antony and Cleopatra* "follows the Greek romance formula faithfully; Shakespeare's transformation is in the conclusion of the love stories." The couples are united only in death instead of marriage.

444 Altmann, Ruth. "Shakespeare's Craftsmanship: A Study of His Use of Plutarch in *Antony and Cleopatra*." *Dissertation Abstracts International* 30 (1969): 2474A (Washington).

Altmann analyzes Shakespeare's method of composition on the basis of the manner in which he used North's Plutarch.

445 Aoyama, Seika. "Magnificence and Folly: A Study of Value in *Antony and Cleopatra*." *Collected Essays by the Members of the Faculty*. No. 13. Kyoritsu, Japan: Kyoritsu Women's Junior College, 1969. In Japanese.

Not seen.

446 Armstrong, John. "*Antony and Cleopatra*." *The Paradise Myth*. London: Oxford UP, 1969, pp. 44-60.

This play's poetic theme "is the marginal, the extreme verge of the formed world" and "the border between the formed and the formless, that alien region with which a great part of the poetry of the last plays occupies itself." The imagery of water, rain and vapor "suggests the outermost verge of the formed order."

447 Barroll, J. Leeds. "Shakespeare and the Art of Character: A Study of Antony." *Shakespeare Studies* 5 (1969): 159-235.

Antony's personal inclination toward voluptuosity has exited independent of Cleopatra. He is proud of this quality in the purely physical sense. He reshapes the concept of war in terms of his own premises.

448 Battenhouse, Roy W. "Anagnorisis and Irony in *Antony and Cleopatra.*" *Shakespearean Tragedy: Its Art and Its Christian Premises*. Bloomington and London: Indiana UP, 1969.

Battenhouse elaborates on the parody-analogy of Antony and Cleopatra's love to that of Christian caritas. He likens Shakespeare's artistic method to Chaucer's ironic telling of Cleopatra's story, but he finds the drama as a whole influenced by patterns "figured" in the Book of Revelation. The number 42 in that book is symbolic of the scope of anti-Christ's reign, and Shakespeare had this in mind when he wrote *Antony and Cleopatra* in 42 scenes. Cleopatra is the great harlot, mistress to three kings, the Apocalyptic harlot. Shakespeare may be applying to Antony the symbolism of the beast with ten horns. At the moment of Antony's suicide, there is an echo of the imagery of a fallen star. From the typological angle, Egypt was known as "a land of fleshpots, sorcerers, and bondage." Antony and Cleopatra's downfall "can be made into Christian tragedy simply by perceiving, more profoundly than Plutarch does, the dimensional range of tragedy's causes and results. Beneath all other causes is man's mislocating of his chief end, in the process of his passionate quest for bliss."

449 Bradbrook, Muriel C. *Shakespeare the Craftsman*. The Clark Lectures 1968. London: Chatto & Windus, 1969. 187 pp.

In this play, "although Antony is descended from the god Hercules, and Cleopatra is the incarnation of Isis, mutability rules." Bradbrook argues that "Fortune rules—the very word occurs again and again; and for the Antony the good and evil aspects of his Fortune are embodied in Cleopatra and Octavia; they correspond to what is divided in Antony himself, the Roman captain and the lover of the Royal Egypt." The play exhibits "a new sense of theatrical pageantry and triumph;" this is "the pageantry of a dream, a masque simultaneously enlarges and reduces the stature of godlike beings."

450 Crawford, John W. "Romantic Criticism of Shakespearian Drama." *Dissertation Abstracts* 30 (1969): 1130-31A (Oklahoma State).

This comprehensive study presents basic views of notable Romantic critics on *Antony and Cleopatra*, *Hamlet*, *Henry V*, and *The Merchant of Venice*.

451 DeCamp, Jacqueline L. "A Study of Punctuation in the First Folio Edition of Shakespeare's *Anthony and Cleopatra*." *Dissertation Abstracts* 29 (1969): 2829A (Michigan).

DeCamp tests two hypotheses: "(1) the punctuation in the First Folio edition of Shakespeare's *Antony and Cleopatra* is a guide to subtleties of meaning and oral delivery" and (2) "in five later editions [from Rowe to Ridley] these subtleties have been eliminated by emendations of Folio punctuation."

452 Fitch, Robert E. *Shakespeare: The Perspective of Value*. Philadelphia: Westminster P, 1969. 304 pp.

Fitch makes numerous references to this play in the context of his argument that "the plays of Shakespeare are saturated with the ideas and imagery of Christianity."

453 Frye, Roland M. "Theological and Non-Theological Structures in Tragedy." *Shakespeare Studies* 4 (1969): 132-48.

Frye points out "a considerable similarity between the basic situations and the treatment of themes" in *Antony and Cleopatra* and Milton's *Samson Agonistes*. Shakespeare "understood the drama and the profession of the dramatist as belonging among those *things* that are Caesar's."

454 Fujita, Minoru. "The Concept of the Royal in Shakespeare." *Shakespeare Studies* (U of Tokyo) 7 (1968-69): 1-32. Reprinted in *English Criticism in Japan: Essays by Younger Japanese Scholars on English and American Literature*. Ed. Earl Miner. Tokyo: Tokyo UP, 1972, pp. 30-48.

The idea of the royal, seen in the tradition of pageantry in history plays, helps explain the nature of the tableau in the final scene of *Antony and Cleopatra*. This scene is a static, iconographic presentation of the idea.

455 Harding, D.W. "Women's Fantasy of Manhood: A Shakespearian Theme." *Shakespeare Quarterly* 20 (1969): 245-253.

Antony and Cleopatra is one of the plays in which Shakespeare tries "to explore the theme of the woman's usurpation of the man's role, though in the setting of a very different relation.." Cleopatra represents "the woman's unreal fantasy of manhood and her own continuing femininity." Her "stubborn insistence on being present in the naval battle and her fatal flight from it are crucial events in the action of the play, and the *action* of the play—perhaps especially in this period of Shakespeare's work—is an integral part of the way he states his theme."

456 Hunter, Robert G. "Cleopatra and the 'Oestre Junocque'." *Shakespeare Studies* 5 (1969): 236-39.

Hunter Makes a case "for a series of equations: Cleopatra=a cow in June=Io=Isis=Cleopatra. Cleopatra, in her flight from Actium, may be a cow, but there is a goddess inside the cow."

457 Lasser, M.L. "Shakespeare: Finding and Teaching the Comic Vision." *English Record* 20 (December 1969): 4-17.

Shakespeare's "comic vision uniquely heightens rather than relieves tension," as in *Antony and Cleopatra* "with the diminution of Antony."

458 Lee, Robin. "'Antony and Cleopatra'. Theme: Structure:Image." *Crux* 3 (1969): 11-16.

Not seen.

459 Moore, John Rees. "Enemies of Love: The Example of Antony and Cleopatra." *Kenyon Review* 31 (1969): 646-74.

Antony and Cleopatra's love "certainly has an aura of animal vitality, but it is based more on an affinity of sporting temperaments than on a lust for physical sex. Each provides the other an ideal audience. They egg each other onto 'outrageous' performance. And the final test of their love is a willingness to give up everything else for it." The two lovers "have escaped from pity into glory; it is Caesar who, calmly oblivious of his own mortality though he seems at this moment, must return to the vile world where even he will not forever escape the need for pity."

460 Morris, Helen. "Queen Elizabeth I 'Shadowed' in Cleopatra." *Huntington Library Quarterly* 32 (1969): 271-78.

Morris tries "to show from contemporary evidence that the portrait of Cleopatra in Shakespeare's main source, North's translation of Plutarch's *Lives*, must in many details have reminded Shakespeare of Queen Elizabeth and that this this resemblance was at the back of his mind while he was writing the play." "A reflection or 'shadow' of Queen Elizabeth" can be found "in certain aspects of Shakespeare's Cleopatra."

461 Nicol, Bernard de Bear, ed. "*Antony and Cleopatra*." *Varieties of Dramatic Experience: discussion on dramatic forms and themes between Stanley Evernden, Roger Hubank, Thora Burnley Jones and Bernard de Bear Nicol*. London: U of London P, 1969, pp. 86-103.

Roger Hubank argues that "this ambiguity of judgement, the difficulty of perceiving rightly, is one of the central features of the play." For him, "The Tragedy is Antony's. He seems to me to embody that magnanimity and self-committal in loyalty and trust which is found nowhere else in the play." Thora Burnley Jones disagrees: "If the tragedy is Antony's, it must be shared with Cleopatra just as his triumph as a man and a lover was shared with her." Nicol proposes that "the world is in fact no place for heroes: this is the central absurdity and to adhere to the truth of this absurdity Shakespeare is driven at times, I think, to replace the 'tragedy' by tragic posturing."

462 Rose, Paul L. "The Politics of *Antony and Cleopatra*." *Shakespeare Quarterly* 20 (1969): 379-89.

Antony and Cleopatra makes one realize that "the death of no man can stop the world, a realization of mortality. But this may itself be the reason for having hope at the end amidst the wreckage."

463 Sakurai, Shoichiro. "Truth and Falsehood: A Study of *Antony and Cleopatra*." *English Literature Quarterly* 7 (1969): 37-55. In Japanese.

Not seen.

464 Schanzer, Ernest. "Plot-Echoes in Shakespeare's Plays." *Shakespeare Jahrbuch* (Heidelberg) 105 (1969): 103-21.

In this play, "echoes play an important part, but they are predominantly not plot-echoes but speech-echoes: echoes of one another in the speeches of the two lovers, as well as in what is said by others about them."

465 Shapiro, Susan C. "Paradox, Analogy, and the Imitation of an Action in Shakespearean Tragedy." *Dissertation Abstracts* 30 (1969): 5420A (Bryn Mawr).

This study of *Antony and Cleopatra* and other plays uses Francis Fergusson's approach to *Macbeth* ("*Macbeth* as Imitation of an Action") to argue that "at the core of each is not simply a central action, but a specifically *paradoxical* action."

466 Simmons, J.L. "The Comic Pattern and Vision in *Antony and Cleopatra*." *ELH: Journal of English Literary History* 36 (1969): 493-510.

This play contains many elements of Shakespearean comedy. "The pure holiday spirit of Egypt encourages the radically comic, sometimes bordering on farce. The conflict of Egypt and Rome engenders critical comedy." In the scenes set in Rome, Shakespeare "even comes close to a comedy of manners, perhaps because for the only time in his career he is treating a historical subject in which the welfare of the state has little relevance." Finally, "the comedy of love is the basis of the protagonists' tragedy."

467 Stock, V.E. "Shakespeare in Translation." *English* 18 (1969): 53-56.

This is a comparison of three French translations of *Antony and Cleopatra* in prose by Victor Hugo (1859-66), André Gide (1920), and A. Rivoallan (1942).

468 Takahashi, Sho. "*Antony and Cleopatra*: The Nobleness of Life." *Cairn* 12 (1969?): 75-91. In Japanese.

Not seen.

469 Takei, Naoe. "Antony and Cleopatra." *A Shakespeare Handbook*. Ed. Jiro Ozu. Tokyo: Nanundo, 1969. In Japanese.

Not seen.

470 Weidhorn, Manfred. "The Relation of Title and Name to Identity in Shakespearean Tragedy." *Studies in English Literature, 1500-1900* 9 (1969): 303-19.

The tragic hero in Shakespeare "undergoes, when faced with severe adversity, a loss of identity. This crisis is signalled by the loss of his title and name. Towards the end of his career, the name—or *some* dignified name—and identity are recovered, but not the title." Cleopatra "sees herself as not 'Madam, Royal Egypt, Empress' but as like the meanest milkmaid and then as wife."

471 Wickham, Glynne. *Shakespeare's Dramatic Heritage*. London: Routledge & Kegan Paul 1969. xviii, 277 pp.

Wickham argues that "the nascent national interest in an imperial future could well have prompted the temporary switching of Shakespeare's interest away from chronicles of English history towards an exploration of those of Roman achievement—primitive, republic and imperial in *Coriolanus*, *Julius Caesar* and *Antony and Cleopatra*."

472 Williamson, Marilyn L. "Patterns of Development in *Antony and Cleopatra*." *Tennessee Studies in Literature* 14 (1969): 129-39.

Williamson argues that "there are throughout the play as a whole similar patterns in Cleopatra's conduct which unify her infinite variety, that there are perceptible stages in her development, and that Shakespeare has so developed the earlier portion of the drama, where he is creating virtually out of whole cloth, that it prepares structurally for the later parts of the play where he is following Plutarch closely."

473 Willson, Robert F., Jr. "A Note on Symbolic Names in *Macbeth* and *Antony and Cleopatra*." *CEA Critic* 31 (May 1969): 7.

Eros has taught Antony how to die.

474 Adelman, Janet. "Shakespeare's *Antony and Cleopatra*: A Study of Allegories on the Banks of the Nile." *Dissertation Abstracts International* 31 (1970): 1256A (Yale).

See item 544.

475 Barroll, J. Leeds. "The Characterization of Octavius." *Shakespeare Studies* 6 (1970): 231-88.

Octavius Caesar is a serious and fully conceived character; his apparent flatness is the result of deliberate techniques. For example, Octavius is known for his sparsity of diction, but he is also surrounded by masters of "glib elocution."

476 Burton, Dolores M. "Aspects of Word Order in Two Plays of Shakespeare." *Computer Studies in the Humanities and Verbal Behavior* 3 (1970): 34-39.

Burton discusses the use of the definite and indefinite article in *Antony and Cleopatra* and *Richard II* as examples of stylistic analysis through a computerized concordance of structure words.

477 Calderwood, James L., and Harold E. Toliver, eds. *Essays in Shakespearean Criticism*. Englewood Cliffs, NJ: Prentice-Hall, 1970, pp. 560-90.

This collection of essays reprints, in whole or in part, the following items found in this bibliography: Arnold Stein and David Kaula.

478 Charney, Maurice. "'This Mist, My Friend, Is Mystical': Place and Time in Elizabethan Plays." *The Rarer Action: Essays in Honor of Francis Fergusson*. Ed. Alan Cheuse and Richard Koffler. New Brunswick: Rutgers UP, 1970, pp. 24-35.

Charney makes a distinction between "what could be accomplished by the staging and what could be evoked imaginatively." Shakespeare used the quick and unspecific scenes in this play "for a panoramic effect," "to compress the amount of time involved and to create a sense of urgency."

479 Enright, D.J. "*Antony and Cleopatra*: Nobody Is Perfect." *Shakespeare and the Students*. London: Chatto & Windus, 1970, pp. 69-118.

Enright offers a rebuttal to "the sharp and only too spontaneous disapproval of both heroine and hero evinced by business-like Singaporean students. In his commentary on each scene he argues against H.A. Mason and suggests that that this tragedy is "patently one of his major works, and written more than sporadically in poetry."

480 Erskine-Hill, H. "Antony and Octavius: The Theme of Temperance in Shakespeare's *Antony and Cleopatra*." *Renaissance and Modern Studies* 14 (1970): 26-47.

When Shakespeare wrote this play, "a play in which we see Octavius become Augustus, he wrote a tragedy in which hyperbole of language, far from being hollow or remote, is endowed with the fullness and variety of everyday speech; and a tragedy which, by contrast with its interwoven Spenserian and Aristotelian theme of Temperance, affirms that in hyperbole of action, licence, a conscious voyaging froth to the extreme, there may be, far from weakness, Magnificence."

481 Fisch, Harold. "*Antony and Cleopatra*: The Limits of Mythology." *Shakespeare Survey* 23 (1970): 59-67.

The myths of Mars and Venus and Isis and Osiris inform the design of the play. But, in her final speeches, Cleopatra suggests Cupid and Psyche. The theme of world history transcends over the myth world of tragedy. At the end, "where the soul is born and its grace is discovered," Paganism "glimpses those permanent and fundamental relations of love which give meaning not only to all human marriages but to the vast and seemingly impersonal march of history."

482 Frye, Roland M. *Shakespeare: The Art of the Dramatist.* Boston: Houghton Mifflin, 1970. 271 pp.

In the course of studying structure, style and characterization in Shakespeare's plays, this work makes about thirty brief references to *Antony and Cleopatra.*

483 Hartstock, Mildred E. "Major Scenes in Minor Key." *Shakespeare Quarterly* 21 (1970): 55-62.

In addition to mirroring the major theme, the music-under-the-ground scene "provides an emotional experience for the audience which defines a major character who might, without the scene, be wrongly interpreted."

484 Herndl, George C. "*Antony and Cleopatra.*" *The High Design: English Renaissance Tragedy and the Natural Law.* Lexington: UP of Kentucky, 1970, pp. 63-70.

This play reflects "an achievement of poetry whose unique and irreducible meaning resists discursive re-presentation; here especially the medium 'creates what it conveys.' In the poetic assimilation of 'Nilus' slime,' of the 'dungy,' 'riggish,' vitality of the animal world to the most exalted possibilities of human experience, it achieves much of its cathartic fruition, a transcendent affirmation of the natural condition." This "is the transcendent vision achieved in the poetry of the final scenes, a glimpse of a possible human greatness learned late and at tragic cost."

485 Homan, Sidney R. "Divided Response and the Imagination in *Antony and Cleopatra.*" *Philological Quarterly* 49 (1970): 460-68.

The "complexities of the aesthetic issues, the praise and ridicule of art and the imagination, qualify a reading of the play which would establish a simple dichotomy between Rome and Egypt, with Shakespeare giving his preference to one or the other."

486 Igata, Hiroshi. "The World of *Antony and Cleopatra*." *Walpurgis* (Kokugakuin U) 1970: 78-94. In Japanese.

Not seen.

487 Kernan, Alvin B., ed. *Modern Shakespearean Criticism: Essays on Style, Dramaturgy, and the Major Plays*. New York: Harcourt, Brace & World, 1970, pp. 407-26.

This collection of essays reprints, in whole or in part, the following item found in this bibliography: John Danby.

488 Mason, H.A. "*Anthony and Cleopatra*." *Shakespeare's Tragedies of Love: An Examination of the Possibility of Common Readings of Romeo and Juliet, Othello, King Lear and Anthony and Cleopatra*. London: Chatto & Windus, 1970, pp. 229-76.

Mason suggests "that we recognize a distinction between fine poetry and dramatic effectiveness; that we follow Shakespeare in his account of Anthony's faults; that we note Shakespeare's refusal to push matters to a fully tragic issue, and the extent to which he merely takes over his 'source'; that we ask ourselves in what sense the play is organized as a dramatic poem."

Opposing Bradley, Mason argues that "in his closing scenes Antony both talks himself out and is talked by others out of reality." This is reinforced by "the admiration Antony thinks they will get from the Elysian spectators." "[I]f we agree with Bradley that this death does not trouble us, if we feel that its import is seriously diminished by the sense that Cleopatra could have died saying 'All's had, nought's spent,' then we can say that the interest aroused by Cleopatra at the end is too ideal, and that she has ceased to be part and parcel of the real. In claiming that the play draws to a fine point, I am expressing a feeling that the end does not bring the whole of our minds into play and as it were set a new pattern on our being."

489 Miyauchi, B. "Preliminary Remarks on *Antony and Cleopatra*, Act V." *Kogoshima Studies in English Language and Literature* 1 (1970): 1-13.

Miyauchi considers Act V as a one-act play.

490 Rice, Julian C. "The Allegorical Dolabella." *College Language Association Journal* (Morgan State College, Baltimore) 13 (1970): 402-07.

Shakespeare derives Dolabella's name from "dolor" and "makes him into an incarnation of his name, which may mean 'beautiful grief'. His compassion and depth of feeling sharply differentiate him from Octavius Caesar, the general to whom Dolabella is the chief aide-de-camp."

491 Tanifuji, Isamu. "Enobarbus' Minor Tragedy in *Antony and Cleopatra*." *Essays and Studies in English Language and Literature* (Tohuku Gakuin Univ., Sendai, Japan) 57 (1970): 51-72. In Japanese.

Not seen.

492 Tanifuji, Isamu. "An Interpretation of *Antony and Cleopatra*—Functions of Enobarbus." *Sendai U Bulletin* 2 (1970?): 1-23. In Japanese.

Not seen.

493 Traci, Philip J. *The Love Play of* Antony and Cleopatra: *A Critical Study of Shakespeare's Play*. Studies in English Literature 64. The Hague: Mouton, 1970. 171 pp.

Antony and Cleopatra "function as both character and symbol . . . as a part of the unified play." Antony "is Phoenix, Adam, and Cleopatra's 'man of men', just as she is both the only woman who cloys not Antony and 'no more but e'en a woman'." Then Traci explains the function of the comic and the bawdy elements. The comedy and the bawdry "function in the interactions of tone, characterization, imagery, structure, and theme." Traci stresses the treatment of the nature and paradoxes of love: "Whatever the nature of love, the play asserts, whether sublime, holy, degrading, or merely comic—or all of these—there is something unreasonable, inexplicable, even magical in its essence." This play, for Traci, "is not so much about intuition and reason, or the East and the West, or Love and Duty as about the nature of the many varieties of love and creation." Shakespeare "leaves us with a question about he nature of love, and we are asked to leave the theatre not purged of thought as well as emotion, but provoked to think toward some conclusions."

494 Wertime, Richard A. "Excellent Falsehood: theme and Characterization in *Antony and Cleopatra*." *Dissertation Abstracts* 30 (1970): 2983A (Pennsylvania).

Wertime stresses character psychology and structural patterns in this play. He considers Antony "as a wishful thinker who tends to assess himself in terms of his immediate context."

495 Williamson, Marilyn. "The Political Context in *Antony and Cleopatra*." *Shakespeare Quarterly* 21 (1970): 241-51.

Williamson's plea is that scholars "cease to neglect those features of the play which relate to the historical narrative and that if we view Antony and Cleopatra as rulers as well as lovers, we shall gain an understanding of the play and insights into their characters which we have missed hitherto." *Antony and Cleopatra* "deals with divided people: strumpet and queen; emperor and debauchee; and so the divided world in which they play out their story reflects and amplifies their wavering loyalties, their deceptions, their policy, their betrayals."

496 Balestri, Charles A. "English Neoclassicism and Shakespeare: A Study in Conflicting Ideas of Dramatic Form." *Dissertation Abstracts* 31 (1971): 6537A (Yale).

Shakespeare's plays like *Antony and Cleopatra* and *The Winter's Tale*, "where the romantic drama's openness of time and space is most fully exploited," are "an implicit apology for the native form at the same time as they transmute it for new purposes."

497 Barton, Anne. "Shakespeare: His Tragedies." *English Drama to 1710*. Ed. Christopher Ricks. Sphere History of Literature in the English Language, vol. 3. London: Barrie & Jenkins, 1971, pp. 215-52. New York: Peter Bedrick, 1987, pp. 195-233.

This play's "is a world of continual flux, in which the ceaseless coming and going of messengers seems to typify the restlessness that informs the whole." It is "a play about the multiple aspects of personality, situation, and of truth itself. But by the end, this bewildering, sometimes disheartening abundance has been converted into a subject for celebration, even for joy."

498 Breasted, Barbara. "I: 'Comus' and the Castlehaven Scandal. II:Public Standards in Fiction: A Discussion of Three Nineteenth-Century Novels—George Eliot's *Middlemarch* and Jane Austen's *Pride and Prejudice* and *Emma*. III:*Antony and Cleopatra*: Theatrical Uses of the Self." *Dissertation Abstracts International* 31 (1971): 4112A (Rutgers).

In *Antony and Cleopatra*, Shakespeare "dramatizes the precariousness of a love affair characterized by a dazzling theatricality."

499 Brodwin, Leonora L. "The Second Pattern: *Antony and Cleopatra*." *Elizabethan Love Tragedy 1587-1625*. London: U of London P; New York: New York UP, 1971, pp. 223-54.

This play "is mankind's supreme poetic tribute to Worldly Love, to that love which can achieve a noble fulfilment in life because it glorifies all that contributes to its finite existence, the corruptions and compromises with the human sovereignty which these help to define." Worldly love can be created only on the basis of "the lover's prior acceptance of the unique significance and value of his own life, of that particularly human individuality which sets him apart as a sovereign entity."

500 Brower, Reuben A. "Heroic Tragedy, Heroic Love: *Antony and Cleopatra*." *Hero & Saint: Shakespeare and the Graeco-Roman Heroic Tradition*. Oxford: Clarendon P, 1971, pp. 346-53.

The subject of this play is the noble act "as it was variously interpreted by writers in the heroic tradition from

Homer to the humanist translators and imitators." Shakespeare "alone gave dramatic life to the history of a noble mind defeated, not by 'charms and poisons,' but by itself." The "'wonderful', the quality that Renaissance critics admired in heroic poetry, is salient in our total impression of *Antony and Cleopatra*, most variously heroic of all Shakespearian tragedies." Shakespeare has given "dramatic life to the history of a noble mind defeated, not by 'charms and poisons,' but by itself." Cleopatra "is not only like Dido a woman capable of jealous fury; she also equals her lover in nobility, as Dido equalled Aeneas." Antony alone "is a truly tragic figure in the tradition of ancient and Renaissance heroic tragedy."

501 Charney, Maurice. *How to Read Shakespeare*. New York: McGraw-Hill, 1971. 150 pp.

In the course of explaining ways of approaching character, structure, poetic meaning, and non-verbal elements, Charney makes numerous references to *Antony and Cleopatra*.

502 Colman, E.A.M. *The Structure of Shakespeare's* Antony and Cleopatra. Sydney: English Association, 1971. 24 pp.

Colman concurs with the "transcendentalist" readings of the play as "an exposition of the ability of sexual love to transcend ordinary human circumstance." He finds evidence for this interpretation from the middle scenes of the play. He concludes that "alongside its defeats, Antony and Cleopatra offers a superb exhilaration: the exhilaration that comes from seeing the urge to idealisation stubbornly asserted and reasserted, even to the point of death."

503 Dunbar, Georgia. "The Verse Rhythms of *Antony and Cleopatra*." *Style* 5 (1971): 231-45.

This is an analysis of prosodic patterns and syntax in the play.

504 Eagleson, Robert D. "Propertied as All the Tuned Spheres: Aspects of Shakespeare's Language." *Teaching of English* 20 (1971): 4-15.

Not seen.

505 Erlich, Richard Dee. "Wise Men and Fools: Values and Competing Theories of Wisdom in a Selection of Tragedies by Tourneur, Marlowe, Chapman, and Shakespeare." *Dissertation Abstracts International* 32 (1971): 5735A (Illinois-Urbana).

Erlich examines *Antony and Cleopatra* in the context of the "great variety of theories of wisdom" and the "various views of the nature man and the nature of the real world in the philosophy and theater of the English late Renaissance."

506 Hapgood, R. "Hearing Shakespeare: Sound and Meaning in *Antony and Cleopatra*." *Shakespeare Survey* 24 (1971): 1-12.

Shakespeare usually takes on the quality of the world it depicts through his style. In this play, "he seems as self-conscious about his use of language as are his characters." Lurking behind the extravagances of Antony and Cleopatra are "disillusionment, grief, or masturbatory fantasizing." Scholars should "range much more widely, surveying the tones that various actors have used for a given speech and scouting out further valid possibilities."

507 Homan, Sidney R. "When the Theater Turns to Itself." *New Literary History* 2 (Spring 1971): 407-17.

Cleopatra's death scene "marks a comment when theater turns to itself, here Cleopatra's imaginative triumph with bad material, if you will, which parallels Shakespeare's own achievement in suggesting highly sensual femininity with what on the Globe stage would be an older boy actor assigned to the queen's part."

508 Jones, Emrys. "Antony and Cleopatra." *Scenic Form in Shakespeare*. Oxford: Clarendon P, 1971, pp. 225-65.

Jones analyzes the general structure of *Antony and Cleopatra*, the structure of individual scenes, and the resemblance between a specific scene in this play and one or more scenes in earlier plays. This analysis requires a detailed commentary on the text.

Jones divides *Antony and Cleopatra* into two scenic sequences: "In the first Antony leaves Cleopatra for Caesar, but in its last scene we learn that he has returned to her. The second movement opens, like the first, with Antony and Cleopatra together; but this time, despite more than one estrangement, he remains with her until his death." *Henry V*, the most recent history play, seems to have provided Shakespeare with "his fundamental layout." The verbal style of *Antony and Cleopatra* performs the function of the Chorus in *Henry V*: " It awakens in the audience a certain attitude to the events it is witnessing on stage."

In the first movement, "the play's scenic contours are very lightly moulded; much of the writing, though always precise and allusive, is curiously unemphatic." In the second movement, "we follow, throughout a single unbroken sequence, the fortunes of Antony and Cleopatra from the day of the first battle to their deaths." The sequence of the second movement "is a marvel of minute plotting—and any illusion of life-likeness should not be confused with the reality of formidable artistry." The order cannot be altered without disturbing the impact of the play.

"The entire play, with its ceaseless wavelike motion," Jones emphasizes, "has mounted an unobtrusive attack on the nerves, but in doing so it has finally placed the audience in an entirely suitable frame of mind for this final movement in which Cleopatra abjures 'the fleeting moon' and scorns a world subject to fortune as 'not worth leave-taking'." In their deaths, Antony and Cleopatra have become icons of Fame: "The contrast between 'breather' and 'statue' seems to have been much in Shakespeare's mind during the writing of a play so much concerned with the private experiences of long-famous personages: the once breathing and intensely animate lives of those who have since become statues standing with fixed postures in the Temple of Fame.."

509 Lee, Robin. *Shakespeare: Antony and Cleopatra*. Studies in English Literature 44. London: E. Arnold, 1971. 64 pp.

Written for students in Sixth Forms and in universities, Lee discusses the nature and structure of the play, central themes and images, characters, and the tragic effect. She argues that "the play finally achieves a supreme balance, seeing all, judging all in turn, but presenting an unresolved ambivalence. It celebrates life, vitality, sensuality, generosity and variousness—all that elevates the glorious Antony and the vital Cleopatra above Caesar, the cold, political animal. Yet, it shows with equal force that in an unfriendly world, such love, vitality and openness lead only to destruction."

510 Lyons, Charles R. "Antony and Cleopatra: The Reality of 'Nilus' Slime' and the Dream of an Eternal Marriage." *Shakespeare and the Ambiguity of Love's Triumph.* Studies in English Literature 68. The Hague: Mouton, 1971, pp. 160-86.

This play is Shakespeare's "first full and 'unprotected' response to the tension between the creative and destructive sexuality of human love." One of the symbols of Antony's union with Cleopatra is "the quickening of the serpent in the fertile slime left by the receding of the annual flood," and "the image of the 'dungy earth' or 'Nilus' slime' is the mortal environment in which that union takes place and which will eventually claim the lovers in the reciprocal process of nourishment and decay." This play "celebrates the infinity of love within the lovers' fantasy and confronts the inevitability of the decomposition of life into death."

511 Matsumoro, Hiroshi. "Defeat and Victory of Antony: An Essay on *Antony and Cleopatra.*" *English Quarterly* 9 (1971): 1-17. In Japanese.

Not seen.

512 Partridge, A.C. "Antony and Cleopatra I.3.66-104." *The Language of Renaissance Poetry: Spenser, Shakespeare, Donne, Milton.* London: Deutsch, 1971, pp. 210-20.

Shakespeare's style in this play "is not classic, but neo-Platonic, glorifying wonder; the art depends on the bold juxtaposition of words." The playwright gains variety in diction "by alternations of realism and romance, and large-scale experiments with words in vicarious functions" and by giving "words new senses through symbolic associations." Antony's "preoccupation with power, and Cleopatra's suspicion of his uneasy fidelity, suggest that Shakespeare's theme is a paradox of misunderstanding, to which the ambiguity of the language contributes magnificently."

513 Rhodes, Ernest. "Cleopatra's 'Monument' and the Gallery in Fludd's *Theatrum Orbi*." *Renaissance Papers 1971*. Ed. Dennis G. Donovan and A. Leigh DeNeef. Durham: Southern Renaissance Conference, 1972, pp. 41-48.

In the original production of this play, Robert Fludd's illustration leads Rhodes to argue that a gallery with a penthouse above the doors was used to represent the "monument."

514 Richmond, Hugh M. "Desdemona, and Cleopatra's Escape from Tragic Virtue." *Shakespeare's Sexual Comedy: A Mirror for Lovers*. Indianapolis and New York: Bobbs-Merrill, 1971, pp. 159-76.

Antony and Cleopatra "is scarcely ever melancholy despite moments of great bitterness," and it "eludes traditional categories so completely that the mere lack of conventional terms of reference has largely contributed to its neglect." This play "also represents the most ambitious ultimate phase of Shakespeare's sexual comedy: its integration into a world of the highest political import whose potentialities are nevertheless shown to be as erratic as those of our own—a world where there are not only quaint misunderstandings such as plague the heroes and heroines of the comedies but also the ever-present possibility that these will suddenly evolve into irreversible international disasters."

515 Slater, John F. "Edward Garnett: *The Splendid Advocate*; *Volpone* and *Antony and Cleopatra*: The Play of Imagination; Self-Concealment and Self-Revelation in Shelley's *Epipsychidion*." *Dissertation Abstracts* 32 (1971): 3332A (Rutgers).

Treating *Volpone* and *Antony and Cleopatra* as examples of "The Play of Imagination," Slater argues that they are similar because "both resist conventional generic classification, both exhibit protagonists familiar with the nomenclature and strategies of theatre, and both draw their imagery from the same areas of human concern."

516 Stratton, John D. "The Dramatic Structures of the Plays in the King's Men's Repertory, 1604-8." *Dissertation Abstracts* 32 (1971): 2711A (Nebraska).

In *Antony and Cleopatra* and other plays, Stratton deals with "the creation of emotional impact through an inductive analysis of the handling of the incidents of the plots and the types of characters."

517 Tanaka, Susumu. "'Antony and Cleopatra': A General Approach." *Studies in English Literature and Language* (Kyushu U, Fukuoka, Japan) 21 (1971): 15-42.

Not seen.

518 Taylor, Michael. "The Conflict in Hamlet." *Shakespeare Quarterly* 22 (1971): 147-61.

While dealing with the problem of ambiguity, Taylor suggests that "a hesitancy in judgment on our part indicating a complex moral world is one of the effects aimed at in *Antony and Cleopatra*."

519 Thompson, Karl F. *Modesty and Cunning: Shakespeare's Use of Literary Tradition*. Ann Arbor: U of Michigan P, 1971. 176 pp.

With this play, Shakespeare "seems bent on a full-scale romanticization of history that results in the elevation of history, or the 'state play,' to the level of tragedy." Shakespeare combines the traditions of history and romance and uses numerous conventions, "often merely suggested in shorthand fashion."

520 Waith, Eugene M. *Ideas of Greatness: Heroic Drama in England*. London: Routledge & Kegan Paul, 1971. 292 pp.

This play is based on "a heroic concept of character." It "works towards a revaluation of Antony's nature, in which his faults seem almost inseparable from his virtues, and his virtues those of a demigod."

521 Wall, Stephen. "Shakespeare: His Later Plays." *English Drama to 1710*. Ed. Christopher Ricks. Sphere History of Literature in the English Language, vol. 3. London: Barrie & Jenkins, 1971, pp. 253-73. New York: Peter Bedrick, 1987, pp. 234-54.

Antony and Cleopatra "and the other plays that followed it are linked by a new adventurousness, almost a new restlessness, of theatrical expression." The playwright's "ability to accommodate such varied moods is an essential preparation for the flexibility of style in *The Winter's Tale*."

522 Weinstock, Horst. "Loyal Service in Shakespeare's Mature Plays." *Studia Neophilologica* 43 (1971): 446-73.

In all his plays, Shakespeare "weaves a tight network of key-words current in Elizabethan times to denote obligations of rank and office, such as allegiance, authority, command, duty, oath, priority, privilege, service, and vow." He "instructs his audience through loyal servants" like Enobarbus.

523 Baba, Yasuko. "Antony and Cleopatra." *Seijo English Literature* (Seijo Univ.) 2 (1972): 9-21. In Japanese.

Not seen.

524 Birkinshaw, Philip. "Heroic Frenzies: Neo-erotic Platonism in *Antony and Cleopatra*." *U of Cape Town Studies in English* 3 (1972): 37-44.

This study identifies the "stages through which 'desolation does begin to make a better life' in *Antony and Cleopatra*. The route lay through suffering and at the end bliss meets agony in the kiss of death." In this play, "with help of Neo-erotic Platonism, [Shakespeare] mocks up an everlasting Cydnus but even so, as his sonnets and last plays reveal, he could not finally bring himself to credit it, and he leaves the problem unsolved."

525 Bose, Amalendu. "Shakespeare's Word-music." *Studies in Elizabethan Literature: Festschrift to Professor G. C. Bannerjee.* Ed. P.S. Sastri. New Delhi: Chand, 1972, pp. 57-63.

The poetry of *Antony and Cleopatra* and *Coriolanus* is wholly attuned to dramatic action, plot, and character. Shakespeare has gone beyond exploiting the lexical and sonal values of words.

526 Entry deleted.

527 Dias, Walter. "Antony and Cleopatra." *Shakespeare: His Tragic World. Psychological Explorations.* New Delhi: Chand, 1972, pp. 450-516.

In this play, Shakespeare "seems to have attempted to explore to its lowest depths this field of interaction of perception and feeling" He shows "the initiation, the progress, and the culmination of the exceedingly interesting, as well as, dangerous fact of the mechanisation of response to the perception." Shakespeare "here seems to strike a note of warning that if the mechanisation of the response to the perception vitiates love, whose highest perfection is the nuclear attribute of the godhead itself, its activity with regard to any lower emotions must be fraught with the most harmful consequences for the subject indeed." In this play, the playwright "enhances the sex-differentia in the lovers, through the interactional contact between personality and personality, and by subordinating others to those, he transforms them into mere automata, with reference to the sexual passion, so that the defect itself by its very excess takes on the glamorous hue of an ethereal beauty."

528 French, A.L. "Antony and Cleopatra." *Shakespeare and the Critics.* Cambridge: Cambridge UP, 1972, pp. 206-35.

French discusses "questions about the mode of the play, in particular the relation of the main comic comments to the interest in love and military honour." This play "isn't a tragedy, but it has its own peculiar sort of desolating clarity about *bovarysme.*" Its characters "try, not so much to make sense of their experience, as to find any experience stable enough, graspable enough, to look at without its shifting and dissolving into something else, or into nothingness."

529 Fujita, Minoru. "The Concept of the Royal in Shakespeare." *English Criticism in Japan: Essays by Younger Japanese Scholars on English and American Literature.* Ed. Earl Miner. Tokyo: Tokyo UP, 1972, pp. 30-48.

Shakespeare created the notion of "the royal" in this play "only in the wake of the long tradition of popular interest in the spectacle of royalty in English peasantry. The dumb show in the concluding scene of the play was the sure and decisive mode of feasting the audience's eyes with the dramatist's final, quintessential poetic vision of 'the royal'."

530 Grant, Michael. *Cleopatra.* London: Weidenfeld & Nicolson, 1972. xviii, 301 pp.

This history of Cleopatra illustrates her influence on the thought of European literature and on Shakespeare.

531 Henn, T.R. "The Images of *Antony and Cleopatra.*" *The Living Image. Shakespearean Essays.* London: Methuen, 1972, pp. 117-36.

This play's "greatness rests on Shakespeare's technique of constantly putting forth tentacles from the dream into the reality." It represents "something which does in fact constitute a transcending of this dream world, a projection beyond it into a world of ultimates where cardinal values move in a kind of elemental simplicity, but with constant and subtle counterpointing of the high and the low styles: which serve both to satirize the tragic dominant, and to restore it."

532 Kawai, Mariko. "Woods, Wilderness, and Sea in Shakespeare's Plays." *Metropolitan* (Tokyo Metropolitan U) 15 (1972): 135-176. In Japanese.

Not seen.

533 Lynch, James Joseph. "The Mediating Figure in Shakespeare." *Dissertation Abstracts International* 33 (1972): 5684A (California-Davis).

A mediating figure like Enobarbus is "a character who, because of his personality, the special relationship which exists between him and the tragic protagonist, and the kinds of functions he performs, acts as a dramatic linking device between the audience and the hero."

534 Muir, Kenneth. "*Antony and Cleopatra*." *Shakespeare's Tragic Sequence*. London: Hutchinson, 1972. Reprint. New York: Barnes & Noble, 1979, pp. 156-71.

Shakespeare disregarded the unities of time and place because "he wanted to show by transporting us from Egypt to Rome and back again that the fate of the Roman Empire and the future of the world depended on what happened." He keeps the unity of action: "Antony is invariably the subject of conversation when he not present on the stage; and Cleopatra is likewise frequently mentioned when she is not present." Antony's tragedy "is due more to vacillation than to lust. He desires power as well as Cleopatra; but in marrying Octavia to preserve the triumvirate he offends Caesar beyond forgiveness." His ruin is definite after that. "Whether the nobleness of life is to do as Antony does or to exercise the arts of power Shakespeare is not concerned to decide; but there is no doubt that he makes the strumpet's fool more sympathetic than Fortune's knave."

535 Nelson, Raymond S. "Eros Lost." *Iowa English Bulletin: Yearbook* 22 (1972): 42-47.

Dryden "worked hard to construct a perfect, classical drama, and he succeeded in a notable way." But the play did not impress the readers because, unlike Shakespeare, "his whole temperament was set against the free play of emotion."

536 Nevo, Ruth. "*Antony and Cleopatra*." *Tragic Form in Shakespeare*. Princeton Princeton UP, 1972, pp. 306-55.

Antony's "tragic distinction is his capacity to serve as the repository of both Rome's and Egypt's values," and he is "as pre-eminent in the man's world of contest as he is in the woman's world of love." He is "a glass of fashion and a mold of form": "The legend of Rome's grandeur rests upon him, not upon Octavius, for its authentication; and by the same token the enkindling vision of 'the nobleness of life' requires his validation of the value claimed for it." Rome and Egypt benefit from Antony's loyalty to them. In Act I, there is a "contest between stoic and epicurean, virtus and voluptas, world mastery and women's mastery, Mars and Venus" which shows that "the current flows toward Rome." Act II, still by means of subtly related contraries, sets the current of attraction and repulsion, of enhancement and disparagement, flowing in the opposite direction." Cleopatra "is another Venus, in her self-created spectacle, or Iris, goddess of love and the fertile Nile: her sign is the asp upon her arm, or upon her breast, the asp of the easy death." What Cleopatra's "great act of faith in the life of the imagination puts to the test is the power of love over death: of that love between man and woman whose mark is mutuality, a consonance of pulse, imagination, and sense; and of the power of such love, such pleasure of life, to neutralize the terror, the pain and the shame of loss and defeat."

537 Platt, Michael David. "Shakespeare's Rome." *Dissertation Abstracts International* 32 (1972): 6999A (Yale).

In order to write about republics while living under a monarch, Shakespeare "requires an art of writing which disguises boldness with indirection." Rome, in Shakespeare's eyes, "is a dismal and forbidding Hell whose study, however, can be neglected only at our peril." In *Antony and Cleopatra*, "the active virtue of the Republic is transferred to erotic East, yet both Rome and Egypt ignore a new order on the horizon."

538 Rackin, Phyllis. "Shakespeare's Boy Cleopatra, the Decorum of Nature, and the Golden World of Poetry." *PMLA: Publications of the Modern Language Association* 87 (1972): 201-12.

Shakespeare defied the rules of decorum and the unities of Time and Place in *Antony and Cleopatra* so that he could "evoke a vision of a transcendent world of the imagination. . . ." Similarly, "his squeaking boy can evoke a greatness that defies the expectations of reason and the possibilities of realistic representation only because we share those expectations and understand the limits of those possibilities." Cleopatra creates a series of shows in the play to challenge the reality of Rome, and Shakespeare's purpose is to reject rational views of reality "in order to present a show that cannot lie because it does not affirm." The spectators are "swept back and forth between the two worlds until the final scene when they are brought to rest in Egypt to behold Cleopatra's suicide, to see in it the nobility Antony saw in her, and thus, several scenes after Antony's death, to see the full significance of his action." Hence, "the ambivalence of our reactions to the first four acts is as important an element of our total experience of the play as is our response to the final scene, which resolves the ambivalence. The golden world of poetry became necessary only after the Fall of man, and the worth of the poet can only be seen when his handiwork is compared to the products of the arts that are bound by the limitations of Nature."

539 Rinehart, Keith. "Shakespeare's Cleopatra and England's Elizabeth." *Shakespeare Quarterly* 23 (1972): 81-86.

Elizabeth I may well have been used as the living model for Cleopatra.

540 Rose, Mark. "*Antony and Cleopatra.*" *Shakespearean Design.* Cambridge, MA: Harvard UP, 1972, pp. 163-68.

This play is built around "the contrast between Egypt and Rome, established at the beginning and kept before us throughout." This opposition enables Shakespeare "to deemphasize overall design and yet multiply scenes at a dizzying rate to achieve an epic effect." Consequently, "the 'heart of the mystery' is not *located* at all, and this may be one reason why this tragedy, while surely one of Shakespeare's greatest, is also one of his most elusive and ambiguous plays."

541 Sen Gupta, S.C. "Happy Valiancy of Style in *Antony and Cleopatra.*" *Aspects of Shakespearian Tragedy.* 1972. 2nd ed. Calcutta: Oxford UP, 1977, pp. 31-60.

In this play, "there are many styles, and some persons speak a variety of styles, all equally characteristic and also equally appropriate to the context." The two main styles "may be named the Roman style, spoken by Caesar and the other Romans, Antony and Enobarbus partly excepted, and the Egyptian style in which Cleopatra is the supreme artist."

542 Whitaker, Juanita J. "*Antony and Cleopatra*: Cosmological Contexts and the Dramatic Achievement." *Dissertation Abstracts* 33 (1972): 736A (Wisconsin-Madison).

Antony and Cleopatra "is patterned after the microcosm-macrocosm analogy," and "within the structure of that analogy the play moves from finitude to infinity."

543 Williamson, Marilyn. "*Antony and Cleopatra* in the Late Middle Ages and Early Renaissance." *Michigan Academician* 5 (1972): 145-51.

Williamson argues that the history of Antony and Cleopatra "was available to artists before the revival of Plutarch." This survey of poets from Dante to Lydgate reveals "an astonishing diversity of treatment of the Antony and Cleopatra story, not only among writers, but also within the works of a single author, or from one part of a long work, like Dante's *Commedia*, to another."

544 Adelman, Janet. *The Common Liar: An Essay on* Antony and Cleopatra. Yale Studies in English 181. New Haven: Yale UP, 1973. 235 pp.

Adelman asks a question about which one to believe. "Critics who wish Antony and Cleopatra to fit Shakespeare's normal tragic mold (if they can decide what it is) will tend to stress the primacy of character and action; those who wish to assimilate the play to the romances will stress the claims of the poetry." Hence she is especially concerned with "the means by which Shakespeare assures both our uncertainty and our final hesitant leap of faith." The characters in this play "do not know each other, nor can we know them, any more clearly than we know ourselves." This play is "essentially a tragic experience embedded in a comic structure": "In that sense it is as treacherous and painful as life itself: each of us has moments in which we experience our lives with a tragic concentration and intensity, but each of us must know that these moments can equally well be experienced as comic, if seen from the perspective of the varying shore."

Adelman explains how Shakespeare uses traditional accounts to suggest conflicts: "Shakespeare can count on the audience to know the story and the traditional interpretations of it; and the conflict of interpretation that the audience brings to the theater becomes part of the play." She focuses on "two traditional pairs of analogies which shape the play decisively: the human analogy of Dido and Aeneas, and the divine analogy of Mars and Venus." Aeneas is an antitype to Antony in the Virgilian tradition. The analogy of Mars and Venus clarifies "the lovers' exchange of clothing and, to some degree, of sexual characteristics." Shakespeare is implying that Antony and Cleopatra "are larger than human, that their union is somehow cosmic like that of their great prototypes, the union of male and female, war and love, strife and friendship."

Adelman proposes that "no one 'meaning' can account for any event in the knot intrinsicate of life." The "ultimate paradox" of *Antony and Cleopatra* is that "even its transcendence is part of the natural world of flux: measure and overflow, flux and stasis, time and eternity, life and deal, are all inseparable, a knot intrinsicate." The play does not conform to a reader's expectations of tragedy, comedy and romance. It "moves among several perspectives, it suggests the futility and the validity of each; only in its generic impurity can it embrace the whole."

545 Alvis, John Edward. "Shakespeare's Roman Tragedies: Self-Glorification and the Incomplete Polity." *Dissertation Abstracts* 35 (1973): 1034A (Dallas).

The thematic unity of *Antony and Cleopatra* and two other Roman tragedies results from Shakespeare's "critique of Roman morality." For Antony, who wants to be admired, "public acclamation replaces the natural sanctions of sexual love, driving him (and Cleopatra) forward through an increasingly consuming cultivation of eros."

546 Barton, Anne. *Nature's Piece 'Gainst Fancy: The Divided Catastrophe in* Antony and Cleopatra. An Inaugural Lecture.

London: Bedford College, 1973. 20 pp. Reprinted in *Essays, Mainly Shakespearean.* Cambridge: Cambridge UP, 1994, pp. 113-35.

In a revision of her 1973 inaugural lecture at Bedford College, Barton compares Shakespeare's divided catastrophes with Sophocles and argues that the device allows the playwrights to modify and alter their vision. Events in life are unpredictable and so are the endings of the plays. Cleopatra, who had been inconstant, becomes "marble constant," and changes the audience's perception of the personal, political and social aspects of her relationship with Antony. The two are transformed into heroic figures.

547 Bell, Arthur H. "Time and Convention in *Antony and Cleopatra.*" *Shakespeare Quarterly* 24 (1973): 253-264.

Antony's character "remains a dramatic triumph not in in spite of, but because of Shakespeare's use of conventions." Antony is seen moving through four conventional stages in time: the Homeric hero, the courtly lover, the Stoic sage, and the man of policy.

548 Berry, J. Wilkes. "Two Hoops in Shakespeare's *Antony and Cleopatra.*" *CEA Critic* 35 (1973): 29-30.

By using the image of the hoop at II.ii.116-18 and II.iii.37-38, Shakespeare arouses suspicions in the mind of the audience concerning the marriage of Antony and Octavia.

549 Burton, Dolores M. *Shakespeare's Grammatical Style: A Computer-Assisted Analysis of Richard II and Antony and Cleopatra.* Austin: U of Texas P, 1973. 364 pp.

Burton examines the style of this play by analyzing such elements as frequency and types of variant questions, proportion of interrogatives to imperatives used by main characters, ratio of interrogatives to imperatives used by main speakers, kinds of adjectival suffixes, kinds of qualifying adjectives, frequency and types pronouns and other topics. She presents this data in forty-three tables in Appendix A and citations to the play in Appendix B. She concludes that it "is a play not about tawdry middle-aged lovers but about the power of imagination to place an Egyptian puppet and a drunken Antony on the stage and, by poetry, to make the audience forget their smaller-than-life reality."

550 Duncan, Charles F. "A Blackboard Model of Shakespearean Irony." *College English* 34 (March 1973): 791-95.

Shakespeare's dramatic irony "in principle is always an exploitation of the distance between character and audience which allows the audience to regard as illusory appearance what the character takes for unassailable fact." Antony cannot achieve "the fruitful harmony of reason and passion" because his loyalties are polarized: "either Egypt or Rome, Cleopatra or Octavius, self-indulgence or self-denial—not both."

551 Godshalk, William Leigh. "The Unstable World of *Antony and Cleopatra*." *Patterning in Shakespearean Drama: Essays in Criticism*. De Proprietatibus Litt. Series Practica, 69. The Hague: Mouton, 1973, pp. 150-63.

"In *Antony and Cleopatra* the pattern of instability and insecurity is basic, and encompasses all elements of the play," Godshalk argues. The plot "is based on this instability and on the struggle to attain some kind of permanence in a world which seems to deny its very existence." Fortune, dissolution, time and other themes "unite in the tragic pattern of sublunary instability." At the end, Cleopatra and Antony "find the stasis which they have desired in suicide and death."

552 Hamilton, Donna B. "*Antony and Cleopatra* and the Tradition of Noble Lovers." *Shakespeare Quarterly* 24 (1973): 245-51.

Many references to Antony and Cleopatra as exempla of noble lovers can be found in antiquity. This "casts doubt on the claims that Shakespeare drew solely upon unfavorable accounts of his characters." This adds another dimension to Shakespeare's artistry. In *Antony and Cleopatra*, "which depends for many of its most powerful effects on hyperbolic statement, Shakespeare has drawn on the tradition of noble lovers to temper the moral emphasis with a dimension of unsurpassable glory."

553 Hawkes, Terence. *Shakespeare's Talking Animals: Language and Drama in Society.* London: Arnold, 1973; Totowa, NJ: Rowman & Littlefield, 1974, pp. 166-93.

Love surpasses language as a means of communication among human beings, because "love's goal is utter communication: the merging of two human beings into one." Since people have been made to communicate with and to love others, they diminish their lives through their inability to love: "To resist the ultimate 'merging' with others, to retain singularity, to remain inviolable, is finally to reject communication itself, and so community."

Shakespeare does not stress a contrast between all and love and between Rome and Egypt: "It is not that 'love' resides in Egypt, 'all' in Rome, or some such sentimental disposition of the demands of existence, but that the distinction itself is a false one, because too readily reductive of the complications of human experience."

"If man's communicative system depends, finally, on two interdependent units, voice and body," Hawkes proposes, "the play assigns voice alone to Rome, body alone to Egypt." "Embracing, as a way of life, proves ultimately sterile, meaningless, only half human. So Cleopatra's physical death mocks her many sexual 'deaths'." Rome is "a place of words" "where precise distinctions are preferred, where men are men and women are women, each accorded a distinct role in the community." This simplistic distinction lies at the heart of tragedy in *Antony and Cleopatra*.

Hawkes also associates the opposition of Rome and Egypt with that of male and female: "If Egypt emphasises the body, one level of language, one sort of 'love', and the concomitant womanly powers of Cleopatra, Rome is a place of works, another level of language, another kind of love, and of self-confident 'manly' prowess." The division of gender signals the breakdown of communication and love.

Hawkes finds a similarity between Antony and Lear. Lear and Antony violate "the complex nature of language by means of reductive objectification and a simplistic and divisive insistence on unitary 'meaning'." If they have a tragic flaw, "it could be characterised as an inability—or refusal—to respond to the full social and moral complexity of oral language; especially the language of love."

554 Hoy, Cyrus. "Jacobean Tragedy and the Mannerist Style." *Shakespeare Survey* 26 (1973), 49-67.

This mannerist play forms a link between the tragedies and the romantic tragi-comedies. The play, "in typically mannerist fashion, sets before us opposing worlds, opposing realities—Rome v. Alexandria, public duty v. private passion, etc.—but there is no real sense in which Antony is found vacillating between the two." *Antony and Cleopatra* "is like nothing so much as one of those soaring, two-storey mannerist paintings wherein the bottom half is occupied with events on what Antony would call 'our dungy earth' (I.i.35), above which the heavens open in a transfiguring blaze that begins with the death of Antony at the end of act IV and keeps ascending to the death of Cleopatra at the end of act V."

555 Hume, Robert D. "Individuation and Development of Character Through Language in *Antony and Cleopatra*." *Shakespeare Quarterly* 24 (1973): 280-300.

In the language of the major characters in *Antony and Cleopatra*, there are striking contrasts in words, rhythm, rhetoric, and speech deviations: "in rhetoric, the logic of Caesar versus the ellipticity of Pompey; in sound, the vowels of Cleopatra against the consonants of Caesar; in imagery, the rich imaginativeness of Antony and Cleopatra versus the barrenness of Caesar."

556 Jewett, Mike. "Shakespeare's Body Politic Imagery." *Dissertation Abstracts* 33 (1973): 5180A (Missouri).

In *Titus Andronicus*, *Julius Caesar*, *Hamlet*, and *Antony and Cleopatra*, "the war within the self is manifested in suicidal tendencies and usually accompanied by military or political imagery in order to suggest the self-destructive effects of a character's actions upon both individual and state."

557 Kearful, Frank J. "''Tis Past Recovery': Tragic Consciousness in *All for Love*." *Modern Language Quarterly* 34 (1973): 227-46.

Dryden acknowledges his debt to *Antony and Cleopatra* in his Preface to *All for Love*, because his play is a "self-consciously literary imitation," or a "conscious imitation of an irrecoverable Shakespearean imagination."

558 Kelly, William J. "The Comic Perspective in Shakespeare's *Henry V*, *Hamlet*, and *Antony and Cleopatra*." *Dissertation Abstracts International* 33 (1973): 6874A (Oregon).

The comic elements have an "influence on our response to character and action." In *Antony and Cleopatra*, "the lovers have a comic aspect, but in spite of it—in fact, because of it—they achieve heroic stature."

559 Kindred, Jerome C. "Unity and Disunity in *Antony and Cleopatra*." *Dissertation Abstracts* 33 (1973): 3588A-3589A (Texas-Austin).

Kindred analyzes the unifying elements like "messengers, secondary characters, imagery and the more intangible devices which are meant to unite Antony and Cleopatra as lovers."

560 Lloyd Evans, Gareth. "The Wide-Ranged Empire: *Antony and Cleopatra*." *Shakespeare V 1606-1616*. Writers and Critics, 72. Edinburgh: Oliver & Boyd, 1973, pp. 24-37.

One thing special about this play is that it is "the myriad incidental truths to human nature and behaviour rather the overall impression which cause us to declare how relevant the play is to human nature—its constituent parts are more affecting than its cumulative whole." Antony and Cleopatra's love is "more important than anything else" and makes its naturalism irrelevant. If the audiences consider this love profligate, "it is profligacy on a giant scale, accompanied by a music and a passion which the stage, after nearly four hundred years, has yet to capture and which the human mind can but wonder at.

561 Mack, Maynard. "*Antony and Cleopatra*: The Stillness and the Dance." *Shakespeare's Art: Seven Essays*. Ed. Milton Crane.

Tupper Lectures on Shakespeare. With Introd. Chicago: U of Chicago for Goe. Wash. U, 1973. 79-113 pp. Reprinted in *Shakespeare: Reflections Chiefly on the Tragedies*. Lincoln and London: U of Nebraska P, 1993, pp. 197-230.

Mack places the play in the medieval tragic tradition of the fall of princes and focuses on "the intricately elaborated context of mobility and mutability within which the fall is shown to occur, so that here as elsewhere in Shakespeare a play's characteristic 'world' and its major action tend to become expressions of each other." In a world in which nothing is permanent, Shakespeare "moves the love affair in the general direction of allegory and myth." Mack also explains how Shakespeare drew upon "the themes and conventions of Renaissance love poetry, notably the sonnet." Mack identifies the conceptions of love-as-space and love-as-war as "the presiding structural ideas of the play." Considering it a paradoxical play, Mack concludes: "As in Erasmus, we have in the play one perspective which knows that Folly is always folly, a consuming and illicit passion always ruinous, and another perspective which sees that some follies may be less foolish than the world's cherished wisdom, an imperium in the embrace of Cleopatra more life-giving than an imperium in Rome."

562 McAlindon, T. "Antony and Cleopatra." *Shakespeare and Decorum*. London: Macmillan, 1973, pp. 167-213.

Among all of Shakespeare's tragedies, "none dwells on the process of fall and change quite so continuously as this one." "In death, and by a deliberate act, Shakespeare's lovers achieve a starry fixity; dolphin-like, they rise above the vast ocean of flux, uncertainty, suspicion, envy and treachery which has been eroding the whole of civilisation."

563 McManaway, James G. "All's Well with Lafew." *Shakespeare's Art: Seven Essays*. Ed. Milton Crane. Chicago: U of Chicago P, 1973, pp. 137-50.

Neither high nor low, characters like Enobarbus "represent a norm of conduct or an attitude by which to measure the actions and utterances of their betters."

564 Payne, Michael. "Erotic Irony and Polarity in *Antony and Cleopatra*." *Shakespeare Quarterly* 24 (1973): 265-79.

In order to show a transcendent world in which oppositions are newly seen as "inter-related polarities," Shakespeare sets up and then demolishes the dualistic concepts of sexuality, ethics, and space-time. Both "irony and polarity function in combination with each other on every level of the play's structure," and its meaning "arises out of an interconnected pattern of polarities which combines the principle of an encompassing myth with that of ironic and seemingly antithetical values and attitudes." Like its thematic polarities, "the play's generic structure is neither tragic nor comic, but both."

565 Quennell, Peter, and Hamish Johnson. *Who's Who in Shakespeare*. London: Dent, 1973. Reprint. Oxford: Oxford UP, 1995. 240 pp.

This is "a guidebook for the reader of the huge Shakespearian canon who wishes to recollect where such-and-such a character occurs, and the function he or she performs."

566 Shaw-Smith, R. "*Antony and Cleopatra*, II.ii.204." *Shakespeare Quarterly* 24 (1973): 92-93.

The Venus to which Enobarbus compares Cleopatra may be an "indecent" figure of the goddess which was popular in pictures of the day.

567 Siemon, James E. "'The Strong Necessity of Time': Dilemma in *Antony and Cleopatra*." *English Studies* 54 (1973): 316-25.

Antony exhibits a tragic dilemma in his character; he is the hero of a tragedy, not a tragic hero.

568 Simmons, Joseph Larry. "'Antony and Cleopatra' and 'Coriolanus', Shakespeare's Heroic Tragedies: A Jacobean Adjustment." *Shakespeare Survey* 26 (1973): 95-101.

These two plays "are distinguished by heroic appeals that are exclusively and definitively aristocratic." Shakespeare "grants that heroes, in an unheroic world, are all but unendurable." He "generates tragedy out of the social disharmony within an audience." Antony and Cleopatra have been destroyed by lust, but there is also something admirable about them. Shakespeare "creates a heroic aspiration beyond that moralism even while aware that the greatness of his tragic Romans must be a limited and qualified one."

569 Simmons, Joseph Larry. "Antony and Cleopatra: New Heaven, New Earth." *Shakespeare's Pagan World: The Roman Tragedies.* Hassocks, nr. Brighton: Harvester, 1973, pp. 109-63.

In this play, Shakespeare "evokes ideals that on the level of imperfect, unredeemed nature are incapable of realization but that ennoble man even they lead to his destruction." His perspective is that of "Christian historiography; it is Augustinian, ecclesiastical, and biblical." In the pagan environment of the play, "their tragedy is inevitable because they demand the perfection of new heaven and new earth without the real means of grace and hope of glory." The greatest irony of the play is that "even the member of the audience who approaches it with Christian expectations is forced, finally, to approve the lovers."

570 Broussard, Mercedes. "Mother and Child: Cleopatra and the Asp." *CEA Critic* 37 (1974): 25-26.

Shakespeare relates Cleopatra to the fertile Nile, thus alerting the audience that procreation is the primary objective of sex. Her "baby," which brings death to her "mother," may be considered the product of Antony and Cleopatra's love.

571 Colie, Rosalie. *Shakespeare's Living Art.* Princeton: Princeton UP, 1974. 370 pp.

In *Antony and Cleopatra* "the abundance of the language seems to match the richness of its subject, the fertility of the Egyptian setting, the emotional largesse of hero and heroine." Colie discusses "style as fundamental morality, style as life." The language of *Antony and Cleopatra* "with its grandioseness and hyperbolical explosions, finally points to the real problem: the efforts of two powerful, wilful, commanding personalities to bring their styles of living, their ingrained alien habits, into line with one another, for no reason other than love." A person's "given style is never merely an alternative way of expressing something: rather, styles arise from cultural sources beyond a character's choice or control."

572 Colman, E.A.M. *The Dramatic Use of Bawdy in Shakespeare*. London: Longman, 1974. 230 pp.

Shakespeare, "as his career developed, quickly became a discriminating user of bawdy, and eventually made it one of the most potent weapons in his dramatic armory." He cites this play as "one of his most 'sexy'" and uses passages from it to illustrate his points.

573 Colombo, Rosa Maria. "'Una creatura umana': *L'Antonio e Cleopatra* di Arrigo Boito ed Eleonora Duse." *Studi inglesi: Raccolta di saggi e ricerche*. Ed. Agostino Lombardo. I. Bari: Adriatica, 1974, pp. 367-407.

Not seen.

574 Costa de Beauregard, Raphaelle. "*Antony and Cleopatra*: A Play to Suit the New Jacobean Taste." *Caliban* 10 (1974): 105-11.

This play "appears Jacobean mainly through the treatment of heroic values in terms of Greek mythology." Antony is compared to Hercules, especially in their anger.

575 Erwin, John W. "Hero as Audience: *Antony and Cleopatra* and *Le soulirer de satin*." *Modern Language Studies* 4.2 (1974): 65-77.

The heroes of Shakespeare and Claudel are passive witnesses who convince the spectators to experience their own freely chosen passivity as a source of power.

576 Foy, Ted C. "Shakespeare's Use of Time: A Study of Four Plays." *Dissertation Abstracts* 35 (1974): 2220A-2221A (Delaware).

In the Roman world of *Antony and Cleopatra*, the "strong necessity of time" (I.ii.42) dictates "the politically expedient, if morally questionable, actions of Octavius and his followers, and at times Antony." The imagery of the death scenes "reconciles spirit and flesh, eternal and temporal."

577 Garber, Marjorie B. *Dream in Shakespeare: From Metaphor to Metamorphosis*. New Haven: Yale UP, 1974. 226 pp.

In this play, "it is just this bold synthesis of major tropes which makes [it] so vast, a many-colored tapestry of titanic actions and gorgeous language." Antony and Cleopatra "are votaries of dream, believers in prophecy and the supernatural," and they "are associated with old heroic values which their world can no longer support. In its tacit relationship to myth-making, this tendency is closely related to the concept of the dream state."

578 Grene, W.D. "Antony and Cleopatra." *Hermathena* (Dublin) 118 (1974): 33-47.

To illustrate his idea of the nobleness of life, Shakespeare "has deliberately chosen a scene of political ruin and moral degeneration." His goal as a poet "is to convince us that here is true greatness existing in a world exactly suited to bring out its meaning." Shakespeare "creates a new poetic reality which has subsumed the original story while freeing it from its obvious implications in sordidness and evil."

579 Gura, Timothy James. "The Function of the Hero in Shakespeare's Last Tragedies." *Dissertation Abstracts* 35 (1974): 3881A (Northwestern).

Antony "both perverts and elevates the devotion, selflessness and sexuality of love." He "effects no change in his world, but joins Cleopatra in a world beyond Octavius' glacial empire."

580 Hoover, Sister M. Frederic, S.N.D. "A Study of Imagery in Shakespeare's *Sonnets*, *Troilus and Cressida*, *Macbeth*, *Antony and Cleopatra*, and *The Winter's Tale*." *Dissertation Abstracts* 34 (1974): 5103A (Case Western Reserve).

Hoover assesses an interaction of imagery with a play's theme, characterization and other elements. She "deals with the bounteous love relationship and the spacious political background of *Antony and Cleopatra*" and "shows how Antony triumphs over time and attains heroic stature."

581 Longo, Joseph A. "Cleopatra and Octavia: Archetypal Imagery in *Antony and Cleopatra*." *University of Dayton Review* 10. 3 (1974): 29-37.

Shakespeare unconsciously relies on the resources of archetypal criticism associated with the conflicts of Dionysian and Apollonian modes.

582 Meredith, Peter. "'That pannelled me at heeles': *Antony and Cleopatra* IV.x.34." *English Studies* 55 (1974): 118-26.

"Pannelled" should be amended to "pantled."

583 Morrison, Mary. "Some Aspects of the Treatment of the Theme of Antony and Cleopatra in Tragedies of the Sixteenth Century." *Journal of European Studies* 4 (1974): 113-25.

In classical times, Cleopatra "was regarded as an arch-enemy of the Roman people." In the Middle Ages, her story "becomes a sort of tale of chivalry, but the Roman attitude of hostility also persists, chiefly on moral grounds." During the Renaissance Shakespeare and other playwrights show "a much more sympathetic attitude to the theme."

584 Payne, Michael. "Erotic Irony and Polarity in *Antony and Cleopatra*." *Irony in Shakespeare's Roman Plays*. Salzburg Studies in English Literature: Elizabethan Studies 19. Salzburg: Institut fur Englische Sprache und Literatur, 1974, pp. 56-85.

In this play, Shakespeare "develops a series of interrelated polarities—Rome-Egypt, masculinity-femininity, space/time boundary-space/time transcendence, death-love—which appear to be mutually exclusive or dualistic concepts but which are finally shown to be polar concepts instead."

585 Smith, Gerald A. "'Good Brother' in *King Lear* and *Antony and Cleopatra*." *Shakespeare Quarterly* 25 (1974): 284

The word "good-brother," when hyphenated in Elizabethan writing, means "brother-in-law."

586 Smith, Gordon R. "The Melting of Authority in *Antony and Cleopatra*." *College Literature* 1 (1974): 1-18.

Analyzing political behavior, this study examines the ways in which Octavius, Antony and other Romans "are manipulated by Shakespeare to set each other off." None of these characters "has the remotest resemblance to that Renaissance image of the perfect prince, he who was just under the angels on the Great Chain, anointed, crowned, and planted as God's vicar, most Christian, wise and just, clement, magnanimous, majestic and serene, as all the various royal rascallitie of that age commonly represented itself to its public."

587 Thomas, Helen S. "'Breeze' and 'Bees,' 'Sailes' and 'Tailes: *Antony and Cleopatra* III.x.17-22." *CEA Critic* 37.1 (1974): 23-24.

In this passage, a cow's *tail* is her *sail*.

588 Waterhouse, Ruth. "Shakespeare's *Antony and Cleopatra* I.iv.12-13 and 44-47." *Explicator* 33 (1974): Item 17.

Lepidus uses a cosmic simile "in reverse" about Antony. Caesar ignores the beauty of the flag iris on the water, calling it vagabond, thus indicating his own blindness to natural beauty.

589 Whitaker, Vigil K. "Shakespeare the Elizabethan." *Rice University Studies* 60.2 (1974): 141-51.

Shakespeare was "often of his own time, even in his greatest plays." The modern reader does not have the right "to expect an Elizabethan, or even a Shakespearean, tragedy to have a clearly articulated plot structure; it may only tell a well-known story." *Antony and Cleopatra*, "though more compelling as a great love story than contemporary plays about Roman wars, and though written with all the magic of Shakespeare's poetry, is little better articulated in plot structure than they."

590 Williamson, Marilyn L. *Infinite Variety:* Antony and Cleopatra *in Renaissance Drama and Earlier Tradition*. Mystic, CT: Verry, 1974 [1975]. 254 pp.

The diversity of treatment of the Antony and Cleopatra story before Shakespeare that they were willing to alter the facts of history.

591 Adlard, John. "Cleopatra as Isis." *Archiv für das Stadium der Neueren Sprachen und Literaturen* 212 (1975): 324-28.

Adlard examines the relationship between Cleopatra and the goddess Isis.

592 Cairncross, Andrew S. "*Antony and Cleopatra*, III.x.10." *Notes and Queries* 22 (1975): 173.

Cairncross emends "ribaudred" to "ribaud."

593 Dorius, R. J. "Shakespeare's Dramatic Modes and *Antony and Cleopatra*." *Literatur als Kritik des Lebens*. Ed. Rudolf Haas, Heinz-Joachim Mullenbrock, and Claus Uhlig. Festschrift zum 65. Geburtstag von Ludwig Borinski. Heidelberg: Quelle & Meyer, 1975, pp. 83-96.

Not seen.

594 Downer, Alan S. "Heavenly Mingle: *Antony and Cleopatra* as a Dramatic Experience." *The Triple Bond: Plays, Mainly Shakespearean, in Performance*. Ed. Joseph G. Price. University Park: Pennsylvania State UP, 1975, pp. 240-54.

Downer argues that "the world of government is ambivalent, the world of love is ambivalent; and yet he [Antony] must choose. And in either choice lies destruction." This is "the idea developed through the dramatic experience. The structure is designed to reveal Cleopatra and Octavius not as lustful figures or dramatic stereotypes but as representations of world-ideas." In this play, "the jaws are Octavius and Cleopatra and what is thrown between is Antony."

595 Dusinberre, Julia. *Shakespeare and the Nature of Women.* London: 1975. New York: Barnes & Noble, 1976. 2nd ed. New York: St. Martin's P, 1996. xlix, 329 pp.

The two editions are identical except that the second one contains a preface, "Beyond the Battle?"

Dusinberre praises Shakespeare because he "saw men and women as equal in a world which declared them unequal. He did not divide human nature into the masculine and the feminine, but observed in the individual woman or man an infinite variety of union between opposing impulses. To talk about Shakespeare's women is to talk about his men, because he refused to separate their worlds physically, intellectually, or spiritually." Shakespeare "gave Cleopatra her own moral law that in being always an artist she was in fact true to her own nature, and this constituted a kind of integrity, the integrity of the player who can only be true to himself by giving himself to his art."

596 Kernan, Alvin. "The full stream of the world (ii): *Antony and Cleopatra.*" *The Revels History of Drama in English.* Ed. J. Leeds Barroll, Alexander Leggatt, Richard Hosley and Alvin Kernan. London: Methuen, 1975, III, 436-45.

This play is a full realization of "man's desire for permanence and the ceaseless change of the world." "The greater rhythms of the world—the ebb and flow of the tides, the rise and fall of the Nile, the ever-shifting shape of the clouds, the continuous process of growth, death and new growth out of death—are, for all the difference in the two characters, the rhythms of the personal lives of Antony and Cleopatra."

597 Labriola, Albert C. "Renaissance Neoplatonism and Shakespeare's Characterization of Cleopatra." *Hebrew University Studies in Literature* 3 (1975): 20-36.

This essay explains "the range and depth of allusion to certain Neoplatonic concepts (especially to the *Anima Mundi* or World Soul and the Stair of Love) that help to define the nature of Cleopatra's love for Antony." In the last scenes of the play, Shakespeare "uses the popular Neoplatonic concept of the World Soul to suggest Cleopatra's heightened appraisal of Antony's worth and value to herself and to the world."

598 Lyman, Stanford M., and Marvin B. Scott. "*Antony and Cleopatra*." *The Drama of Social Reality*. New York: Oxford UP, 1975, pp. 54-98.

Lyman and Scott treat this play as a "global drama" which focuses on "civilizational encounter and conflict. Its outcome indicates the triumph of one over the other, and the victory of Rome over Egypt is a symbolic foreshadowing of the modern world." Octavius Caesar personifies the new world "in which we are all enclosed. Its cold and efficient bureaucracy invites our concern. Its meaninglessness prepares us to understand it with a sociology of the absurd."

Lyman and Scott treat the Roman and Egyptian cultures as "a contrast between the Apollonian and the Dionysian," and "Antony is desperately, helplessly, and ultimately, fatally, caught between the two." They also comment on the play as "tragedy of forbidden social regression" and the main characters' "egocentric withdrawal, with the discharge of all energies directed exclusively at the self."

599 Martin, Leslie Howard. "'All for Love' and the Millenarian Tradition." *Comparative Literature* 27 (1975): 289-306.

Instead of adapting *Antony and Cleopatra*, Dryden shared with Shakespeare a popular historical subject.

600 Maxwell-Mahon, W.D. "Character and Conflict in 'Antony and Cleopatra'." *Crux* 9 (Aug. 1975): 39-44.

Not seen.

601 Miyazaki, Yukoh. "Heavenly Miracle: A Reading of *Antony and Cleopatra*." *Journal of Human and Cultural Sciences* (Musashi U) 5.3-4 (1975): 41-73. In Japanese.

Not seen.

602 Otsuki, Kenji. *Psychoanalytic Insight of the Poet_Shakespeare: Analytic Appreciation of his Five Great Tragedies*. Tokyo: Sozo-bunka-sha Press, 1975. In Japanese.

Not seen.

603 Patrick, J. Max. "The Cleopatra Theme in World Literature up to 1700." *The Undoing of Babel: Watson Kirkconnel, The Man and His Work*. Ed. James R.C. Perkin. Toronto: McClelland & Stewart, 1975, pp. 64-76.

In this survey, Patrick praises Shakespeare for his "copiousness in treatment, complexity of characterization, exploitation of a cosmic panorama, and richness."

604 Praz, Mario. "The Life of Antony and Cleopatra." *Hauptwerke der englischen Literature: Darstellungen und Interpretationen*. Ed. Manfred Pfister. Munich: Kindler, 1975.

Not seen.

605 Shanker, Sidney. "Antony and Cleopatra and Vanishing Ideology." *Shakespeare and the Uses of Ideology*. Studies in English Literature 105. The Hague and Paris: Mouton, 1975, pp. 195-212.

This play "deals with the primal essence of being, of its contradictions, paradoxes, and finite limits." It "deals with the eternal problems of living in the real world, of finding value and meaning for and by oneself." It "deals with the nature of human interactions, of their harmfulness and wonderfulness, with the fact that evil and death can befall a man through the operation of his own essence and not through a guilt or sinfulness of any man."

606 Shapiro, Susan C. "To 'O'erflow the Measure': The Paradox of the Nile in *Antony and Cleopatra*." *Studies in the Humanities* 4.2 (1975): 36-42.

This play "is surely the 'brightest,' shading off toward the romances in tone and mood." Its central paradox is that "the destruction which comes about through excess necessarily precedes and is an integral part of the process of creation." In this play, "it is the carrying to excess of the opposing values of Rome and Egypt which causes both the destruction and subsequent creation."

607 Sircar, Bibhuti Bhusan. "Antony and Cleopatra." *An Appreciation of William Shakespeare: Ten Plays with Critical Estimates*. Calcutta: South Calcutta P and Sircar, 1975, pp. 579-675.

Sircar comments on sexual morality and the dissipated characters of Antony and Cleopatra. "Against all his pricks of conscience, his greater sense of propriety and judgement," Antony "proceeds with half-opened eyes to indulge indiscriminately in the worthless frivolities of a dissipated life with disastrous consequences. And that appears to be the object lesson of the character of Mark Antony, as the essence of its merits, the key-note of its critical estimate and all."

608 Taft, Roberta Jill. "A Rhetorical Perspective of *Romeo and Juliet*." *Dissertation Abstracts International* 37 (1975): 342A (California-Berkeley).

Taft explains the techniques Shakespeare "uses to create and control a theater audience's understanding and experience of the plays." In comparison with *Romeo and Juliet*, in *Antony and Cleopatra* "these devices appear but in a strategically more complex fashion."

609 Weitz, Morris. "Literature without Philosophy: *Antony and Cleopatra*." *Shakespeare Survey* 28 (1975): 29-36.

Weitz identifies in this play "the theme of generation and corruption, of coming into being and passing away, a theme as old as ancient Greek philosophy." It is a "pre-Socratic tragedy" in which Shakespeare presents "the contrast and unity of external and internal vastness; the infinite variety and enigma of Cleopatra; Antony's role as a middle-aged hero who has experienced the gap of boredom; and the human as well as demi-god in Antony and Cleopatra, both of create gaps in nature by their presence and absence."

610 Whatley, Janet. "L'Orient desert: *Berenice* and *Antony and Cleopatra.*" *University of Toronto Quarterly* 44 (1975): 96-114.

Shakespeare and Racine treat the orient quite differently. The "Shakespearean Orient of swarming fecundity" stands in contrast with the "Racinian Orient of staticity and sterility."

611 Wilson, Robert Benjamin. "A Survey of Stoicism and Neostoicism in the Dramatic Works of Chapman, Marston, and Shakespeare." *Dissertation Abstracts International* 36 (1975): 8038A (Southern Illinois).

In his delineation of Antony, Cleopatra, and King Lear, Shakespeare "uses the Boethian concepts of love as a divine and compelling force which raises its adherents above the vicissitudes of the world into another realm."

612 Ardinger, Barbara R. "Cleopatra on Stage: An Examination of the Persona of the Queen in English Drama, 1592-1898." *Dissertation Abstracts* 37 (1976): 3634A (Southern Illinois).

Ardinger examines the treatment of Cleopatra's persona in eleven plays in English. These plays reflect the three motifs created by Roman propaganda: "Cleopatra is a divine figure, a love figure, and a political figure." In the plays focusing on Antony and Cleopatra, "she is the reigning Queen of Egypt who bargains with Octavian before her suicide to preserve her throne for her heirs." There is "an anti-feminist bias at work in both propaganda and drama."

613 Bayley, John. ""'Antony and Cleopatra' and 'Coriolanus'." *The Uses of Division: Unity and Disharmony in Literature.* New York: Viking, 1976, pp. 234-44.

Antony and Cleopatra "have nothing to do but be actors; nothing but to utter the golden speeches, make the heroic assertions, touch us at times and leave us sceptical at others." Paradoxically, "for this very reason actors find the two great parts almost impossible to play—as they understand playing parts." In this play Shakespeare "rightly found himself content with a situation which his intelligence, in the imaginative working out, sensed to be all on the surface, in a way that could none the less be rendered with a felicitous bravura."

614 Benoit, Raymond. "The Prophecy in the Play: *Antony and Cleopatra.*" *Greyfriar* (Siena College) 17 (1976): 3-7.

In 5.2.21-33, Benoit finds evidence of Christian terminology and the Annunciation.

615 Bradbrook, M.C. "*Antony and Cleopatra.*" *The Living Monument: Shakespeare and the Theatre of His Time.* Cambridge: Cambridge UP, 1976, pp. 176-83.

In this play, "the variety of points of view, the contradictions and paradoxes mean that strong identification alternates with cool detachment." The principal characters are "ruled by the Fortune." The "immense range of setting has prepared for such cosmic enlargement at death," and Cleopatra is shown in "a prolonged, eloquent ritualistic death scene."

616 Brand, Alice G. "Antony and Cleopatra and the Nature of Their Sexuality." *The Bard* (London) 1 (1976): 98-107.

Brand analyzes the imagery associated with the figures of Antony and Cleopatra and underlines its centrality to the play.

617 Cantor, Paul A. *Shakespeare's Rome: Republic and Empire.* Ithaca: Cornell UP, 1976. 228 pp.

This study examines the "way in which the political story and the love story integral to one another." Shakespeare "has taken pains to ground his love story in a very specific political and historical setting, a setting which gives the love its particular character and significance," and "in the Empire portrayed in *Antony and Cleopatra* political honors have come to seem empty precisely because of the nature of those who do the honoring." In this political environment, the issue of loyalty or fidelity "is also the central problem in the love story of *Antony and Cleopatra* and provides the closest point of contact between public and private life in the play." Hence, this play's keynote is "the need for tests of love in a world in which old forms of loyalty have given way to new." The real test of love "is how much one is willing to sacrifice for one's beloved, so that Antony's losses become a pledge of his faith to Cleopatra, and her willingness to stand by him in his downfall becomes in turn her token of allegiance." Their "loyalty in defeat must finally extend to loyalty in death, and suicide seems to offer the one unambiguous—and hence final—deed of love."

Antony and Cleopatra "are governed in their public and private lives by the same principles," and they "never make any attempt to keep their love affair strictly private but are instead proud to flaunt it in the public eye." This play "underscores the subjectivity of the lovers' experience." Consequently it can be paradoxically described as a tragedy and a comedy. "To the extent that Antony and Cleopatra take their private vision with them to the grave, their story remains a tragedy. But to the extent that they do leave behind them believers in the legend of their love, their story becomes a comedy." But it must be added that "for their story to be a comedy, it would have to be a kind of divine comedy."

618 Champion, Larry S. "*Antony and Cleopatra.*" *Shakespeare's Tragic Perspective*. Atlanta: U of Georgia P, 1976, pp. 239-65.

In this play, Shakespeare "achieves his most powerful delineation of these secular values between which man struggles to make the choices for a successful life. Gone is a clear distinction between virtue and vice, between material and spiritual choice." The play "operates within the world of man, within the conflict created out of the struggle for power and influence between a Roman emperor and an Egyptian queen. And the values of these two worlds are equally tainted."

619 Christopher, Georgia B. "The Private War and Peace in *Antony and Cleopatra.*" *A Festschrift for Professor Marguerite Roberts, on the Occasion of Her Retirement from Westhampton College, University of Richmond, Virginia*. Ed. Frieda Elaine Penninger. Richmond: U of Richmond, 1976, pp. 59-73.

Christopher analyzes elements of "private war and peace" in this play.

620 Hallett, Charles A. "Change, Fortune, and Time: Aspects of the Sub-Lunar World in *Antony and Cleopatra*." *Journal of English and Germanic Philology* 75 (1976): 75-89.

In this play, "Shakespeare has given us an almost clinical analysis of eros, its power and glory, but also its ultimate inability to sustain itself and those who venture all in its cause." The play gives the impression that "there would be no virtues; everything would resolve itself into ambiguity and relativism." The instability that the characters "detect in the universe and the state renders them unable to make final judgments."

621 Heffner, Ray L., Jr. "The Messengers in Shakespeare's *Antony and Cleopatra*." *ELH: Journal of English Literary History* 43 (1976): 154-62.

In this play, "the dispersed locations, sweeping scope, and rapid turns of the action required a heavy use of reporters and intermediaries."

622 Honigmann, E.A.J. "Antony versus Cleopatra." *Shakespeare, Seven Tragedies: The Dramatist's Manipulation of Response*. London: Macmillan; New York: Barnes & Noble, 1976, pp. 150-69.

Analyzing Shakespeare's manipulation of the audience's response to his characters, Honigmann discusses the two Antonies—"the heroic Antony and the perpetual loser." Antony appears to be rigid; for Cleopatra, Shakespeare "invented an extraordinary range of special gestures, so that her physical expressiveness intimates a corresponding emotional and intuitive mobility." About the middle of the play, Cleopatra's humour against Antony ceases, Antony becomes serious and begins to dominate her. At the time of his death, Antony has gained a fresh clarity of vision. Cleopatra stages a scene during her suicide, which makes her sincerity questionable. It is not certain that she has transcended "baser life," but it is a possibility.

623 Long, Michael. "Antony and Cleopatra and the Song of Dionysos." *The Unnatural Scene. A Study in Shakespearean Tragedy*. London: Methuen, 1976, pp. 241-59.

Shakespeare's tragedies "look closely at how men attach themselves to a social structure and shape their identities thereby, and at how this attachment creates habits of perception, behaviour and evaluation which are radically delimiting." Critics often miss the comedy in *Antony and Cleopatra* and how the Rome of its first half "is seen with airy and scurrilous comedy as absurd." In Egypt, "Dionysos is brought alive as a breeding chaos of self-replenishing energies creating kinds of luxury and magnificence which have nothing to do with mere 'ornament' or 'ostentation'." In this play, "the whole tangle of Dionysiac elements can only be taken as being of a piece, the whole chaos of it all taken as it is in the certain knowledge, imparted by this great romanticism, that without these grotesqueries there will be no creative life, without these indignities (painfully there when Antony botches his suicide, for example) there will be no possibility of Egyptian 'fire and air'."

624 McFarland, Ronald E. "The Rhodian Colossus in Renaissance Emblem and Poetry." *English Miscellany* 25 (1975-76): 121-34.

In this play, Shakespeare refers to "the bestriding Colossus with upraised arm." He "is aware of the pictorial tradition of the Rhodian Colossus, and his allusions to the statue are more precise and more effective than those of Chapman."

625 Marsh, D.R.C. "*Antony and Cleopatra*." *Passion Lends Them Power: A Study of Shakespeare's Love Tragedies*. Manchester: Manchester UP, 1976, pp. 141-200.

In this tragedy, "love triumphs, but since the two central figures cannot simply abdicate from their positions of importance in the world, their concentration on their love leaves them exposed to the worldly dangers which their political importance has attracted." The two lovers "die because they no longer care to protect themselves," and "their love's triumph brings about their deaths: when they die, as the play makes very clear, the act by which they acknowledge love's supreme importance ends love and life together." Shakespeare "concentrates on the worth of a love that is allowed both intensity and scope."

626 Mourgues, Odette de. "Deux triomphes de l'hyperbole." *De Shakespeare à T.S. Eliot: Mélanges offerts à Henri Fluchère*. Ed. Marie-Jeanne Durry, Robert Ellrodt, and Marie-Thérèse Jones-Davies. Etudes anglaises 63. Paris: Didier, 1976, pp. 73-79.

Shakespeare in *Antony and Cleopatra*, V.ii.76-99, and Maurice Sceve in *Deli* show that they used hyperbole as a device for rendering the intensity and the infinite power of expression.

627 Platt, Michael. *Rome and Romans According to Shakespeare*. JDS 51. Salzburg: Inst. fur eng. Sprache & Lit., Univ. Salzburg, 1976. 295 pp.

This play "makes us long for a better world, for world where the beauty we apprehend fitfully and uncertainly in these lovers will be strong, constant and viable, where what is passionate tension in them is knit whole." The readers are "struggling to judge these lovers aright, a task they struggle with too; it also means never denying either what scepticism sees or wonder divines in them."

628 Powell, Henry W. "Shakespeare's Rome: Major Themes in the Late Political Plays." *Dissertation Abstracts* 37 (1976): 1568A (North Carolina-Chapel Hill).

Antony and Cleopatra has been written "in a mixed mode—part tragedy, part comedy, and, most important, partly a myth play which invites its audience to participate in the enactment of commonly held values."

629 Ray, Robert H. "The 'Ribaudred Nagge' of *Antony and Cleopatra* III.x.10: A Suggested Emendation." *English Language Notes* 14 (1976): 21-25.

All the explanations given by editors are inadequate or far-fetched concerning the textual problem of "ribaudred." It should be simply emended to read "Ribauld red."

630 Rothschild, Herbert B., Jr. "The Oblique Encounter: Shakespeare's Confrontation of Plutarch with Special Reference to *Antony and Cleopatra*." *English Literary Renaissance* 6 (1976): 404-29.

Shakespeare "himself was concerned with the relationship between drama and historiography when he began transferring Plutarchan materials into plays," and, "beginning with *Antony and Cleopatra*, this relationship and the questions it generates are central issues in the dramatic action."

631 Schulman, Norma M. "A 'Motive for Metaphor': Shakespeare's *Antony and Cleopatra*." *Hebrew University Studies in Literature* 4 (1976): 154-74.

In this play there is a conflict "between the autonomous, creative attempt to shape and determine one's world, and the surrender to an intransigent, external reality." Cleopatra "has the strongest 'motive for metaphor' in the play since her antipathy to routine, fact, and, even, ultimately, the limitations of mortality is deepest." "For not only does she exercise 'poetic licence' in viewing reality selectively, but with her unpredictable whims and capricious provocations of others, she virtually 'acts out' the process of metaphor, if metaphor is a process of asserting changes."

632 Stansfield, Dale Bryan. "Montaigne and Shakespeare, Renaissance or Baroque?" *Dissertation Abstracts* 36 (1976): 6075A (Wisconsin-Madison).

Hamlet, *King Lear*, and *Antony and Cleopatra* are "best designated as Baroque, not Renaissance," because they "portray the general affirmation of human values in a state of crisis" and "are permeated by the critical spirit of reappraisal of the human condition typical of Baroque realism."

633 Steiner, George. *After Babel: Aspects of Language and Translation*. 1976. 2nd. ed. New York: Oxford UP, 1992. 538 pp.

While discussing the complexities of translating this and other plays into French, Steiner refers to André Gide's rendering of *Antony and Cleopatra*. He argues that "it is probably a part of Shakespeare's strategy, and of the strategy of spoken drama as such, to allow indecision, to let different possibilities of meaning 'hover' around the principal axis."

634 Stilling, Roger. "*Antony and Cleopatra.*" *Love and Death in Renaissance Tragedy.* Baton Rouge: Louisiana State UP, 1976, pp. 278-89.

Shakespeare defines "the disabling division of consciousness" in Antony "quite explicitly in terms of the opposing ideologies of love that have dominated this study—the romantic and the antiromantic. Thus, the vision of eros that we see in *Antony and Cleopatra* as distinctly *Roman* is also the typical Renaissance antiromanticism that manifests itself elsewhere in the drama." The ending leaves one with a feeling of "ripeness: love completed by death, not undermined—drawing the lovers in metaphor and image to the love marriage that they never gave each other in life."

635 Waller, Gary F. "'Things in Motion'—the Time-Worlds of *Troilus and Cressida* and *Antony and Cleopatra.*" *The Strong Necessity of Time: The Philosophy of Time in Shakespeare and Elizabethan Literature.* The Hague and Paris: Mouton, 1976, pp. 109-21.

These two plays "are deeply concerned with the conflict between the public world and the world of private motives and inner promptings, and both play extend and deepen into tragedy Shakespeare's examination of time and mutability in the political world." Antony and Cleopatra's "is a world dominated by a restless, unpredictable Fortune, a dangerous world except for the most single-minded and ruthless opportunist."

636 Alvis, John. "Unity of Subject in Shakespeare's Roman Plays." *Publications of the Arkansas Philological Association* 3 (1977): 68-75.

Alvis argues that "the Roman protagonists are not speculative men (not even Brutus), nor do they often have opportunity to engage in prolonged exercises of private introspection. Their life is lived out in a public arena where hortatory rather than deliberative rhetoric prevails." Antony and Cleopatra do not "dwell upon questions concerning the nature of love itself." In the Roman plays, "ignorance and intellectual misconceptions, rather than conscious malice, cause the ills that befall society and individuals."

637 Beckerman, Bernard. "Past the Size of Dreaming." *Twentieth Century Interpretations of Antony and Cleopatra.* Ed. Mark Rose. Englewood Cliffs, NJ: Prentice-Hall, 1977, pp. 99-112. Reprinted in *Shakespeare: The Theatrical Dimension.* Ed. Philip C. McGuire and David A. Samuelson. New York: AMS, 1979, pp. 209-23.

Cleopatra's teasing and testing and Antony's sense of rapture are a paradigm for the play's action and full of contradictions like these. "Idealized love can and cannot exclude the demands of Rome." "Cleopatra's detached and calculated mockery is a necessary yet finally unsatisfactory stimulant of Antony's rapture." "The boundless love envisioned by Antony is expressed in the limited act of wandering the streets." By "subjecting these contradictions to the breaking point, Shakespeare refines the love so deliberately aroused by Cleopatra and so facilely rhapsodized by Antony."

The play is about Antony trying to acquire selflessness, and "the subtle motions of the play dramatize the growth of the still moments of communion in the teeth of the unstable shifts of will, passion, and calculation with which Antony and Cleopatra habitually meet the world." It does not matter that Antony and Cleopatra suffer defeat as kings; "their painful struggle to touch each other truly is what finally holds our attention."

638 Browne, Marlene Consuela. "Shakespeare's Lady Macbeth and Cleopatra: Women in a Political Context." *Dissertation Abstracts* 38 (1977): 274A (Brown).

Browne explains "the theoretical political context of Shakespeare's time and woman's place in it." She believes that "the fear of women rulers affects the portrayals of Lady Macbeth and Cleopatra."

639 Camé, J.F. "A Note on Shakespeare's *Antony and Cleopatra* and Milton's *Dalila.*" *Cahiers Elisabéthains* 12 (1977): 69-70.

It seems likely that Milton had Shakespeare in mind when he "uses some features of Enobarbus' famous description, in order to degrade Dalila each time." Camé argues that "Dalila is a degraded Cleopatra, still able to seduce, but obviously unable to love, as the end of the scene with Samson will show."

640 Farmer, Harold. "'I'll give thee leave to play': Theatre Symbolism in *Antony and Cleopatra.*" *English Studies in Africa: A Journal of the Humanities* (Johannesburg) 20 (1977): 107-19.

In this play, "the significance of love is explored through metaphors and symbols related to matters of style, particularly acting style, while questions of histrionic style and purpose are, simultaneously, explored through the paradigm of the love story."

641 Felperin, Howard. *Shakespearean Representation: Mimesis and Modernity in Elizabethan Tragedy*. Princeton: Princeton UP, 1977. 199 pp.

In *Antony and Cleopatra*, "it is the principals themselves who attempt to impose, in characteristic Shakespearean fashion, a morality structure upon themselves and their world, a structure closely analogous to the by now familiar one adopted by Hal in the earlier moral history, *Henry IV, Part 1*." Juxtaposed against this is the heroic model of the Renaissance epic which treats Cleopatra as "a figure of deceit and corruption, seducing the hero from his true mission of self-realization through heroic conquest." Each of these models "enables us to see the weakness or inadequacy of the other as a model of conduct." The play "moves toward the joyful reunion with its implied models that characterizes Shakespearean comedy and romance rather than toward the unsettling divergence that characterizes Shakespearean tragedy." But these models are "mutually contradictory to the end, which is also what finally maintains the play within the mode of tragedy."

642 Ferrara, Fernando. "Sesso e potere. Le truffe di Cleopatra." *Annali-Anglistica* 22 (1977): 27-80.

In the character of Enobarbus can be found echoes of some themes and situations typical of the *Sonnets*.

643 Fitz, Linda T. "Egyptian Queens and Male Reviewers: Sexist Attitudes in *Antony and Cleopatra* Criticism." *Shakespeare Quarterly* 28 (1977): 297-316.

Fitz argues that critical approaches to this play "have been coloured by the sexist assumption the critics have brought with them to their reading." She thinks that "many critics feel personally threatened by Cleopatra and what she represents to them." In the case of Cleopatra, "critical attitudes go beyond the usual condescension toward female characters or the usual willingness to give critical approval only to female characters who chaste, fair, loyal, and modest: critical attitudes toward Cleopatra seem to reveal deep personal fears of aggressive or manipulative women." She is "seen as the archetypal woman: practiser of feminine wiles, mysterious, childlike, long on passion and short on intelligence—except for a sort of animal cunning." The "wicked and manipulative" Cleopatra can be contrasted with "the chaste and submissive" Octavia.

In their assessments of Antony and Cleopatra, critics apply double standards: "What is praise-worthy in Antony is damnable in Cleopatra." The most lamentable sign of sexism "is the almost universal assumption that Antony alone is its protagonist." Cleopatra needs to be examined "without the assumption that readers and theatregoers will never be able to treat her as anything more than an exotic and decadent puzzle, inaccessible to rational thought, remote from human feeling."

644 Godshalk, W.L. "Dolabella as Agent Provocateur." *Renaissance Papers 1977*. Ed. Dennis G. Donovan and A. Leigh DeNeef. Durham: Southern Renaissance Conference, 1977, pp. 69-74.

Caesar's enigmatic remarks about Dolabella in 5.1.71-72 suggest that Dolabella has provoked Cleopatra to commit suicide on Caesar's orders. Shakespeare wants the audience to question Dolabella's actions, and "if we read the last scene as Caesar's ultimate triumph over Cleopatra, it does not harm a basic tension in the play, the struggle between the two manipulators, Caesar and Cleopatra."

645 Harris, Duncan S. "'Again for Cydnus': The Dramaturgical Resolution of *Antony and Cleopatra*." *Studies in English Literature, 1500-1900* 17 (1977): 219-31.

This play "achieves a satisfying conclusion, despite the lack of knowledgeable and reliable characters to give our responses to the last scene." Harris argues that "guidance exists and encourages us to take the side of the lovers," but he does not argue that the end of the play "provides the intellectual clarity found at the ends of the major tragedies." He argues "only that Shakespeare put his thumb on the scale, not that he removed the counterweights."

646 Kastan, David Scott. "More Than History Can Pattern." *Cithara* 17 (1977): 29-44.

Kastan considers this as one of the plays in which "the movement beyond the tragic finds its first mature voice." "Defeat and death are discovered to be not merely the terms of tragic loss but paradoxically also the terms of victory and transcendence." In this play, "the resistance to tragic closure exists in the imaginations of the lovers, while in the romances it exists in the imagination of the playwright, but in both cases it is love that is recognized as the perfecting agent."

647 Kernan, Alvin. "Place and Plot in Shakespeare." *Yale Review* 67 (1977): 48-56.

The Romes of *Antony and Cleopatra*, *Julius Caesar*, *Titus Andronicus*, *Cymbeline*, and *Coriolanus* are very different towns.

648 Kozikowski, Stanley J. "Shakespeare's *Antony and Cleopatra* V.ii.309-311." *Explicator* 35 (1977): 7-8.

Cleopatra's usage of "ass" means that she is mocking the historical "signe" of Caesar's victory over Antony.

649 Kranz, David Lord. "Shakespeare's Roman Vision." *Dissertation Abstracts* 38 (1977): 4846A (California-Berkeley).

Shakespeare's particular view of Roman history "provides the homogeneity others have sensed in the so-called 'Roman plays'."

650 Kuriyama, Constance Brown. "The Mother of the World: A Psychoanalytic Interpretation of Shakespeare's *Antony and Cleopatra.*" *English Literary Renaissance* 7 (1977): 324-51.

Instead of "treating the play as a clear or ambiguous *statement* about something—which only leads to endless debate over whether the world is well-lost, ill-lost, or both—we might try reading the play as a richly elaborated rendering of a basic human sexual fantasy (*liebestod*) which also explores and mediates the psychological conflicts attending the fantasy."

651 Leary, William G. *Shakespeare Plain: The Making and Performing of Shakespeare's Plays.* New York: McGraw-Hill, 1977. 298 pp.

Most of Shakespeare's plays "cannot be made plain—meaning *simple*—without falsifying them." But by studying "the ways he worked as he set about composing and then produced these plays," one can "gain a plain view of both the plays and their performances." In this play, Shakespeare presented "an outsized world of seemingly infinite spaciousness within which oscillate the two lovers of mythic proportions who both fuse and transcend the smaller worlds of Rome and Egypt that they emblemize."

652 Nochimson, Richard. "The End Crowns All: Shakespeare's Deflation of Tragic Possibility in *Antony and Cleopatra.*" *English* (London) 26 (1977): 99-132.

This "untragic" play presents "a mundane world, inhabited by very ordinary people with inflated visions of themselves, and dominated by foolishness." Generally, "in mood and theme *Antony and Cleopatra* is very similar to the ironic view expressed in *Troilus and Cressida* that fair is fool, that neither heaven nor spectator should care very much about what happens to the characters in the play because the absence of value to be lost makes the losses that occur meaningless and untragic, that Shakespeare has deliberately taken the tragic element inherent in the story of Antony and Cleopatra and reduced it so much that his version of the story no longer evokes a tragic response in the spectator."

653 Ozaki, Yoshiharu. "Shakespeare no Boy Cleopatra." Nihon Kyokai, ed. *Shakespeare no Engekiteki Fudo.* Tokyo: Kenkyusha, 1977, pp. 289-318. In Japanese.

Not seen.

654 Rahesoo, Jask. "The First Complete Shakespeare Edition in Estonian: Background and Perspectives." *Shakespeare Jahrbuch* (Weimar) 113 (1977): 178-84.

This is an account of the playwright in Estonian culture on the occasion of the publication of the first complete translation between 1959 and 1975 in seven volumes.

655 Rose, Mark, ed *Twentieth Century Interpretations of* Antony and Cleopatra: *A Collection of Critical Essays.* Twentieth-Century Interpretations. Englewood Cliffs, NJ: Prentice-Hall, 1977. 138 pp.

This collection of essays reprints, in whole or in part, the following items found in this bibliography: Maurice Charney, Julian Markels, Reuben A. Brower, John F. Danby, John Holloway, Robert Ornstein, Bernard Beckerman, George Bernard Shaw, Northrop Frye, Janet Adelman, and Maynard Mack.

In his introduction, Rose argues that, unlike the heroes of Renaissance epic, "with its dual focus on love and war and its recurring figure of the great hero torn between his love for a beautiful enchantress and the claims of glory, duty, and the battlefield," Antony "never does quite break his Egyptian fetters." The play is concerned with "becoming" and also "with the idea of selfhood, of individuality brought to fulfillment." This tragedy "leaves us with a special feeling of fulfillment, for what we witness at end is the spectacle of life becoming history, of Antony and Cleopatra at last becoming 'themselves' as we who have observed their lives across a great gap of time have always known them to be."

656 Schwartz, Murray M. "Shakespeare through Contemporary Psychoanalysis." *Hebrew University Studies in Literature* 5 (1977): 182-98. Reprinted in *Representing Shakespeare: New Psychoanalytic Essays*. Ed. Murray M. Schwartz and Coppélia Kahn. Baltimore and London: Johns Hopkins UP, 1980, pp. 21-32.

This play contains "a 'dialectic of contrariety' almost impossible in the earlier tragedies. For me, Antony acts out an intensely ambivalent struggle between masculine hardness and feminine fluidity, finally choosing—both, and neither, a new synthesis."

657 Shintri, Sarojini. *Woman in Shakespeare*. Research Publication Series 32. Dharwad: Karnatak U, 1977. 313 pp.

In her analysis of daughters, lovers, wives, mothers, low women, and other female characters in Shakespeare, Shintri comments on Cleopatra, Octavia, Iras and Charmian. Cleopatra "is one of those women who are eternally young in body and mind and in whom the pleasures of youth are glorified. Nowhere do we experience in the play the beauty of mind and heart of Cleopatra; only her physical beauty, her crown, her royal robe, her golden barge, and her delicate cheeks and lips catch and dazzle our imagination." Cleopatra "never allows herself to be analyzed" and "is more elusive and deceptive than a mirage." Octavia does not make "a single complaint against Antony or Cleopatra. There lies the beauty of Octavia's character and her triumph over Cleopatra."

658 Smith, Stella T. "Imagery of Union, Division, and Disintegration in *Antony and Cleopatra*." *Claflin College Review* (Orangeburg, South Carolina) 1, 2 (1977): 15-28.

This is an analysis of the imagery of unity and disintegration in the play.

659 Speaight, Robert. "Roman Questions." *Shakespeare: The Man and His Achievement*. London: Dent, 1977, pp. 308-21.

Antony and Cleopatra "are, each in their different way, too fallible to realize the love which at the same time unites and so nearly destroys them." Shakespeare "does not skimp its ambivalence; yet his purpose is not to moralize but to mediate, and the instrument of his mediation is a poetry which I can only describe as sacramental, in the sense that material things are invested with spiritual meaning without losing anything of weight or shape or colour."

660 Sujaku, Shigeko. "Fall and Fortune of Antony." *Eibei Bungaku Kenkyu* (Baiko Women's College) 13 (1977): 231-42. In Japanese.

Antony destroys himself not because he has fallen in love with Cleopatra but because his fate is controlled by the turns of the wheel of fortune.

661 Tanifuji, Isamu. "Aspects of Love in *Antony and Cleopatra*." *Jour. of Eng. Inst.* (Tohoku Gakuin Univ.) 7-8 (1977): 1-34. In Japanese.

Not seen.

662 Tomokiyo, Yoko. "The Dramatic World of *Antony and Cleopatra*." *Chofu Gakuen Woman's Junior College Kiyo* 10 (1977): 50-75.

This tragedy is on the way to the world of "romances." The difference is that Antony and Cleopatra can realize the dream only when they are dying.

663 Venet, Gisele. "Images et structure dans *Antoine et Cléopâtre*." *Etudes Anglaises: Grand-Bretagne, Etats-Unis* 30 (1977): 281-302.

The images of dissolution and fusion function as the two focal points of a structure of mutability. The tragedy is elliptic because it combines double focus and unity, and it looks ahead to the baroque universe of *The Tempest*, which constitutes a new vision of the world founded on paradox and ambivalence.

664 Alvis, John. "The Religion of Eros: A Re-Interpretation of *Antony and Cleopatra*." *Renascence: Essays on Value in Literature* 30 (1978): 185-98.

Alvis proposes that "we can best apprehend Shakespeare's ironic appraisal of Antony and Cleopatra by seeing their erotic experience in opposition to another ideal of love evident from from the sonnets and comedies."

665 Acki, Kazuo. "An Essay on Antony and Cleopatra." *Ippan Kenkyu Kokoku* (Seikei University) 14 (1978): 1-45. In Japanese.

The uniqueness of the play can be discovered partly in the vacillation of the characters and partly in their humanistic generosity.

666 Asahara, Sanae. "Myth-Ritual Patterns in *Antony and Cleopatra.*" *Edgewood Review* (Kobe Jogakuin University) 5 (1978): 1-26. In Japanese.

Considered in the light of reality, Antony and Cleopatra lose their grand stature. However, Shakespeare presents them as mythological figures toward the end of the play.

667 Brandao, Nielson das Neves. "Defeat in *Antony and_Cleopatra.*" *Signal* (Univ. Federal da Paraiba) 1 (1978): 101-16. Eng. and Port. sums.

The play's main theme is the decline and subsequent defeat of a man; political and military defeats are a consequence of man's infatuation with a woman; This leads to the decay of an empire; paradoxically, death leads to triumph.

668 Brennan, Anthony S. "Excellent Dissembling: Antony and Cleopatra Playing at Love." *Midwest Quarterly: A Journal of Contemporary Thought* (Pittsburg, KS) 19 (1978): 313-29.

In *Antony and Cleopatra* can be found Shakespeare's "view of the world as theatre."

669 Brito, Joao Batista B. de. "Duality in *Antony and Cleopatra.*" *Signal* (Univ. Federal da Paraiba) 1 (1978): 32-46. Eng. and Por. sums.

Based on the possible implication of numbers, Brito analyzes *Antony and Cleopatra* from the angle of duality as expressed in the frequent use of antitheses throughout the play.

670 Coates, John. "'The Choice of Hercules' in *Antony and Cleopatra*." *Shakespeare Survey* 31 (1978): 45-52.

"The linking of the 'Choice of Hercules' with *Antony and Cleopatra* gives a fuller value to Enobarbus's death, strengthens the case for accepting Antony's courage at the end as genuine, and above all, allows us to accept the poetry of acts IV and V as what it surely is, the real expression of something real: nothing so callow as 'the world well lost' but a statement of Pleasure reconciled to Virtue."

671 Costa, Maria Glaucia de V. "The Moon and Cleopatra: A Case of Parallelism in *Antony and Cleopatra*." *Signal* (Univ. Federal da Paraiba) 1 (1978): 47-64. Eng. and Port. sums.

The moon imagery is associated with Cleopatra and, indirectly, with the myths of Demeter, Aphrodite, Isis, and Cybele. Comparing Antony to Hercules, particularly in their anger, this study considers the play "Jacobean mainly through the treatment of heroic values in terms of Greek mythology."

672 Crawford, John. "*Antony and Cleopatra*." *Romantic Criticism of Shakespearian Drama*. Romantic Reassessment 79. Salzburg: Universitat Salzburg, 1978, pp. 82-123.

This is a revised version of the author's dissertation on the romantic and historical criticisms of this play. Critics like A.C. Bradley and G. Wilson Knight consider it "as a kind of lyrical poem which exalts love as the greatest value in life and which shows love triumphant over death and the world." Historical scholars "see the actions of the lovers as they appear in the play and thus view it as an exposure of human weakness and corruption."

673 Dawson, Anthony B. *Indirections: Shakespeare and the Art of Illusion*. Toronto: U of Toronto P, 1978. 194 pp.

Dawson examines Shakespeare's plays "from the point of view of reflexivity, that is, their use of self-conscious techniques which radically affect the relation of the audience to the play." In this play, "the characters manifest a consciousness of *story*, an awareness that they are playing a part in a significant action." Dawson focuses on the two suicide scenes, which "are full of what ought to be comic devices." The play defines Antony and Cleopatra "in terms of *acting*." Their tragedy "merges with the tragedy of society, a society which cannot accommodate the self-emptying and self-fulfillment of the central characters, a society which must, in fact, destroy that commitment in order to ensure its own survival."

674 Dias, Walter. "Cleopatra." *Voices from Shakespeareana. Dramatic Autobiographies*. New Delhi: S. Chand, 1978, pp. 113-23.

Not seen.

675 Dorius, R.J. "*Antony and Cleopatra*." *How to Read Shakespearean Tragedy*. Ed. Edward Quinn. New York: Harper, 1978, pp. 293-354.

This play presents a unity of "the heroic, tragic, romantic and satiric modes." It thus "achieves an equilibrium which is as subtle and challenging to some readers as it is puzzling or disturbing to others." Dorius reviews criticism of the play under such categories as "The Critics and the Love Affair" and "Tragedy and the Heroic."

676 Erlich, Bruce. "Structure, Inversion, and Game in Shakespeare's Classical World." *Shakespeare Survey* 31 (1978): 53-63.

In this structuralist interpretation, Shakespeare "constructs drama upon internal between multiple and conflicting axes which allow no mediation between their antithetic terms: what is signified is permanent, irredeemable opposition." Every significant axis in the play "is crossed by others which contradict it, thus complicating the protagonists' choices and the audience's response." What Antony and Cleopatra "attempt and fail to mediate is the *encounter* of two value-systems, each of which represents an *already* formed civilization and each of which is the inversion of the other.

677 Fergusson, Francis. "Poetry and Drama." *Symbolism and Modern Literature: Studies in Honor of Wallace Fowlie*. Ed. Marcel Tetel. Durham: Duke UP, 1978, pp.13-25.

This is an Aristotelian analysis of passages from *Antony and Cleopatra*, *Antigone*, a *Canzone* by Dante, and "Gerontion." The exchange in 4.14 of *Antony and Cleopatra* "is analogous to the Sophoclean choral ode." Antony "is its persona, and his action is to see through the cloudy shapes before him to himself, as he really is."

678 Foreman, Walter C., Jr. "Antony and Cleopatra." *The Music of the Close: The Final Scenes of Shakespeare's Tragedies*. Lexington: U P of Kentucky, 1978, pp. 175-201.

Shakespeare's "experiments in the art of the play, his 'conclusions,' are a way of experiencing a world that, like the cloud Antony sees in the setting sun, is always blowing away from the shapes we impose on it." This play, "more than the other tragedies, sees life whole and sees the activity of living in terms of the activity of being an artist." Cleopatra can be considered "an image of human creative energy dealing with a world that is constantly regenerating itself in new forms."

679 Fuzier, J. "*Antony and Cleopatra*'s Three-Stage Tragic Structure: A Study in Development." *Cahiers Elisabéthains* 13 (1978): 69-74.

This play follows the three-stage structure: the supposed death of the loved woman; the suicide of the lover; the loved woman's suicide.

680 Hiraiwa, Toshio. "Assimilation and Alienation in Shakespeare's Dramas." Gaikokugo Kenkyu (Aichi Kyoiku University) 15 (1978): 129-46. In Japanese.

Hiraiwa discusses *Romeo and Juliet*, *Antony and Cleopatra*, *Othello*, and *King Lear* to argue that characters are assimilated and then alienated by the act of love.

681 Kalmey, Robert P. "Shakespeare's Octavius and Elizabethan Roman History." *Studies in English Literature 1500-1900* 18 (1978): 275-87.

Kalmey explains the difference between "Cleopatra's scathing assessment of the character of Octavius" and the popular view of him as an "ideal prince" by saying that Elizabethan histories distinguished his character before and after his coronation as emperor.

682 Levith, Murray J. "Antony and Cleopatra." *What's in Shakespeare's Names*. Hamden, CT: Archon Books, 1978, pp. 59-61.

This study generalizes about Shakespeare's naming practices and thus provides "a helpful handle to Shakespeare, perhaps even refine our understanding of authorial tone in the plays."

683 Lloyd Evans, Gareth, and Barbara Lloyd Evans. *The Shakespeare Companion*. New York: Scribner's, 1978. 368 pp.

This companion is divided into four sections: The Man and his Times; Shakespeare in Performance; The Works; Stratford-upon-Avon and Shakespeare. There is information about Shakespeare and about his period, and the section on performance covers the period from 1590 to 1978. There are summaries of plays, a list of characters, and a glossary.

684 Maguin, J.M. "A Note on Shakespeare's Handling of Time and Space Data in *Antony and Cleopatra*." *Cahiers Elisabéthains* 13 (1978): 61-67.

Maguin assembles data on "Time, Space, and Action" in the form of a "synoptic table" to show that the play "is a complex and cleverly fitted puzzle in time and space."

685 Miyauchi, Bunshichi. *Immortal Longings: The Structure of Shakespeare's* Antony and Cleopatra. Tokyo: Shinozaki Shorin, 1978. 369 pp.

Miyauchi analyzes Shakespeare's design of tragedy, the structure of this play, and this play as acme of Shakespeare's tragedy. "The cumulative pattern of *action* is chiefly caused by the uproars of the queen in the early part of the play, but it is by and by compensated by a chapter of torrential events that take place by the temporal context from Octavia's return onward in the latter part." Antony "is first of all reduced from his licentious dotage to his noble death through the catalyst of the Roman honour, which is purposely manipulated by Cleopatra. At the next stage, she is reduced as well from her wile of seduction to her 'immortal longings' in death through the catalyst of Antony's nobility." What makes Antony and Cleopatra's tragic love "genuine" is that "they stand firm on the foothold of undaunted will. They did truly defy all the earthly honours, never wailing their destiny, nor seeking for the lost cause." Shakespeare's "ruling idea of *Antony and Cleopatra* is that life's drama begins with death and ends in death."

686 Nunes, Herta Maria F. de Q. "Enobarbus: 'He Is of Note'." *Signal* (Univ. Federal de Paraiba) 1 (1978): 10-31. Eng. and Port. sums.

Enobarbus changes in character and personality when, from the eyewitness of the early scenes, he becomes critic and commentator on the action. Like Antony, he succumbs, broken-hearted, after receiving his master's last display of generosity. Enobarbus' intriguing death contrasts with Eros' and Antony's, both clear cases of suicide.

687 Rackin, Phyllis. "*Antony and Cleopatra*." *Shakespeare's Tragedies*. World Dramatists. New York: Ungar, 1978, pp. 123-36.

If Shakespeare's Cleopatra "is played by a boy, we are likely to notice disturbing similarities between his tragedy and the Roman comedy Cleopatra rejects." Cleopatra "is a dedicated contriver and performer of shows—so much so that we are never sure how to take her."

688 Richmond, Velma B. "Shakespeare's Women." *Midwest Quarterly* 19 (1978): 330-42.

In Cleopatra, Shakespeare "extends his exploration of women's roles into simultaneous public and private spheres. The woman of 'infinite variety' is his most complex character."

689 Smith, Maria Selma Ataide. "Last Farewells in *Antony and Cleopatra*." *Signal* (Univ. Federal da Paraiba) 1 (1978): 65-77. Eng. and Port. sums.

Antony and Cleopatra's love is reflected in their farewells to each other and to others.

690 Smith, Michael Harold. "Men of Ice: The Dehumanizing Effects of Ambition in Shakespeare's *Antony and Cleopatra*." *Signal* (Univ. Federal da Paraiba) 1 (1978): 117-26. Eng. and Port. sums.

Octavius Caesar is ambitious and cold; he is a calculating politician who suppresses his warmer instincts.

691 Tolmie, L.W. "'Least cause'/'All cause': Roman Infinite Variety: An Essay on *Antony and Cleopatra*." *Southern Review: Literary and Interdisciplinary Essays* (Adelaide, Australia) 11 (1978): 113-31.

Shakespeare has composed this play according to a formula: "This formula is: the Roman oscillates, is 'sad-merry-sad,' in effect simultaneously ; Cleopatra reads this oscillation, responds to the relativism absolutely."

692 Uphaus, Robert W. "Shakespearean Tragedy and the Intimations of Romance." *The Centennial Review* 22 (1978): 299-318.

King Lear and *Antony and Cleopatra* "intimate or dramatize versions of 'worlds elsewhere'," and "these 'worlds elsewhere' subsequently become the periential realm beyond tragedy which is fully enacted in the romances." *Antony and Cleopatra* "has it both ways—tragedy and tentative romance."

693 Van Laan, Thomas F. *Role-Playing in Shakespeare*. Toronto: U of Toronto P, 1978. 267 pp.

This study explores Shakespeare's concern with role-playing by analyzing the stage images and recurring verbal theatrical metaphors. Antony is searching "for a setting that will be sufficiently spacious and diverse." His "potential identity is vast and various, but he cannot actually perform it because neither of his settings will him to play all the specific roles he must assume if he is to make his potential identity actual." In the last act of the play, Cleopatra's "attempt to impose her own will on reality, to become a dramatist of life, constitutes a new and striking example of an action motif that often appears in the tragedies and forms a chief element of Shakespeare's earliest tragic practice." This play cannot be considered tragic. Antony "experiences to some extent the felt loss of identity and the accompanying glimpse of the void which stand at the core of the tragic pattern, but, unlike any tragic hero before him, he passes through the void to the other side, so that the audience's final awareness of him is as of someone who has triumphed—and without having to delude himself." In this play, "it is the dream that triumphs and, in its triumph, reduces history to insignificance. *Antony and Cleopatra* thus rejects tragedy and history both."

694 Van Woensel, Maurice J. F. "Revelry and Carousing in Shakespeare's *Antony and Cleopatra.*" *Signal* (Univ. Federal da Paraiba) 1 (1978): 78-100. Eng. and Port. sums.

The lexical and semantic forms of the language of "revelry and carousing" demonstrate its thematic significance in *Antony and Cleopatra.*

695 Vincent, Barbara Cutts. "The Anatomy of Antony: A Study of the Literary Worlds in Shakespeare's *Antony and Cleopatra.*" *Dissertation Abstracts* 39 (1978): 904A (Rutgers).

Vincent "interprets *Antony and Cleopatra* as an encyclopedic and culminating work, which reveals the roots and reflects on the nature of Shakespeare's art." One of the main actions here is "the elevation of the world of comedy to include and complete tragedy."

696 Wilders, John. *The Lost Garden: A View of Shakespeare's English and Roman History Plays*. London: Macmillan, 1978. 154 pp.

This is "a play of irreconcilable worlds, of opposing personalities and ways of life." "Totally engaged in the movement of events," Antony "allows himself to be carried in whatever direction they, or his own impulses, lead him."

697 Yokomori, Masahiko. "An Essay on *Antony and Cleopatra*." *Kenkyu Kiyo* (Shujutoku University) 12 (1978): 83-98. In Japanese.

Not seen.

698 Acharya, Shanta. "An Analysis of Sylvia Plath's 'Edge'." *Literary Criterion* 14.2 (1979): 52-57.

Acharya explains several references which connect the dead protagonist of Plath's poem to Shakespeare's Cleopatra.

699 Alvis, John. "The Coherence of Shakespeare's Roman Plays." *Modern Language Quarterly* 40 (1979): 115-34.

Antony and Cleopatra and other Roman plays "attest their common focus by strongly marked intrinsic similarities of tone, style, imaginative scope, and moral content." Roman heroes "move with a comparatively temperate atmosphere wherein the stark moral turbulence and agonized metaphysical inquiries give way to dramas that suggest detached and predominantly ironic treatments of a distinctly Roman style of consciousness." These Romans "restrict their attention to this world, where they look to find happiness, or at least dignity, in the recognition they acquire from some form of public endeavor." These plays represent "the corporate tragedy engendered by a Roman ethos." They "imply a critique of the glory-enamored soul, a skeptical judgment upon Roman claims to the title of history's noblest regime, and a challenge directed toward Renaissance enthusiasts to rethink the grounds of their admiration for things Roman."

700 Anderson, Donald K., Jr. "A New Gloss for the 'Three-Nook'd World' of *Antony and Cleopatra.*" *English Language Notes* 17 (1979): 103-06.

The words "three-nook'd world" mean a "three-sectored world."

701 Bono, Barbara Jane. "'Sunt hic etiam . . . mentem mortalia tangunt' (*Aen.* I.161-162): Renaissance Transvaluations: From Vergilean Epic to Shakespearean Heroic Drama." *Dissertation Abstracts* 39 (1979): 5520A (Brown).

Shakespeare has written "a true heroic drama" than a Vergilian tragedy. In *Antony and Cleopatra*, "while recognizing the historical, tragic action," he "ends with a hope for a greater heroism of the epic-erotic imagination."

702 Booth, Stephen. "Speculations on Doubling in Shakespeare's Plays." *Shakespeare: The Theatrical Dimension*. Ed. Philip C. McGuire and David A. Samuelson. New York: AMS, 1979. 103-31.

Booth argues that the roles of Dolabella and Proculeius were doubled.

703 Brecht, Bertolt. *Diaries 1920-1922*. Ed. Herta Ramthun. Trans. John Willett. New York: St. Martin's P, 1979. xiii, 182 pp.

Brecht remarks (dated 17 August 1920) that *Antony and Cleopatra* is "a splendid drama which really gripped me. The more central the place apparently taken by the plot, the richer and more powerful are the developments open to its exponents."

704 Coursen, Herbert R. "Agreeing with Dr. Johnson." *Ariel* 10.2 (April 1979): 35-42.

Shakespeare "was anticipating *Antony and Cleopatra* even as he wrote *Macbeth*." In each of these plays, "the disorder created by great warriors who would defy the premises of the worlds they inhabit is firmly replaced by realistic politics."

705 Dillon, Janette. "'Solitariness': Shakespeare and Plutarch." *Journal of English and Germanic Philology* 78 (1979): 325-44.

The common factor in the experience of Plutarch's Antony, Coriolanus and Timon is "solitude, whether physical, spiritual, or both." "As Shakespeare adapts history to drama, solitude becomes the essential structural element on which their tragedies are made to hinge."

706 Evans, Bertrand. "The High Professionals: *Antony and Cleopatra*." *Shakespeare's Tragic Practice*. London: Oxford UP, 1979, pp. 223-80.

This "is the only tragedy in which Shakespeare seems actually to prefer inexplicitness to explicitness in his management of awareness." Antony, Cleopatra, and Caesar both win and lose "in this game of secret motives and marked cards dealt by high professionals." Antony "never learns what a prize he had in Cleopatra, and loses his life and empire, but he successfully shields from the world his shameful secret and leaves behind him a magnificent fiction—that he had lost all for love." Cleopatra "loses her kingdom and her life and never did secure the mind and heart of Antony, but she momentarily deceives Caesar, wins the right to be notable to herself, and in the next life can anticipate a second chance at an Antony who is no longer intimidated by Caesar." And Caesar "loses his one crucial skirmish with Cleopatra, so that his triumphal procession at Rome will lack its prize trophy; but he has made himself sole sir of the world."

707 Green, David C. "Antony and Cleopatra." *Plutarch Revisited: A Study of Shakespeare's Last Roman Tragedies and Their Source*. JDS 78. Salzburg: Inst. fur Anglistik & Amerikanistik, Univ. Salzburg, 1979, pp. 12-129.

A reader may feel at first reading that Shakespeare "has sacrificed unity beyond the bounds of dramatic art, but comparison of source and play will reveal that, although Antony and Cleopatra is loosely constructed, its structure is nevertheless as well planned and as carefully put together as in any piece of work Shakespeare penned."

708 Grudin, Robert. "*Antony and Cleopatra*." *Mighty Opposites: Shakespeare and Renaissance Contrariety*. Berkeley: U of California P, 1979, pp. 165-79.

What gives this play "its memorable tonality" is "paradox," and "paradoxical structures of language occur more than one hundred times." "Verbal paradox buttresses or parallels larger contradictions that are psychological, geographical, or structural." The play "reiterates two major principles of contrariety: that experience, to the extent that it is strong or 'real,' is based on the interaction of conflicting forces; and that extreme courses lead to their own opposites." It "is thus a kind of Problem Comedy in reverse—a play in which tragic form and comic content unite unfamiliarly to effect a positive appreciation of life's evanescent joys."

709 Hymel, Cynthia D. "Shakespeare's *Antony and Cleopatra*." *Explicator* 37 (1979): 2-4.

In V.ii.243-78, Shakespeare makes puns on "lie," "die," and "honest" to suggest sexual meanings that relate to the value of sex, Cleopatra's emotions towards Antony, and her sometimes ambivalent attitude, and to establish the motivation for her suicide.

710 Johnson, Anthony L. *Readings of Antony and Cleopatra and King Lear*. Pisa: ETS Disenciclopedia 2, 1979. 174 pp.

Not seen.

711 Matthews, R. "The Shakespeare Line: A Study of *Antony and Cleopatra*." *Dissertation Abstracts* 39 (1979): 4694C (Trinity College, Dublin).

Abstract not available.

712 Oki, Hiroko. "A Study of *Antony and Cleopatra*—with Special Reference to Cleopatra." *Eigo Eibeihungaku Ronso* (Beppo University) 12 (1979): 23-64. In Japanese.

Not seen.

713 Shirley, Frances A. *Swearing and Perjury in Shakespeare's Plays*. London: Allen & Unwin, 1979. 174 pp.

Shirley cites some of her examples from this play, in which "the oaths range from the satiric to the angry, a variety not found in the other Roman plays."

714 Suzuki, Hisako. "Enobarbus as an Excellent Supporting Actor in *Antony and Cleopatra*." *Eibungaku Kenkyukai Kaishi* (Ferris Women's College) 12(1979): 11-18. In Japanese.

Not seen.

715 Tobin, J.J.M. "Apuleius and *Antony and Cleopatra*, Once More." *Studia Neophilologica: A Journal of Germanic and Romance Languages and Literature* 51: 225-28.

Tobin discusses Cleopatra as Isis.

716 Wells, Henry W., and H.H. Anniah Gowda. "*Antony and Cleopatra* and Tragic Love." *Style and Structure in Shakespeare*. New Delhi: Vikas, 1979, pp. 206-13.

The play's final impression "is one of passion not within limits, for it becomes possessive and infects other characters—Eros, Enobarbus, Charmian and Iras—who die through love and loyalty. . . . The poetic building-up is conducive to the invocation *sringara*. Here is the dominant play of *sringara*—the *rasa* of love."

717 Bergren, Paula S. "The Woman's Part: Female Sexuality as Power in Shakespeare's Plays." *The Woman's Part: Feminist Criticism of Shakespeare*. Ed. Carolyn R.S. Lenz, Gayle Greene, and Carol T. Neely. Urbana: U of Illinois P, 1980, pp. 17-34.

"Nursing the asp, voluptuous even as she prepares to die," Cleopatra "assumes a posture that apparently was a medieval emblem of the dull earth. Yet at the last this enchanting queen triumphs over physical nature, readjusts the elements themselves, and sublimates herself into fire and air." Cleopatra undergoes a metaphorical rebirth in her death, and this relates the play to the last romances which deal with "rebirth as miracle and as physical achievement."

718 Bloomfield, Morton W. "Personification-Metaphors." *Chaucer Review* 14 (1979-80): 287-97.

The allegorical sense of Enobarbus speech in praise of Cleopatra (2.3.190-218) can be understood by relating it to classical rhetoric. In personifying metaphors, Shakespeare used the verb, not the noun, to provide animation.

719 Blythe, David Everett. "Lear's Soiled Horse." *Shakespeare Quarterly* 31 (1980): 86-88.

Antony's tragedy "is that of a 'lust-dieted' man whose heroic capacities have been enervated by lethal superfluity."

720 Clemon-Karp, Sheila. "The Female Androgyny in Tragic Drama." *Dissertation Abstracts International* 41 (1980): 2096A (Brandeis).

The non-stereotypical female characters or "androgynes" like Cleopatra and Hedda Gabler "commit themselves to causes greater than themselves, they dare, and they die in the service of these self-selected goals." For Cleopatra and Hedda, "the self-determined action is suicide."

721 Davidson, Clifford. "*Antony and Cleopatra*: Circe, Venus, and the Whore of Babylon." *Shakespeare: Contemporary Critical Approaches*. Ed. Harry R. Garvin. Lewisburg: Bucknell UP, 1980, pp. 31-55.

Cleopatra's character depends on "uniquely opposing elements," and Shakespeare has drawn her "with apparent paradigms: the Whore of Babylon described in the Apocalypse, Circe, and Venus and Mars." The sympathies of the audience may depend upon "the sensuous Cleopatra, but the earthly Venus is purged of her baser elements and transformed by the immortality of art."

722 Degenhart, Karen. "*Anthony and Cleopatra*: Psychic Elements in Conflict." *Lapis* (Homewood, IL) 6 (1980): 29-39.

The psychic and archetypal conflict between masculine and feminine forces is resolved by the suicides of Antony and Cleopatra.

723 Fegan, James. "Philo's sonnet in Antony and Cleopatra: The Fact, Features and Possible Interpretative Implications." *ILT News* 70 (1980): 90-112.

Philo's opening lines before the entrance of Antony and Cleopatra in the play are "a hidden sonnet." When read as a sonnet, these lines help "to define the presence, character and importance of the *Apocalyptic* element in the play."

724 Fichter, Andrew. "*Antony and Cleopatra*: 'The Time of Universal Peace'." *Shakespeare Survey* 33 (1980): 99-111.

Pax Romana is a foreshadowing of Pax Christiana in *Antony and Cleopatra*; the play looks toward Christian revelation. Cleopatra and the serpent are anticipations of Madonna and Child. "As Antony and Cleopatra paradoxically assert for themselves a love transcending death and a triumph emerging from defeat we are meant to recognize an impulse that is completed in Christian miracle; but we are also meant to realize that in the pre-Christian world of Shakespeare's play the transcendence to which the lovers aspire is tragically impossible."

725 George, Kathleen. *Rhythm in Drama*. Pittsburgh: U of Pittsburgh P, 1980. 194 pp.

George praises this play as "an excellent model of the rhythm of a changing scene" and other rhythms like that of gesture.

726 Gohlke, Madelon. "'I wooed thee with my sword': Shakespeare's Tragic Paradigms." *The Woman's Part: Feminist Criticism of Shakespeare*. Ed. Carolyn R.S. Lenz, Gayle Greene, and Carol T. Neely. Urbana: U of Illinois P, 1980, pp. 150-70.

Antony and Cleopatra "recalls the ritual marriage conclusion of the comedies as it deepens the sexual dilemma of the tragic hero." Antony's "relation both to Cleopatra and to Caesar may be read in terms of his anxieties about dominance, his fear of self-loss in any intimate encounter."

727 Green Brian. "'Single Natures double name': An Exegesis of *The Phoenix and Turtle*." *Generous Converse: English Essays in Memory of Edward Davis*. Ed. Brian Green. Cape Town: Oxford UP, 1980, pp. 44-54.

Antony and Cleopatra is one of the love tragedies which "is created by the interaction between three attitudes to sexual love: the vulgar, the sublime, and the chaste."

728 Hibbard, G.R. "Feliciter Audax: *Antony and Cleopatra I,i,1-24*." *Shakespeare's Styles: Essays in Honour of Kenneth Muir*. Ed. Philip Edwards, Inga-Stina Ewbank, and G.K. Hunter. Cambridge: Cambridge UP, 1980, pp. 95-109.

An analysis of *Antony and Cleopatra*'s opening lines that "there is an unbounded confidence in the potentialities of language, which seems capable of encompassing anything and everything, except the monstrous and the unspeakable, which it is not called on to do."

729 Hughes, Derek. "*Aphrodite katadyomene*: Dryden's Cleopatra on the Cydnos." *Comparative Drama* 14 (1980): 35-45.

Dryden's play can be compared with Shakespeare's where Dryden is influenced by Shakespeare and Plutarch in relating Cleopatra's "grandiose self-deification" on the Cydnos.

730 Ide, Richard S. "The Improbable Heroics of *Antony and Cleopatra*." *Possessed with Greatness: The Heroic Tragedies of Chapman and Shakespeare*. Chapel Hill: U of North Carolina P, 1980, pp. 102-31.

Chapman's *Bussy D'Ambois* "did have a negative influence on *Antony and Cleopatra*, one that enabled Shakespeare to clarify his own conceptions of Herculean heroism, heroic passion, feminine frailty, amatory idealism, and human heroism by distinguishing them from those of Chapman." The "fundamental difference between the plays may be focused on the humanizing vision and humane tone of *Antony and Cleopatra*—its naturalistic characterization, its intrepid realism, its frivolous, wry, and poignant humor, its credible expression of impossible dreams." The tragic folly of Shakespeare's play "is human, and so, too, is its conception of heroism and grandeur." The grandeur of Antony and Cleopatra's love "is predicated on the acceptance of human frailty in themselves and in others; its value stems from a reckless disregard for reality that the worldly wise would judge to be foolish."

731 Kimura, Teruhira. "Roman Historic Figures and Shakespeare: A Historical Approach to Shakespeare's Roman Plays with Special Reference to Plutarch—*Antony and Cleopatra.*" *Eibungaku Hyoron* (Kyoto University) 43 (1980): 73- 92. In Japanese.

Not seen.

732 Kinsley, Dominic Alfonso. "The Voice of Interpoler: Essays on Three Shakespearean Characters." *Dissertation Abstracts International* 41 (1980): 2614A (Yale).

This is an analysis of three minor characters, Jack Cade, Mercutio, and Enobarbus. Enobarbus is characterized as "a man of the body rather than a man of judgment" who "plays Bacchus to Cleopatra's Venus."

733 Novy, Marianne. "Shakespeare's Female Characters as Actors and Audience." *The Woman's Part: Feminist Criticism of Shakespeare*. Ed. Carolyn Ruth Swift Lenz, Gayle Greene, and Carol Thomas Neely. Urbana: U of Illinois P, 1980, pp. 256-70.

The image of the woman as actor is "problematic" in the tragedies, because "the heroes' suspicion of female pretense darkens their view of women, whether pretending or not." *Antony and Cleopatra* "is the only Shakespearean tragedy that focuses on and indeed glorifies the woman as actor in both senses, doer and pretender, and, not coincidentally, as sexually active."

734 Paulin, Bernard. "L'element pastoral dans *Antoine et Cléopâtre* de Shakespeare." *Le genre pastoral en Europe du XVe au XVIIe*

siècle. Ed. Claude Longeon. Saint-Etienne: Pubs. de l'Univ. de Saint-Etienne, 1980, pp. 161-67.

This is an analysis of such pastoral elements in the play as intrigue, characters, themes, language, and method.

735 Ross, Gordon N. "Enobarbus on Horses: *Antony and Cleopatra*, III.vii.7-9." *Shakespeare Quarterly* 31 (1980): 386-87.

Enobarbus is suggesting that "if horses and mares are both employed in battle, the horses will mount the mares and thus be 'lost' with regard to their intended function." The pronunciation of "merely" and "bear" explains the bawdy reference.

736 Snyder, Susan. "Ourselves Alone: The Challenge to Single Combat in Shakespeare." *Studies in English Literature 1500-1900* 20 (1980): 201-16.

In *Antony and Cleopatra* and other plays "which set up the challenge to single combat in a context of mass warfare, its associations of a personal chivalry outmoded but none the less compelling comment critically on the ways of the modern political machine."

737 Snyder, Susan. "Patterns of Motion in *Antony and Cleopatra*." *Shakespeare Survey* 33 (1980): 113-22.

There is "a pattern of kinetically linked images" in Shakespeare's plays which can "support, even embody, a major movement of the dramatic action." In *Antony and Cleopatra*, Shakespeare "has set images of solid fixity or speedy directness against images of flux and of motion unpurposive but beautiful to express kinetically the opposition of Rome and Egypt and, through their incompatibility, the nature of Antony's tragic dilemma."

738 Spriet, Pierre. "Regard et verbe: La Metamorphose du heros dans quelques pieces de Shakespeare." *La Metamorphose dans la poesie baroque francaise et anglaise: Variations et resurgences.* Actes du Colloque Inonal de Valenciennes, 1979. Ed. Gisele Mathieu-Castellani. Etudes Litteraires Francaises 7. Tubingen: Gunter Narr; Paris: Jean-Michel Place, 1980, pp. 203-9.

This is a study of Macbeth, Lear, Prospero, *A Midsummer Night's Dream* characters, Caesar and Cleopatra as interlocutors to show that Shakespeare is a Baroque poet in his construction of reality through language.

739 Stallings, Alden Page. "'When I perceive Your Grace': Patterns of Vision in Shakespeare." *Dissertation Abstracts International* 41 (1980): 4048A (Virginia).

Antony's mind is divided between the conflicting claims of love and the world, but "his final defeat unites his soul in luminous apprehension of love's transcendent value."

740 Steppat, Michael. *The Critical Reception of Shakespeare's* Antony and Cleopatra *from 1607 to 1905*. BAS 9. Amsterdam: Gruner, 1980. 619 pp.

This is a comprehensive survey of criticism from the seventeenth century to A.C. Bradley. An appendix discusses criticism under topics like general assessments, theme, relation of the play to history, technique, and characters. There is a bibliography covering the years 1607-1977.

741 Tamaizumi, Yasuo. "Kureopatora wa naze Shinunoka—Shakespeare no Sakugekihou ni tsuite no ichi Kousatsu [Why Must Cleopatra Die? 'Palinode' and Medievalism in Shakespeare]." *Poetry and Drama in the English Renaissance—In Honour of Professor Jiro Ozu*. Ed. Koshi Nakanori and Yasuo Tammaizumi. Tokyo: Kinojuniya Shoten, 1980, pp. 75-103. In Japanese.

Not seen.

742 Uchiyama, Hitoshi. "The Function of Words in *Antony and Cleopatra*." *Jinbun Kagaku Ronshu* (Shinshu University) 14 (1980): 105-20. In Japanese.

Not seen.

743 Wheeler, Richard P. "'Since first we were dissevered': Trust and Autonomy in Shakespearean Tragedy and Romance."

Representing Shakespeare: New Psychoanalytic Essays. Ed. Murray M. Schwartz and Coppélia Kahn. Baltimore and London: Johns Hopkins UP, 1980, pp. 150-69.

Antony and Cleopatra belongs "in the trust-merger group" of plays in which "the effort to establish power and autonomy is ultimately subordinated to what proves to be a stronger need for a lost or jeopardized relation of mutuality." In this play, Shakespeare "dramatizes value in a dream of fulfillment plainly incompatible with pragmatic reality."

744 Wigginton, Waller B. "'One way like a Gorgon': An Explication of *Antony and Cleopatra*, 2.5.116-117." *Papers on Language and Literature* 16 (1980): 366-75.

Cleopatra's Gorgon, signifying rage, "derives primarily from Sir Thomas Elyot's translation of, and commentary on, a passage from Ovid's *Art of Love*, and secondarily from Christopher Marlowe's echo of a line from Spenser's *Faery Queene*."

745 Yamada, Teruo. "A Study on *Antony and Cleopatra*—Shakespeare's Adjustment to the Jacobean Taste." *Aichi Gakuin University Goken Kiyo* 5.i (1980): 25-52. In Japanese.

Not seen.

746 Yamaura, Takuzo. "Egyptian and Roman—Music in *Antony and Cleopatra*." *Hirosaki Gakuin University Kiyo* 16 (1980): 1-18. In Japanese.

Not seen.

747 Yoshioka, Fumio. "*Antony and Cleopatra*: A Paradoxical Universe of Love." *Attempts in Liguuistics and Literature* (International Christian University) 8 (1980): 15-35. In Japanese.

Not seen.

748 Yoshitomi, Sakae. "After the High Roman Fashion—A Study on the Double Climax in *Antony and Cleopatra*." *Essays*

Presented to Professor Hiroshige Yashida. Japan: Shhinozaki Shorin, 1980, pp. 171-85. In Japanese.

Not seen.

749 Bayley, John. *Shakespeare and Tragedy.* London and Boston: Routledge & Kegan Paul, 1981. 228 pp.

The idea of fatality dominates this play. Fate here "has something almost good-natured about it, relaxed and familiar. The tone of poetry, simultaneously terse and expansive, easy and strenuous, reinforces this impression."

750 Berek, Peter. "Doing and Undoing: The Value of Action in *Antony and Cleopatra.*" *Shakespeare Quarterly* 32 (1981): 295-304.

Despite the "mighty opposites" in *Antony and Cleopatra*, most of the characters possess a "common understanding of the possibilities for action the world of the play makes available to them." This is supported by the recurring use of the forms of "do" in the script. In spite of the differences in their behaviors, they "are in substantial agreement about what 'doing' is worth." They may not agree on the right time to act, "they agree that there are grim limits to the joy one can take in earthly achievements."

751 Bosworth, Denise Mary. "'Fail not our Repast': The Dramatic Significance of Shakespeare Repasts." *Dissertation Abstracts* 42 (1981): 710A (Oregon).

The references to food and drink in *Antony and Cleopatra* "emphasize the sexual aspects of the lovers' union, while at the same time they give the relationship an everyday reality and a vitality which prepare for the transcendence of the couple from earth and water to fire and air."

752 Bellman, James F., and Kathryn Bellman. *Antony and Cleopatra. Notes.* Cliff Notes. Lincoln, Nebraska: Cliff Notes, 1981. 70 pp.

This is a study guide for students.

753 Chaudhuri, Sukanta. *Infirm Glory: Shakespeare and the Renaissance Image of Man*. London: Oxford UP, 1981. 231 pp.

In *Antony and Cleopatra* "we have the concepts of standard Scepticism, raised to epic power and thereby transformed beyond recognition." Rome and Egypt "are incompatible, not so much by the difference between their values as by the opposite modes of experience they imply." This "is the first play where experience becomes eternally significant as an enlarging or liberating force, an 'infinite virtue' (IV.viii.17); and it is the only play where this force is generated from purely human impulse."

754 Clayton, Thomas. "'Mysterious by this Love': The Unregenerate Resurrection of *Antony and Cleopatra*." *Jadavpur University Essays and Studies III: A Festschrift in Honor of S. C. Sengupta*. Calcutta: Jadavpur U, 1981, pp. 95-116.

Not seen.

755 Cohen, Brent Martin. "Sexuality and Tragedy in *Othello* and *Antony and Cleopatra*." *Dissertation Abstracts International* 42 (1981): A 5127 (California-Berkeley).

Using a psychological and psychoanalytic approach, Cohen argues that *Antony and Cleopatra*, "although a tragedy itself, regains the power of celebration felt unselfconsciously in *Romeo and Juliet*."

756 Cullum, Graham. "'Condemning Shadows Quite': *Antony and Cleopatra*." *Philosophy and Literature* 5 (1981): 186-203.

Cullum explores the problem created by the awareness that Shakespeare's plays "take unto themselves, and, in doing that, reveal *our* selves" and "we know they are only plays—things made and acted—about which it is the business of the critic to make judgments." This play "forces us to hold several seemingly incompatible truths in mind at one and the same time" and presents "the structured aggregation of these varied, often contesting truths."

G. "Union of Roles: *Antony and Cleopatra.*"
ding, and Power: Women in Shakespeare's Plays.
lumbia UP, 1981, pp. 208-48.

are "dramatizes the question of the meaning of ...onship between a man and a woman by creating two rulers who love one another." The playwright "presents the conflicts between them, conflicts frequently born of the struggle for mastery of one human being over another" and "stresses the concept of mutuality nourishing the complete development of each of them." Since Cleopatra "owns herself and is not dependent except when she herself wills a dependency, Antony has great difficulty trusting her." By showing Antony's death in the fourth act and by giving the last act to Cleopatra alone, Shakespeare "forces us to observe her as the one character who spans the entire drama."

758 Dent, R.W. *Shakespeare's Proverbial Language: An Index.* Berkeley and London: U of California P, 1981. 289 pp.

This index "is a revision and expansion of that provided on pp. 803-808 of M.P. Tilley's *A Dictionary of the Proverbs in England in the Sixteenth and Seventeenth Centuries.*" The entries for *Antony and Cleopatra* are found on pp. 32-33. Appendix A lists all entries in the index itself. Appendix B lists the proverbial phrase, its OED location and earliest date, and instances in Shakespeare. Appendix C gives any of the excluded entries that do not appear in Appendix A.

759 French, Marilyn. *Shakespeare's Division of Experience.* New York: Summit Books, 1981, pp. 251-65.

French stresses that the "basic distinction in human social order since the beginning of recorded history has been gender." The masculine principle is about the attainment of power-in-the-world and the female has to do with "acceptance of simple confrontation, of present pleasure, of surrender to mortality." The tragic drama emerges from the opposition between masculine and feminine, where what is at issue are those social institutions in and through which constancy is defined. "Constancy is totally integrated with the united feminine principle and provides what is, to my mind, the most profound vision possible of human constancy." "More than Antony, Cleopatra, and Octavius, more than Rome versus Egypt," she argues, "the play is concerned with portraying the opposition of the gender principles in the world."

The Roman masculine "values—order and degree, power-in-the-world, structure and possession—do not create harmonious order and a protective pale for procreation. They create contention and rivalry, one order superseding another, and a thin, pleasureless, stiff experience." The feminine principle "may be doomed; it may always be defeated. But in the meantime it offers the richness of emotional and erotic dimensions of life—pleasure, play, and sex. At the end of *Antony and Cleopatra*, Caesar has the world; Antony and Cleopatra had the living."

760 Halle, Louis J. "*Antony and Cleopatra*." *The Search for an Eternal Norm: As Represented by Three Classics*. Washington, DC: UP of America, 1981, pp. 195-213.

Halle reads this play as a poem full of moments "that for me are unmatched in their eloquence, their poignancy, and their sheer verbal beauty." Antony represents "a type of the eternal masculine, as Cleopatra represents a type of the eternal feminine." Antony and Cleopatra have no moral stature, but the play is a tragedy "because of the transfiguration of Cleopatra, who in the end achieves a perfect dignity, realizing in her matured self some divinity that had all along been hidden in the spoiled child."

761 Hirsh, James E. *The Structure of Shakespearean Scenes*. New Haven and London: Yale UP, 1981. 230 pp.

Hirsh argues that "the present division of Shakespeare's plays into acts and scenes be replaced by the division of the plays simply into scenes numbered sequentially." He divides *Antony and Cleopatra* into forty-five scenes.

762 Homan, Sidney. "Love and the Imagination in *Antony and Cleopatra*." *When the Theatre Turns to Itself. The Aesthetic Metaphor in Shakespeare*. Lewisburg, PA: Bucknell UP; London: Associated University Presses, 1981. pp. 177-91.

Homan argues that "the theater becomes truly dramatic when it arouses a variety of responses from its spectators, a variety richer than we could afford to have in the real world." The play is "neutral" because "it presents sharply and brilliantly many viewpoints. All are confined in a work of art finite and unchanging in a way that life cannot be." Cleopatra's "imaginative world is a paradox since Cleopatra offers us not an empire, nothing as solid as Rome, but merely words, words, words." "Even as it allows for an extraordinary variety of responses to the lovers, the play itself offers extremes in the celebration and condemnation of art and the imagination—the very process that calls *Antony and Cleopatra* into being."

763 Jaffa, Harry V. "The Unity of Tragedy, Comedy, and History: An Interpretation of the Shakespearean Universe." *Shakespeare as Political Thinker*. Ed. John Alvis and Thomas G. West. Durham: Carolina Academic P, 1981, pp. 277-303.

Antony's "political incapacity is a cause of grief not only for his supporters; it is mourned by no one more eloquently than by Octavius." Shakespeare reminds his audience that "this Roman empire will become the Holy Roman Empire, and be a feudal empire, in which the Emperor will indeed be regarded—at least in theory—as the universal landlord." In his plays, Shakespeare "displays a cycle of regimes, beginning in the republicanism that results in the overthrow of Tarquin, and ending in the establishment of Caesarism." Shakespeare's "understanding of Roman republicanism follows closely Machiavelli's account."

764 James, Max H. "'The Noble Ruin': *Antony and Cleopatra*." *College Literature* 8 (1981): 127-43.

Scarus' speech (3.10.19-24) expresses the central paradox of the play: the ruin of nobility and the "nobility of ruin." The play "is about *ruin*. Decay, dissipation, dissolution flow in the language, comprise a main current, and carry its central theme." This play has a "realism scarcely equalled in any" of Shakespeare's other tragedies" and "embodies a very complex view of life, good and evil being almost inseparably intermingled."

765 Jeske, Jeffrey M. "Antony as a Source for *Pierre*: The Saga of the Male Psyche." *American Transcendental Quarterly* 50 (1981): 117-28.

This study "examines both the nature and the extent of the Roman play's influence on *Pierre*—an influence apparently greater than that of any other Shakespearean work."

766 Kennedy, William J. "Audiences and Rhetorical Strategies in Jodelle, Shakespeare, and Lohenstein." *Assays: Critical Approaches to Medieval and Renaissance Texts*. Ed. Peggy A. Knapp and Michael A. Stugrin. Vol. 1. Pittsburgh: U of Pittsburgh P, 1981, pp. 99-116.

Kennedy analyzes the use of tradition and rhetorical strategies in the three playwrights to show the shift in audience attitudes and expectation from Renaissance to Baroque.

767 Keyes, Laura Catherine. "Silence in Shakespeare." *Dissertation Abstracts International* 42 (1981): 1847A (SUNY Buffalo).

Antony and Cleopatra and other Roman plays "equate speech with power," and "the weak—women, children and the dispossessed—are silenced."

768 Manlove, Colin N. "Relationship in *Antony and Cleopatra*." *The Gap in Shakespeare: The Motif of Division from Richard II to The Tempest*. Totowa, NJ: Barnes & Noble, 1981, pp. 91-100.

This play "presents one of the most striking portraits of the lack of relationship and development in love in Shakespeare's plays: here a love-bond would seem to be central to the play, and yet in fact, as a bond, it is not." Shakespeare, "for whatever reason, is simply incapable of portraying a love relation that lasts through time and develops under its pressure."

769 Pitt, Angela. *Shakespeare's Women*. London: David and Charles; Totowa, N.J: Barnes & Noble, 1981. 224 pp.

Cleopatra cannot be considered a tragic figure because she does not have "a fatal weakness, revealed by a progressive worsening of her character." "The whims, the paradoxes, the mystery and above all the supreme grandeur of Cleopatra, create a goddess-figure rather than a tragic heroine."

770 Weightman, Franklin Case. "Politics in Shakespeare's Roman Plays." *Dissertation Abstracts International* 42 (1981): 2692A (North Carolina-Chapel Hill).

In this analysis of the four Roman plays, Weightman "explores a pattern of thematic development in them and concludes that by dramatizing certain motifs Shakespeare is stressing certain political ideas which were important to his age."

771 Wheeler, Richard P. *Shakespeare's Development and the Problem Comedies*. Berkeley: U of California P, 1981. 229 pp.

In this play, "an explicitly sexual relation is directly implicated in a crisis of trust, but often, as in *King Lear*, the sexual dimension is absent from the surface structure of key bonds." Antony longs for a union with Cleopatra; this longing "at once allows him to achieve a richer, more inclusive humanity and estranges him from political resources established by Caesar's deflection of all human impulse into the quest for power." In this play more than any other, Shakespeare "dramatizes value in a dream of fulfillment plainly incompatible with pragmatic reality."

772 Adler, Doris. "The Unlacing of Cleopatra." *Educational Theatre Journal* 34 (Dec. 1982): 451-66.

Adler traces four different stage images of Cleopatra from the early seventeenth to the end of the nineteenth century.

773 Bamber, Linda. *Comic Women, Tragic Men: A Study of Gender and Genre in Shakespeare*. Stanford: Stanford UP, 1982. 211 pp.

Bamber identifies and discusses three Cleopatras: First, she is "the embodiment of Egypt and a symbol of our antihistorical experience." "As Egypt, Cleopatra is radically ambiguous and can never be finally known." Second, she "represents the Other as against Antony's representation of the Self." The dialectic between Self and Other "begins with the refusal of the Other, develops into misogynist rage, and resolves into kindness and connectedness." Third, Cleopatra "is a character like Antony himself, facing failure and defeat, motivated by the desire to contain or rise above her losses." The third Cleopatra "faces Nature independently of Antony and differently from him; it is her own self-centredness that leads her back to him."

774 Bowers, Fredson. "The Concept of Single or Dual Protagonists in Shakespeare's Tragedies." *Renaissance Papers 1982*: Ed. A. Leigh DeNeef and M. Thomas Hester. Raleigh: Southern Renaissance Conference, 1983, pp. 27-33.

Shakespeare dramatizes a wide span of history in this play. "In such circumstances a dual protagonist within the looser structure of a history in basic form might be accepted on technical grounds even though, literally, the phrase is something of a contradiction in terms."

775 Entry deleted.

776 Estrin, Barbara. "'Behind a Dream': Cleopatra and Sonnet 129." *Women's Studies* 9 (1982): 177-88.

Cleopatra's pursuit and loss of Antony can be examined in terms of the description of the process of lust in Sonnet 129.

777 Greenwood, Kathy Lynn. "The Transforming Eye: The Poetic Fictions of Falstaff and Cleopatra." *Dissertation Abstracts International* 42 (1982): 4458A (Ohio State).

Falstaff and Cleopatra "alter reality or transform reality as it is established for us in the play." Their "'innocent' transformations engage us even as we recognize them to be 'fictive' versions of reality."

778 Hawkins, Peter S. "The Truth of Metaphor: The Fine Art of Lying." *Massachusetts Studies in English* 8.4 (1982): 1-14.

In his analysis of Enobarbus' speech in Act 2, scene 2, Hawkins suggests that the "primary sources of poetic metaphor" are "the capacity for multiple statement which we find in a single line of Shakespeare" and "the ability to evoke not only diverse but contradictory realities."

779 Kastan, David S. "Shakespeare and 'The Way of Womenkind'." *Daedalus* 111 (1982): 115-30.

In this play, "the lovers are 'a mutual pair' (1.1.37), who ultimately reject the historical world that Caesar controls, and commit themselves to an emotional realm that they alone dominate." In Shakespeare's histories, "we see the exclusion of women from the centers of power and value; in the tragedies, we learn the full human cost. In the histories, women are marginal; in the tragedies, they are destroyed." The two lovers "verbally escape tragic necessity, but only in the romances does Shakespeare redeem the tragic pattern."

780 Kranz, David L. "Shakespeare's New Idea of Rome." *Rome in the Renaissance: The City and the Myth*. Ed. Paul A. Ramsey. Medieval and Renaissance Texts & Studies 18. Binghamton, NY: Medieval and Renaissance Texts and Studies, Center for Medieval & Early Renaissance Studies, 1982, pp. 371-80.

In the Renaissance, Rome was known "for her civilized arts and for her great stoical nobility," but it was also "notorious for her bloody 'gargoyles', her civil wars." In this and other Roman plays, Shakespeare imagined "a psychological and ethnological interpretation which explained how such apparently positive cultural attributes could result in such tragic waste."

781 Lesser, Wendy. "Hitchcock and Shakespeare." *Threepenny Review* 11 (Fall 1982): 17-19.

Hitchcock's films share such thematic concerns with *Antony and Cleopatra* as "sexual animosity and attraction," "betrayal and trust," and "conflicting desires that can never be fulfilled."

782 Maghab, Ali Mosa. "The Stage History of William Shakespeare's *Antony and Cleopatra*." *American Doctoral Dissertations 1980-1981* (1982): 297 (Maryland).

Abstract not available.

783 Makhzangi, A.D.R. "An Account of the Criticism of *Antony and Cleopatra*." *Index to Theses* 32 (1982): 197 (Birmingham).

This thesis gives a critical account of the play in five areas: Its sources in Plutarch, Ovid, the Senecan dramatists, topical influences, Biblical echoes; its structure; its themes like the relationship of the lovers, political readings, and theological interpretations; its characters; its imagery, rhetorical modes, versification, metrication, syntax.

784 Mulryne, J.R. "The Paradox on the Stage: *Antony and Cleopatra*." *Le Paradoxe au temps de* la *Renaissance*. Ed. Marie-Thérèse Jones-Davies. Univ. de Paris-Sorbonne Inst. de Recherches sur les Civilisations de l'Occident Moderne, Centre de Recherches sur la Renaissance 7. Paris: Jean Jouzott, 1982, pp. 155-68.

Mulryne's guiding idea here is that "the theatrical paradox while glorifying theatre's visions, uses theatre's means to call into question the assertions of theatre." He argues that, for example, "within the paradox of the theatre, the monument scene stresses that earthbound quality that opposes theatre's more ethereal, more 'radiant' tendencies." Shakespeare's treatment of her final words is another example of a "parallel between Cleopatra's dying and the literature of paradox." In this scene, "the theatre-presentation does all it can, by way of interruption, noise and busyness to undermine the solemnities of ritual. and hence to maintain the doubleness of paradox."

785 Raeburn, Anna. "*Antony and Cleopatra*." *Shakespeare in Perspective*. Ed. Roger Sales. Vol. 1. London: Ariel Books, BBC, 1982, pp. 263-69.

One of the themes of this play is "the fragility of human beings when they place themselves totally at risk."

786 Shapiro, Michael. "Boying Her Greatness: Shakespeare's Use of Coterie Drama in *Antony and Cleopatra*." *Modern Language Review* 77 (1982): 1-15.

Drawing on the coterie traditions, *Antony and Cleopatra* "is richer in its ways of evoking sympathy for Cleopatra than a stock neo-classical play like Daniel's *Cleopatra*, more truly sophisticated in theatrical self-consciousness than a private-theatre pathetic-heroine like *Sophonisba*." From Marlowe and Nashe, Shakespeare "may have learned to present his classical lovers not only from their own self-idealizing perspective but also from persistent and pervasive ironic viewpoints within and beyond the play, but he outdid them by incorporating ironies far more potentially destructive than any they had confronted."

787 Shibata, Fumiko. "Three Essays on Shakespeare's Women." *Kiyo* (Niimi Women's Junior College) 2 (1982): 98-119. In Japanese.

Not seen.

788 Slater, Ann Pasternak. *Shakespeare the Director*. Totowa, NJ: Barnes & Noble, 1982. 244 pp.

Slater uses a number of passages from this play to illustrate her points about "Shakespeare's direction of his plays, analysing the implications of theatrical effects especially engineered by him."

789 Traversi, Derek. "The Imaginative and the Real in *Antony and Cleopatra*." *The Literary Imagination: Studies in Dante, Chaucer, and Shakespeare*. Newark: U of Delaware P, 1982, pp. 197-227.

Shakespeare had a lifelong concern with "the deeper implications of the dramatic illusion." Hence, in this play, his theme "is the relationship of the imaginatively creative to the obstinately real, of the 'reality' that, following an inherent compulsion of our nature, we 'make' for ourselves to the ineluctable 'reality' with which that making is required to come to come to terms." For Shakespeare, "who was in this as in other respects a uniquely self-conscious artist, these are questions involved in the very decision to set up a group of actors to present 'characters' to an audience in the interlocking and developing action of a play: and they are, perhaps, as subtly addressed in *Antony and Cleopatra* as anywhere in his work."

This balance between the imaginative and the real in the development of the play leads to this conclusion. "The balancing of the generosity that Antony's folly sometimes seems to imply against Caesar's successful, necessary, but limiting practicality: the gradual ascent of the love imagery from earth and 'slime' to 'fire and air,' are are seen at the last to be one great process that tends to death as its completion. For death, which often in Shakespeare—in some of the most eloquent of the sonnets and in the tragedies—seemed to offer incontrovertible evidence of the subjection of the most cherished human values to time's dissolving action, now becomes an instrument of release, the necessary condition of an experience that, though dependent on the temporal dimension that limits all human experience in the act of bringing it into being, is by virtue of its value and intensity incommensurate with it: that is, 'immortal'."

790 Vincent, Barbara C. "Shakespeare's *Antony and Cleopatra* and the Rise of Comedy." *English Literary Renaissance* 12 (1982): 53-86.

The conflict of genres is one of the play's structuring motifs, according to Vincent. In the interaction of comedy and tragedy, one can see the way the Egyptian "irrational world of monstrous fertility" poses a challenge to the tragic one of realism and restraint in Rome. Cleopatra "is the primary desire in the play, and she also plays a prominent role in creating Antony's ultimate identity." Her "desires so govern her perception of reality that she has great difficulty crediting news, such as Antony's marriage to Octavia, which contradicts them."

"The central action in the play's vision of literary history is a movement from a world in which the mythos of tragedy dominates to one in which that of comedy does. The perspectives of tragedy are not, however, disallowed, as many readings of the play attest. It is the nature of the comic vision to include, not to reject, and Shakespeare revitalises the values and vision of his literary forebears at the same time that he encompasses them in his own more capacious structure."

791 Weis, René J.A. "The Myth of the Androgyny: A Study of a Neoplatonic Fiction in Relation to Renaissance Literature and Particularly Shakespeare and *Antony and Cleopatra*." *Index to Theses* 32 (1982): 197 (University College, London).

Abstract not available.

792 Wolf, William D. "'New Heaven, New Earth': The Escape from Mutability in *Antony and Cleopatra.*" *Shakespeare Quarterly* 33 (1982): 328-35.

Antony and Cleopatra "presents one mutable world of changing alliances, relationships, emotional states, and attitudes." The two lovers try to escape both instead of having to choose between earthly love and duty: "The escape occurs in the death scenes, which drive home the irony of death as both an end of temporal, material life and a beginning of union outside the boundaries and necessities of time."

793 Abraham, Lyndall. "Alchemical Reference in *Antony and Cleopatra.*" *Sydney Studies in English* 8 (1982-83): 100-104.

Abraham interprets Lepidus' lines "Your serpent of Egypt" (2.7.26-27) in terms of alchemical imagery and allusion.

794 Ansari, A.A. "*Antony and Cleopatra*: An Image of Liquifaction." *Aligarh Journal of English Studies* 8 (1983): 79-93.

Ansari analyzes images of water, melting and dissolution which serve as a theatrical forces to clarify the play's essential ambiguity.

795 Blake, Norman F. *Shakespeare's Language: An Introduction.* London: 1983.

This study seeks to analyze "limits to our understanding of the language." In his response to prevailing linguistic attitudes, Shakespeare sought "to indulge in linguistic expressiveness involving wit and sound." Elizabethan English "contained more euphony and variety and less subordination than ours" and "different structure with fewer grammatical words." Shakespeare and contemporaries "were carried away by sound and theme to the detriment of grammatical sense." Blake cites twenty-seven passages from *Antony and Cleopatra* in his analysis.

796 Bliss, Lee. *The World's Perspective: John Webster and Jacobean Drama*. New Brunswick, NJ: Rutgers UP, 1983. 246 pp.

Antony cannot be "both Rome's and Cleopatra's" because the values of these empires are "antithetical." The playwright is "deheroizing" Antony because his "stature at his death remains debatable, for his assertions build upon the sand of Cleopatra's lie." The plays of Webster, Chapman and Shakespeare "redefine heroism and nobility, but, with the partial exception of Antony and Cleopatra's transcendent assertion, much of that redefinition remains implicit or unavailable as consolation to the suffering protagonist."

797 Bowers, John M. "'I Am Marble-Constant': Cleopatra's Monumental End." *Huntington Library Quarterly* 46 (1983): 283-97.

"Working from an imagination steeped in native lore concerning monumental tombs and deaths of royal ladies," Shakespeare "invented two discrete episodes—the interlude with the Clown and the suicide itself (V.ii.207-318)—which derive some important measure of their inspiration from the funereal surroundings and, in close sequence with one another, inform the mood and meaning of the tragedy during its final catastrophe."

798 Clayton, Thomas. "'Is This the Promis'd End?' Revision in the Role of the King." *The Division of the Kingdoms: Shakespeare's Two Versions of* King Lear. Ed. Gary Taylor and Michael J. Warren. Oxford: Clarendon P, 1983, pp. 121-41.

Clayton finds a similarity between deaths of Lear in the Folio and Cleopatra: "a primary design in both cases seems to be to convey the emotional conviction that we are witnessing one side of a sort of mystical communion transcending death." They are also similar "in the way they frame the protagonists and introduce their prospective tragic passions."

799 Erskine-Hill, Howard. *The Augustan Idea in English Literature*. London: E. Arnold, 1983. 379 pp.

In this play, Octavian becomes Augustus. Shakespeare "wrote a tragedy in which hyperbole of language, far from being hollow or absurd, is endowed with the fullness and variety of everyday speech; and a tragedy which, by contrast with its interwoven Spenserian theme of Temperance, affirms that in hyperbole of action, licence, a conscious voyaging forth to the extreme, there may be, far from weakness, Magnificence."

800 Fumio, Yoshioka. "Passage to 'New Heaven, New Earth': A Study of Identity in *Antony and Cleopatra*." *Studies in English Literature* (Tokyo) 60 (1983): 275-291.

Not seen.

801 Goldberg, Jonathan. *James I and the Politics of Literature*. Baltimore and London: Johns Hopkins UP, 1983. 292 pp.

The Roman plays "reflect the style of the monarch and James's sense of himself as royal actor. They bear, as *romanitas* does in the Renaissance, a strong notion of public life, the continuities of history, the recreation of Rome as England's imperial ideal."

802 Greenwood, John Philip Peter. "The Mannerist Shakespeare." *Dissertation Abstracts International* 44 (1983): A2771 (Toronto).

In *Antony and Cleopatra* and other plays of the Jacobean period, Shakespeare realized "a learned, self-conscious, and highly artificial new art form" which "mocks, conceals, and elaborates art."

803 Gregson, J.M. "*Antony and Cleopatra*." *Public and Private Man in Shakespeare*. London and Canberra: Crom Helm; Totowa, NJ: Barnes & Noble, 1983, pp. 217-31.

In this play, Shakespeare dramatizes the limitations of reason and calculation and "the attractiveness of a reckless disregard of them." There are "tensions between private thought and public behaviour." The playwright celebrates "sexual love and the urge to see it as a manifestation of spiritual values." He explores "a tragic weakness which brings an otherwise great man to ruin." He develops the "private personalities of the great public figures and the part played by these in great historical events."

804 Jones, Gordon P. "The 'Strumpet's Fool' in *Antony and Cleopatra*." *Shakespeare Quarterly* 34 (1983): 62-68.

In 1.2.79, Enobarbus may have referred to Antony as a woman because, in the opening scene, Antony may have been shown as a "strumpet's fool" both in his costume and his behaviour. Similarly, Antony was often compared with Hercules, who had donned Omphale's clothes. Thus Shakespeare "contrived a prominently-located piece of theatrical cross-dressing in order to establish efficiently and conclusively the unmanning of Antony by the power of love."

805 Jose, Nicholas. "*Antony and Cleopatra*: Face and Heart." *Philological Quarterly* 62 (1983): 487-505.

Antony and Cleopatra "is a play about personalities, a tragedy of love founded upon the continuous presence and being of the protagonists, beyond any roles they may splendidly or ineptly fall in." The triumph of "their love over any other commitment is certified only in their mutual destruction."

806 Kiefer, Frederick. *Fortune and Elizabethan Tragedy.* San Marino, CA: Huntington Library, 1983. 354 pp.

In this play, Cleopatra "wins a victory of sorts" to the extent that she imposes her will on circumstance and confronts her death with dignity." But she gains this at a heavy cost. "For Cleopatra must suppress the qualities that have made her personality so distinctive and appealing; she must adopt a Stoic rigidity; and she must forfeit her very life."

807 Kimura, Teruhira. "Roman Historic Figures and Shakespeare—A Historical Approach to Shakespeare's Roman Plays with Special Reference to Plutarch, Part II: On *Antony and Cleopatra* (III)." *Eibungaku Hyoron* (Kyoto University) 48 (1983): 1-12. In Japanese.

Not seen.

808 Miola, Robert S. "Antony and Cleopatra: Rome and the World." *Shakespeare's Rome*. Cambridge: Cambridge UP, 1983, pp. 116-63.

This play "examines the struggle of Romans with Rome, portrayed as physical locality and an imagined ideal." It "explores the resulting conflict between private needs and public responsibilities by again focusing on the Roman code of honor, shame, and fame; the paradoxes implicit in Roman ceremony and ritual; the political motifs of rebellion and invasion." Shakespeare dramatizes "the predicament of the living human beings who must define themselves against the oppressive background of Roman tradition and history." Rome has lost its status as an imperial city by the end of the play. Cleopatra's monument "finally occupies the center of our interest and sympathies, and the entering Romans appear as impious invaders."

809 Notani, Akira. "Who Is Your Cleopatra?" *Shiga Eibungakukai Ronshu* (Shiga University) 2(1983): 1-22. In Japanese.

Not seen.

810 Roberts, G. J. "Shakespeare and 'Scratching'." *Notes and Queries* ns 30 (1983): 111-14.

Cleopatra is called a witch, and there is a reference to scratching in 4.12.37-39: "The queen's spell, momentarily seen as loathsome *maleficium*, would be removed by the wronged wife scratching the face of the witch."

811 Weis, René J.A. "*Antony and Cleopatra*: The Challenge of Fiction." *English: The Journal of the English Association* 32 (1983): 1-14.

Cleopatra is one of the unique tragic characters "who consciously tries to transcend the limits of fiction through affirming, in the face of death, valid, but ultimately impossible, alternate fictions." Hence it is "peculiarly fitting" that "her defeat, through the generic law of tragedy, should be partly redeemed through translating flamboyantly into a final vindication of her love for Antony which 'needs death to complete it.' The tragic 'reality' in *Antony and Cleopatra* demands a death, but it also ensures that a love-death becomes an integral part of their relationship in the fiction, leaving us with a sense of wonder and fulfilment."

812 Yagi, Tsuyoshi. "A Visionary Dream of Royal Egypt: Death and Marriage in *Antony and Cleopatra*." *Eigo Eibungaku Ronshu* (Seinan Gakuin University) 24.2 (1983): 1-28. In Japanese.

Not seen.

813 Yoshioka, Fumio. "A Passage to 'New Heaven, New Earth'." *Studies in English Literature* (University of Tokyo) 60.2 (1983): 275-91. In Japanese.

Not seen.

814 Andrews, Michael Cameron. "Cleopatra's 'Salad Days'." *Notes and Queries* ns 31 (1984): 212-13.

"Salad days" alludes to Cleopatra's sex life: "Once she was cold and green; now—emphatically—she is neither." "The present transforms the past, making it seem paltry, childish. Her salad days behind her, Cleopatra has become Cleopatra."

815 Aoyama, Seiko. "*Antony and Cleopatra* as a Pre-Romance: The Dramaturgy of Shakespeare's Romances (3)." *Kiyo* (Ferris Women's College) 19 (1984): 255-52. In Japanese.

Not seen.

816 Barroll, J. Leeds. *Shakespearean Tragedy: Genre, Tradition, and Change in 'Antony and Cleopatra'*. Folger Books. Washington, DC: Folger Shakespeare Library; London: Associated University Presses, 1984. 309 pp.

Barroll situates Shakespeare and this play in the western tradition of tragedy. He argues that "the world of the tragic vision requires the presence of embracing ordinances. These natural or supernatural imperatives are crucial, for they are the efforts of dramatic art to make man's world something more than meaningless. If we just obeyed such cosmic Laws, tragedy argues, then perhaps life could avoid disaster." The tragic view is the "warp and woof of Western civilization with its continually urgent need to explain catastrophe and sudden death as part of some sane scheme of existence."

Barroll makes a distinction between major and minor characters. "Those figures who have been called 'minor'—the Eroses—have no personality, while the 'major' figures are conceived as imitated personalities." Barroll proposes that "some kind of rule prohibits us from thinking of Eros as a person with complex motives," and Caesar also falls into this category. Shakespeare "had to shape his imagining of human beings according to the rigorous demands of an art composed only in part of a psychological and philosophical tradition concerning the nature of man. The other part demanded the creation of fictive lives in human beings standing on a stage."

In *Antony and Cleopatra*, Shakespeare "carried the sophistication of his way with the tragic 'person' in the new kind of drama to difficult, and thus illustrative, extremes. For the poet has made the facts about Cleopatra and Antony available only from the ways they converse with others, from the actions they initiate and respond to, from the contradictory comments of different 'minor' figures around them, and only very occasionally from soliloquies." "The strangeness of desire is Shakespeare's basic framework for 'talking about' the character of Mark Antony," and "where Shakespeare makes Antony especially interesting is in the fact that the hero is proud of this voluptuary mode in himself. In truth, the pleasures of the flesh and of combat and of the idea of women are his personal way to a sense of exaltation which he sees as the gates to a kind of transcendence." In Cleopatra, Antony sees "a mirror of himself." This explains Antony's failure as a commander.

Barroll offers a defence of Cleopatra by saying that she achieves tragic proportions. After the disaster at Actium, Cleopatra "bolts in the panic of inexperience. She has no deep, vile plots to betray Antony. Nor can she be blamed for any great tactical errors in the disposition of her forces." The play "so far has emphasized the vagueness of the queen's concepts of political and military cause and effect and, indeed, her message to Caesar after the disaster emphasizes her removal from the reality of war." "A tragic figure whom the poet has driven, perhaps further than he drove Lear, to a delirium of desperation," Cleopatra "has been stripped, as Lear, of grandiose conception after grandiose conception—in the melting of the godhood of Antony and his empire, the lapse of her own greatness, the death of her lover, Caesar's utter indifference—and still she concedes nothing." Cleopatra "insists on her sense of her own, towering self." Barroll concedes that "the difficulty of Cleopatra's death is its very spectacle." Barroll looks "at Cleopatra's story as of a kind similar to Lear's or Coriolanus's, we cannot casually grant the Egyptian enchantress even the pagan truth in her magniloquent vision. For her concept of death as a floating to meet Mark Antony in a physical afterlife to attain marriage and 'that kiss which is my heaven to have' was a vision which few if any of the intelligent thinkers of the ancient world would have granted her, especially those whom Shakespeare and his contemporaries were likely to know." Cleopatra's "only aesthetic course is to go down, losing all, like Lear and Richard stripped figuratively and literally to a nakedness."

Barroll stresses that "love is around Antony." "It is Antony alone, for a moment and between delusions, who most nearly approaches something which has not been imagined by the other. And his failure is the ethical tragedy of Shakespeare's drama." Antony's tragedy "becomes the tragedy of his world too. The greed that is Rome infects him and, in the end, he cannot escape it." Antony's "one great truth is his loving and the love he causes in others. His tragedy and the the tragedy of his world is that he does not hold this truth any more strongly than he finally holds his sword. In the end, he is too much of Rome."

817 Booth, Stephen. "Poetic Richness: A Preliminary Audit." *Pacific Coast Philology* 19 (1984): 68-78.

Booth makes a detailed analysis of a short scene (3.10) to show that literary "works really are or really mean what they have not previously suggested to be or mean." He stresses that "the elements that inspire us to use the label *poetic* are as subtle and as vital as they are dry, wispy, and dull."

818 Britton, Elizabeth Lindsey. "The Dido-Aeneas Story from Vergil to Dryden (Ovid, Chaucer, Shakespeare)." *Dissertation Abstracts International* 45 (1984): 246A (Virginia).

Britton discusses *Antony and Cleopatra* in the context of two opposite interpretations of the Dido-Aeneas story, one stressing Aeneas' morality and duty and the other emphasizing Dido's love and personal commitment.

819 Casey, John. "The Noble." *Philosophy and Literature*. Ed. A. Phillips Griffiths. Royal Institute of Philosophy Lectures Series 16. Cambridge: Cambridge UP, 1984, pp. 135-53.

The idea of the noble in Shakespeare "is assumed but questioned, asserted and denied in a way that makes it possible for us to see how it is not simply an historical idea, a survival of the aristocratic ethic of the Renaissance, but a way of probing human values." In plays like *Othello*, *Antony and Cleopatra* and *Coriolanus*, "Shakespeare presents the noble as intimately involved in the most profound and general choices men may make of their values."

820 Dollimore, Jonathan. *Radical Tragedy: Religion, Ideology and Power in the Drama of Shakespeare and His Contemporaries*. Chicago and London: U of Chicago P, 1984, pp. 204-17.

One of the exponents of cultural materialism, Dollimore explains the link between "signification and legitimation: the way that beliefs, practices and institutions legitimate the dominant social order or *status quo*—the existing relations of domination and subordination." He suggests that *Antony and Cleopatra* and *Coriolanus* "effect a sceptical interrogation of martial ideology and in doing so foreground the complex social and political relations which hitherto it tended to occlude." The tragic subject is constituted in and through the contradictions which reside at the heart of Jacobean culture, and which ideology functions to mediate. In *Antony and Cleopatra* "those with power make history yet only in accord with the contingencies of the existing historical moment." "Those around Antony and Cleopatra see their love in terms of power; languages of possession, subjugation and conspicuous wealth abound in descriptions of the people." Antony's "sexuality is informed by the very power relations which he, ambivalently, is prepared to sacrifice for sexual freedom; correspondingly, the heroic *virtus* which he wants to reaffirm in and through Cleopatra is in fact almost entirely a function of the power structure which he, again ambivalently, is prepared to sacrifice for her." If the play "celebrates anything it is not the love which transcends power but the sexual infatuation which foregrounds it."

821 Hill, James L. "The Marriage of True Bodies: Myth and Metamorphosis in *Antony and Cleopatra.*" *REAL—The Yearbook of Research in English and American Literature* 2 (1984): 211-37.

Hill analyzes the way mythological allusions relate to the subject of metamorphosis, especially the surrender of good sense to appetite in *Antony and Cleopatra.*

822 Ingram, Angela J.C. "Cleopatra." *In the Posture of a Whore: Changing Attitudes to "Bad" Women in Elizabethan and Jacobean Drama.* Salzburg Studies in English Literature: JDS 93. Salzburg: Institut fur Anglistik and Americkanistik, Universitat Salzburg, 1984, pp. 298-329.

This is a commentary on the work of Countess of Pembroke, Daniel and Shakespeare. Shakespeare has written "an expansive, exuberant 'Elizabethan' play from the point of view of a sceptical Jacobean, creating in Cleopatra a figure whose intricacies of character seem perfectly to embody the qualities of 'bad' women of the contemporary drama." This Cleopatra "represents dangerous elements of disorder in a man's world." Shakespeare "took advantage of every possible ambiguity in both the Cleopatra legend and in the language and dramatic craft available to him."

823 Kranz, David L. "'Too Slow a Messenger': The Certainty of Speed in *Antony and Cleopatra.*" *CEA Critic* 47 (1984): 90-98.

Kranz elaborates the motif of speed in the play as "a dramatic element which enlists rational certainty on Cleopatra's side, reinforcing the imaginative claims of her art while shocking, at least for a moment, Caesar's and our own certainty in his worldly victory." Shakespeare juxtaposes "relatively quick scenes in Rome and langurously slow ones in Egypt."

824 Lyons, Clifford. "The Dramatic Structure of Shakespeare's *Antony and Cleopatra*." *Renaissance Papers 1983*. Ed. George Walton Williams. Durham: Southern Renaissance Conference, 1984, pp. 63-77.

This play has four structural divisions which direct the audience to a theme of "Cleopatra as dark enchantress."

825 Magnusson, Augusta Lynne. "Studies in Shakespeare's Later Style." *Dissertation Abstracts International* 45 (1984): 2887A (Toronto).

This study "describes the tendencies in Shakespeare's syntax, diction, and prosody that emerge in *Antony and Cleopatra* and *Coriolanus* and become more pronounced in the plays from *Cymbeline* to *The Two Noble Kinsmen*."

826 Marchant, Robert. "Cleopatra's Masterpiece." *A Picture of Shakespeare's Tragedies*. Retford, Nottinghamshire: Brynmill P, 1984, pp. 141-80.

In Shakespearean tragedy, "the intelligible but inexplicable passion, elation or despair in the protagonist's actions constitutes the last judgement upon him, as it shows his actions to be actions he wills and cannot avoid willing." The question "Why can he not avoid willing his actions?" cannot be given an explanation because "it belongs to the recognition of a picture of things." Cleopatra "braves death out in the splendid flesh—and her splendour is pathetic. The pathos runs right through the play, informing alike Antony's brave resolve to put an end to the dalliance of the love and Cleopatra's sublime sacrifice in the last act."

827 Matchett, William H. "Reversing the Field: *Antony and Cleopatra* in the Wake of *King Lear*." *Modern Language Quarterly* 45 (1984): 327-37.

This play "seems to follow most directly from *King Lear*" and "shows Shakespeare facing into the problem and finding his creative bearings again." *King Lear* "asserts a value, then wipes it out; *Antony and Cleopatra* challenges us to evaluate." "By reversing the field allows the open dialectic of drama to continue, and the greatest drama provides us with profound experience while leaving our questions open."

828 Nishizawa, Yasuo. "The Logic of 'Scene' and the Dynamism of Drama in *Antony and Cleopatra.*" *Kyoikugakubu Kenkyu Hokoku* (Gifu University) 32 (1984): 844-96. In Japanese.

Not seen.

829 Novy, Marianne. *Love's Argument: Gender Relations in Shakespeare.* Chapel Hill: U of North Carolina P, 1984. 237 pp.

In her brief comments on this play, Novy stresses it as "the only Shakespearean tragedy that focuses on and indeed glorifies the woman as actor in both senses, doer and pretender, and, not coincidentally, as sexually active."

830 Pearson, Jacqueline. "Romans and Barbarians: The Structure of Irony in Shakespeare's Roman Plays." *Shakespearian Tragedy.* Ed. Malcolm Bradbury and David Palmer. New York: Holmes & Meier, 1984, pp. 159-82.

This play is "teasing in its contrasts of opposed values which are defined as Roman and Egyptian." In the course of action, "though, our sense of the equality of these contrasting values is increasingly disturbed. The Roman values increasingly seem harsh and reductive, the Egyptian values deeply flawed but still more humane." The play "ends not with a blurring but with a triumphant reconciliation of its contrasting values." Through her suicide, Cleopatra "resolves all conflicts, and has become a figure who is at once comic and tragic, male and female, Roman and Egyptian." This and other Roman tragedies "centre on ambiguous and paradoxical characters, and typical structural devices are ironic parallelism, juxtaposition and contrast."

831 Rice, Juanita Jean Patterson. "Shakespeare's Dramatic Structuring of Prose, Verse and Verse Variations: A Computer-Assisted Analysis of Eight Plays (Editing, Performance, Othello,

Antony, Henry IV)." *Dissertation Abstracts International* 45 (1984): A944 (California-Berkeley).

Rice argues that "Shakespeare's use of prose, verse, and verse variations correspond to dramatic conventions which governed performance style."

832 Robertson, Patricia R. "'This Herculean Roman': Shakespeare's Antony and the Hercules Myth." *Publications of the Arkansas Philological Association* 10 (1984): 65-75.

Shakespeare employs the Hercules myth to "clarify Antony's paradoxical behavior, underline and deepen his basic insecurity, and affirm his capacity for tragic greatness."

833 Rossky, William. "*Antony and Cleopatra*, I.ii.79: Enobarbus' 'Mistake'." *Shakespeare Quarterly* 35 (1984): 324-25.

Enobarbus "is not mistaking an 'Herculean' Antony in Cleopatra's clothes for the Queen but rather is accurately, though ironically, assessing the relationship between the principals, making the familiar point that Antony has become effeminate, a leader led by a woman."

834 Rubinstein, Frankie Ruda. *A Dictionary of Shakespeare's Sexual Puns and Their Significance.* London: Macmillan, 1984. 334 pp. 2nd ed. New York: St. Martin's P, 1995. 372 pp.

This dictionary provides a comprehensive list of words used by nine characters in *Antony and Cleopatra* and sheds light on the speaker and the one addressed or the one spoken about. For example, the word "abominations" in 3.6.94 contains a sexual pun and refers to Antony's bisexuality and sodomy.

835 Sekimoto, Eiichi. "On Cleopatra and Her Death." *Seasons in Shakespeare*. Tokyo: Shinozaki Shorin, 1984, pp. 161-69.

Not seen.

836 Summers, Joseph H. "A Definition of Love: *Antony and Cleopatra*." *Dreams of Love and Power: On Shakespeare's Plays*. London: Oxford UP, 1984, pp. 115-36.

Summers argues that "in the sexual battles and the transformation of lust into love which make up, I believe, the primary action of the play, the lovers achieve their miracle not at all by abandoning sexuality but by committing themselves to their loves, ultimately uniting Roman and Egyptian values in their pristine brightness." The spectators "have watched the passionate and disorderly history of Antony and Cleopatra as it was transformed into a 'great solemnity' of love, and we have sensed in its final moments a state and an 'order' both 'high' and mysterious."

837 Thuot, Eugene F. "Love, Politics, and the Emergence of the Christian Soul: A Commentary on Shakespeare's *Antony and Cleopatra*." *American Doctoral Dissertations 1982-1983* (1984): 343 (Chicago).

Abstract not available.

838 Tucker, Kenneth. "Psychetypes and Shakespeare's *Antony and Cleopatra*." *Journal of Evolutionary Psychology* 5 (1984): 176-180.

Antony and Cleopatra "is one of the first literary works to investigate differences between psychological types as the modern world has come to understand them." Much of the conflict in the play "results from the opposition of thinking and feeling types." This opposition "gives depth to the struggle between Antony and Octavius and emerges in Enobarbus' problematic relationship with Antony." Cleopatra also is a feeling type.

839 Woodbridge, Linda. *Women and the English Renaissance*. Urbana and Chicago: U of Illinois P, 1984. 364 pp.

Enobarbus is a misogynist. He "has a soldier's contempt for women, and the woman he dislikes most is Cleopatra; not despite his recognizing her extreme attractiveness (the greatest accolades to Cleopatra's beauty and charm are his), but because he recognizes her extreme attractiveness." As stage misogynist, Enobarbus is "a foil" to Cleopatra.

840 Baker, W. *Brodie's Notes on William Shakespeare's Antony and Cleopatra.* Pan Study Aids. London: Pan, 1985. 127 pp.

This is a study guide for students.

841 Barber, Charles L. *The Theme of Honour's Tongue: A Study of Social Attitudes in the English Drama from Shakespeare to Dryden.* Gothenburg Studies in English 58. Gothenburg: Acta Universitatis Gothoburgensis, 1985. 171 pp.

In this play, "Rome and Egypt represent two different ways of life and sets of attitudes, Rome broadly representing the public world, and Egypt the private, personal world." The play's tragedy "is that of Antony, who belongs to both worlds, and is destroyed by this fact."

842 Bulman, James C. *The Heroic Idiom of Shakespearean Tragedy.* Newark: U of Delaware P, 1985. 254 pp.

Shakespeare invoked the heroic tradition to conform to his audience's expectations, but he also questioned and modified it. Hence he "incorporated allusions to and conventions from his literary and dramatic heritage to serve as models from which to evolve a more authentic representation of heroism." Antony and Cleopatra are both heroic and non-heroic characters. In this play, Shakespeare uses these conventions in such a way "that they appear artificial, old-fashioned, and finally inadequate to describe a heroic reality; and by doing that, he allows us, if we so choose, not to credit them at all." According to Bulman, "The conflict between heroic hyperbole and a diminished human reality in *Antony and Cleopatra* is too fundamental, too pervasive to allow us to make a leap of faith." Shakespeare's art can be appreciated only with "an awareness of the tension he creates between demands for rational analysis and persuasions to give in to the fiction."

843 Cluck, Nancy A. "Shakespeare Studies in Shame." *Shakespeare Quarterly* 36 (1985): 141-51.

Cleopatra's sensual nature changes Antony "from a man of reason, honor, and integrity to a man of weakness, irresoluteness, and cowardice." She "tames the great Roman hero" who "is womanized, and the shame that overcomes him during the course of the play threatens his self-identity." Having been compelled to examine himself closely, Antony at the end "reorders his identity and ultimately reaches tragic understanding."

844 Davies, H. Neville. "Jacobean *Antony and Cleopatra*." *Shakespeare Studies* 17 (1985): 123-58

James I associated himself with Caesar Augustus, and Shakespeare may have modelled his Octavius on James I. The playwright may have based his shipboard scene on the shipboard entertainment that marked the end of the visit of Christian IV of Denmark to England in the summer of 1606. "Like Antony, Christian was extravagant, physically strong, and able to take pleasure in the company of all sorts and conditions of men."

845 Erickson, Peter. "Identification with the Maternal in *Antony and Cleopatra*." *Patriarchal Structures in Shakespeare's Drama*. Berkeley, 1985, pp. 123-47.

Shakespeare shows a tolerant attitude toward the weaknesses of men and women in this play. Antony "is preoccupied with the 'new heaven, new earth' (1.1.17) that a woman seems to have revealed to him, a revelation that Antony's intermittent attacks of jealousy are not permitted permanently to obscure." Antony deviates from the custom of male bonding because of his commitment to Cleopatra, but "the claims of traditional manliness are reasserted at the end of the play through the military success of Octavius." By suggesting that Octavius stands for the reality principle, Shakespeare "can legitimately insist on the escapist aspect of Antony and Cleopatra's suicidal action and thus regard them with a safe mixture of admiration and criticism."

846 Faber, M.D. "*Antony and Cleopatra*: The Empire of the Self." *Psychoanalytic Review* 72 (1985): 71-104.

Faber argues that the "lovers' empire is the need for an integrated self."

847 Fuller, David. "Writing Criticism and Discussing Literature: A Polemical Essay on Subjectivity and Creativity in Criticism." *Durham University Journal* 78 [NS 47] (1985): 145-65.

Fuller points out the personal element in criticism by commenting on G. Wilson Knight's and L.C. Knights's evaluations of *Antony and Cleopatra*: "Clearly this meaning is personal. Its full articulation, like all personal writing, will have an extra-personal validity and interest if the self articulated is broad enough and the mining of that self sufficiently deep."

848 Goldman, Michael. "*Antony and Cleopatra*: Action as Imaginative Command." *Acting and Action in Shakespearean Tragedy*. Princeton: Princeton UP, 1985, pp. 112-39.

This play is about greatness, which "is primarily a command over other people's imaginations. It depends on what people think of you and what you think of yourself." There are several audiences for greatness: "it is, first, the small group of people on stage at any time; second, the entire known world to whom Antony and Cleopatra constantly play and which seems always to regard them with fascination; it is also a timeless, superhuman audience, the heroes of history and legend and the gods themselves; finally, it is the audience of posterity, of whom we in the theatre are a part." In this play, Shakespeare "found a subject that richly indulged the ambiguity of the poet's position, a story that both challenged the claims of raw imaginative power and seductively breathed them forth." Hence the play "mounts no case against morality and public order; for certain instants, it simply leaves them behind." The play's action "puts a premium on sensual indulgence, on the unabashed exploitation of what is immediately attractive." The audiences "must be won over by the actors' ability to make the experience of sensation itself admirable and fulfilling—to demonstrate their commitment to pleasure in a way that makes an audience willing to entertain it as 'the nobleness of life'."

849 Gruber, William E. "The Actor in the Script: Affective Strategies in Shakespeare's *Antony and Cleopatra*." *Comparative Drama* 19 (1985): 30-48.

The methods of characterization and visual rhetoric in Renaissance drama cannot be understood unless one sees that the whole notion of 'character' may be complicated by the actors' presence." There is a difference in the "patterns of audience expectation and the rhythms of histrionic performance." The spectators get interested in the play "not by mechanisms of expectation and fulfillment but by processes more accurately defined as identification." Shakespeare "created in Cleopatra a role designed explicitly to extend the concept of maleness against an obvious extreme limitation: properly speaking, 'boying' Cleopatra is an innovation upon man's estate."

850 Jorgensen, Paul A. "*Antony and Cleopatra*." *William Shakespeare: The Tragedies*. TEAS 415. Boston: Twayne, 1985, pp. 110-25.

This "tragedy must, at least first of all, be seen as the disgrace and defeat of a Herculean hero." Antony's inner struggle has to do with his power to free himself from sensuality. This "struggle will have a lingering and poignant afterlife once Antony has decided, in his moral choice, to give up the struggle; it will give give him his major source of suffering after his total surrender to Cleopatra." Cleopatra makes, "at least toward the end of the play, an attempt not only to honor but also to match the nobility of her fallen Antony." Her nobility and loyalty are "the measure of her true greatness," and this virtue alone, "if the loves meet the traditional challenge, justify the passion of the two monarchs as something more than an entertainment of game and betrayal." In Antony's decline, "there begins both a heroically grand suffering and a swelling eloquence lamenting his threatened loss of nobility." Cleopatra also struggles to be noble, and "it is a struggle as worthy of tragic stature as her infinite variety was of her wanton days." In this play, Shakespeare "has created more than uncertainties: he has eternally united this pair in nobility."

851 Kelly (Varisco), Lois. "Multiplicity and Meaning in Three Shakespearean Plays: *Titus Andronicus*, *Antony and Cleopatra*, and *Othello*." *Dissertation Abstracts International* 46 (1985): 707A (SUNY Buffalo).

Using Roland Barthes's approach to interpretative process, Kelly's commentary on these plays "celebrates the triumphant plural as it breaks away from any ideology of totality."

852 Leary, Daniel. "Shaw and Shakespeare: Why Not!" *Independent Shavian* 23 (1985): 6-8.

In *Caesar and Cleopatra*, "Shaw was playing with Shakespeare, distorting, augmenting, fooling around with audience expectations based on their spotty high school education and their reluctant exposure to *Julius Caesar*, *Antony and Cleopatra*, and odds and ends of the Shakespearean corpus."

853 Macdonald, Ronald R. "Playing till Doomsday: Interpreting *Antony and Cleopatra*." *English Literary Renaissance* 15 (1985): 78-99.

This play reflects "a highly self-conscious interrogation of the [classical] rules, a studied and often playful attempt to suggest alternate modes of representation, and to explore the consequences of committing oneself to *any* system of construction." Shakespeare's attitude led him "beyond the relatively circumscribed domain of literary theory into an historical questioning of classicism in general, the peculiar prestige accorded it in learned Renaissance circles, and its centrality for European culture." This play "asks us to see the meanings of history as indeterminate. It sees the past as an open possibility, a collection of meanings in competition, a field as radically ambiguous as the play we have witnessed."

854 Nakasato, Toshiaki. "The Snake and the Sword—Antony and Cleopatra." *Eibeibungaku Ronso* (Nihon University) 33 (1985): 1-18. In Japanese.

Not seen.

855 Neely, Carol Thomas. "Gender and Genre in *Antony and Cleopatra*." *Broken Nuptials in Shakespeare's Plays*. New Haven and London: Yale UP, 1985, pp. 136-65.

In this play, "gender roles are not exchanged or transcended, but played out in more variety than in the other tragedies." Consequently, "the generic boundaries of *Antony and Cleopatra* are expanded to include motifs, roles, and themes found in Shakespeare's comedies, histories, problem plays, and romances." This analysis "illuminates both the gender relations characteristic of different Shakespearean genres and the unique generic mix of *Antony and Cleopatra*, a play which, like Egypt's crocodile, is shaped only like 'itself'." Cleopatra, "like the heroines of comedy, engenders Antony's growth and her own, controlling the ending to glorify her submission to him." Resembling the heroine of the problem comedies, "she endures sexual degradation and uses sexuality fruitfully." Her death is "self-willed and self-fulfilling," but it "serves Caesar's political needs, confirming historical control; serves Antony's emotional needs, reaffirming the nobleness of his 'shape'; and serves Shakespeare's aesthetic needs, allowing him to make Cleopatra's death, like her life, 'eternal in [his] triumph' (5.1.66)."

856 Rozett, Martha Tuck. "The Comic Structures of Tragic Endings: The Suicide Scenes in *Romeo and Juliet* and *Antony and Cleopatra*." *Shakespeare Quarterly* 36 (1985): 152-64.

Shakespeare repeats in *Antony and Cleopatra* a pattern he had tried in *Romeo and Juliet*. They "conclude with a tragic sequence consisting of the feigned death of the heroine, followed by the suicide of the lover, then the heroine's 'resurrection', and finally, a second suicide." Foremost among the mysteries of human nature in these plays "is the paradoxical way in which lovers alternately torment and celebrate one another, which is one of the most timeless subjects of comedy."

857 Sano, Akiko. "A Queen and a Woman—An Aspect of Women's Nature." *Bungakubu Kiyo* (Teikyo University) 16 (1985): 79-96. In Japanese.

Not seen.

858 Simmons, Joseph L. "Shakespeare's Treatment of Roman History." *William Shakespeare: His World, His Work, His Influence*. Ed. John F. Andrews. 3 vols. New York: Charles Scribner's, 1985, II, 473-88.

In this play, Shakespeare "manipulates the audience from point to point of view until in the final scene his Cleopatra, in a comically exalted fashion, brings us to a common coign of vantage just at the turning point of Roman and, from the Elizabethan perspective, universal history." The playwright's "historiographical perspective establishes the pagan world against the only standard by which it becomes meaningfully pagan, by an appeal to events in 'the time of universal peace' that will presage 'new heaven, new earth'."

859 Steppat, Michael Payne. "Octavius Cold and Sickly." *Notes and Queries* ns 32 (1985): 53-54.

Shakespeare's portrayal of Octavius may have been influenced by "Suetonius' graphic picture of the emperor's periodic suffering from cold temperament."

860 Tanigami, Reiko. "Cleopatra, the Snake of Mandala." *Shigakudai Eibungaku Ronso* (Otani Women's University) 21 (1985): 1-30. In Japanese.

Not seen.

861 Taylor, Anthony Brian. "The Non-Existent Carbuncles: Shakespeare, Golding and Raphael Regius." *Notes and Queries* ns 32 (1985): 54-55.

In 4.8.28-29, the notion of the Sun-god's jewel-encrusted chariot may derive from Ovid, *Metamorphoses*, ii.107-9.

862 Aoyama, Seiko. "*Antony and Cleopatra*: Notes about Its Mythological Background." *Kiyo* (Ferris Women's College) 21 (1986): 27-41. In Japanese.

Not seen.

863 Banerjee, Ron D.K. "Space: Form and Feeling in *Antony and Cleopatra*." *Shakespeare*. Ed. Debabrata Mukherjee. Proceedings of a Conference on Shakespeare and Recent Trends in Shakespeare's Scholarship, 1984. Jadavpur University Essays and Studies 5. Calcutta: Jadavpur University, 1986, pp. 55-71.

Not seen.

864 Barber, C.I., and Richard P. Wheeler. *The Whole Journey: Shakespeare's Power of Development.* Berkeley: U of California P, 1986. 354 pp.

This play is the "most complete expression of human, fully sexual love." It "reaches toward a mode of fulfillment that poses a radical alternative to the dominant patterns of social and familial relationships."

865 Battenhouse, Roy. "Augustinian Roots in Shakespeare's Sense of Tragedy." *Upstart Crow* 6 (1986): 1-7.

Shakespeare's imagery "frequently echoes Bible language or paradigm, even when the play's setting is pagan." In 4. 2, Shakespeare may be echoing Christ's premonition of death in Antony's fellowship speeches. Antony may be "enacting unwittingly a perverted likeness to Christ, a dark analogy to divine love." Cleopatra "becomes a parody of the Virgin Mary when she supplies an asp to her breast and describes the serpent as the 'baby' she nurses to give suck to 'immortal longings'."

866 Carducci, Jane Shook. "'Our hearts you see not': Shakespeare's Roman Men (Androgyny, Feminist Criticism, Silent Men)." *Dissertation Abstracts International* 46 (1986): 139A (Nevada-Reno).

Shakespeare's Roman hero "represents the extreme stereotype, boasting qualities universally considered to be masculine; he is a stoic, aggressive, and independent warrior, completely out of touch with his feminine side." Antony "moves between the plain style of Rome and the hyperbole of Egypt, neither offering him an avenue to express feelings."

867 Cioni, Fernando. "'The Fancy Outwork Nature': Enobarbo e la sua descrizione di Cleopatra." *Analysis: Quaderni di Anglistica* 4 (1986): 73-93.

Cioni points out the significance of Enobarbus as a character and the eroticism of his description of Cleopatra in its dramatic and theatrical contexts.

868 Cook, Elizabeth. "*Antony and Cleopatra.*" *Seeing Through Words: The Scope of Late Renaissance Poetry*. New Haven and London: Yale UP, 1986, pp. 72-93.

The Sonnets and *Antony and Cleopatra* "explore romantic lovc, not as the source of tragedy or the proper end of comedy, but as a mode of thought, a way of seeing and organising experience. Love is not madness but elucidation." In this play, "the cramped real world has given way to the conceptual and imaginative freedom of the lovers—an internal freedom which ignores the constrictions of Rome/room." Antony, "Colossus-like, straddles both of the play's worlds and operates in both kinds of room, material and internal."

869 Danobeitia Fernandez, Maria Luisa. "Cleopatra's Role Taking: A Study of *Antony and Cleopatra.*" *Revista Canaria de Estudios Ingleses* 12 (1986): 55-73.

This study analyzes Cleopatra's character to reveal the game and play element in her political situation; it also shows when she is playing games through role-playing or role-taking.

870 Durbach, Errol. "*Antony and Cleopatra* and *Rosmersholm*: 'Third Empire' Love Tragedies." *Comparative Drama* 20 (1986): 1-16.

Durbach is suggesting "the possibility of a third term emerging: some Hegelian Aufhebung to oppose against the violent falling apart of opposite, or at least some value to salvage from the collapse of paganism and the failure of civilization." Even though Shakespeare's play is pre-Christian and Ibsen's post-Christian, both of them "resolve their dialectical impasse in similar intimations of a 'third empire'."

871 Edwards, Philip. *Shakespeare: A Writer's Progress*. London: Oxford UP, 1986. 204 pp.

Edwards proposes that this play "is not a a love-and-honour tragedy, weighing Egyptian luxury against austere Roman virtue, though Antony sees it that way. There is no either/or in it." Antony "wants to be remembered as the great soldier and not the fated lover." Shakespeare has chosen "the royal harlot Cleopatra" as the one "in whom to portray a richness in sexual love which has a mysterious though almost inaccessible power to redeem the spirit."

872 Fang Ping. "Better Impassioned Than Passionless—On *Antony and Cleopatra*." *Shashibiya yanjiu* 3 (1986): 73-122. In Chinese.

Not seen.

873 Frye, Northrop. "Antony and Cleopatra." *Northrop Frye on Shakespeare*. Ed. Robert Sandler. Markham, Ontario: Fitzhenry and Whiteside, 1986, pp. 122-39.

Shakespeare's character is the theatre, and Cleopatra is "the essence of theatre." She has the biggest role in drama, and her "identity is an actress's identity." She "is a woman possessed by vanity, and vanity is a rather disarming vice."Antony and Cleopatra's heroic dimensions "are too big for the world as we know it, and so become distinctive. The chaos is social as well as cosmic." Frye also touches on the mythological and Biblical elements like the Biblical Egypt.

874 Ghosh, Gauri Prasad. "*Antony and Cleopatra*: The First Recoil from the Tragic Impasse." *Journal of the Department of English, University of Calcutta* 22.2 (1985-86): 1-20.

Antony and Cleopatra is "a recoil from the darkly realistic tragic vision that had been haunting the poet's imagination;" it "is the transitional link between Tragedies and the Romances."

875 Guillory, John. "Dalila's House: Samson Agonistes and the Sexual Division of Labor." *Rewriting the Renaissance: The Discourses of Sexual Difference in Early Modern Europe*. Ed. Margaret W. Ferguson, Maureen Quilligan, and Nancy J. Vickers. Women in Culture and Society. Chicago and London: U of Chicago P, 1986, pp. 106-22.

Milton's rhetorical description of Dalila's "instruments of seduction" in *Samson Agonistes* draws on details of Cleopatra's barge in Shakespeare's play.

876 Hill, James L. "'What, are they children?'" Shakespeare's Tragic Women and Boy Actors." *Studies in English Literature 1500-1900* 26 (1986): 235-58.

The adult male actors on stage "are given roles in which the inner world of the character must be revealed explicitly to the audience; with the female characters, that inner world remains for the most part implicit, to be inferred by the audience." What the spectators see of Cleopatra "may well be a result of having to write for a boy actor." Shakespeare's "thought can be glimpsed only through the limiting filter of the boy actor's act."

877 Huzar, Eleanor G. "Mark Antony: Marriages vs. Careers." *Classical Journal* 81 (1986): 97-111.

This is a historical and biographical narrative of Mark Antony's life with his five wives, and there are three references to *Antony and Cleopatra.*

878 Johnson, Anthony L. "Semiotic Systems and Lexical Clues in *Antony and Cleopatra.*" Alessandro Serpieri, ed. *Retorica e immaginario.* Parma: Pratiche, 1986, pp. 125-60.

Not seen.

879 Kabbani, Rana. *Europe's Myths of Orient.* Bloomington: Indiana UP, 1986. 166 pp.

Kabbani argues that "the voyage to the Orient and the contact with the Oriental is often tinged with danger." Antony "embarked on that voyage a 'firm Roman,' but as the play opens, he has been captivated by its erotic possibilities, fallen into the lassitude of love hours, fallen from his former stature—fallen, in short, into the East (which is set as a foil to Rome)." Cleopatra, an Eastern woman, "was a narrative creation that fulfilled the longings of Western imagination."

880 Krohn, Janis. "The Dangers of Love in *Antony and Cleopatra.*" *International Review of Psycho-Analysis* 13 (1986): 89-96.

The action and imagery of this play "express the fantasy that Antony's impassioned attachment to Cleopatra leads him continually to feel emasculated, forcing him repeatedly away from her sphere in order to replenish his sense of manhood in the company of other men." This unconscious fantasy destroys the couple more than the pressure of outside obstacles.

881 Kusunoki, Akiko. "'Nature Piece 'Gainst Fancy': Cleopatra and Women of English Renaissance." *Bungaku* (Iwanami Shoten) 54.iv (1986): 135-48. In Japanese.

Not seen.

882 Mehl, Dieter. "*Antony and Cleopatra.*" *Shakespeare's Tragedies.* Cambridge: Cambridge UP, 1986, pp. 152-78.

Mehl argues that this play "underlines the dangerous and destructive aspects of this love as much as its potential happiness and its exemplary character." It is in this play alone that "the ennobling and the destructive potentialities of love are inextricably linked; Cleopatra combines the characteristic qualities of Juliet and Cressida, of the ideal beloved and the humiliating seductress." The play "gives an astonishingly faithful impression of the fascinating variety and the forceful realism of Plutarch's account, enriched by exuberant poetry and complexity of characterization; yet there is no consistent effort to make these anecdotic scenes conform to any strict rules of tragedy." Plutarch paid attention to "the inextricable tangle of historical crises and unpredictable personalities, and these intriguing contrasts are brought out even more sharply in Shakespeare's dramatization, whereas they get largely lost in those neoclassical tragedies that attempt to remodel Antony and Cleopatra according to the precepts of conventional tragic practice." Mehl "argues against a particularly significant thematic relationship between *Antony and Cleopatra* and Shakespeare's romances, such as has occasionally been suggested, because in those later plays, the nature of evil and human corruptibility is examined with far greater intensity."

883 Moseley, C.W.R.D. "Cleopatra's Prudence: Three Notes on the Use of Emblems in *Anthony and Cleopatra.*" Deutsche Shakespeare Gesellschaft West. *Jahrbuch 1986*: 119-37.

Shakespeare uses three emblematic images—the Colossus image, the choice of Hercules in relationship to Antony, and Prudence holding a serpent to her breast in relation to Cleopatra—to suggest wisdom and prudence. Shakespeare examines and redefines these concepts "in such a way that the areas we might have thought to be covered by a consensus are seen as much more problematized."

884 Oshima, Hisao. "Time and Heroism: A Study of *Antony and Cleopatra.*" *Bungaku Kenkyu Ronshu* (Seinan Gakuin University) 5 (1986): 109-34. In Japanese.

Not seen.

885 Riemer, Seth Daniel. "National Biases in French and English Drama. *Dissertation Abstracts International* 46 (1986): 2686A (Cornell).

Shakespeare's *Antony and Cleopatra* and Corneille's *Cinna* are discussed "in context of their contemporary milieus, and this discussion serves as a basis for comparing the two national theaters."

886 Siegel, Paul N. *Shakespeare's English and Roman History Plays: A Marxist Approach.* Rutherford, NJ: Fairleigh Dickinson UP, 1986. 168 pp.

Siegel suggests that "the idea underlying the Roman history plays is that of the greatness of Rome and of its subsequent degeneration; a degeneration that caused its fall." In *Antony and Cleopatra*, "the degeneration of Rome deepens." Rome is invaded by such Egyptian values as pleasure-seeking, luxury and self-indulgence: "The world is well lost for Antony and Cleopatra not when they throw off the cares of government to drown themselves in pleasure; it is well lost when they renounce its pomps and pleasures for the spiritual values they attain in death. In giving up the world, they are paradoxically immortalized in its history, for they have given it an example of the self-sacrifice and regeneration in which lies its hope." Antony "in being most true to Roman values in his death transcends these values."

887 Sigurdson, Paul A. "To Weet or Not To Weet." *Shakespeare Newsletter* 36 (1986): 52.

In 1.1.38-39, "to weet" should be read as "to eat."

888 Tanner, John S. "'Here Is My Space': The Private Mode in Donne's Poetry and Shakespeare's *Antony and Cleopatra*." *Iowa State Journal of Research* 60 (1986): 417-30.

Tanner has discovered "several remarkable similarities" between Donne's *Songs and Sonnets* and *Antony and Cleopatra*. Both of them are "conspicuously paradoxical, ironic, and hyperbolic." They contrast the "metaphysical 'private mode' against the public sphere." They "repeatedly inscribe this tension between public and private spheres in the language of empire."

889 Verma, Rajiva. "Winners and Losers: A Study of *Macbeth* and *Antony and Cleopatra*." *Modern Language Review* 81 (1986): 838-52.

Verma seeks "to establish the opposition between the two plays and to show that it operates on the aesthetic level as well as the psychological." Dealing with the opposites, Shakespeare showed himself "capable of empathy with radically opposed states of mind and opposite kinds of aesthetic experience."

890 Worthen, W.B. "'The Weight of Antony:' Staging Character' in *Antony and Cleopatra*." *Studies in English Literature 1500-1900* 26 (1986): 295-308.

Shakespeare wants the audience "to weigh both the story and its acting, and to find in the case of these huge spirits the specific gravity of the stage." Antony and Cleopatra "opens by showing legendary characters claiming a resonantly theatrical 'space', one in which their actions seem both to confirm and to belie the texts of 'character' provided by others in the play, and by the familiar traditions of judgment that the play recalls." This play "closes in a similarly evocative space, in which the performed characters relinquish the discandying flesh of the stage" and "take their place among the less ephemeral monuments of art, in 'story', 'chronicle', tomb, perhaps even in dreams."

891 Wymer, Rowland. *Suicide and Despair in the Jacobean Drama.* Brighton, Sussex: Harvester, 1986. 193 pp.

There is "a tradition in which Antony and Cleopatra were regarded as *exempla* of lust and finally, for despair." But Shakespeare did not follow it. Antony and Cleopatra's "suicides are able to balance contrary kinds of positive in a precarious stasis, thanks to the varied implications of suicide even when separated from despair."

892 Bai Niu. "The Essence of Antony's Tragedy." *Wuhan daxue xuebao* [Journal of Wuhan University] 1 (1987): 100-04. In Chinese.

Antony is a tragic hero of the Hamlet type. His tragedy is partly the consequence of his character flaws, but the principal cause lies in the age he lives in, which does not permit him to combine love with reason.

893 Birringer, Johannes H. "Texts, Plays, and Instabilities." *South African Theatre Journal* 1.1 (1987): 4-16.

Birringer employs "the sexual undercurrent of Antony's death (4.15) in an examination of the theoretical underpinnings of a semiotics of theatre."

894 Boorman, Stanley C. "Antony and Cleopatra." *Human Conflict in Shakespeare.* London and New York: Routledge & Kegan Paul, 1987, pp. 235-52.

Antony and Cleopatra "remains the final point of Shakespeare's movement from 'plays of plot' to 'plays of character-in-situation', when a play based closely on the events of history has ended by rising above those events into the private and personal world of the two main characters." It shows the "unconquerable strength of the human spirit, and it is characteristic of Shakespeare that here this strength is shown to spring from human love: thus, in a strange but very true sense, *Antony and Cleopatra* is religious in the real meaning of the word, and a special manifestation of the tragic spirit."

895 Calderwood, James L. "Antony and Cleopatra." *Shakespeare and the Denial of Death*. Amherst: U of Massachusetts P, 1987, pp. 184-87.

This study suggests "how often and how variously Shakespeare dramatizes the human desire for symbolic immortality." The Clown speaks the truth: "For the biting of stage snakes is theatrically immortal in the sense of not being mortal in the least, as Cleopatra's reappearance tomorrow will prove."

896 Fox, Levi, ed. *The Shakespeare Handbook*. Boston: G. K. Hall, 1987. 264 pp.

The focus of this handbook is Shakespeare's life and times, his complete works, and the performances, songs, operas, and films they have inspired. A summary of the play can be found on pp. 142-43.

897 Gajowski, Evelyn Jacqueline. "The Art of Loving: An Inquiry into the Nature of Love in Shakespeare's Tragedies (Women: Juliet, Desdemona, Cleopatra)." *Dissertation Abstracts International* 48 (1987): 1774A (Case Western Reserve).

Cleopatra "shares with Desdemona and Juliet a depth and totality of concept of love that includes but is not confined to the sexual." Unlike the other two, Cleopatra "successfully tutors her 'husband' in love, allowing Antony's transformation from a soldier to a lover."

898 Greene, James J. "*Antony and Cleopatra*: The Birth and Death of Androgyny." *Hartford Studies in Literature* 19.2-3 (1987): 24-44.

This play "is the story of a man who attempts to redefine his own manhood, his sexuality, his humanity, and of a woman who has already defied the conventional Roman sense of the appropriate. That the attempt ends in the deaths of the two lovers does not lessen the significance or daring of that attempt."

899 Griffin, John. *Antony and Cleopatra: Advanced Teaching Pack*. English Literature 1. London: E. Arnold, 1987.

This is a portfolio with teachers' notes.

900 Hart, B. "Shakespeare and the Idea of Metamorphoses." *Dissertation Abstracts International* 48 (1987): 55C (Kent-Canterbury).

In *Antony and Cleopatra* and other plays, Shakespeare had been influenced by Ovid's conception of metamorphosis and his view of literature and society and the poet's role.

901 Hedayet, A.A.E.A. "Cleopatra in English Literature from Chaucer to Thomas May." *Index to Theses with Abstracts* 35 (1987): 43.

Antony and Cleopatra is in the tradition of the romantic and heroic visions of the story in its exemplary and ethical interpretations and in the portrayal of Cleopatra's death. One chapter deals with the significance of mythology, emblem, and pageantry in the play.

902 Hendricks-Wenck, Aileen Alana. "Sexual Politics in *Antony and Cleopatra*." *Theatre Southwest* 15.2 (May 1988): 18-22.

If the audience considers *Antony and Cleopatra* "as an example of sexual politics, then the understanding and meaning of the human action portrayed takes on a tragic significance that explains the dual nature of the main characters and theme."

903 Hillman, Richard. "Antony, Hercules, and Cleopatra: 'The Bidding of the Gods' and 'the Subtlest Maze of All." *Shakespeare Quarterly* 38 (1987): 442-51.

Shakespeare initiated the movement of the triumph and beauty as the lovers go to their doom by using "the Hercules scene in a pivotal way" and by exploiting its ambiguity. He enriched the ambiguity by inserting "Neoplatonic resonances." Antony and Cleopatra's spiritual victory over death, "sealed by Cleopatra as *Venus victrix*, uniting in herself now masculine and feminine, signals a transcendence also of moralistic eschatology." In the labyrinth of beauty, which follows that of human actions, "the contraries are even more intricately interwoven."

904 Hooks, Roberta. "Shakespeare's *Antony and Cleopatra*: Power and Submission." *American Imago* 44 (1987): 37-49.

The mother-child dilemma is the model for the unresolved tensions of adult sexuality in *Antony and Cleopatra*. Antony is plagued by conflicting forces, political and sexual compulsions, which he finds difficult to deal with. "The psychosis at the core of the play involves issues of differentiation from a maternal environment and the difficulties of maintaining an integrated, reality-oriented perspective toward the love object."

905 Jankowski, Theodora A. "'On a tribunal silver'd': Cleopatra, Elizabeth I, and the Female Body Politic." *Shakespeare Newsletter* 37 (1987): 22.

Shakespeare's image of Cleopatra "as a powerful female ruler who insists upon the wholeness of both her natural and political bodies is iconoclastic because it subverts traditional Renaissance ideologies regarding the powerlessness of women."

906 Levin, Harry. "Two Monumental Death-Scenes: *Antony and Cleopatra*, 4.15; 5.2." *Shakespeare, Text, Language, Criticism: Essays in Honour of Marvin Spevack*. Ed. Bernhard Fabian and Kurt Tetzeli von Rosador. Hildesheim: Olms, 1987, pp. 147-63.

Levin argues that "since tragedy views death as an unhappy ending—or, at any rate, a dark curtain—this is calculated to enhance our feeling for life in its more sensuous and most vital moments. Nowhere has that hedonistic awareness proclaimed itself more magnificently than in Shakespeare's *Antony and Cleopatra*."

907 Levine, Laura Ellen. "Men in Women's Clothing: Anti-Theatricality and Effeminization from 1579 to 1642 (England)." *Dissertation Abstracts International* 49 (1987): 511A (Johns Hopkins).

In *Troilus and Cressida* and *Antony and Cleopatra*, Shakespeare "suggests that anti-theatrical anxieties ultimately require theatrical expression, need to be 'acted out' or staged through others in order to be allayed."

908 Logan, Robert A. "The Sexual Attitudes of Marlowe and Shakespeare." *Hartford Studies in Literature* 19.2-3 (1987): 1-23.

This play presents "the fullest treatment of romantic sexual love and the importance of bonded love." Through their love, Antony and Cleopatra "fulfill themselves and reach self-hood, and with such energy and regal splendor that they achieve immortality in legend." The play "articulates in its portrayal of romantic love what is at the center of Shakespeare's view of human existence—namely, the need for bonding and the myth-making faculty necessary to make it possible."

909 Lombardo, Agostino. "Antonio e Cleopatra: L'Eros come arte." *L'Eros in Shakespeare*. Ed. Alessandro Serpieri and Keir Elam. Parma: Pratiche Editrice, 1988, pp. 47-62.

This play explores in aesthetic terms the nature of *eros*, accomplished through death.

910 Melltzer, Gary Stephen. "The Comic Side of the Tragic Mask: The Role of Comic Perspective in Shaping Tragic Vision." *Dissertation Abstracts International* 49 (1987): 812A (Yale).

Seneca's *Thyestes*, Shakespeare's *Antony and Cleopatra*, and Anouih's *Antigone* "all suffer psychic and spiritual disintegration which makes them susceptible to an array of techniques of comic subversion."

911 Miles, Thomas Geoffrey. "'Untir'd spirits and formal constancy': Shakespeare's Roman Plays and the Stoic Tradition." *Dissertation Abstracts International* 50 (1987): 3238A (Oxford).

See item 1145.

912 Perez Martin, Maria Jesus. "A Brief Reflection on the Apotheosis in the Final Act of Shakespeare's *Antony and Cleopatra*." *Anglo-American Studies* 7.2 (November 1987): 149-52.

Two monologues by Octavius (V.i.35-48) and Cleopatra (V.ii.76-92) show their power of language, prosody, sonority, diction, imagery, and their creation of a "pedestal and statue effect."

913 Scott, Mark W., ed. "*Antony and Cleopatra.*" *Shakespearean Criticism*. Detroit: Gale, 1987, VI, 11-240.

This volume provides a critical history of the reception of the play and extensive excerpts of criticism from the seventeenth century to the 1980s.

914 Shaheen, Naseeb. "Antony and Cleopatra." *Biblical References in Shakespeare's Tragedies*. Newark: U of Delaware P, 1987, pp. 175-86.

Shakespeare's use of the book of Revelation in this play is "outstanding." He also refers to the Apocalypse and Exodus. There are thirty-two passages in which biblical influences can be identified.

915 Singh, Jyotsna. "The Artist and His Inheritance: A Metadramatic Study of Shakespeare's *Troilus and Cressida* and *Antony and Cleopatra*." *Dissertation Abstracts International* 48 (1987): 1212A (Syracuse).

Shakespeare "is the typical Renaissance artist, transforming and improvising upon received materials such as classical texts and historical chronicles, even while acknowledging their influence." *Antony and Cleopatra* "shows the artist in the positive role of a bricoleur who transforms received models into distinctive self-representations."

916 Stockholder, Kay. "The Sweetened Imagination of *Antony and Cleopatra*." *Dream World: Lovers and Families in Shakespeare's Plays*. Toronto: U of Toronto P, 1987, pp. 148-68.

Antony's distinguishing mark is "his self-awareness." He displays "changing levels of emotional immediacy and degrees of awareness." It is "in the play's framework and structure of action that Antony confronts the unconscious dimensions of the ideas and fears that polarize the Roman martial honour and the Egyptian gratification by both of which he defines them." Such characters "yield to the force of their unacknowledged desires, as

Antony does when his sense of himself dissolves into the aura of magic with which he has surrounded both Cleopatra and Octavius."

917 Sun Jiaxiu. "Reflections on *Antony and Cleopatra*." *Xiju* [Drama: The Journal of the Central Academy of Drama] 3 (1987: 32-40; 4 (1987): 12-22. In Chinese.

Not seen.

918 Tanner, Jeri. "The Power of Names in Shakespeare's *Antony and Cleopatra*." *Names: Journal of the American Name Society* 35 (1987): 164-74.

Shakespeare "uses names to characterize, to reveal attitudes, prejudices, and superstitions, to show conflict or concord, to enhance themes, and to add humorous and serious dimensions to his dramatic narrative."

919 Tanner, Tony. "*Antony and Cleopatra*: Boundaries and Excess." *Hebrew University Studies in Literature* 15 (1987): 78-104.

The body is seen as the final boundary by the lovers who cannot be contained, even by words, and who triumph as they move to the unbounded spaces of infinity.

920 Wine, Martin L. *Antony and Cleopatra*. With an Introduction by Harold Brooks. Macmillan Master Guides. Basingstoke and London: Macmillan, 1987. 104 pp.

Not seen.

921 Astington, John H. "Shakespearian Rags." *Modern Drama* 31 (1988): 73-80.

In his *Long Day's Journey into Night*, Eugene O'Neill drew from *Antony and Cleopatra* "both the mood and the imagery of enervation, dissolution, and despair."

922 Bloom, Harold, ed. *William Shakespeare's* Antony and Cleopatra. Modern Critical Interpretations. New York: Chelsea, 1988. 182 pp.

This collection of essays reprints, in whole or in part, the following items found in this bibliography: Janet Adelman, Anne Barton, Rosalie L. Colie, Howard Felperin, John Bayley, Linda Bamber, Jonathan Dollimore, Laura Quinney.

923 Cahn, Victor L. "*Antony and Cleopatra.*" *The Heroes of Shakespeare's Tragedies.* American University Studies. Series IV: English Language and Literature 56. New York: Peter Lang, 1988, pp. 143-66.

In this play, Shakespeare "has dramatized the power of love and understanding." Antony and Cleopatra are "eminent figures trapped between public and private needs and responsibilities." Normally they would compromise, but "such moderation is impossible, particularly for Antony. A man's first duty is to his own humanity, no matter what the cost."

924 Dunn, T.A. "The Imperial Bawd." *Literature and the Art of Creation.* Ed. Robert Welch and Suheil Badi Bushrui. Gerrards Cross, Bucks.: Colin Smythe; Totowa, NJ: Barnes & Noble, 1988, pp. 26-32.

This study examines Shakespeare's treatment of the theme of love, with special focus on characterization of Cleopatra. Shakespeare "gives a realistic view of life and an adult view of love and the problems connected with sex." The play is unsatisfactory because "it is too specific, too much tied to the literal matter of the chronicles, of history." Hence it does not "move from the world of specifics into the world of myth."

925 Gallwey, Kay. "Shakespeare's Cleopatra: Strumpet or Good Angel?" *CRUX: A Journal on the Teaching of English* (South Africa) 22 (1988): 47-59.

Critics from Dowden and A.C. Bradley to T. McAlindon have held divergent opinions on Cleopatra's character. The language of the play indicates that Cleopatra is no strumpet, even though she may not be an angel either.

926 Grene, David. "Antony and Cleopatra: The Triumph of Fantasy." *The Actor in History: A Study in Shakespearean Stage Poetry.*

University Park and London: Pennsylvania State UP, 1988, pp. 13-35.

Grene's objective is "to consider the relation which Shakespeare establishes between the values of the supreme world of Elizabethan and Jacobean reality, that of the kinds and soldiers at the top of the tree, and his own domain, the poetry of the theater." Antony and Cleopatra "almost consciously seek and explore the theatrical in their situation, and theirs is, in its effect upon the audience, a most brilliant, imaginative victory over the hard core of a more conventional reality which appears to overwhelm them. Their moment of victorious defeat lives in action, but action strengthened and transformed by the magnificence of poetry."

927 Hamer, Mary. "Cleopatra: Housewife." *Textual Practice* 2 (1988): 159-79.

The variations in visual representations of Cleopatra indicate "the reinforcing and renegotiation of gender differences that took place in early modern Europe." A study of Cleopatra in art and literature to the seventeenth century suggests that, except in *Antony and Cleopatra*, she "receives translation into domesticity which closes off all ambiguity and threat."

928 Houston, John P. "Syntactical Tone in *Antony and Cleopatra*." *Shakespearean Sentences: A Study in Style and Syntax*. Baton Rouge and London: Louisiana State UP, 1988, 179-97.

This play's style "is marked by a notable use of sentence forms and grammatical devices that are associated with speech, as opposed to the written language, although some of them belong to both, an ambiguity that Shakespeare exploits in shifting tone and mood while maintaining a unified syntactic surface." In this case, Shakespeare "abandoned the density of highly developed sentences, so conspicuous somewhat earlier in his plays, for a more restrained distribution of lengthy and hypotactic structures."

929 Jankowski, Theodora Ann. "Women in Power in the Jacobean Drama: Shakespeare's *Antony and Cleopatra* and Webster's *The Duchess of Malfi*." *Dissertation Abstracts International* 49 (1988): 258A (Syracuse).

This dissertation "explores the representation of women sovereigns in *Antony and Cleopatra* and *The Duchess of Malfi* as these plays participate in the discursive construction of Renaissance woman, especially as they reveal the contradictions in the notion of a female ruler."

930 Keiko Beppu. "'O, rare for Emily': Dickinson and Antony and Cleopatra." *After a Hundred Years: Essays on Emily Dickinson*. Kyoto: Apollon-sha, 1988.

Antony and Cleopatra served as a catalyst to crystallize Dickinson's concept of love, a love "inextricably associated with death and immortality."

931 Leggatt, Alexander. "Antony and Cleopatra." *Shakespeare's Political Drama: The History Plays and the Roman Plays*. London and New York: Routledge, 1988, pp. 161-88.

Shakespeare presents characters in their doubleness, their shadow and substance; one idealizes the other. He reverses the normal order of shadow and substance: "the imagined Antony is the work of nature; it is prosaic reality that is a fantasy-world of shadows." Antony and Cleopatra see something godlike in each other, and "characters seem most vivid and powerful when they are absent, living in the imagination of those who remember them." Through their imagination, the characters "are constantly trying to create new heaven, new earth, in which Caesar and Antony are at war in the realm of the spirit and Antony and Cleopatra are avatars of Mars and Venus." There are contrasted visions of Rome and Egypt; "compressed and foreshortened, the business of history begins to look trivial, while the frivolities of Egypt, dramatized in a relaxed and detailed way, look solid and real." The playwright separates the real from the heroic Antony, when "one is seen, the other talked of." Cleopatra does the same when she wants to be recognized as the Queen of Egypt, a sly politician, who "outwits Caesar." In this play, Shakespeare "allows us glimpses of human grandeur working through the vicissitudes of time and through closely observed reality. Its method is not selection but fusion." The playwright's political thinking can be summarized thus: "The most impressive characters in Shakespeare's political world are not the winners but those who have confronted and absorbed the experience of loss, whose achievement is not to order a state but to assert themselves against inevitable ruin."

932 Levine, Laura E. "Men in Women's Clothing: Anti-Theatricality and Effeminization from 1579 to 1642." *Dissertation Abstracts International* 49 (1988): 511A (Johns Hopkins).

In *Troilus and Cressida* and *Antony and Cleopatra*, Shakespeare suggests that "anti-theatrical anxieties ultimately require theatrical expression, need to be 'acted out' or staged through others in order to be allayed."

933 Mitchell, Robin Norman. "Tragic Identity: Studies in Euripides and Shakespeare." *Dissertation Abstracts International* 49 (1988): 2211A (Brown).

Using the theories of Rene Girard on mimetic desire, Mitchell examines *Antony and Cleopatra* as a "tragedy of mimesis as Antony engages in mimetic rivalries with Cleopatra and Octavius, creating a political crisis which leads to the scapegoating of Antony."

934 Muir, Kenneth. *Antony and Cleopatra: A Critical Study*. Harmondsworth: Penguin, 1988.

Not seen.

935 Murr, Priscilla. *Shakespeare's Antony and Cleopatra: A Jungian Interpretation*. European University Studies Series 14: Anglo-Saxon Language and Literature 187. Bern, Frankfurt am Main, New York, and Paris: Peter Lang, 1988. 196 pp.

What the play has defined as "Rome" could "be understood in Jungian terms to represent persona values: work, duty, commitment to outer, social reality. In contrast the anima stands at the entrance to the unconscious and represent love, feeling values, the watery world of Cydnus. It is this feminine world of inner values which erupted into Antony's Roman world of outer, adapted values. Egypt lost."

Egypt and Cleopatra "had presented Rome with an opportunity to expand its horizons beyond the world of mechanic slaves. Unfortunately the split was too great; Antony and Cleopatra were unable to deal with their own inner problems, were unable to get their new perceptions onto solid ground." Hence, Octavius, "a representative of Rome and the persona, is a necessary consequence."

936 Quinney, Laura. "Enter a Messenger." *William Shakespeare's* Antony and Cleopatra. Ed. Harold Bloom. New York: Chelsea, 1988, pp. 151-67.

Quinney analyzes the differences in Antony's language before and after the battle of Actium: "While Antony is still a pillar of the world, his language shares in the contented dexterity of his power. But after his fall at Actium—from which point, until his death, he dominates the stage—his language suddenly comes into a range and an urgency that it had not had, at the same time that he comes into a fragility prophesied by the other characters' insistent apostrophes to him."

937 Song, Nina. "Death in the Tragedies of William Shakespeare and Eugene O'Neill." *Dissertation Abstracts International* 49 (1988): 1139A (SUNY Albany).

In *Hamlet*, *Othello*, *King Lear*, and *Antony and Cleopatra*, physical death "carries spiritual values, such as tragic perceptions, spiritual sublimation, and a sense of a new beginning and new order."

938 Thomas, Shirley Forbes. "'One that's dead is quick': A study of Counterfeit Death and Resurrection in Relation to Plot, Character, and Theme in the Plays of William Shakespeare." *Dissertation Abstracts International* 49 (1988): 1812A (Arkansas).

Thomas examines Shakespeare's "use of supposed, feigned, and staged death and resurrection in relation to overall plot structure, characterization, and theme" in *Antony and Cleopatra* and fourteen other plays.

939 Wiggins, Martin. "An Early Misinterpretation of *Antony and Cleopatra.*" *Notes and Queries* ns 35 (1988): 483-84.

The description of Caesar, Pompey and Antony in an anonymous moralistic pamphlet of 1614 about a recent murder "is clearly based on a memory of Shakespeare's treatment." There are several verbal similarities between the two.

940 Wilders, John. "*Antony and Cleopatra.*" *New Prefaces to Shakespeare*. Oxford: Blackwell, 1988, pp. 224-30.

Wilders wrote these introductions as the Literary Consultant to the BBC Television Series. For him, "the stage pictures can often sum up the meaning of the drama at a particular stage." "No situation, no relationship, in this play remains stable and fixed but is shown to be in a ceaseless state of motion, transformation and flux." Evidence of this flux can be found in "the frequent and rapid shifts of location," "the violent, sudden shifts in the moods of the characters," and the "references to melting and decomposition." The play forces the audience "continually to revise our judgements of what we see on stage." The spectators will never know whether Cleopatra's "suicide is the victory she thinks it is, or merely her last splendid delusion."

941 Wright, George T. *Shakespeare's Metrical Art*. Berkeley: U of California P, 1988. 349 pp.

In late plays from *Antony and Cleopatra* to *Cymbeline*, speech "tends to be abrupt and agitated, the rift between phrase and line a constant feature of the verse." Their style "bespeaks a distrust of sententious rhetoric, of the deceitful uses and users of language such as they all touch and turn on."

942 Ahrens, Rudiger. "The Critical Reception of Tragedies in Twentieth-Century Germany." *Shakespeare: Text, Subtext and Context*. Ed. Ronald Dotterer. Susquehanna University Studies. Cranbury, NJ: Associated University Presses, 1989, pp. 97-106.

Shakespeare's reception "has taken a variety of forms based on scientific, political, and theatrical justifications." *Antony and Cleopatra* had been banned in the 1920s "for obvious moral and ethnic reasons."

943 Canfield, J. Douglas. "*Antony and Cleopatra.*" *Word as Bond in English Literature from the Middle Ages to the Restoration.* Philadelphia: U of Pennsylvania P, 1989, 291-300.

The world in this play is "presided over by the fickle goddess Fortuna and including mobs and inconstant rulers." The action of the play "is a visual metaphor for inconstancy" because "the extraordinarily proliferated scenes change with dizzying speed." Its poetry "fills the vacancy of desire and gives us the mythic mermaids of Presence that enable us to endure the inconstancy of word and world around us. The Logos manifests itself as simply the Word of the poet." In the whole play, Shakespeare "undercuts Antony and Cleopatra's heioic diction, revealing it to be the rhetoric of desire, an attempt to acquire transcendence through language."

944 Conway, Daniel J. "Erotic Arguments: Rhetoric and Sexuality in Seventeenth Century English Stage Adaptations of Plutarch." *Dissertation Abstracts International* 50 (1989): 1139A (Minnesota).

Antony and Cleopatra is "a play about sexuality that argues, on both sides of the question, the fundamental heroism of its central characters."

945 Coppedge, Walter R. "The Joy of the Worm: Dying in *Antony and Cleopatra.*" *Renaissance Papers 1988* . Ed. Dale B.J. Randall and Joseph A. Porter. Durham: Southern Renaissance Conference, 1988, pp. 41-50.

Cleopatra gives up the sphere of "sublunary activity to align herself with a higher principle in her spiritual journey." She, "radiant with love, firm in her resolve, takes the joy of the worm and becomes a dish for the gods."

946 Entry deleted.

947 Dutton, Richard. *William Shakespeare: A Literary Life.* Macmillan Literary Lives. London: Macmillan, 1989.

Dutton finds it "difficult to isolate the pressure that prompted Shakespeare back into his most sustained contemplation of classical history around this time." *Antony and Cleopatra* "shares with *King Lear* and *Macbeth* (and most of the late tragi-comedies) a fascination with imperial destinies, albeit not those of Britain; human weakness, folly and vice all contribute, by some perverse miracle, to the possibility of a more secure and splendid future."

948 Hall, Michael. "The Gap in Nature: *Antony and Cleopatra*." *The Structure of Love: Representational Patterns and Shakespeare's Love Tragedies*. Charlottesville: UP of Virginia, 1989, pp. 140-65.

"By using most of the large variety of traditional views of the historical Antony and Cleopatra but refusing to give priority to any one, or even to any cohesive combination," Hall argues, "Shakespeare produces a play that forces us to accept the kind of divided unity that destroys Troilus's universe: the idea that a relationship can be its most decadent at the same time that it is most nearly ideal." For Antony, "as finally for us, the movement toward the final ecstatic union is too compelling to be resisted. But *Antony and Cleopatra* makes us understand that such a union can only be purchased at a terrible price."

949 Honigmann, E.A.J. "Past, Present and Future in *Macbeth* and *Antony and Cleopatra*." *Myriad-minded Shakespeare: Essays, Chiefly on the Tragedies and Problem Comedies*. London: Macmillan, 1989, pp. 93-111.

In Antony and Cleopatra's love-relationship, "as in the general historical situation, the past is massively and disquietingly present, implicitly questioning the values of the here and new." The characters brood on the instability of the present, and "foreknowing the future" is important in differentiating between Antony and Cleopatra. *Julius Caesar* may be the model for *Antony and Cleopatra*.

950 Jankowski, Theodora A. "'As I Am Egypt's Queen': Cleopatra, Elizabeth I, and the Female Body Politic." *Assays: Critical Approaches to Medieval and Renaissance Texts* 5 (1989): 91-110.

Cleopatra represents an allegory of the problems Elizabeth I faced in exercising power in a patriarchal England. The two queens secured their thrones by combining their natural and political bodies. Elizabeth defines herself as a virgin and becomes mistress to her subjects; Cleopatra sleeps with her enemies and bears their children. Hence *Antony and Cleopatra* is not about a voluptuous prostitute, but rather a "text of female political theory."

951 Larson, Marilyn. "The Fallen World of Shakespeare's *Antony and Cleopatra.*" *Encyclia: The Journal of Utah Academy of Sciences, Arts, and Letters* 66 (1989): 79-86.

Shakespeare's use of the "snake-in-a-basket device" is, "by its echoes of serpents and fig leaves, an echo of Eden," and is "the most accessible symbol Shakespeare has for telling his audience of a fallen world."

952 Loomba, Ania. *Gender, Race, Renaissance Drama.* Manchester: Manchester UP, 1989. 178 pp.

Loomba's objective is "to insert the dimension of gender more fully into such proto-Brechtian multiplicity and montage, and to suggest that the epic structure is at least partly derived from and closely related to the drama's interrogation of gender roles and patriarchal authority." She focuses on the "non-linear, non-climatic, episodic structure and montage" which reveals "the *construction* of identity and social relations."

"The geographical turbulence of the first three acts involves a redefinition of femininity and of female space: patriarchal Rome contests Egyptian Cleopatra for her geographical and sexual territory. Into the contest is woven the theme of imperial domination. Dominant notions about female identity, gender relations and imperial power are unsettled through the disorderly non-European woman."

As "foul Egyptian," Cleopatra "will always stand outside Roman society: Antony can never fully trust her and will marry safe and obedient women like Octavia to ensure his stability within that society." Cleopatra's sex "renders her political unacceptable, her political status problematises her femininity, and her racial otherness troubles, doubly, both power and sexuality." "The narrative of masculinity and imperialism regains control but Cleopatra's final performance, which certainly exposes her own vulnerability, not only cheats Caesar but denies any final and authoritative closure."

953 Morse, David. *England's Time of Crisis: From Shakespeare to Milton: A Cultural History*. London: Macmillan, 1989. 391 pp.

This play reflects the contemporary feeling that "the center as a locus of power, authority and truth is progressively demystified." It "so insistently reiterates the Roman perspective and yet manages to contradict it quite comprehensively." Shakespeare's audiences "would have caught more than a glancing allusion to the tragic fate of the Earl of Essex, executed for treason in 1601."

954 Peirce, Carol. "'One other gaudy night': Lawrence Durrell's Elizabethan *Quartet*." *Into the Labyrinth: Essays on the Art of Laurence Durrell*. Ed. Frank L. Kersnowski. Ann Arbor: UMI Research P, 1989, pp. 101-15.

Defining Durrell's style and vocabulary as "Elizabethan"–that is, "archaic as well as current, poetic as well as prosaic"–Peirce offers numerous parallels between the *Quartet* and Shakespeare's *Antony and Cleopatra*. She shows how Durrell uses Shakespeare's play to color his characters.

955 Reynolds, Kelly. "Imaginary Forces: Reading and Performance in *Antony and Cleopatra* (Shakespeare)." *Dissertation Abstracts International* 51 (1989): 1241A (South Florida).

Reynolds opposes the tradition of explicating texts-as-text and stresses how "every signifier in a play is a call to action."

956 Rowse, A.L. *Discovering Shakespeare*. London: Weidenfeld and Nicolson, 1989. 177 pp.

This play is "a celebration of a world-famous love; yet there is something curiously ambivalent about it, something nostalgic, not without a suggestion of disillusion—no illusion anyway."

957 Ryan, Rory. *Notes on Antony and Cleopatra: Study Guides for Standard 10*. Achiever Series. Pretoria: Via Afrika Ltd.; Hodder & Stoughton Educational, 1989. 35 pp.

This is a study guide for students.

958 Singh, Jyotsna. "Renaissance Antitheatricality, Antifeminism, and Shakespeare's *Antony and Cleopatra*." *Renaissance Drama* 20 (1989): 99-121.

"This ideology of exclusion through which the Romans perceive the power relations—and gender relations—of their world is repeatedly dismantled by Cleopatra as she represents, and in the scene of cross-dressing literally reconstitutes, the Roman divisions between the masculine and the feminine." "Read in relationship to the anti-theatrical and anti-feminist tracts," *Antony and Cleopatra* "seems both to reproduce and to contest their conception of a social order in which women and actors are seen as duplicitously subverting the 'natural' boundaries of social and sexual difference." "Human identity, as Cleopatra dramatises it, is multiple, varied, and protean, and the playwright affords her many occasions to exult in her playful disruptions of the Roman gender polarities. Thus both dramatic text and public debates, when read in relationship to each other, present a complex picture of Renaissance society caught between the pressures of mobility and a desire for stasis."

959 Sprengnether, Madelon. "The Boy Actor and Femininity in *Antony and Cleopatra*." *Shakespeare's Personality*. Ed. Norman Holland, Sidney Homan, and Bernard J. Paris. Berkeley: U of California P, 1989, pp. 191-205.

A boy actor playing Cleopatra is central to Shakespeare's equivocal representation of femininity; it illuminates his portrayal of gender conflict and reveals something of his attitude toward women. Shakespeare's plays "satisfy the radical impulse to subvert established structures of authority, along with a certain masculine need to incorporate aspects of femininity, yet they do not propose any serious alternative to the patriarchal understanding of woman as 'other'." If there is any glimpse of an alternative, it is in "the portrayal of Cleopatra, in its temporary suspension of the question of gender and the creative ambiguity that entails."

960 Suzuki, Mihoko. "Epilogue: *Antony and Cleopatra.*" *Metamorphoses of Helen: Authority, Difference, and the Epic.* Ithaca: Cornell UP, 1989, pp. 258-63.

Shakespeare "celebrates his Cleopatra from an Egyptian perspective." Cleopatra and Helen in Egypt "function as figures of mutability and difference—the sea god Proteus guards Helen in Egypt, and Cleopatra's 'infinite variety' identifies her with the overflowing Nile." In each of these cases, "mutability does not preclude a racial constancy: Helen's loyalty to Menelaus and Cleopatra's to Antony."

961 Thomas, Vivian. "Realities and Imaginings in *Antony and Cleopatra.*" *Shakespeare's Roman Worlds*. London: Routledge, 1989, pp. 93-153.

In an analysis of Shakespeare's departures from his sources, Thomas argues that Shakespeare "transformed" Antony into a much more attractive" and diminished the significance of Octavia's relationship with Antony. Octavius has "none of the attractive features delineated by Plutarch." The playwright "accentuates Cleopatra's charm, vivacity and consciousness" and turns Enobarbus into a major character. This play "disconcerts because it explores the guile and folly of reality along with the attainment of immortality and the *process* of the creation of myth."

962 Toliver, Harold. "Cleopatra's Phantom Marriage." *Transported Styles in Shakespeare and Milton*. University Park: Pennsylvania State UP, 1989, pp. 65-86.

"In their retrospective moments," Toliver argues, "plays have ample time to remember the presences we have just witnessed, which gives them the chance—if they wish to go a little past the catastrophe itself—to emphasize both loss and reconstruction." Primarily because of Cleopatra, this play "is remarkable for its prolonged parting and recasting. Antony's early removal gives the off-going a twofold rhythm—first his departure, recollected by Cleopatra, and then hers, as eventually recollected by Plutarch and Shakespeare. After such leave-takings, one version of their story will beget another and then another, each rendering some reasonable facsimile that varies from the postures of a fizgig to stately poses."

963 Wells, Charles. *The Northern Star: Shakespeare and the Theme of Constancy.* Upton upon Severn: Blackthorn P, 1989. 222 pp.

Wells argues that "the search for 'constants' in a world of mutability is a thread that runs through all the plays and poems." By writing this play, Shakespeare "seems to have burst out from the dark tunnel of *Othello*, *Lear*, and *Macbeth* into a new world of vivid colour." Here he "sees a superior reality latent within the moment as though frozen there and waiting to be dissolved out in the heat of actualisation." The two lovers "seek to escape from the painful isolation of their own separate subjectivity by dissolving into the present moment and into the higher reality of each other."

964 Whittier, Gayle. "The Sublime Androgyne: Motif Three Shakespearean Works." *Journal of Medieval and Renaissance Studies* 19 (1989): 185-210.

In *Sonnet* 20, *Romeo and Juliet*, and *Antony and Cleopatra*, androgyny centers not on transvestism but on the hermaphrodite "as a symbol of marriage, but marriage as itself a symbol of the necessary concord of opposite on which the world depends and individual welfare also."

965 Aubrey, Bryan. "Quantum Physics and the Experience of Shakespeare." *Aligarh Critical Miscellany* 3 (1990): 111-31.

Expanding Norman Rabkin's thesis in his *Shakespeare and the Problem of Meaning*, Aubrey argues that unified field theories of quantum physics can, by analogy, assist the reader in understanding the experience that Shakespeare has provided by the end of plays like *King Lear*, *Antony and Cleopatra*, and *Hamlet*.

966 Bennett, Paula. "'The Orient Is in the West': Emily Dickinson's Reading of *Anthony and Cleopatra*." *Re-Visions of Shakespeare: On the Responses of Dickinson, Woolf, Rich, H. D., George Eliot, and Others*. Ed. Marianne Novy and Carol Thomas Neely. Urbana: U of Illinois P, 1990, pp. 108-22.

In her analysis of Emily Dickinson's use of *Antony and Cleopatra* and its influence on her Oriental imagery, Bennett argues that in this play Dickinson "found the justification and validation for the vision of romantic love and poetic imagination that shaped her poetry and her life."

967 Bloom, Harold, ed. *Cleopatra*. Major Literary Characters. New York and Philadelphia: Chelsea House, 1990. 269 pp.

This selection of criticism about the character of Cleopatra in Shakespeare, Dryden and Bernard Shaw reprints, in whole or in part, selections from H. Goddard, F. Dickey, J. Bayley, I. Dash, J. Leeds Barroll, A. Leggatt, and L.J. Mills, M. Williamson.

968 Carducci, Jane S. "Antony as Roman Soldier in Shakespeare's *Antony and Cleopatra:* 'Under the service of a child'." *Language and Literature* 15 (1990): 79-107.

Antony does not become effeminized or androgynous, nor does he develop a balanced disposition. He exhibits childish behavior when he indulges in dishonesty, evasiveness, histrionics, self-pity, tantrums and irresponsibility; this behavior "denies him a balanced, and finally admirable humanity."

969 Charnes, Linda Anne. "'So Unsecret to Ourselves': Notorious Identity in Shakespeare's *King Richard III*, *Troilus and Cressida*, and *Antony and Cleopatra* (Legendary Characters)." *Dissertation Abstracts International* 52 (1990): 1336A (California-Berkeley).

This dissertation "is about Shakespearean figures who are trapped by their own notorious intertextual identities." Charnes elaborates the way *Antony and Cleopatra* "stages a battle between the conflicting representational modes of narrative and spectacle, and the different kinds of politics and subjects—discursive and histrionic—they produce."

970 Cheadle, Brian. "'His Legs Bestrid the Ocean' as a 'Form of Life'." James Redmond, ed. *Drama and Philosophy*. Themes in Drama 12. Cambridge: Cambridge UP, 1990, pp. 87-106.

In this play Shakespeare draws on his earlier precedents in two ways: he "brings Antony (like Troilus, Othello, and Hamlet) to the experience of a world-dissolving scepticism after Cleopatra has deserted him," and he confronts "Cleopatra (like Lear) with the problem of continuing in a meaningful way after the death of the one whose love has been all." Cleopatra's speech (5.2.82ff.) is "pivotal in the dramatic structure," and is "as much forward-looking as retrospective in presenting Cleopatra's attempt to re-establish grounds for action after Antony's death." Cheadle tries "to place Antony's experience of dissolution and recovery in relation to Wittgenstein's arguments concerning certainty and doubt in his late work *On Certainty*;" then he introduces Wittgenstein's notion of "forms of life" which he then brings to bear on Cleopatra's "His legs bestrid the ocean" speech.

971 Cunningham, John E. "*Antony and Cleopatra*: The World Well Lost." Linda Cookson and Bryan Loughrey, eds. *Critical Essays on Antony and Cleopatra*. Longman Literature Guides. Harlow, Essex: Longman, 1990, pp. 105-15.

Antony "did indeed lose his world, but whether well or ill, whether for love or folly, Shakespeare does not tell us: he leaves such certainties for lesser men like Dryden."

972 Davis, Timothy C. "Shakespeare's *Antony and Cleopatra*." *Explicator* 48 (Spring 1990): 176-78.

On the surface, Antony's crocodile speech in 2.7.42-51 "mocks Lepidus, but within this jest lurk a cutting criticism of Caesar and a clue to interpreting Caesar's paraded love for Octavia."

973 Dollimore, Jonathan. "Shakespeare, Cultural Materialism, Feminism and Marxist Humanism." *New Literary History* 21 (1990): 471-93.

This is a reiteration of the author's argument in *Radical Tragedy* that "sexual desire is not that which transcends politics and power, but the vehicle of politics and power." Antony's "masculinity and sexuality are informed by the contradictions of the very history which is rendering him obsolete."

974 Ellis, Mark Spencer. "A Cloud That's Dragonish." Linda Cookson and Bryan Loughrey, eds. *Critical Essays on Antony and Cleopatra*. Longman Literature Guides. Harlow, Essex: Longman, 1990, pp. 93-104.

One of the themes of this play is that "the real 'cloud that's dragonish' is the crippling acceptance of the arbitrary and the contingent as if they were inevitable and eternal, a final clinging to empty terms."

975 Farley-Hills, David. "King James and Barnes's *Devil's Charter*." *Notes and Queries* ns 37 (1990): 205-06.

In his Act IV, scene v, Barnes plagiarizes an extensive excerpt from Shakespeare's play.

976 Farr, Judith. "Emily Dickinson's 'Engulfing' Play: *Antony and Cleopatra*." *Tulsa Studies in Women's Literature* 9 (1990): 231-50.

Farr proposes that Dickinson's liking for Antony and Cleopatra resulted from "the voluptuousness as well as the austerity of her imagination" in examining her use of metaphors and symbolism from the play. She argues that Dickinson used the Shakespeare play in her writings "as an emblem for the domination of one person by another; for the conflict between honor and duty on one hand and pleasure and charm on the other." Dickinson treated the play as "an allegory of all that was Roman, or Puritan, in herself and all that attracted her in what she thought Egyptian scintillation."

977 Fawkner, H.W. *Shakespeare's Hyperontology: Antony and Cleopatra*. Rutherford, NJ: Fairleigh Dickinson UP, 1990. 199 pp.

Fawkner suggests that *Antony and Cleopatra* "traces a crucial (non)structure, that this (non)structure is hyperontological, and that the hyperontological trace engages the polar opposites 'following' and 'leaving'."

978 Fawkner, H.W. "The Concept of Taste in the Post-modernist Era." *Criticism in the Twilight Zone: Postmodern Perspectives on Literature*. Ed. Danuta Zedworna-Fjellestad and Lennart Bjork. Stockholm: Almqvist & Wiksell, 1990, pp. 101-12.

In the context of current theoretical debates, Fawkner uses this play "as a work that will exemplify theory, provide an example." In this way, "inside the 'concrete' example, (*Antony and Cleopatra*, Shakespeare) the 'abstract' (theory, law, conceptuality, thought paradigm) is already opening up. The problematic can be formulated in post-structuralist terms: Can we separate the inside from the outside? Can we hold apart example and theory?"

This play, "as the dramatic performance of its own rule and essence, seems to me to be a peculiarly interesting work—a peculiarly interesting example—in this theoretical context, since what it stages, in the innermost furnace of its imaginative thinking, is not only exemplariness, but also this very difference between following and imitation."

979 Ferreira-Ross, Jeanette. "A Comparison between Two Tragedies: Shakespeare's *Antony and Cleopatra* and Racine's *Berenice*." *French Studies in Southern Africa* 19 (1990): 11-27.

The main conflict in the two plays arises from "externalization of deep-seated psychic processes." Their imagery stresses the dichotomy of metaphoric space, and death is praised as symbol of intimacy.

980 Fox, Jan. "*Antony and Cleopatra*: 'Something rich and strange . . .'." *Viewpoints on Shakespeare*. Ed. Brian McFarlane. Melbourne: Longman Cheshire, 1990, pp. 210-20.

Not seen.

981 Gardiner, Alan. "Leadership in *Antony and Cleopatra*." *Critical Essays on Antony and Cleopatra*. Ed. Linda Cookson and Bryan Loughrey. Longman Literature Guides. Harlow, Essex: Longman, 1990, pp. 18-27.

Shakespeare is interested "in the forces that drive people to seek power, the ways in which power changes hands and the nature of the psychological burden that those in positions of authority must carry." This is how he approaches Antony, Caesar and Pompey in *Antony and Cleopatra*: "the triple pillars of the world can be touchy, ill-tempered and hysterical, and are seen shedding tears and getting drunk." Antony "loses in the struggle between the triumvirs because Caesar's character is ideally suited to the world of Roman politics while his is not."

982 Gearin-Tosh, Michael. "Love and *Antony and Cleopatra*." *Critical Essays on Antony and Cleopatra*. Ed. Linda Cookson and Bryan Loughrey. Longman Literature Guides. Harlow, Essex: Longman, 1990, pp. 53-60.

This play ends "with a warm if costly and anarchic triumph of love, of life so enriched by love that death is 'as a lover's pinch'."

983 Heinemann, Margot. "'Drama for Cannibals?' Notes on Brecht and Shakespearean Characterization." *Shakespeare Jahrbuch* (Weimar) 126 (1990): 135-39.

According to this Brechtian reading, Antony and Cleopatra's "relationship cannot be romanticised. Their self-fashioned identities as godlike lovers and rulers, identities always shown as fragile, in face of military and political catastrophe are seen painfully to fall apart and dissolve, and the language enacts this disintegration." The play "is not just about these two but also about the splitting of an empire and the disintegration of a world, with the dissolution of the old republican Rome into military rat race, hard-faced ambition, ruthless scheming, destructive warlordism."

984 Holderness, Graham. "'Some squeaking Cleopatra': Theatricality in *Antony and Cleopatra*." *Critical Essays on Antony and*

Cleopatra. Ed. Linda Cookson and Bryan Loughrey. Longman Literature Guides. Harlow, Essex: Longman, 1990, pp. 42-52.

In 5.2.207-21, Cleopatra's self-dramatising vision indicates that "both her greatness and her sexuality will be negated, as she is imitated on stage by common player in the 'squeaking' voicc of a mere boy."

985 Hollindale, Peter. "Music Under the Earth: The Suicide Marriage in Antony and Cleopatra." *Critical Essays on Antony and Cleopatra.* Ed. Linda Cookson and Bryan Loughrey. Longman Literature Guides. Harlow, Essex: Longman, 1990, pp. 28-41.

The "vision of reunion" in this play "is a part of a complex pattern of associations which cumulatively reinforces its power, including certain ambiguities of vocabulary and dramatic effect which enable the drama to take on its unique transformative quality."

986 Hughes-Hallett, Lucy. *Cleopatra: Histories, Dreams and Distortions.* New York: Harper and Row, 1990. 338 pp.

This book is about the "dream-Cleopatras, and about the reasons why they took their particular and diverse forms." In Shakespeare, the story "becomes an infinitely subtler, less censorious thing than Roman propaganda and prejudice had made it, but it is full of echoes of the ancient themes." "In demonstrating the deathliness of excessive passionate love Shakespeare makes clear that he considers such love, thrilling and grand though it may, to be inimical to life."

987 Kinney, Clare. "The Queen's Two Bodies and the Divided Emperor: Some Problems of Identity in *Antony and Cleopatra.*" *The Renaissance Englishwoman in Print: Counterbalancing the Canon.* Ed. Anne M. Haselkorn and Betty S. Travitsky. Amherst: U of Massachusetts P, 1990, pp. 177-86.

Kinney argues that "the equation of the woman so completely with her state conflates the monarch's 'two bodies' and breaks down, or rather denies, the barrier between her public and private selves." Cleopatra's life "encompassed Egypt, all possible versions of womankind, and the male principle too; the

Roman rulers can only 'become' Rome in their absence, self-suppression, or self-diminishment." Cleopatra "is not so much subordinating herself to Roman value systems as adding a couple of new 'beginnings' to her play of identity."

988 Laub, Martin. "Love's Violence in Shakespeare." *Dissertation Abstracts International* 50 (1990): 2065A (Loyola-Chicago).

In *Measure for Measure*, *Othello*, and *Antony and Cleopatra*, Shakespeare "offers two opposing view of love: one which sees it as spiritual and elevating and another which sees it as impetuous and self-deluding."

989 MacKenzie, Clayton G. "*Antony and Cleopatra*: A Mythological Perspective." *Orbis Litterarum: International Review of Literary Studies* 45 (1990): 309-29.

Shakespeare manipulates mythological figures in this play to suggest "a movement away from a view of a world structured purely in terms of traditional Classical mythology." Antony and Cleopatra's "love myth emerges to challenge the Roman military ethos," and it is clear "in its emphasis on the worth of the human bond and interpersonal obligations."

990 Makaryk, Irena Rima. "'Let's make the best of it': The Late Tragedies of Shakespeare." *Ukrainska Shakespiriiana na Zakhodi/Ukrainian Shakespeariana in the West*. Vol. 2. Edmonton, Canada: Slaverta, 1990, II, 27-39.

The uneasiness many scholars feel about *Antony and Cleopatra*, *Coriolanus* and *Timon of Athens* arises from Shakespeare's use of comic structures and strategies that result in the audience siding with society against the hero.

991 Mallery, Mary Aileen. "The Changing Face of Fortune in Six English Versions of the Tragedy of Antony and Cleopatra (Shakespeare, Dryden, Hobbes)." *Dissertation Abstracts International* 51 (1990): 885A (CUNY).

This study "traces the development and changes in the depiction of the goddess Fortune" in *Antony and Cleopatra* and other plays.

992 Mooney, Michael E. "Directing Sympathy in *Antony and Cleopatra.*" *Shakespeare's Dramatic Transactions.* Durham and London: Duke UP, 1990, pp. 170-91.

Mooney argues that "the experience of a play is circumscribed by the creation and the dissolution of the illusion and that the audience, the playwright, and the players must conspire to create the world of the play." During a performance, the ambivalent or conflicting impressions disappear. Antony lost all for love. He "is a bungler, but he is also one of the most 'remarkable' men 'Beneath the visiting moon'." Cleopatra may be "riggish" and "cunning past man's thought," but she is also "a lass unparallel'd." "The confluence, and not the multiplicity, of perspectives channels response to *Antony and Cleopatra*, and it is time to acknowledge that while Shakespeare may have built ambiguities into the play, he has also woven into it means to guide us."

993 Moseley, Charles. "Speaking Pictures: Visual Symbol in *Antony and Cleopatra.*" *Critical Essays on Antony and Cleopatra.* Ed. Linda Cookson and Bryan Loughrey. Longman Literature Guides. Harlow, Essex: Longman, 1990, pp. 84-91.

Antony's "being hoisted aloft, and Cleopatra's immortal longings, suggest they have found a paradoxical wisdom that is no plant that grows on mortal soil."

994 Mullini, Roberta. "'Fatale monstrum': Note sul fascino di Cleopatra." *Antony and Cleopatra dal test alla scena.* Ed. Mariangela Tempera. Bologna: Cooperative Libraria Universitaria Editrice, 1990, pp. 81-87.

Mullini discusses the Cleopatra myth.

995 Reynolds, Kelly. "Imaginary Forces: Reading and Performance in *Antony and Cleopatra.*" *Dissertation Abstracts International* 51 (1990): 1241A (South Florida).

Reynolds explicates "the text-as-action" by combining post-structuralism and performance criticism, and she concludes that "reading for performance values" forms a "vital adjunct in the pedagogy of English Studies."

996 Reynolds, Peter. "The Divided Self: The Public and Private Lives of Antony and Cleopatra." *Critical Essays on Antony and Cleopatra.* Ed. Linda Cookson and Bryan Loughrey. Longman Literature Guides. Harlow, Essex: Longman, 1990, pp. 72-83.

This is a discussion of the conflict between public and private lives in the portrayal of Pompey, Octavius Caesar, Antony, and Cleopatra. Shakespeare "recognised the vital importance to political leaders of being able to present and sustain a positive, appropriate, and preferably charismatic public presence," but he also "explores the difficulty of sustaining such an image, for the lives of Antony and Cleopatra are shown as a constant struggle between the conflicting demands of their public and private lives."

997 Riemer, Seth Daniel. *National Biases in French and English Drama.* Garland Studies in Comparative Literature. New York and London: Garland, 1990. 172 pp.

Their cultural context produces national biases in *Antony and Cleopatra* and Pierre Corneille's *Cinna*: "Corneille flatly rejects moral legitimacy of a world order based on the notion of shared responsibility or common understanding, while Shakespeare presents his inquiry in a socially-affirmative way." *Antony and Cleopatra* stresses "the power of moral conventions to curb the impulses of man's private will and heighten his sense of responsibility."

998 Royle, Nicholas. "Some Thoughts on *Antony and Cleopatra* by Moonlight." *Telepathy and Literature: Essays on the Reading Mind.* Oxford: Blackwell, 1990, pp. 142-59.

This play is full of "the concatenation of the foreseeing of 'death,' reading the future, prophecy, the text of telepathy." It is "a telepathic vision." "For there are all kinds of telepathic threads, of only those which ensnare history and prophecy, which entangle the lunatic death-drive of an Enobarbus, or weave the shirt of Nessus for an Antony." Antony and Cleopatra is "a war poem not only because it concerns wars in and of the Roman

Empire, nor yet because it dramatizes that other war, the undecidedly 'tragic' and erotic one between Antony and Cleopatra."

999 Sacerdoti, Gilberto. *Nuovo cielo, nuova terra: La riverlazione Copernicana di Antonio e Cleopatra di Shakespeare*. Bologna: Il Mulino, 1990.

This is a reading of *Antony and Cleopatra* in the context of the neoplatonic-hermetic-cabalistic tradition, mediated in England by Giordano Bruno. He explains the play as a celebration of the union of the New Heaven and New Earth, representing the new universal harmony embodied in the Copernican universe.

1000 Singh, Jyotsna. "Renaissance Antitheatricality, Antifeminism, and Shakespeare's *Antony and Cleopatra*." *Renaissance Drama* (Northwestern University) NS 20 (1990): 99-121.

Singh elaborates the link between Cleopatra's histrionics and the blurring of gender boundaries to the analysis of women and theatre in antifeminist and antitheatrical tracts of the Renaissance. *Antony and Cleopatra* "seems both to reproduce and to contest their conception of a social order in which women and actors are seen as duplicitously subverting the 'natural' boundaries of social and sexual discourse."

1001 Smidt, Kristian. "I' the East My Pleasure Lies." *Unconformities in Shakespeare's Tragedies*. New York: St. Martin's P, 1990, pp. 163-79.

This play "has a poetic splendour, a grandeur of historical and geographical perspective, and a magnificence in its conception of characters which give it a place apart in Shakespearean canon." The play's ambiguities "may be seen chiefly as the result of Shakespeare's effort to present them [characters] as complex." Antony and Cleopatra are the ones "in whom different but equally strong and equally genuine impulses are in conflict."

1002 Tempera, Mariangela. "Narrazione e descrizione in *Antony and Cleopatra*." *Antony and Cleopatra dal test alla scena*. Ed.

Mariangela Tempera. Bologna: Cooperative Libraria Universitaria Editrice, 1990, pp. 89-107.

This is a study of Shakespeare's handling of descriptions and his use of reticence as narrative method in *Antony and Cleopatra.*

1003 Tilak, Raghukul, ed. *Antony and Cleopatra.* Rajhans English Literature Series. 3rd. ed. Meerut, India: Rajhans Prakashan Mandir, 1990, pp. 1-81, 268-396.

This edition gives an outline of Shakespeare's life and work, a summary of the play, and a discussion of thematic concerns. It is intended for college students in India.

1004 Tomlinson, Maggie. "Antony and Cleopatra: Making Defect Perfection." *Viewpoints on Shakespeare.* Ed. Brian McFarlane. Melbourne: Longman Cheshire, 1990, pp. 180-91.

Not seen.

1005 Walker, Steven F. "Les mythes dans la tragedie: Nouvell perspectives jungiennes." *Toward a Theory of Comparative Literature.* Ed. Mario J. Valdes. Vol. 3. New York and Bern: Lang, 1990, pp. 87-96.

Jung's theory involving identification with an archetype can be used to examine the Aristotelian concept of hamartia and its relationship to the tragic hero in *Antony and Cleopatra.*

1006 Watts, Cedric. "Antony and Cleopatra: The Moral and the Ontological." *Critical Essays on Antony and Cleopatra.* Ed. Linda Cookson and Bryan Loughrey. Longman Literature Guides. Harlow, Essex: Longman, 1990, pp. 61-71.

Watts argues that "throughout *Antony and Cleopatra* Shakespeare has set up a variety of orthodox ethical tests around the two central figures." This play "is largely about the sense that each of us holds more potential life than circumstances allow us to actualise."

1007 Barroll, J. Leeds. *Politics, Plague, and Shakespeare's Theater. The Stuart Years*. Ithaca and London: Cornell UP, 1991. 249 pp.

Barroll reiterates here "the possibility that *King Lear, Antony and Cleopatra*, and *Macbeth* may all have first appeared, not only in the same year, but even in the same two-month holiday season at court, December-February 1606-7."

1008 Blythe, David-Everett. "Shakespeare's *Antony and Cleopatra*." *Explicator* 49 (Winter 1991): 77-79.

In 3.7.7-9, the figure "stems from a common liability of horses: stallions with riders ('The horse') will try to 'serve' mounted mares. Female horses may thus 'bear' (uphold) 'A Soldier and his horse,' for in close proximity, ridden, ungelded males ordinarily attempt to mount ridden mares. In this way is 'The horse' 'lost' (distracted) as mares support their riders, their mounters, and their mounters' riders, in a gross depiction that Enobarbus dare not express directly to the queen."

1009 Brown, John Russell, ed. *Shakespeare, Antony and Cleopatra: A Casebook*. Rev. ed. Casebook Series. London: Macmillan, 1991. 214 pp.

Brown reprints brief excerpts from criticism before 1900; reviews and accounts of performances; excerpts from A.C. Bradley, H. Granville-Barker, J.M. Murry, M. Charney, L.C. Knights, H.A. Mason, M. Long, L. Tennenhouse, K. Stockholder; and a revised excerpt from F.M. Dickey.

1010 Bushman, Mary Ann. "Representing Cleopatra." *In Another Country: Feminist Perspectives on Renaissance Drama*. Ed. Dorothea Kehler and Susan Baker. Metuchen, NJ: Scarecrow, 1991, pp. 36-49.

"Deprived of a voice and objectified by the masculine gaze," Bushman argues, "the female character in tragedy recedes into the blanks of failed speech." Cleopatra "seems one of the few characters in Shakespeare's plays to elude this silence. Using the actor as subject to authorize her control, she reveals a social model of selfhood that resists completion, that refuses to defer identity to a more 'authentic' private self." Shakespeare's play "revises the rhetoric of representing self-consciousness and turns it to different functions for this female character."

1011 Cahn, Victor L. *Shakespeare the Playwright: A Companion to the Complete Tragedies, Histories, Comedies, and Romances.* Westport, CT: Greenwood P, 1991. 888 pp.

Cahn finds it hard to assess this play as a tragedy. For him, "it has no pervasive evil nor are the characters' emotions tragically intense." At the end, he does "not feel the world redeemed or a society purified. Instead we see a glorious, if turbulent, romance that burgeons amid circumstances that prohibit its fulfillment, and from the insoluble predicament emerges a sense of loss." This feeling of loss, "coupled with the characters' stature and the political consequences of their lives, invests the play with tragic grandeur."

1012 Cartwright, Kent. "The Audience in and out of *Antony and Cleopatra*." *Shakespearean Tragedy and Its Double: The Rhythms of Audience Response.* University Park: Pennsylvania State UP, 1991, pp. 227-70.

Cartwright argues that "spectatorship, reciprocally with acting, stands as a dominant activity in *Antony and Cleopatra*, so much as to constitute the paradigm of its tragic action." This play "creates a domain of action in the positionings of characters toward each other—their emotional distances, their maneuverings for psychological advantage—beyond the Aristotelian rise and fall of their fortunes. They play for legendry as much as for victory." This drama "engages audiences in the 'double' of that action, characterized by the spectator's heightened self-awareness of 'meaning' as contingent upon distance. The spectatorial paradigm does not resolve the uncertainties of *Antony and Cleopatra*; rather, it unveils, with criticism and delight, the mechanics by which characters make meaning—and playgoers too."

1013 Cunico, Juliette Marie. "Audience Attitudes toward Suicide in Shakespeare's Tragedies (Romeo and Juliet, Othello, Julius Caesar, Antony and Cleopatra)." *Dissertation Abstracts International* 52 (1991):2560A (New Mexico).

Cunico explains "the audience's perceptions of the effects of Shakespeare's suicides and demonstrates how their beneficial results caused the audience to weigh, but finally to approve of and sympathize with" Cleopatra, Antony and other characters.

1014 Dean, Paul. "*Antony and Cleopatra*: An Ovidian Tragedy?" *Cahiers Elisabéthains* 40 (October 1991): 73-77.

Shakespeare "may draw his source material from Plutarch but he suffuses it with an Ovidian awareness of metamorphosis which places the emotional conflicts of the protagonists within a universe permeated by flux and instability."

1015 Di Miceli, Caroline. "Le corps eclate: Antoine et Cléopâtre, Coiolan, et Othello." *Shakespeare et les corps a la Renaissance.* Societe Francaise Shakespeare Actes du congres 1990. Ed. Marie-Thérèse Jones-Davies. Paris: Les Belles Lettres, 1991, pp. 17-28.

This is an analysis of the macrocosmic and microcosmic significance of the imagery of the broken body in *Antony and Cleopatra*, *Coriolanus*, and *Othello.*

1016 Hall, Joan Lord. "Double-edged Theatrics: *Antony and Cleopatra.*" *The Dynamics of Role-Playing in Jacobean Tragedy.* New York: St. Martin's P, 1991, pp. 115-35.

The lovers of this play "are energetic chameleons; Cleopatra, even in death, escapes the sombreness of being reduced to one fixed form." Shakespeare "examines the ambivalence at the heart of the histrionic impulse: the way that the self may be transformed creatively, and not necessarily diminished, through playing roles." The delineation of Antony "suggests how projection into different personae, often a means of creative self-expression, can ultimately dissipate any unified self; the Roman hero dies unable to synthesise the conflicting roles of lover and warrior." Cleopatra's staging of death "vindicates the histrionic mode as a vehicle for affirming and consolidating a complex identity." Considered "as a vibrant stage image," "her death goes some way towards resolving those dualities—between the contrived and the natural—, the mutable and the stable—that her behaviour continually raises in the play." In this play, Shakespeare "sets the human talent for shaping life alongside the other type of 'play' as constant acting. The completed act, whether perfect fashioning of death or the imaginative creation of a life-enhancing myth, is a ballast against the endlessly shifting, self-renewing and self-destroying roles that individuals must play on the stage of life."

1017 Hall, Joan Lord. "'To the very heart of loss': Rival Constructs of 'Heart' in *Antony and Cleopatra*." *College Literature* 18.1 (1991): 64-76.

The Romans understood "heart" as "manly courage. For Egyptians, though, 'heart' is understood in its more common sense as the 'seat of love or affection,' and is sometimes paired with the term 'affection' to connote passion as well as emotional warmth." The play presents a dialectic of these two meanings.

1018 James, Heather. "The Fatal Cleopatra: Imitation, Gender, and Cultural Criticism in Shakespeare's Translations of Empire." *Dissertation Abstracts International* 53 (1991): 1526A (California-Berkeley).

"In his translations of empire," Shakespeare "develops a practice of literary imitation and conflation analogous to the punning, Cleopatra-like language which exasperates Johnson not because it is meaningless but because it generates more meanings than it can possibly authorize and order."

1019 Levitan, Alan. "Love-Metrics and Death-Metrics in Antony and Cleopatra." *Love and Death in the Renaissance*. Ed. Kenneth R. Bartlett, Konrad Eisenbichler, and Janice Liedl. Ottawa: Dovehouse, 1991, pp. 73-93.

The lines spoken by Egyptians are distinguished from those spoken by and about Romans by a distinct 3/4 time musical lift; this metrical distinction reflects the love-death opposition in the play.

1020 McAlindon, Thomas. "*Antony and Cleopatra*." *Shakespeare's Tragic Cosmos*. Cambridge: Cambridge UP, 1991, pp. 220-57.

Antony and Cleopatra "may be called a tragedy of Fortune, where Fortune is conceived, not a cruel and meaningless mischance, nor as a retributive agent of divine providence, but as a manifestation of inevitable change in the cyclic order of history and nature; and where the tragic effect stems mainly from a perception that what has been swept away in the process of change is irreplaceable—two of Nature's masterpieces 'which not to have have been blest withal would have discredited' humanity (1.2.148-9)." Ovid's poem and Shakespeare's play "embody an expansive imaginative world which comprehends the human and the divine, the historical and the mythical; a fluid paradoxical world where change and permanence are reconciled and loss in the natural order is counterbalanced by transmutation, transmigration, regeneration, apotheosis." Antony's death "accords with the Roman and Stoic conception of a noble constancy." Cleopatra's death "unites courage and love, firmness and sensuousness, Stoicism and Epicureanism, death and birth, gravity and play, tragedy and comedy, becoming and being." This play should be studied "in the context of Ovid's *Metamorphoses* and Plutarch's 'Of Isis and Osiris'." Shakespeare's "tragic art is radically informed by essentialist notions of a transhistorical human nature and of unchanging laws encoded in universal nature."

1021 Quinones, Ricardo J. *The Changes of Cain: Violence and the Lost Brother in Cain and Abel Literature*. Princeton: Princeton UP, 1991.

In identifying a motif of violence in this play, Quinones suggests that "division is still to be endemic and necessary, and the other, the mysterious brother, who here represents vital qualities and energies, must once again be sacrificed."

1022 Sharma, T.R. "The Indian View of *Purusha* and Shakespeare's Cosmic Form in *Antony and Cleopatra*." *Meerut Journal of Comparative Literature and Language* 4.2 (1991): 60-76.

Antony and Cleopatra are cast in the mold of *Purusha* (the Hindu concept of the all-pervading power that creates and controls the universe, and that links the transient with the ultimate). Cleopatra is all fire and air; Antony has a face like the heavens. They transcend their human dimensions to assert their cosmic affinity.

1023 Westerweel, Bart. "Eros and Thanatos in *Antony and Cleopatra*." *Love and Death in the Renaissance*. Ed. Kenneth R. Bartlett, Konrad Eisenbichler, and Janice Liedl. Ottawa: Dovehouse, 1991, pp. 163-82.

Dramatically and rhetorically, Shakespeare exploits Eros as character and linguistic sign in relationship to such concerns as love, death, friendship, and loyalty.

1024 Yachnin, Paul. "'Courtiers of Beauteous Freedom': *Antony and Cleopatra* in Its Time." *Renaissance and Reformation/Renaissance et Reforme* 15 (1991): 1-20.

Yachnin argues that "the meanings of the play in 1606-1607 were on the whole more political and certainly more topical than they are now." "In terms of the political culture of the early Stuart period," this play's "account of the shift from the magnificent but senescent Egyptian past to the pragmatic but successful Roman future can be seen as a critical register of the symbolic constructions and political ramifications of the shift from the Elizabethan to the Jacobean style of rule."

1025 Adelman, Janet. "*Antony and Cleopatra*." *Suffocating Mothers: Fantasies of Maternal Origin Shakespeare's Plays, "Hamlet" to "The Tempest."* New York: Routledge, 1992, pp. 174-92.

In *Timon of Athens* and *Antony and Cleopatra*, Shakespeare "exposes this [autonomous] masculinity in its most naked form and then attempts to move beyond it, reimagining both sexual union and masculine identity in a new relation to the maternal as it is invested in Cleopatra; and the final alliance of his own creativity with hers opens the way toward the romances."

"Insofar as the memory of Cleopatra's womb becomes the nurturant space that holds the fullness of Antony's masculine bounty, insofar as she herself becomes the model and the source of that bounty," Adelman argues, "*Antony and Cleopatra* is Shakespeare's most strenuous attempt within the tragedies to redefine the relationship of masculinity to the maternal, hence to redefine tragic masculinity itself." Through Cleopatra, Shakespeare allows himself to imagine a fully masculine selfhood that can overflow its own rigid boundaries, a masculinity become enormous in its capacity to share in the female mystery of an endlessly regenerating source of supply, growing the more it is reaped." All of *Antony and Cleopatra* overflows the measure; in its interpretative openness, its expansive playfulness, its imaginative abundance, it seems to me lead directly to *The Winter's Tale*, where trust in female process similarly bursts the boundaries of the tragic form."

1026 Baker, J. Robert. "Absence and Subversion: The 'O'erflow' Gender in Shakespeare's *Antony and Cleopatra.*" *Upstart Crow* 12 (1992): 105-15.

Baker suggests that, in this play, "Shakespeare seems to be playing on his own era's anxieties about gender. The Elizabethans were particularly conscious of gender, for theirs was an age headed by a queen and, simultaneously, determinedly patriarchal." Antony and Cleopatra, "in stepping outside the normal space assigned to their genders, threaten order and stability, particularly in the Roman world of the play." In the final scenes, "what they enter into, despite Antony's fears and Cleopatra's ambitions, is not so much tragedy as a place where each assumes the very person of the other and fashions it anew, where each assumes the gender of the other and makes it more than it was alone, and where tragedy assumes the very resonance and expansiveness of comedy."

1027 Charnes, Linda. "What's love got to do with it? Reading the Liberal Humanist Romance in Shakespeare's *Antony and Cleopatra.*" *Textual Practice* 6 (1992): 1-16.

Liberal-humanist love stories coerce readers into identifying with what otherwise they would reject. Love in *Antony and Cleopatra* forms part of the theme of power relations.

1028 Curtis, Mary Ann. "The Joining of Male and Female: An Alchemical Theme of Transmutation in *Antony and Cleopatra.*" *Upstart Crow* 12 (1992): 116-26.

Antony and Cleopatra's "love for each other is an archetypal union that transcends both Rome and Egypt. Such a joining of opposites, of male and female, is, in fact, representative of the inner quest for unity that was not fully expressed until it found voice in the Jungian theories of the human psyche." It may be that Shakespeare and Jung "were drawing on the same sources in alchemy, that mysterious quest for transmutation which has its historical roots in the ancient soil of Egypt."

1029 Davies, H. Neville. "In the Public Eye: Antony and Cleopatra Now." *Shakespeare from Text to Stage*. Ed. Patricia Kennan and Mariangelo Tampora. Bologna: Cooperativa Lib. Univ. Editrice Bologna, 1992, pp. 111-30.

Davies argues that anyone fascinated by this play "will also be hungry for knowledge about what can be learnt of *Antony and Cleopatra* from reports of its life in the theatre, hungry to discover what is revealed about a dramatic work that performers dare to transfer, before the eyes of the public, *from text to stage*." Readers "will want to use evidence from the theatre primarily to sharpen their response to the play."

1030 Entry deleted.

1031 Eastwood, David R. "A Drama Hypothesis." *Hypotheses: Neo-Aristotelian Analysis* 3 (1992): 8-9.

The lack of symmetry in Shakespeare's delineation of Antony and Cleopatra relates to their moral parity; Cleopatra gains in stature after Antony's death.

1032 Eggert, Katherine E. "Ravishment and Remembrance: Responses to Female Authority in Spenser and Shakespeare." *Dissertation Abstracts International* 53 (1992): 1525A (California-Berkeley).

This dissertation "investigates how literary productions of English Renaissance reflected, and reflected upon, cultural unease about queenship." Chapter 4 "addresses Jacobean nostalgia for queenship in terms of *Antony and Cleopatra*'s radical revision of marginalized feminine theatrical power. The play proposes that the queen's ravishing nature constitutes theatricality itself, and compels an audience to take pleasure in her spectacle."

1033 Flesch, William. *Generosity and the Limits of Authority: Shakespeare, Herbert, Milton*. Ithaca, NY: Cornell UP, 1992. 277 pp.

Flesch elaborates the experience of loss or solitude or mortality in *Richard II*, *King Lear*, and *Antony and Cleopatra.* Shakespeare's "tragic figures experience, and describe the experience of, an exhaustion of the generosity of being that they imagined they had embodied." Antony's "absolute generosity or bounty manifests itself in an absolute imperiousness of language that never fails, even when confronted with its own absolute poverty."

1034 Fraser, Russell. *Shakespeare. The Later Years*. New York: Columbia UP, 1992. 379 pp.

Shakespeare wrote this play probably no later than the spring of 1608 and thus finished the tragic cursus. The tragedy, "not notably dramatic, resembles the swan's-down feather Antony tells of. Held by conflicting currents, it goes back and forth between extremes." There is no midway point for Antony between them.

1035 Gajowski, Evelyn. "*Antony and Cleopatra*: Female Subjectivity and Orientalism." *The Art of Loving: Female Subjectivity and Male Discursive Traditions in Shakespeare's Tragedies*. Newark: U of Delaware P, 1992, pp. 86-119.

In his love tragedies like *Antony and Cleopatra*, Shakespeare stresses the problems of mutual realization of self and other (or intersubjectivity), with focus on such problems as obstacles to the love relationship, the destructive potential of male friendship for heterosexual relationships, and the power and language of the women characters.

Following Edward Said, Gajowski suggests that "*Orientalism* is to culture as Petrarchism and Ovidianism are to gender. All three are constructions of colonized or sexual others by imperialistic or patriarchal dominant ideologies. All three

Roman constructions of other operate powerfully, from Philo's opening lines, throughout the play." Shakespeare's representation of Cleopatra "humanizes her, disrupting centuries of treatment of the legend of the two lovers." In *Antony and Cleopatra*, "women are most emphatically *not* as they are valued by men. More so than is true of any of Shakespeare's female protagonists, Cleopatra's estimation of herself is independent of male estimations of her."

For the Romans, "women are objects that satisfy men's sexual appetites; they are prizes of war; they are political pawns to be used as the means of cementing opportunistic alliances." From their perspective, "Cleopatra is but the supreme erotic delight among the vast array of exotic experiences that the conquest of diverse cultures offers up to the policemen of the empire." Shakespeare "presents male delusions about female betrayal in *Antony and Cleopatra* as in *Othello* only to accentuate the reality of female constancy and to expose male inconstancy." Shakespeare's women are "remarkable for their totality of being that eludes and defies, disrupts and subverts male constructions of the female."

1036 Grene, Nicholas. "*Antony and Cleopatra*." *Shakespeare's Tragic Imagination*. Basingstoke: Macmillan, 1992, pp. 223-48.

There is not in this play "in any real sense a conflict between the values of East and West." Here "the focus is almost entirely on Antony and Cleopatra's capacity to imagine identities for themselves, to create and sustain their parts in the story in the face of the ironies and disbelief which surround them." Since it does not have absolutes of faith or feeling, it "seems in some ways a strikingly modern play." Antony and Cleopatra "are what they make themselves rather than what they history made them, or at at least they play out with their own wilfulness the parts in which history has cast them."

1037 Hanson, Ellis. "Sodomy and Kingcraft in *Urania* and *Antony and Cleopatra*." *Homosexuality in Renaissance and Enlightenment England: Literary Representations in Historical Context*. Ed. Claude J. Summers. Research on Homosexuality. New York and London: Haworth, 1992, pp. 135-51.

James I's probable homosexual relationship with Robert Carr, Earl of Essex, and his subsequent separation from Queen Anne may have inspired "two literary accounts of kingship confounded by sex." Shakespeare's play represents the excessive extravagance of the Jacobean court. Cleopatra's role is similar to that of Somerset, and "Antony's vacillation between pleasure and duty" is reminiscent of James's writing on sodomy and statecraft.

1038 Heinemann, Margot. "'Let Rome in Tiber melt': Order and Disorder in 'Antony and Cleopatra'." *Shakespeare Jahrbuch* (Weimar) 128 (1992): 39-48.

This play "represents the disintegration and transmutation not only of a passionate relationship, but of a whole world and its values. The chaos looks more radical and shocking, the supposed restoration of order at the end less firm and reassuring, if we see it in the light of history. Win or lose, the struggle between the triumvirs marks the end of the republic, so admired and idealised in the European Renaissance for its stern Roman virtues and the anti-absolutist principles of its aristocracy."

1039 Helms, Lorraine. "'The High Roman Fashion': Sacrifice, Suicide, and the Shakespearean Stage." *PMLA: Publications of Modern Language Association* 107 (1992): 554-65.

In *Antony and Cleopatra* and other Roman tragedies, "the most venturesome representations of sacrifice and suicide are animated not by the popular tradition but by Senecan tragedy and its distant descendant, the ensembles of the children's companies." Cleopatra's "suicide, like the wife's in Greek tragedy, constellates death and marriage in ancient symbols of female heroism."

1040 Hughes, Ted. "The Tragic Equation Makes its Soul: *Timon of Athens, Coriolanus, Antony and Cleopatra*." *Shakespeare and the Goddess of Complete Being*. New York: Farrar, Straus, and Giroux, 1992, pp. 283-320.

Antony and Cleopatra is a bridge between the tragedies and the romances. "Though Antony and Cleopatra die, physically, within the Tragic Equation, Antony killing himself—like Othello—when he believes his Tarquinian frenzy has killed

Cleopatra, and Cleopatra killing herself because his death leaves her no life, nevertheless, at the same time, in the most resplendent and undeniable fashion, both Antony and Cleopatra transcend their tragic fates (and their deaths) by rising together above the Tragic Equation (and the Rival Brothers), on to a sharply defined, higher, metaphysical plane, where such worldly sufferings are redeemed." This play reflects Shakespeare's attempt to solve the Tragic Equation and "marks the point of substantial transformation between those plays in which man destroys himself and his world through his misunderstanding and rejection of Divine Love, and those in which Divine Love redeems him in spite of his misunderstanding and its consequence." *Antony and Cleopatra* "is the tragedy of the God of Love himself, the tragedy of Eros, compelled to suffer not only the cruel moral tyranny of that other god, but also the inescapable tragedy of being an Immortal, the God of 'immortal longings', the God of Life itself in the mortal body."

1041 Jankowski, Theodora A. "Exercising the Body Politic: William Shakespeare's *Antony and Cleopatra* and John Webster's *The Duchess of Malfi*." *Women in Power in the Early Modern Drama*. Urbana and Chicago: U of Illinois P, 1992, pp. 174-88.

Antony and Cleopatra and *The Duchess of Malfi* "attempt to examine the various questions and problems associated with a woman who holds political power, in particular, the relationship of her natural to her body politic." In the case of Cleopatra, Shakespeare "has created a female figure within whose seemingly gratuitous voluptuousness lies a clever strategy for successful rule. Uniting her body natural and her body politic has allowed Cleopatra to use the former's sexuality as a means by which she can gain power in the latter."

1042 Kay, Dennis. *Shakespeare: His Life, Work, and Era*. New York: William Morrow, 1992. 446 pp.

Shakespeare builds this play around oppositions of "Rome and Egypt, love and duty, honor and pragmatism" and "constructs for the audience two contrasting experiences: one of juxtaposition, paradox, fragmentation; the other of unity, coherence, wholeness."

1043 Kim, Jong-hwan. "Shakespeare in Korea: 1906-1989." *Dissertation Abstracts International* 53 (1992): 504A (Nebraska).

This study examines "how Koreans received, translated, produced, and studied Shakespeare from 1906 to 1989."

1044 King, Laura Severt. "Blessed When They Were Riggish: Shakespeare's Cleopatra and Christianity's Penitent Prostitutes." *Journal of Medieval and Renaissance Studies* 22 (1992): 429-49.

In *Antony and Cleopatra* Shakespeare "dramatizes competing versions of the penitent prostitute: one that creates a sexual profligacy transformed by conversion and one that insists on a sexual profligacy eliminated by conversion." Cleopatra's death "is not triumphant but tragic, in part because she repudiates her supernaturally potent eroticism, trading the iconography of Isis for that of the Virgin Mary."

1045 Kujawinska-Courtney, Krystyna. "Derrida's *The Truth in Painting*." *Explicator* 50 (Winter 92): 124-25.

Although Derrida does not acknowledge his debt to Shakespeare, he "follows the dramatist's conception of Antony's brobdingnagian attributes as able to be presented only in narrative speeches." They are never shown on stage; they are "almost unpresentable." Therefore Shakespeare's *Antony and Cleopatra* 5.2 "becomes a gloss that we can use to refine Derrida's definition of 'Colossal' in art."

1046 Lehmann, Elmar. "Love Stories: Antony and Cleopatra Plays of the 16th and 17th Centuries." *Telling Stories: Studies in Honour of Ulrich Broich on the Occasion of His 60th Birthday.* Amsterdam and Philadelphia: Gruner, 1992, pp. 56-68.

Lehmann argues that this play "does contain a love story, but it is a love story that is not, and quite clearly cannot be, emplotted. There are too many stories decentering it, and there seems to be only room for the careful plotting of time and space that allows all these stories to mushroom, but to be confined within the limits of play or to function according to the constraints of a 'logic of signification'."

1047 Little, Geoffrey "The Womanning of Cleopatra's Barge." *Sydney Studies in English* 17 (1991-92): 43-45.

Little's reading of Enobarbus's speech in 2.2 "puts the gentlewomen at the bows and at the stern, handling the barge, with Cleopatra reclining amidships shaded beneath the pavilion and flanked by the pretty boys." These "pretty boys produce an artificial breeze; it is the women who make use of the real one."

1048 Mahood, Molly M. "The Varying Tide in *Antony and Cleopatra.*" *Bit Parts in Shakespeare's Plays*. Cambridge: Cambridge UP, 1992, pp. 180-204.

"The complexity of response elicited by the strong poetic undertow in Philo's opening lines is awakened time and again in *Antony and Cleopatra,*" Mahood explains, "and those lesser figures whose function extends beyond their usefulness in delivering messages contribute richly to that complexity." This play's "incidental figures have responded sharply and immediately to the events they witness. In this their function is in large part to ensure that our view of the main characters does not solidify."

1049 Maquerlot, Jean-Pierre. "Playing within the Play: Towards a Semiotics of Metadrama and Metatheatre." *The Show Within: Dramatic and Other Insets, English Renaissance Drama (1550-1642).* Montpellier: Publications de Universite Paul Valery—Montpellier III, 1992, pp. 39-49.

This is a semiotic analysis of the dramatic and theatrical codes that Shakespeare exploits in three metadramatic, metatheatrical sequences: *Julius Caesar* 3.1.111-16; *Antony and Cleopatra* 5.2.215-20; *Richard II* 4.1.181-89.

1050 Margolies, David. "*Antony and Cleopatra.*" *Monsters of the Deep: Social Dissolution in Shakespeare's Tragedies.* Manchester: Manchester UP, 1992, pp. 103-19.

In this play, there is no "sense of contradiction at the ending, where the picture of the present turning into the future cannot quite live up to the grandeur of what has preceded it." This may be "because the positive aspects of Antony and Cleopatra were never made part of the reality of the playworld;

they remained an image of what had once been, a twilight of the remembered past. The defeat of the humane attitudes by soulless calculation in inevitable—the image is not a substitute for reality. This sunset vision was warming but it could not last."

1051 Miller, Anthony. *Shakespeare's Antony and Cleopatra.* Horizon: Studies in Literature. Sydney: Sydney UP, 1992. 76 pp.

This study is designed for Year 12 students and undergraduates; it discusses stage history, sources, the role of judgment and the imagination, politics, love, and mutability.

1052 Riemer, A.P. "Wine, Woman and Song: *Antony and Cleopatra* Revisited." *Sydney Studies in English* 17 (1991-92): 3-21.

Reconsidering his *A Reading of Shakespeare's Antony and Cleopatra* in light of recent concepts of literature and feminist and other practices of criticism, Riemer "see[s] no compelling reason . . . to dissent from the interpretation of the play it contains."

1053 Sacerdoti, Gilberto. "'Cosa significan questo?' Sopra uno 'stran trueco' Shakespeariano in *Antonius e Cleopatra.*" *Intersezioni* 12 (1992): 35-62.

Cleopatra's questions "What means this? (4.2.13) and "What means he?" (4.2.23) and Enobarbus's description of Antony's preparations for his "last supper" as "odd tricks" (4.2.14) point to further meanings, and the scriptural references in this and previous scenes suggest a reading of Antony's behavior in terms of Giordano Bruno's and Thomas Harriot's Machiavellian doctrines.

1054 Saksena, Divya. "Shakespeare's Cleopatra: The Forgotten Factor of Ancient Egypt." *Bulletin of the Shakespeare Society of India* (1990-92): 5-6.

Cleopatra should be seen in relation to Egypt rather than through Roman eyes.

1055 Suhamy, Henri. "Man and Divinity in *Antony and Cleopatra.*" *Mythes, croyances et religions dans le monde anglo-saxon* 10 (1992): 33-41.

The interplay of human spirituality and paganism helps in understanding the eschatology of the play.

1056 Ueno, Yoshiko. "A Double Perspective in *Antony and Cleopatra.*" *Chaucer to Shakespeare: Essays in Honour of Shinsuke Ando*. Ed. Toshiyuki Takamiya and Richard Beadle. Woodbridge, England: Brewer, 1992.

Like anamorphic paintings, *Antony and Cleopatra* offers dual perspectives, for example, Roman/Egyptian, political/private.

1057 Bate, Jonathan. *Shakespeare and Ovid.* Oxford: Clarendon P, 1993. 292 pp.

Shakespeare "was an extremely intelligent and sympathetic reader of Ovid," and "his readings are embedded in his own works. The references to Mars and Venus and Aeneas and Dido are drawn from Ovid. The play "celebrates the fame of the lovers, seeks to make their story 'toto notissima caelo'." *The Heroides* "are important for *Antony and Cleopatra* because they see the male hero from the woman's point of view. More generally, they provide Shakespeare with examples of female characters who are witty as well as amorous, not merely moody but also full of vitality, linguistically adept and good at arguing." For Ovid and Shakespeare, "myth is a creative resource, not a set of prescriptions: to believe Antony's 'Dido and her Aeneas shall want troops' and Cleopatra's 'Husband, I come' is to believe in the possibility that history, which these myths encode in archetypal form, can be rewritten. To make Aeneas not Rome's but Dido's—'*her* Aeneas'—is to question the primacy or empire."

1058 Blake, Norman Francis. "*Antony and Cleopatra* II.ii.56-58." *Lore and Language* 11 (1992-93): 223-26.

After discussing Nicholas Rowe's and M. R. Ridley's readings of these lines, Blake sides with Ridley and argues that "the tone which characterises the scene up to this point is hostile."

1059 Brink, Jean R. "Domesticating the Dark Lady." *Privileging Gender in Early Modern England.* Ed. Jean R. Brink. Sixteenth Century Essays and Studies 23. Kirksville, MO: Sixteenth Century Journal Publications, 1993, pp. 93-108.

Shakespeare's characterization of Cleopatra "supports the view that female power and sexuality cannot be reconciled with patriarchy and patriotism." Cleopatra, "like the Dark Lady and Tamora, violates the behavioral norms specifying that virtuous women should be chaste, silent, and obedient, but she never exhibits power except through her sexuality and never achieves recognition as a political figure."

1060 Brown, John Russell. *Shakespeare's plays in performance.* New and revised ed. New York and London: Applause Books, 1993, pp. 32-33, 199-200.

Brown stresses that physical actions modify and extend the implications of words. In some of the scenes, the spectators on stage are watching a show and represent the audience in the theatre.

1061 Charnes, Linda. "Spies and Whispers: Exceeding Reputation in *Antony and Cleopatra*." *Notorious Identity: Materializing the Subject in Shakespeare.* Cambridge, MA: Harvard UP, 1993, pp. 103-47.

Shakespeare uses legendary figures like Antony and Richard the Third to explore the ideological foundations of infamous notoriety. Their notoriety "emerges both as an effect—and as a symptom—of an emergent capitalism, of textual and theatrical reproduction, and the influences that both are exercising on the changing conditions of identity in early modern England." *Antony and Cleopatra* "enacts what one imagines might have been both a tactical and a strategic fantasy for the playwright: how to appropriate for theatrical authorship figures whose meanings had been massively overdetermined by their prior constructions in 'legendary' narratives; how to 'poach' on the texts of others, and how then to claim as 'new' what is produced on the stage out of the most overly 'known' of stories."

1062 Farley-Hills, David. "The Position of Antony and Cleopatra in the Canon." *Notes and Queries* ns 40 (1993): 193-97.

Antony and Cleopatra precedes *Macbeth* in date of composition.

1063 Gibbons, Brian. "Unstable Proteus: Marlowe and *Antony and Cleopatra*." *Shakespeare and Multiplicity*. Cambridge: Cambridge UP, 1993, pp. 182-202.

Marlowe's *Tragedy of Dido* anticipates the "sensuous language and sensuous personality" of Cleopatra. "The imperial theme exalts Antony and Cleopatra to a heroic scale, in struggles to master empires and nations, and the directions of armies in war, but also involves them in bitter Machiavellian politics, so that they are degraded and soiled by ugly and sordid personal and public actions." The heroic rhetoric and mythological imagery "owe much to *Tamberlaine*; but the relation of Shakespeare's tragedy to Marlowe's *Tragedy of Dido* is perhaps more decisive for its depiction of the multiple textures of experience in its dramatic narrative."

1064 Hansen, Carol. *Woman as Individual in English Renaissance Drama: A Defiance of the Masculine Code*. American University Studies, Series 4: English Language and Literature 156. New York: Lang, 1993. 217 pp.

Shakespeare and his contemporary dramatists asked the right questions about the predicament of the woman in a male-dominated society because, as artists, they were free to speak "with great insight." They "could show in the tragedies that the masculine code led to disintegration, defiance, and death for women, and to madness for men."

Shakespeare "was no conventional moralist," and in his hands "the blackened name of Cleopatra became one of beaten gold, something finer than it was before." Cleopatra alone "defies the masculine control of Rome, largely because she has the weight of another culture which recognizes the existence of goddesses, as well as gods, to back her." "Out of the Egyptian culture," Shakespeare "found the missing link to the mystery of the female principle and fashioned Cleopatra first as a wanton, then as a wife, and finally, into an 'eastern star'."

1065 Hawkins, Harriett. "Disrupting Tribal Difference: Critical and Artistic Responses to Shakespeare's Radical Romanticism." *Studies in the Literary Imagination* 26, 1 (1993): 115-26. Revised Version. "Shakespeare's Radical Romanticism: The Popular Tradition and the Challenge to Tribalism." *Shakespeare in the New Europe*. Ed. Michael Hattaway, Boika Sokolova, and Derek Roper. Sheffield: Sheffield Academic P, 1994, pp. 278-93.

In *Antony and Cleopatra* and some of the other tragedies, romantic love is "set against a background of tribal conflict and compared *positively* to the interminable feuds, wars, political backstabbings, or racial and sexual hatred that oppose it." Shakespeare broke new ground when he gave "equal billing to male and female characters, as well as in their gloriously, defiantly anti-tribal love." There "are culturally based reasons why critical patriarchs generally disapprove of Shakespeare's most romantic plays and characters, and very important counter-reasons why women as well as men in love tend to respond to them with sympathy and admiration."

1066 Humes, James C. *Citizen Shakespeare: A Social and Political Portrait*. New York: Praeger, 1993. 192 pp.

Humes argues that, "though only in his mid-forties, the playwright found his energies waning." Consequently, "he ransacked the pages of Plutarch for two more plots—*Timon of Athens* and *Antony and Cleopatra*."

1067 Jackson, R.L.P. "Imagining Anthony and Cleopatra." *Sydney Studies in English* 18 (1992-93): 3-28.

The play's "central thrust" is the struggle in Shakespeare's imagination to find a balance between "licence and proportion," the 'looseness' of Egypt and the authority of Rome, the urge toward expansive life and the need for structure and 'resolution'." This play contains echoes of the tragedies which preceded it and foreshadows the ones which followed it.

1068 Kolin, Philip C. "Cleopatra of the Nile and Blanche DuBois of the French Quarter." *Shakespeare Bulletin* 11 (1993): 25-27.

Shakespeare's Cleopatra influenced Tennessee Williams's characterization of Blanche DuBois.

1069 Kujawinska-Courtney, Krystyna. "Antony and Cleopatra: The Narrative Construction of the Other." *"Th' Interpretation of the Time": The Dramaturgy of Shakespeare's Roman Plays.* ELS Monograph Series 57. Victoria, BC: English Literary Studies, U of Victoria, 1993, pp. 59-90.

This is a study of the effects of the interplay of mimesis and diegesis on the audience. In *Antony and Cleopatra*, Roman diegesis is subverted by Egyptian mimesis. This play "makes hungry where most it satisfies, since the reconciliation of diegesis and mimesis challenges the observers." Hence, "the ongoing agon between the mimetic and the diegetic becomes a dramaturgical analogue to other polarities in the play."

1070 Lombardo, Agostino. "La memoria in *Antony and Cleopatra.*" *Shakespeare e la sua eredita.* Ed. Grazia Caliumi. Parma: Edizioni Zara, 1993, pp. 79-87.

Cleopatra's "death is the death of memory," the annulment of present, past, and future; freedom from memory is tantamount to the conquest of absolute freedom.

1071 Marienstras, Richard. "Les prix des choses et des etres dans quelques textes de Shakespeare." *Shakespeare et l'argent.* Ed. M.T. Jones-Davies. Paris: Les Belles Lettres, 1993, pp. 137-48.

Love is valued in economic terms in *Antony and Cleopatra* and other plays.

1072 Marshall, Cynthia. "Man of Steel Done Got the Blues: Melancholic Subversion of Presence in *Antony and Cleopatra.*" *Shakespeare Quarterly* 44 (1993): 385-408.

In the light of Hank Williams's ballad, Antony, who calls himself a "man of steel," "feels himself undone by the conflicting pressures of love and masculine bravado." "Nostalgia, frustration, ambivalence, loss, incorporation--the various terms of melancholy parse the character of Antony, a lover, as he is presented in the play and experienced by an audience." *Antony and Cleopatra* "shows love and melancholy to be the mutually constituting terms of a subject's identifications."

1073 McJannet, Linda. "Antony and Alexander: Imperial Politics in Plutarch, Shakespeare, and Some Modern Historical Texts." *College Literature* 20 (October 1993): 1-18.

Antony and Cleopatra "lends itself to an approach indebted to the new history." Plutarch and Shakespeare's representations of Antony's politics can be compared with those of twentieth-century historians like Cyril E. Robinson, Ian Scott-Kilvert, and Guglielmo Ferrero.

1074 McJannet, Linda. "Gesta Romanorum: Heroic Action and Stage Imagery in *Antony and Cleopatra*." *Shakespeare Bulletin* 11 (1993): 5-9.

The stage business, stage imagery, and gestures associated with political and martial deeds define Antony and Caesar and their concepts of Romanness.

1075 Miller, Anthony. "*Insignia Triumphalia*: The Roman Triumph in *Antony and Cleopatra*." *Shakespeare and the World Elsewhere*. Ed. Robin Eaden, Heather Kerr, and Madge Mitton. Studies in Shakespeare 2. Adelaide: Australian and New Zealand Shakespeare Association, 1993, pp. 15-22.

The "triumph as political gesture, as token of victory in war or in love, as all-licensed revel, becomes a recurring dramatic issue in *Antony and Cleopatra*."

1076 Miller, Anthony. "The Metamorphic Tragedy of Antony and Cleopatra." *Sydney Studies in English* 18 (1992-93): 29-47.

Instead of voicing only Plutarchan censoriousness of Antony, Shakespeare "adds generosity towards human weakness. He adds admiration of the spectacle of human excess—excess in folly as well as in heroic aspiration. He adds awe at the irresistible powers of Eros and mutability—powers that are by turns life-giving and destructive." These are the voices of Ovid's *Metamorphoses. Antony and Cleopatra* "is most profoundly faithful to Ovid's metamorphic vision in its representation of a world ruled—or capriciously overruled—by instability."

1077 Mulherin, Jennifer, and Gwen Green. *Antony and Cleopatra.* Shakespeare for Everyone. Bath: Cherrytree P, 1993. 31 pp.

The authors provide a summary of the play for young readers and discuss the characters.

1078 Wells, Charles. "Antony and Cleopatra—Duty, Service and Betrayal" and "Love." *The Wide Arch: Roman Values in Shakespeare*. London: Bristol Classical, 1993, pp. 138-72.

Central to this play "is the theme of loyal service and betrayal. It is this which connects the protagonists' fevered passion with the political and military aspects of the play." Its language "is full of references to service given or withheld." In Antony and Cleopatra, "passion and politics are inextricably mingled—indeed each becomes, in some sense, an expression of the other." Cleopatra "understands her partner's need to maintain his Roman honour, irksome to her though its consequences are. Antony's status as 'world sharer' earns her chronicle as well as his, and in it her love for him is spectacularly affirmed." The play's "central metaphor of fluidity and evanescence contrasts with a Rome that appears stolid, angular and marmoreal."

1079 Yachnin, Paul. "Shakespeare's Politics of Loyalty: Sovereignty and Subjectivity in *Antony and Cleopatra.*" *Studies in English Literature 1500-1900* 33 (1993): 343-63.

Antony and Cleopatra "displayed 'absolutist loyalty' in such elaborate detail that absolutism's deeply conflicted dependence on 'sovereign subjectivity' was able to emerge into the consciousness of the members of its 1606-1607 audiences."

1080 Archer, John Michael. "Antiquity and Degeneration: The Representation of Egypt and Shakespeare's *Antony and Cleopatra.*" *Genre* 27 (1994): 1-27.

When examined in the context of historical, geographical, and travel literature of the early modern period, *Antony and Cleopatra* illustrates that "bodily fantasies of sexual and racial difference are produced and consumed in sharply dissimilar ways in both Shakespeare's play and the representation of Egypt that intersects it."

1081 Barfoot, C.C. "News of the Roman Empire: Hearsay, Soothsay, Myth and History in *Antony and Cleopatra*." *Reclamations of Shakespeare*. Ed. A.J. Hoenselaars. Amsterdam: Rodopi, 1994, pp. 105-28.

Messengers and messages "prompt the action, forward the action, stimulate emotional responses, and kept in motion" in *Antony and Cleopatra*, and hearsay contributes to the "play's sense of its own status as history and myth."

1082 Bartholomeusz, Dennis. "Shakespeare Imagines the Orient: The Orient Imagines Shakespeare." *Shakespeare and Cultural Traditions*. Ed. Tetsus Kishi, Roger Pringle and Stanley Wells. Newark: U of Delaware P; London and Toronto: Associated University Presses, 1994, pp. 188-204.

Shakespeare conceived and used the Orient in *Antony and Cleopatra*, *Othello*, and *Henry VIII*; "China, India, and Japan have been moved to imagine and recreate Shakespeare's plays in performance and in terms of their own sociopolitical structures and theatrical traditions." Bartholomeusz argues that "Shakespeare's imaginative encounter with the Orient extended and enriched his vision of life, while his plays in their turn have, for all their difference, extended and enriched the cultures of the Orient." He suggests that "when Imperial Rome attempts to take over the Orient, which is Egypt in [*Antony and Cleopatra*], Shakespeare confronts it with the brilliant complex presence of Cleopatra, the 'serpent of old Nile'." Bartholomeusz opposes any "hopelessly racist and colonial reading of the text, as if one saw it entirely from Philo's point of view, that of a simple-minded, prejudiced soldier."

1083 Battenhouse, Roy, comp. "*Antony and Cleopatra*." *Shakespeare's Christian Dimension. An Anthology of Commentary*. Bloomington: Indiana UP, 1994, pp. 494-506.

Battenhouse argues that, in this play, "a surprising amount of imagery is biblical." Antony himself "in his 'hill of Basan' roaring is a parody of the Messiah-figure of Psalm 22." This anthology contains excerpts from Clifford Davidson, Andrew Fichter, and David Scott Kastan.

1084 Bevington, David. "Shakespeare and Recent Criticism: Issues for a Christian Approach to Teaching." *Shakespeare and the Christian Tradition*. Ed. E. Beatrice Batson. Lewiston, Queenston, and Lampeter: Mellen, 1994, pp. 1-18.

Postmodern approaches like new historicism, feminism, and deconstruction pose problems for those who adopt a Christian approach in teaching plays like *Antony and Cleopatra*.

1085 Dollimore, Jonathan. "Playing in the Shadows of History." *Political Shakespeare: Essays in Cultural Materialism*. Ed. Jonathan Dollimore and and Alan Sinfield. 2nd edition. Ithaca and London: Cornell UP, 1994, pp. 114-49.

For Dollimore, "Camp is a form of transgressive reinscription, turning the artifice of the theatre against what it represent, reconfiguring the natural as the most deeply inadequate of all ontologies—a post without style." He would like to see a woman playing Antony and a boy playing Cleopatra because this "would confuse the very idea of sexual difference and sexual identity upon the romantic, the moralistic, the sexist, the racist, and other decadent interpretations all at some stage rely."

1086 Drakakis, John, ed. *Antony and Cleopatra*. New Casebooks. New York: St. Martin's P, 1994. 341 pp.

This collection of essays reprints, in whole or in part, the following items found in this bibliography: John F. Danby, Janet Adelman, Phyllis Rackin, Terence Hawkes, H. Neville Davies, Margot Heinemann, Linda T. Fitz, Barbara C. Vincent, Jonathan Dollimore, Marilyn French, Ania Loomba, and Jyotsna Singh.

Drakakis outlines the critical assessments of the play by John F. Danby and Janet Adelman and several critics of 1980s from Phyllis Rackin to Jyotsna Singh. Bradley and others were "concerned with the question of locating a single meaning in the text, which will lead to some 'truth' at its centre which is in some sense beyond language." In the 1980s emerged "a critical practice which involves a much fuller, more problematical articulation of the conditions, sometimes unconscious, which govern a text's construction, as well as those which govern its reconstitution and reception."

1087 Frank, Marcie. "Fighting Women and Loving Men: Dryden's Representation of Shakespeare in *All for Love*." *Queering the Renaissance*. Ed. Jonathan Goldberg. Durham: Duke UP, 1994, pp. 310-29.

Frank seeks to "emphasize the disruptive moments in *All for Love* and its preface in order to make visible that underwriting Dryden's representation of Shakespeare as a cultural inheritance is the suppression of any relations between poets except an oedipal one and to note the strategies by which they are suppressed."

1088 Glasser, Marvin. "Dramaturgical Uses of Visual Forms in Shakespeare's *Antony and Cleopatra*." *Upstart Crow* 14 (1994): 89-104.

Shakespeare used multiple planes of depth, foregrounding, perspective and multiple points of view to create "a space beyond that of this world, a space that continues to the vanishing point of infinity, that gives the play the tone of one of the late romances rather than of tragedy."

1089 Han, Kang-Sok. "Shakespeare's Idea of Nothing." *Dissertation Abstracts International* 55 (1994): 201A (Calgary).

Han "investigates how the conflicting East and West in Antony and Cleopatra, the aesthetic world of 'becoming' (Egypt) and the critical world of 'being' (Rome), are reconciled in the poetic 'airy' vision."

1090 Harris, Jonathan Gil. "'Narcissus in thy face': Roman Desire and the Difference It Fakes in *Antony and Cleopatra*." *Shakespeare Quarterly* 45 (1994): 408-25.

Through his analysis of the relation between Elizabethan versions of Ovid's Narcissus myth and *Antony and Cleopatra*, Harris "challenges orthodox understandings of gender difference in the play, in particular the status of Cleopatra as the quintessentially female object and origin of heterosexual desire—both the desire of her Roman suitors and, perhaps just as important, the desire of her heterosexual male spectators and readers, past and present." Shakespeare presents Cleopatra as "a threatening Other to both Roman and Jacobean body politic" and "as the *same*."

1091 Heinemann, Margot. "'Let Rome in Tiber melt': Order and Disorder in 'Antony and Cleopatra'." *Antony and Cleopatra*. Ed. John Drakakis. New Casebooks. New York: St. Martin's P, 1994, pp. 166-81.

Antony and Cleopatra "represents the disintegration and transmutation not only of a passionate relationship, but of a whole world and its values. The chaos looks more radical and shocking, the supposed restoration of order at the end less firm and reassuring, if we see it in the light of history."

1092 Kim, Yongtae. "The Jacobean Roman Tragedies of Shakespeare and Jonson in their Political Context (Shakespeare, William, Jonson, Ben)." *Dissertation Abstracts International* 55 (1994): 33852A (Nebraska).

Following the New Historical approach, Kim argues that "Antony's amorous relationship with Cleopatra, which reflects the contemporary political corruption in James's court, is subversive to the health of the body politic represented by the politically more powerful Caesar."

1093 Kramer, David Bruce. *The Imperial Dryden: The Poetics of Appropriation in Seventeenth-Century England.* Athens and London: U of Georgia P, 1994.

Dryden's *All for Love* stands in opposition to Shakespeare's style and to *Antony and Cleopatra*, and Dryden assimilates Shakespeare's authority by misquoting him.

1094 Laroque, François. "Le Nil dans *Antoine et Cléopâtre.*" *Le fleufe et ses metamorphoses.* Ed. François Piquet. Paris: Didier Erudition, 1994, pp. 437-42.

The ebb and low of the Nile in this play has semantic, mythic, and metaphoric significance, and the river serves as an analogue to the protean Cleopatra.

1095 Levine, Laura. *Men in Women's Clothing: Anti-Theatricality and Effeminization, 1589-1642.* Cambridge Studies in Renaissance Literature and Culture 5. Cambridge and New York: Cambridge UP, 1994. 185 pp.

In *Antony and Cleopatra, Troilus and Cressida* and other plays, Renaissance dramatists addressed the antitheatrical attacks that costume could affect the gender of the male body and effeminatize men.

1096 McDonald, Russ. "Late Shakespeare: Style and the Sexes." *Shakespeare Survey* 46 (1994): 91-106.

The changes in the style of the late plays are related to Shakespeare's "imaginative recovery of the feminine" as he moves from tragedy to romance, and the binary structure of *Antony and Cleopatra* reflects the relationship of language to gender.

1097 McGuire, Philip C. *Shakespeare: The Jacobean Plays.* English Dramatists Series. New York: St. Martin's P, 1994. 217 pp.

Under the social and cultural circumstances in which the King's Men first performed it, *Antony and Cleopatra* "may have helped differentiate James's reign from Elizabeth's by allowing audiences to see the final phase of the process by which the Roman empire and its first emperor came into being." James's propagandists believed that his reign was "the re-embodiment of that empire on British soil."

1098 Newton, Allyson Paix. "Jesting at Scars: Shakespeare's Sceptics and the Problem of Belief (Characterization)." *Dissertation Abstracts International* 55 (1994): 3893A (Rice).

Skeptics like Enobarbus "involve us not just in characterological subtleties but in issues which have to do with the impingement of skepticism on the 'illusion' of theatrical embodiment."

1099 Sacerdoti, Gilberto. "Tre re, Erode di Guidea e un bambino." *Intersezioni* 14 (1994): 171-209.

Charmian's mention of "herod of Jewry" (1.2.25-30) supports a neoplatonic-apocalyptic reading of the play, based on the doctrines of Giordano Bruno filtered through the Ralegh circle.

1100 Simonds, Peggy Munoz. "'To the very heart of loss': Renaissance Iconography in Shakespeare's *Antony and Cleopatra*." *Shakespeare Studies* 22 (1994): 220-76.

The iconographic underpinnings of language and imagery help the audience in associating Cleopatra with the goddess Fortuna in their response to the play. Antony and other characters "describe Cleopatra herself in terms of the attributes widely associated with the pagan goddess Fortuna."

1101 Song, Won-Moon. "Racial Otherness: The Representation of Colored Minorities in Shakespeare and Restoration Drama." *Dissertation Abstracts International* 55 (1994): 3929A (Wisconsin-Madison).

Song discusses "the Western 'rape mentality' about 'other' cultures and women through investigating how women of color were represented in *Antony and Cleopatra* and Dryden's *All for Love*."

1102 Whitney, Charles "Charmian's Laughter: Women, Gypsie, and Festive Ambivalence in *Antony and Cleopatra*." *Upstart Crow* 14 (1994): 67-88.

The independence of Cleopatra, Charmian, and Iras, and the references to gypsies "can provide a powerful basis for understanding how festivity, tragedy, power, and gender are related" in *Antony and Cleopatra*, especially as the factive ambivalence of the play encourages sympathy for marginalized groups.

1103 Wilkes, G.A. "'Excellent dissembling': A View of *Antony and Cleopatra*." *Sydney Studies in English* 19 (1993-94): 31-39.

The theatrical quality of *Antony and Cleopatra* precludes the inner struggle that defines for A.C. Bradley the great tragic protagonists.

1104 Cheney, Donald. "'A Very Antony': Patterns of Antonomasia in Shakespeare." *Connotations* 4 (1994-95): 8-24.

The Roman characters tend to understand the world "by naming, characterizing, [and] describing it by means of epithets." and this creates "a static and necessarily inadequate verbal formula" in the play.

1105 Cluck, Nancy. "The Fearful Summons: Death in the Opening Scenes of Shakespearean Tragedy." *Entering the Maze: Shakespeare's Art of Beginning*. Ed. Robert F. Willson, Jr. Studies in Shakespeare 2. New York: Peter Lang, 1995. 181 pp.

Cluck studies how Shakespeare establishes the motif of death at the beginning of *Antony and Cleopatra* and other plays.

1106 Cohen, Ralph. "Staging Comic Divinity: The Collision of High and Low in *Antony and Cleopatra*." *Shakespeare Bulletin* 13.3 (1995): 5-8.

In their disjunction of language and actions, the closing scenes (from 4.14 on) are comic and, thus, debase "Caesar and the Roman 'high order' that needs to look on the story of Antony and Cleopatra as a tragedy."

1107 Conway, Katherine M "Material Girls: Gender and Property in Shakespeare." *Dissertation Abstracts International* 56 (1995-96): 3135A (Massachusetts).

Shakespeare uses English land laws in *Antony and Cleopatra* and other plays, by means of which he "was able to make politics—from the marriage market of Padua to Caesar's world politics—local politics for his contemporary audience."

1108 Dessen, Alan C. *Recovering Shakespeare's Theatrical Vocabulary*. Cambridge: Cambridge UP, 1995. 283 pp.

Based on a survey of stage directions, this study of images and stage effects cites a number of passages from *Antony and Cleopatra.*

1109 Ferguson, Elaine Murman. "Dialectic and Antony and Cleopatra. (Shakespeare)." *Dissertation Abstracts International* 56 (1995): 1985A (Texas A&M).

Shakespeare "shapes *Antony and Cleopatra* in order to focus on the merits of a dialectical balance between alternate points of view." He "uses this play to dramatize the need to balance the claims of a printed text's avowals to be a container of objective truth with a discursive process which could be a means to subjective mutuality."

1110 Flesch, William. "The Ambivalence of Generosity: Keats Reading Shakespeare." *ELH* 62 (1995): 149-69.

Antony and Cleopatra is a source for "To Autumn" in which Keats "tries to free himself" from the influence of Shakespeare. Antony "is a precursor for the ambivalent imago that Autumn represents for Keats."

1111 Fusini, Nadia. "Eroine shakespearina: 1. L'eros di Cleopatra." *Republica* 25 August 1995.

Cleopatra sacrifices her femininity in exchange for Antony's renunciation of his virility.

1112 Hall, Kim F. *Things of Darkness: Economies of Race and Gender in Early Modern England.* Ithaca and London: Cornell UP, 1995. 319 pp.

This play "perhaps is most closely concerned with the ways an African queen threatens empire. Cleopatra's darkness makes here the embodiment of an absolute correspondence between fears of racial and gender difference and the threat they pose to imperialism." The Nile River is "a sign of overwhelming sexuality and social disorder and associates Cleopatra with the kind of overflow and excess characteristic of the female grotesque." This play "provides an object lesson in imperial history; Antony becomes a warning against the dangers of overinvolvement with the reputed sexual excess of black women."

1113 Hawkins, Harriett. *Strange Attractors: Literature, Culture, and Chaos Theory*. New York and London: Prentice Hall-Harvester Wheatsheaf, 1995. 180 pp.

Hawkins follows the premise that "concepts and metaphors from chaos science, most notably 'the butterfly effect,' 'fractals' and 'the strange attractor,' as they have been appropriated by modern artists of altogether different kinds, also provide important *theoretical* perspectives on the persistent instability that characterizes the dynamical interaction between order and disorder both in canonical and popular fictions." Cleopatra "can be seen as deterministic chaos personified, since she instigates and orders her own forms of chaos." In a paradoxical way, "her chaotic components are as poetically positive as they are political disruptive." As the plot unfolds, "the ageing Cleopatra is simultaneously associated with the artifice of eternity inhabited by pagan gods and goddesses and classic lovers such as Dido and Aeneas, and with a highly subjective view of the world (she sees Antony in epic and romantic terms beyond the range of others), as well as with natural forces and physical laws."

1114 Held, George F. *The Good That Lives after Them: A Pattern in Shakespeare's Tragedies*. Anglistische Forschungen 231. Heidelberg: Winter, 1995. 247 pp.

Held argues that one of the features of Shakespeare's great tragedies is that "if the protagonist grieves over the death of the person he loves most, he subsequently dies from grief and from or for love; his death hence is to some extent a love sacrifice." *Antony and Cleopatra* is not a great tragedy because "its protagonists do not seem quite as tragic as those of the other four plays." Antony's and Cleopatra's deaths are not love sacrifices.

Antony wants to kill himself, "not out of grief over her death but in order to avoid the 'disgrace and horror' that are his since he has been conquered by Octavius Caesar." Cleopatra "does in fact kill herself not out of grief over Antony's death but in order to avoid the disgrace and horror of being displayed in Caesar's triumphal procession."

1115 Hunt, Maurice. "Elizabethan 'Modernism," Jacobean 'Postmodernism': Schematizing Stir in the Drama of Shakespeare and His Contemporaries." *Papers on Language and Literature* 31 (1995): 115-44.

In *King Lear*, *Antony and Cleopatra*, and *The Winter's Tale*, Shakespeare "solved an aesthetic problem of the relationship of flux to ordering stasis to a degree not attained by other Jacobean playwrights. Certain strategies of postmodernism vis-a-vis defunct Elizabethan 'modernism' create a model for fully comprehending his achievement."

1116 Kernan, Alvin. *Shakespeare, the King's Playwright: Theater in the Stuart Court 1603-1613*. New Haven and London: Yale UP, 1995. 230 pp.

Shakespeare did not portray James I directly on the stage. But his audiences "at Whitehall that Christmas would have been aware that the character of Octavius, representing order and rationality in conflict with anarchy and sensuality, figured James Stuart in his official position as the governor of the court and the representative of state morality." The question Shakespeare focused on "was Stuart court corruption, which was reflected in the excesses of Egypt and the Roman Antony's submersion in them"

1117 Kim, Yongtae. "The Jacobean Roman Tragedies of Shakespeare and Jonson in their Political Context." *Dissertation Abstracts International* 55 (1994-95): 3852A (Nebraska-Lincoln).

After discussing the contemporary historical context and its relationship to meaning in *Antony and Cleopatra* and *Coriolanus*, Kim suggests that Antony's dalliance with Cleopatra reflects the corruption in the court of James I.

1118 Lee, Hee-Won. "Histrionic Cleopatra as a Critic of Patriarch: A Feminist Study of *Antony and Cleopatra*." *Shakespeare Review* (Seoul) 27 (1995): 191-212.

Cleopatra criticizes the Roman patriarchy as she performs her various roles in *Antony and Cleopatra.*

1119 Leimberg, Inge. "The Scarrus-Episode in *Antony and Cleopatra*: A Response to Roy Batttenhouse, *Shakespearean Tragedy*." *Connotations* 4 (1994-95): 251-65.

The validity of Battenhouse's Christian approach is questionable, especially in his reading of the Scarrus episode in the play.

1120 Lindblade, Thomas Wendel. "Tactical Measures: The Interactions of Drama with Music (Shakespeare, Bertolt Brecht, Germany, Samuel Beckett, Ireland, France, Robert Wilson." *Dissertation Abstracts International* 56 (1995): 2046A (Stanford).

In plays like *Antony and Cleopatra*, *Hamlet*, *Othello* and *King Lear*, Shakespeare "utilizes the medieval concepts of musica humana, musica mundana, and musica instrumentalis as an aesthetic triumvirate to unify the text, explore character, and create a heightened awareness through a disjunctive technique of lexicon pitted against melody."

1121 Lombardo, Agostino. *Il fuoco e l'aria. Quattro studi su Antonio e Cleopatra.* Piccola biblioteca shakespeariana 9. Rome: Bulzoni, 1995. 103 pp.

This is a collection of Lombardo's previously published articles (see items 224, 234, 909, 1070).

1122 Magoulias, Michael, ed. *Shakespearean Criticism: Excerpts from the Criticism of William Shakespeare's Plays and Poetry, from the First Published Appraisals to Current Evaluations*. Vol. 27. New York: Gale, 1995. xi, 423 pp.

This is a selection of excerpts from criticism (principally since 1960) about Shakespeare and classical civilization in *Antony and Cleopatra*, *Timon of Athens*, *Titus Andronicus*, and

Troilus and Cressida, along with a selective annotated bibliography of additional studies of each work and cumulative index of topics. The section on Shakespeare and classical civilization (pp. 1-80) organizes the material under these headings: Overviews, Rome, Vergil and Ovid, Greece. The headings in the section on *Antony and Cleopatra* (pp. 81-153) are: Structure, Language, Myth, Rome vs. Egypt, Cleopatra.

1123 Marriot, John Eric. "Challenging Cultural Stereotypes: Women Tragic Protagonists in Jacobean Drama (Women Characters, Shakespeare, Francis Beaumont, John Ford, Thomas Middleton, John Webster)." *Dissertation Abstracts International* 56 (1995): 980A (UBC).

For Shakespeare's Desdemona and Cleopatra, "sexuality is an integral part of the love they offer Othello and Antony who, however, stereotypically see women's sexuality as wantonness and temptation."

1124 Newton, Allyson P. "At 'the very heart of loss': Shakespeare's Enobarbus and the Rhetoric of Remembering." *Renaissance Papers 1995*. Ed. George Walton Williams and Barbara J. Baines. Raleigh: Southern Renaissance Conference, 1996, pp. 81-91.

The varied memories and memorials of Enobarbus characterize Cleopatra. "Unlike the Cydnus speech, with its calculating presentation of Cleopatra as the mistress of appearances and theatrical effects, Enobarbus' memory seems to glimpse Cleopatra when she is not aware of being seen, in a moment to which Enobarbus somehow has been accidentally privy."

1125 Nochimson, Richard L. "The Establishment of Tragic and Untragic Patterns in the Opening Scenes of *Hamlet*, *Macbeth*, *Antony and Cleopatra*, and *Troilus and Cressida*." *Entering the Maze: Shakespeare's Art of Beginning*. Ed. Robert F. Willson, Jr. New York: Peter Lang, 1995, pp. 75-94.

Nochimson's focus is "the assumptions and expectations that Shakespeare creates for the spectator at the beginning of a potentially tragic play to prepare the spectator for the tragic or, alternatively, for the ironic reactions that should follow." Shakespeare "has deflated our expectations for Antony and Cleopatra, diminishing their potential for tragic status by avoiding the opportunity to depict larger forces in control of their destinies."

1126 Raizada, Seema. *Problem Plays of Shakespeare: Double Vision in Character and Action*. Delhi: Sharad, 1994.

Analyzing *Antony and Cleopatra* and other plays, Raizada suggests that "the duality of Shakepeare's vision of creative imagination and intellect, of the secular and the spiritual, of appearance and essence, and even of life and death, indicates not only the richness of his vision but also a deliberate design on his part to present life's contradictions, ambiguities, and ambivalences."

1127 Ronan, Clifford. *"Antike Roman": Power Symbology and the Roman Play in Early Modern England 1585-1635*. Athens and London: U of Georgia P, 1995. xiii, 233 pp.

In Antony and Cleopatra and other Roman plays, Shakespeare reflected contemporary artistic, ethical, and political concerns.

1128 Sacerdoti, Gilberto. "'What means this?' An 'odd trick' in Shakespeare's *Antony and Cleopatra*." *Counting and Recounting. Measuring Inner and Outer Space in the Renaissance*. Ed. Paolo Bottalla and Michela Calderaso. Trieste: La Mongolfiera, 1995, pp. 209-31.

This is a reading of the play in the context of neoplatonic and hermetic doctrines derived from Giordano Bruno.

1129 Sanders, Eve Rachele. "Inscribing Selves: Gender and Literacy in the English Public Theater (William Shakespeare, Mary Sidney, Robert Garnier, Samuel Daniel, Samuel Brand." *Dissertation Abstracts International* 56 (1995): 3980A (California-Berkeley).

Analyzing sex-specific models of reading in "educational treatises and conduct manuals," it appears that "Antony and Cleopatra figure as anti-ideals to the model English Gentleman and English Gentlewoman that sex-specific practices of reading were intended to form." In the early modern period, "men and women learned to read and write in ways that fostered differences between them," and the theater "both aided and disrupted" this process.

1130 Singh, Sukhbir. "Shakespeare's 'Dolphin' in Eliot's Drawing Room: *The Waste Land* II, line 96." *English Language Notes* 33.2 (1995): 59-62.

Eliot's reference to "a carved dolphin" in "The Game of Chess" alludes to Cleopatra's eulogy for Antony and to Oberon's description of a mermaid's song in *A Midsummer Night's Dream.*

1131 Smith, Peter J. "Social Geography of the Renaissance: On the Imagery of *Antony and Cleopatra.*" *Social Shakespeare: Aspects of Renaissance Dramaturgy and Contemporary Society.* Basingstoke: Macmillan; New York: St. Martin's P, 1995, pp. 62-91.

Antony and Cleopatra "is built upon a mesh of imagery and the structural dialectic of the play (Rome versus Egypt) is the genesis of the double standard upon which so much of that imagery rests." These images do "not form a consistent correlative for something"; they are "redefined upon each occasion" and are hence "environmentally conditioned." For this reason, "the relativity which underlies a play like *Antony and Cleopatra* dramatises the moment of separation of mankind and the natural world." This play "is built upon infinitely regressive ironies: the stage, the cast, the characters, the characters' ideas and lastly the ideas themselves and we are show that in the smallest of these Chinese boxes where we would expect an absolute standard, we in fact find only a relativity which undermines our most fundamental conceptions about the interplay between female and male."

1132 Song, Won-Moon. "Racial Otherness: The Representation of Colored Minorities in Shakespeare and Restoration Drama." *Dissertation Abstracts International* 55 (1994-95): 3525A (Wisconsin-Madison).

This is a comparative study of the treatment of colored minorities in Shakespeare's *Antony and Cleopatra*, *Othello*, *The Tempest*, and *Titus Andronicus* and some of the Restoration plays.

1133 Vinson, Pauline H. "Chastity on Display: Gender, Theater, and Problems of Representation in English Renaissance Drama." *Dissertation Abstracts International* 56 (1995-96): 2700A (Northwestern).

Antony and Cleopatra and other plays trace the ways in which the Renaissance theatre and contemporary male concerns about female chastity intersect and affect "modes of theatrical production."

1134 Baines, Barbara J. "Girard's Doubles and *Antony and Cleopatra.*" *Antony and Cleopatra.* Ed. Nigel Wood. Theory in Practice. Buckingham and Philadelphia: Open UP, 1996, pp. 9-39.

Antony and Cleopatra "come together within the context of the rivalry between two Roman brothers who divide the world between them. The coming together and the togetherness of Antony and Cleopatra can, in fact, be understood only within the complex patterns of mimetic desire and rivalry that govern action and characterization in *Antony and Cleopatra.*"

1135 Brown, John Russell. *William Shakespeare: Writing for Performance*. New York: St. Martin's P, 1996. 184 pp.

Brown cites a few passages from this play to illustrate his arguments about writing for the theatre.

1136 Callaghan, Dympna. "Representing Cleopatra in the Post-Colonial Moment." *Antony and Cleopatra.* Ed. Nigel Wood. Theory in Practice. Buckingham and Philadelphia: Open UP, 1996, pp. 40-65.

This play "is an important cultural document in the history of the West's eroticization, and thence subjugation, of the raced woman as Other, a complex male fantasy and projection. Indeed, it is because the Other is always a projection, a complex and culturally necessary fantasy, that Cleopatra cannot represent authentic alterity." Cleopatra's voice may be "hubristic and voluble," but it is merely an instance of elaborate Western ventriloquism." A critic's "more complex and more urgent" job is "to show that even in the process of ostensibly being represented, the category of radical female alterity is absent as ever, its representation barred by a cunning simulation."

1137 Davis, Philip. *Sudden Shakespeare: The Shaping of Shakespeare's Creative Thought*. London: Athlone, 1996. 259 pp.

"There is a bursting feeling about the plays; almost too much seems to be happening simultaneously." Shakespeare is "first of all a technical writer, getting himself into tight configurations of space and time which bring forth words—and only then meanings, arising out of them." His sense of form "is protean, as a packed content pushes and probes blindly amidst countervailing forces to find shape, name, action and expression for itself." Shakespeare "sets going a process through scene after scene which of itself seems a model or a site for all those questions about life as it comes into being that one could ever ask—without himself being initially committed to anything other than the technical creation of the process."

1138 Hamer, Mary. "Reading *Antony and Cleopatra* through Irigaray's Speculum" *Antony and Cleopatra*. Ed. Nigel Wood. Theory in Practice. Buckingham and Philadelphia: Open UP, 1996, pp. 66-91.

Shakespeare was one of the Renaissance artists and writers who "began to rework the figure of Cleopatra as they renewed their identification with the Roman tradition. They had to square her not only with their sense of the imperial past but also with current attempts in the cities where they lived, in Augsburg, Haarlem or Florence to lay down the terms for women's lives and for relations between the sexes. It was with one eye on the new institution of Christian marriage that they told the story of Cleopatra." The question of Cleopatra's race cannot be overlooked. "Shakespeare's imagination may be able to reconcile her with less privileged women, but it preserves a chasm between her dark self and the white women of Rome."

1139 Date, Toshohiro. "A Bridge between Shakespeare and the Traditional Theatre of Japan." *Shakespeare East and West.* Ed. Minoru Fujita and Leonard Pronko. New York: St. Martin's P, 1996, pp. 77-102.

Shakespeare in this play and Chikamatsu in *Sonezaki Shinju* (*The Love Suicides at Sonezaki*, 1703) "have the same penetrating look into the potentiality of pure love and human dignity in worldly love affairs."

1140 Hodgdon, Barbara. "'Doing the Egyptian': Critical/Theatrical Performances, Oxford and London, 1906." *Antony and Cleopatra.* Ed. Nigel Wood. Theory in Practice. Buckingham and Philadelphia: Open UP, 1996, pp. 268-96.

Hodgdon's objective "is to illuminate the meanings of *Antony and Cleopatra* to particular readers and spectators in a specific sociohistorical moment and so to contribute to discussions about how reading and theatrical effects shape the cultural destiny of a text as well as that of its central icon."

1141 Hyland, Peter. *An Introduction to Shakespeare: The Dramatist in His Context.* New York: St. Martin's P, 1996. 224 pp.

Antony's tragedy "does arise from a conflict between duty and desire, between the military code of Rome embodied in Caesar and the pull of erotic love embodied in Cleopatra, between public and private worlds." In this play, "the tragic and the comic are not different modes but inextricable components of each other."

1142 James, Heather. "The Politics of Display and the Anamorphic Subjects of *Antony and Cleopatra.*" *Shakespeare's Late Tragedies.* Ed. Suzanne L. Wofford. New Century Views 13. Upper Saddle River, NJ: Prentice Hall, 1996, pp. 208-34.

This essay "seeks to retie *Antony and Cleopatra*'s concerns with sexuality and politics into a 'knot intrinsicate' and, more generally, to argue that sexuality, gender, and a refurbished notion of character should be reconsidered as indispensable terms of—not arbitrary metaphors for—political questions in the emergent Roman empire of the play, in Jacobean England, and in the Shakespearean theater."

1143 Kiernan, Pauline. "*Antony and Cleopatra* as 'A Defence of Drama'." *Shakespeare's Theory of Drama*. Cambridge: Cambridge UP, 1996, pp. 154-90.

Kiernan discusses Antony *and Cleopatra* as part of her thesis about Shakespeare's theory of drama premised on "the primacy of the human body in his art" and on "an insistence on the fictitious status of his drama." What distinguishes this play from Plutarch is that Shakespeare makes Cleopatra a physical, concrete figure of flesh bound by time and decay; hers is the immediate world of the senses. Shakespeare identifies time with biological processes of birth and death, "and it is the indissoluble link between organic process and time that powers the play." Kiernan points out this link: "All we are given is Cleopatra's body, standing on a bare stage: 'I am again for Cydnus' announces the dramatist's triumph over all insubstantial versions of Cleopatra that have gone before, including that of Enobarbus in this play. The body that stands before is 'nature's piece, 'gainst fancy, / Condemning shadows quite'." The playwright's achievement in his characterization of Cleopatra "lies in her power to surpass nature while remaining within nature."

1144 McDonald, Russ. *The Bedford Companion to Shakespeare. An Introduction with Documents*. New York: St. Martin's P, 1996. 240 pp.

A number of references to *Antony and Cleopatra* deal with topics like female roles, language, sources, stages, and the genre of tragedy.

1145 Miles, Geoffrey. *Shakespeare and the Constant Romans*. Oxford English Monographs. Oxford: Clarendon P, 1996, pp. 169-88.

Miles examines the play in the context of the Stoic ideal of constancy as steadfastness and consistency: "More than any other of Shakespeare's plays, Antony and Cleopatra is dominated by a sense of mutability." Unlike the Romans, Antony "can only define what is proper for him in terms of his own continually changing self." From a Stoic perspective, Antony is 'a man whose surrender to fortune leaves him without the inner strength to withstand adversity." He acquires a fixed and constant identity only in his death: "Antony's Stoic death seems like a tragicomic attempt to attain stability in a world whose chaotic mutability undercuts any such attempt." The motives and manner of Cleopatra's death "are very close to those of the traditional Stoic suicide as defined by Seneca and practised by Cato or Brutus." Cleopatra "does not reject her un-Roman, un-Stoic qualities—emotionalism, sensuality, frivolity, capriciousness, changeableness—but combines them with a new Stoic dignity and resolution."

1146 Weber, A.S. "New Physics for the Nonce: A Stoic and Hermetic reading of Shakespeare's *Antony and Cleopatra*." *Renaissance Papers 1995*. Ed. George Walton Williams and Barbara J. Baines. Raleigh: Southern Renaissance Conference, 1996, pp. 93-107.

On the basis of its stoic cosmology, this play should be situated within the English anti-Aristotelian movement. The playwright had been influenced by the strong Stoic bias of his education and the developments in technical astronomy. "The play's patterns, including Christian resurrection symbolism, alchemical imagery, and Herculean cosmic allegory, coalesce in the striking image of Antony's apotheosis in Cleopatra's dream in Act V."

1147 Wilcher, Robert. "*Antony and Cleopatra* and Genre Criticism." *Antony and Cleopatra*. Ed. Nigel Wood. Theory in Practice. Buckingham and Philadelphia: Open UP, 1996, pp. 92-124.

This play can "be seen as a text which problematizes the tendency to allow meaning to be shaped by the generic perspective adopted by writer and reader." The "direct experience" of the play "must bring to bear what is known about the 'generic horizon' within which the text was first created, if it is to offer anything more than a collection of subjective and historically ungrounded impressions."

1148 Wofford, Suzanne L., ed. *Shakespeare's Late Tragedies*. New Century Views 13. Upper Saddle River, NJ: Prentice Hall, 1996. 304 pp.

This anthology reprints, in part or in whole, material by Jonathan Dollimore, Heather James, Ania Loomba, Michael Goldman, and Barbara Hodgdon.

1149 Wortham, Christopher. "Temperance and the End of Time: Emblematic *Antony and Cleopatra*." *Emblem, Iconography, and Drama*. Ed. Clifford Davidson, Louis R. Gamez, and John H. Stroupe. Kalamazoo, MI: Medieval Institute Publications, Western Michigan U, 1995, pp. 1-37.

The "Jacobean mentality that operates through a discourse of ideological expression" in this play can be reconstructed by focusing on how Shakespeare's emphasis on temperance links emblematic representations of Mars and Hercules with Antony to a biblical dimension that stresses the apocalypse, and how all of this serves as a compliment to James I.

1150 Zhang, Xiao Yang. *Shakespeare in China: A Comparative Study of Two Traditions and Cultures*. Newark: U of Delaware P, 1996. 279 pp.

This study "describes many differences and similarities between Shakespeare and traditional Chinese drama." It "examines the nature and significance of the interaction between Shakespeare and traditional Chinese drama. It "explores the interaction between Shakespeare and Chinese culture." Zhang also comments on the productions of *Antony and Cleopatra* by the Shanghai Youth Spoken Drama Troupe in 1984.

1151 Hunter, G.K. *English Drama 1586-1642: The Age of Shakespeare*. Oxford History of English Literature VI. Oxford: Clarendon P, 1997. 623 pp.

In his brief discussion, Hunter argues that this play "is clearly designed to bring the heroisms of empire and sexual passion not only into tension against one another but also into a mutually supportive grandeur of world-contemning, death-defying experience." Antony and Cleopatra "take a dionysiac delight in transgressing the boundaries that convention sets between male and female, drunk and sober, human and divine, tragic and comic, serious and playful, spiritual and physical, royal and vulgar."

What saves the two of them from disgrace "is that decline and failure lead them not to hide but discover selves they can die with."

1152 Wells, Stanley. *Shakespeare: The Poet and his Plays*. Rev. ed. London: Methuen, 1997. 411 pp.

Wells argues that this play "resembles the sonnets in its emphasis on the destructive power of time, but it resembles them too in its counterbalancing suggestions that the power of human love, and of the imagination, can transcend the effects of time." He suggests that "the geographical scope of the action, wide enough in itself, gains in effect from the hyperbolical terms in which the protagonists are portrayed and indeed in which they think of themselves." Shakespeare presents Cleopatra, "not as a woman who steadily develops, maturing finally into a dignified and immaculate tragedy queen, but as a woman to be wondered at in her complexity to the end."

Sources and Background

1153 Skeat, W. W., ed. *Shakespeare's Plutarch.* London: Macmillan, 1875. xxxi, 332 pp.

This is a reprint of the 1612 text of North's Plutarch.

1154 Rouse, W.H.D., ed."The Life of Marcus Antonius." *Plutarch's Lives: Englished by Sir Thomas North.* The Temple Plutarch. 10 vols. London: J.M. Dent, 1898-1899, IX, 1-118.

This text is based on the first edition of 1579: The spelling has been modernised, except in a few words where it testified to the ancient pronunciation; but old grammatical have been kept unchanged." There are brief notes and vocabulary at the back.

1155 Anders, H[enry] R. D. *Shakespeare's Books: A Dissertation on Shakespeare's Reading and the Immediate Sources of his Works.* Schriften der Deutschen Shakespeare-Gesellschaft 1. Berlin: G. Reimer, 1904. xx, 316 pp.

Anders identifies the sources of *Antony and Cleopatra* in Plutarch, Ovid, Pliny, the Psalms, and others.

1156 Brooke, C.F.L. Tucker, ed. "The Main Sources of *Antony and Cleopatra.*" *Shakespeare's Plutarch.* 2 Volumes. London: Chatto & Windus, 1909.

Tucker Brooke has selected here the North text of 1579. In his introduction he stresses that the minor characters in this play "are for the most part elaborated by Shakespeare out of very scanty suggestions."

1157 Taylor, George Coffin. *Shakespeare's Debt to Montaigne.* Cambridge, MA: 1925. Reprint. New York: Phaeton P, 1968. 66 pp.

Taylor cites parallels between passages, "in which it is possible to detect the most convincing evidences of an immediate relation between Shakespeare and Montaigne." Seven of the quotations are taken from *Antony and Cleopatra.* They "justify the inference that he had read the [John] Florio [translation of Montaigne's *Essays* in English, published in 1603] practically from cover to cover."

1158 Ellehauge, Martin. "The Use of His Sources Made by Shakespeare in *Julius Caesar* and *Antony and Cleopatra.*" *Englische Studien* 65 (1930): 197-210.

Commenting on action, character and language, this study focuses on what Shakespeare "copies, what he changes, and what he gains by it."

1159 Clark, Eva Lee Turner. "*Antony and Cleopatra.*" *Hidden Allusions in Shakespeare's Plays.: A Study of the Oxford Theory based on the Records of Early Court Revels and Personalities of the Times.* New York: William Farquhar Payson, 1931, pp. 202-13.

North's translation of Plutarch in 1579 "was ready to hand material for a drama that would commemorate the visit in August, 1579, of Alencon, Prince of France, to Elizabeth, Queen of England, by portraying a romantic and somewhat similar situation in ancient history, the visit of Antony, Consul of Rome, to Cleopatra, Queen of Egypt, albeit the play may be said to end in a warning to Elizabeth not to ally herself with the French Prince" (202).

1160 Murry, John Middleton. "North's Plutarch." *Centuries of the Mind, 2nd. Series.* Oxford: Oxford UP, 1931. Reprint. Freeport, NY: Books for Libraries P, 1968, pp. 78-96.

Shakespeare based his play on North's Plutarch "steadily and completely" and "used North's language because he had none better."

1161 Noble, Richmond. *Shakespeare's Biblical Knowledge and Use of the Book of Common Prayer.* Oxford: Society for Promoting Christian Knowledge, 1935, pp. 238-40

Shakespeare "often alludes to or makes use of a Biblical incident in some way or other without mentioning any proper names at all; if the audience cares to fill in the name it can do so, but as far as the author is concerned no name which might divert the attention from the main issue is indicated." For example, 2 Pet. iii.13 can be found in *Antony and Cleopatra* I.i.117.

1162 Craig, Horace S. "Duelling Scenes and Terms in Shakespeare's Plays." *University of California Publications in English* 9.1 (1940): 1-28.

In the course of documenting the background for duelling and swords, Craig comments on the "he at Philippi" passage in *Antony and Cleopatra.*

1163 Law, Robert Adger. "The Text of Shakespeare's Plutarch." *Huntington Library Quarterly* 6 (1942): 197-203.

Since the list of ladies given by Titania in *A Midsummer Night's Dream* is drawn from the 1579 edition of the life of Theseus in North's translation of Plutarch, Shakespeare must have used this version, not the later ones.

1164 Draper, John W. *The Humors and Shakespeare's Characters.* Durham: Duke UP, 1945. 126 pp.

Elizabethans believed in the Greek theory of humors, and the inner psychology of a character can be grasped according "to the individual's physique, the humor or fluid that dominated his body, and the associated planet, metal, colors, and the rest." Shakespeare delineates Antony as "a phlegmatic voluptuary, heedless of martial glory and honor." Cleopatra is a mercurial type, "who, womanlike, founded her power on her weakness." According to Draper, "Cleopatra's subduing of Antony's martial choler to a luxurious phlegm by a round of exhausting pleasures shows her an even cleverer practical psychologist than Petruchio, whose heroic treatment was certainly less pleasing to the patient."

1165 Starnes, DeWitt T. "Shakespeare and Apuleius." *PMLA: Publications of the Modern Language Association* 60 (1945): 1021-1050.

Identifying Apuleius as one of the sources, Starnes proposes that "to posit the Cleopatra of Enobarbus' description as a synthesis of the matter from Apuleius and Plutarch is to offer a satisfactory explanation of the highly controversial phrases and to state a theory entirely in accord with Shakespeare's art."

1166 Westbrook, Perry D. "Horace's Influence on Shakespeare's *Antony and Cleopatra*." *PMLA: Publications of the Modern Language Association* 62 (1947): 392-98.

Shakespeare may have drawn Cleopatra's tragic heroism from Horace's Cleopatra Ode, suggesting that it is "royal pride that brings her to self-destruction" and not "the frenzy of a desperate minds" as in Plutarch. Shakespeare relied on *Epode* 9 for his image of the hostile Roman attitude toward Cleopatra.

1167 Nyland, Waino S. "Pompey as the Mythical Lover of Cleopatra." *Modern Language Notes* 64 (1949): 515-16.

Nyland discusses a source of statements in *Antony and Cleopatra*, 1.5.31-34, and 3.13.116-18.

1168 Dennet, Dayton N. "Samuel Daniel's Tragedy of Cleopatra: A Critical Edition." Diss. Cornell. *Index to American Doctoral Dissertations 1951/52* , p. 140.

Abstract not available.

1169 Jorgensen, Paul A. "Enobarbus' Broken Heart and *The Estate of English Fugitives*." *Philosophical Quarterly* 30 (1951): 387-392.

Jorgensen argues that Enobarbus' death by heartbreak, which contradicts Plutarch's account, was suggested to Shakespeare by Sir Lewis Lewkenor's book (1595), which purports to describe the grief and unexplained deaths of English renegades in Spain.

1170 Reeves, John D. "A Supposed Indebtedness of Shakespeare to Peele." *Notes and Queries* 197 (1952): 441-42.

Peele's Queen Elinor-Mayoress episode was not Shakespeare's source, and his horrific scene of death by snakebite has little to do with Shakespeare.

1171 Ribner, Irving. "Shakespeare and Peele: The Death of Cleopatra." *Notes and Queries* 197 (1952): 244-46.

Ribner finds a source of Cleopatra's death-scene in Plutarch, and particularly of V.ii.311-13 of *Antony and Cleopatra*, in Peele's *Edward the First*.

1172 Thomson, J.A.K. *Shakespeare and the Classics*. London: Allen & Unwin, 1952. 254 pp.

In a brief discussion of *Antony and Cleopatra*, Thomson lists parallels between Ovid and other classical writers and Shakespeare. Thomson suggests that Shakespeare "was but a perfunctory reader of the classics, and that like most of us who are not Latin scholars he used translations when they came to hand, and only turned to the original when his interest or curiosity was aroused."

1173 Hankins, John Erskine. *Shakespeare's Derived Imagery.* Lawrence: U of Kansas P, 1953. Reprint. New York: Octagon Books, 1967 and 1977. 289 pp.

Hankins argues that "Shakespeare's imagery was derived from earlier authors and that some of their words survive in his expression of the images." He explicates about ten passages from *Antony and Cleopatra.*

1174 Bradbrook, Frank W. "Thomas Nashe and Shakespeare." *Notes and Queries* 199 (1954): 470.

Cleopatra's speech in 5.2 may have been influenced by Thomas Nashe's *Christ's Tears over Jerusalem* because it has "the vividness with which the present is *seen*, and the imagery of the heavens, the sun and moon is identical."

1175 Oakeshott, Walter. "Shakespeare and Plutarch." *Talking of Shakespeare.* Ed. John Garrett. London: Hodder & Stoughton, 1954, pp. 111-25.

A major difference in Plutarch's interpretation of Antony and that of Shakespeare's is that "Shakespeare divined the prejudices of the Stoic Plutarch and saw through them to a truer Antony."

1176 Michel, Laurence, and Cecil D. Seronsy. "Shakespeare's History Plays and Daniel: An Assessment." *Studies in Philology* 52 (1955): 549-77.

Verbal parallels between *Antony and Cleopatra* and Daniel "add a little to the argument for the priority of Shakespeare's play—an argument that rests mainly, if uncertainly, on the structural changes Daniel made in the 1607 version."

1177 Norgaard, Holger. "The Bleeding Captain Scene in *Macbeth* and Daniel's *Cleopatra*." *Review of English Studies* ns 6 (1955): 395-96.

Daniel's *Cleopatra* "furnished several hints for *Antony and Cleopatra*."

1178 Norgaard, Holger. "Shakespeare and Daniel's 'Letter from Octavia'." *Notes and Queries* ns 2 (1955): 56-57.

Shakespeare may have drawn on the second stanza of Daniel's *Letter* in his presentation of Antony's response to the messenger with letters from his wife.

1179 Simpson, Percy. *Studies in Elizabethan Drama*. Oxford: Clarendon P, 1955. 265 pp.

Simpson discusses Shakespeare's use of Latin authors in *Anthony and Cleopatra* and other plays and "the pause a supreme factor" in Shakespeare's versification.

1180 Norman, Arthur M.Z. "Source Material in 'Anthony and Cleopatra.'." *Notes and Queries* ns 3 (1956): 59-61.

Norman explains how Shakespeare read and assimilated Plutarch.

1181 Schanzer, Ernest. "'Antony and Cleopatra' and the Countess of Pembroke's 'Antonius'." *Notes and Queries* ns 3 (1956): 152-54.

Numerous parallels in the language suggest that Shakespeare had read *Antonius* before or during the composition of *Antony and Cleopatra*.

1182 Schanzer, Ernest, ed. *Shakespeare's Appian: A Selection from the Tudor Translation of Appian's "Civil Wars."* English Reprints Series 13. Liverpool: U of Liverpool P, 1956. xxviii, 101 pp.

This is a reprint of one of the probable sources for the play.

1183 Starnes, DeWitt T., and Ernest W. Talbert. *Classical Myth and Legend in Renaissance Dictionaries*. Chapel Hill: U of North Carolina P, 1956. 517 pp.

Although Plutarch was Shakespeare's principal source for this play, "it seems not improbable that he had also read and remembered the sketch of Cleopatra in Cooper's *Thesaurus*." From Cooper he derived the application of the word "dotage" and "the manner of Cleopatra's death."

1184 Thomas, Mary Olive. "Plutarch in *Antony and Cleopatra*." Diss. Chicago. *Index to American Doctoral Dissertations 1955/56*, p. 139.

Abstract not available.

1185 Muir, Kenneth. "*Antony and Cleopatra*." *Shakespeare's Sources*. Vol. 1. London: Methuen, 1957, pp. 201-19. *The Sources of Shakespeare's Plays*. London: Methuen, 1977, pp. 220-37.

Muir analyzes the sources for plot and the use Shakespeare made of them. He gives excerpts from Plutarch, Appian, the Countess of Pembroke, Daniel, and the Book of Revelation.

1186 Barroll, J. Leeds. "Shakespeare and Roman History." *Modern Language Review* 53 (1958): 327-343.

In terms of tragedy and of history, Shakespeare wrote *Julius Caesar* and *Antony and Cleopatra* "in a tradition which was fostered and dominated by the Countess of Pembroke's

Circle." The recent writings of this circle, not Plutarch, "may have directed Shakespeare's attention to the story."

1187 Potts, Abbie Findlay. "*Antony and Cleopatra.*" *Shakespeare and* The Faerie Queene. Ithaca and London: Cornell UP, 1958, pp. 199-207.

Shakespeare's literary ideas "bear a close resemblance to the literary ideas" of Spenser. The fact that "Shakespeare has seen the truth in Cleopatra, the possible Una in the actual Duessa, the possible holiness or magnificence in the actually faithless Antony, give him complete control of his ethical action."

1188 Honigmann, E.A.J. "Shakespeare's Plutarch." *Shakespeare Quarterly* 10 (1959): 25-33.

Shakespeare has been more broadly indebted to Plutarch than scholars have recognized. Most frequently ignored have been the "comparison" chapters as they apply to Antony.

1189 Lloyd, Michael. "Cleopatra as Isis." *Shakespeare Survey* 12 (1959): 88-94.

Shakespeare may have Cleopatra's most striking qualities from his knowledge of the cult of Isis in Plutarch and Apuleius.

1190 Norman, Arthur M.Z. "'The Tragedie of Cleopatra' and the Date of 'Antony and Cleopatra'." *Modern Language Review* 54 (1959): 1-9.

Antony and Cleopatra "was written some time in 1606 or 1607," in which Shakespeare "echoed one of the 1594-1605 editions of Daniel's *Cleopatra.*" Daniel "witnessed a performance of Shakespeare's play and found in it the spur he needed to reconsider his early tragedy."

1191 Stamm, Rudolf. "Elizabethan Stage Practice and the Transmutation of Source Material by the Dramatists." *Shakespeare Survey* 12 (1959): 64-70.

There is a close relation between this play and its source in North's Plutarch.

1192 Rees, Joan. "Shakespeare's Use of Daniel." *Modern Language Review* 55 (1960): 79-82.

Daniel's "Letter from Octavia to Marcus Antonius" is a "device of the imagined reception of the letter" which Shakespeare uses in this play. It is significant to note "the way in which [Shakespeare] changes and stabilizes the idea," and he "charges even such a small fragment with the complexities of motive and character that underlay the whole play."

1193 Turner, Paul, ed. *Selected Lives from the Lives of the Noble Grecians and Romans*. Centaur Classics. 2 vols. Carbondale: Southern Illinois UP, 1963.

This is a reprint of the 1579 text, with an introduction by the editor.

1194 Rees, Joan. *Samuel Daniel*. Liverpool: Liverpool UP, 1964. 184 pp.

The purpose of Daniel's revision of *Cleopatra* in 1607 "was not to emulate Shakespeare nor to compete with him on his own ground, but to show how the bounds of neo-classic drama could be enlarged beyond the narrow limits of the earlier Pembroke examples and yet remain uncontaminated by sensationalism and technical 'licence'."

1195 Jones, Eldred. *Othello's Countrymen: The African in English Renaissance Drama*. London: Oxford UP, 1965. 158 pp.

Shakespeare "may have based Antony's description of the measurement of the Nile" on a passage in John Pory's 1600 translation of *The History and Description of Africa* by Leo Africanus.

1196 Bullough, Geoffrey. *Narrative and Dramatic Sources of Shakespeare*. Vol. 5. New York: Columbia UP, 1966, pp. 215-449.

Bullough provides an introduction (215-53 pp.), and extensive excerpts from Plutarch, Lucan, Appian, Robert Garnier, Samuel Daniel, and Simon Goulart's *Life of Augustus*.

1197 Griffin, Alice. *The Sources of Ten Shakespeare Plays*. New York: Thomas Y. Crowell, 1966. 312 pp.

In her analysis of Shakespeare's use of sources, Griffin suggests that Shakespeare shows sympathy for the lovers from the beginning and Plutarch does so only towards the end.

1198 Satin, Joseph. "*Antony and Cleopatra*." *Shakespeare and his Sources*. Boston: Houghton Mifflin, 1966, pp. 573-623.

Satin reprints large sections from Plutarch's *Parallel Lives* and the Countess of Pembroke's *Antonie*, along with a brief headnote and sources for further study.

1199 Sampson, Sr. Helen Lucy. "A Critical Edition of Samuel Daniel's *The Tragedie of Cleopatra*." *Dissertation Abstracts* 27 (1967): 3017A (St. Louis).

This is an edition with introduction and explanatory notes. It shows the relationship of the 1607 version to *Antony and Cleopatra* and concludes that it is "exceedingly difficult to present conclusive proof of his [Daniel's] actual borrowing."

1200 Spencer, T.J.B., ed. *Shakespeare's Plutarch*. Penguin Shakespeare Library. Harmondsworth: Penguin, 1964. 365 pp.

This is a reprint of the 1595 edition of North's Plutarch. The editor has provided at the foot of the page the passages from Shakespeare "in which his language or his treatment of an episode follows North."

1201 Friedman, Stanley. "*Antony and Cleopatra* and Drayton's *Mortimeriados*." *Shakespeare Quarterly* 20 (1969): 481-484.

Since there are a number of parallels between Drayton's heroic poem and *Antony and Cleopatra*, Shakespeare may have used Drayton's work as a source supplementing North's Plutarch.

1202 Muir, Kenneth. "Elizabeth I, Jodelle, and Cleopatra." *Renaissance Drama* ns 2(1969): 197-206.

Muir suggests that "Shakespeare knew Jodelle's play *Cléopâtre captive* as well as *Antonie* in the Countess of Pembroke's translation and Daniel's *Cleopatra*." Muir also points out parallels between the behavior of Queen Elizabeth and that of Cleopatra. He believes that "in two scenes where Cleopatra's conduct has been stigmatized as unregal, Shakespeare came uncannily close to contemporary examples of queenly behavior—closer, indeed, than Samuel Daniel did in his statuesque portrait."

1203 Walter, J. H. "Four Notes on *Antony and Cleopatra*." *Notes and Queries* ns 16 (1969): 137-39.

1. "Her infinite variety" in 2.3.236 may have been suggested to Shakespeare by Plutarch. 2. "Shards" in 3.2.20 means "patches of dung." 3. The conceit in 3.3.158-67 is "evocative of divine threats preceding the plagues that befell the Egyptians (*Exodus* vii. 14-xii.33)." 4. "Poor passion" in 4.15.73-75 may refer to "*hysterica passio*, or the Mother, a condition common to women according to Elizabethan medical views."

1204 Gourlay, Patricia S. "Shakespeare's Use of North's Plutarch in the Roman Plays, with Special Reference to *Julius Caesar*." *Dissertation Abstracts* 31 (1971): 1757A (Columbia).

In *Antony and Cleopatra*, Shakespeare "opposes Cleopatra's romantic idealization of Antony to the Roman judgment of him, which reflects Plutarch's ethic only in fragmented and distorted form."

1205 Williamson, Marilyn L. "Did Shakespeare Use Dio's Roman History?" *Shakespeare Jahrbuch* (Heidelberg) 107 (1971): 180-90.

Shakespeare "borrowed from Dio to develop what he found in Plutarch:" the inspiration for Ventidius' campaign and for the function of Enobarbus in the play.

1206 Thomas, Mary O. "The Opening Scenes of *Antony and Cleopatra.*" *South Atlantic Quarterly* 71 (1972): 565-72.

The similarities between the play's opening scenes and Plutarch are "sufficient to indicate that the scenes' basis in Plutarch is broader than has been generally recognized, and the nature of the connections suggests how a great artist may achieve rich subtleties by building upon a pre-existing work of art."

1207 Leavenworth, Russell E. *Daniel's "Cleopatra:" A Critical Study.* Salzburg Studies in English Literature: Elizabethan and Renaissance Studies 3. Salzburg: Institut fur Englische Sprache und Literatur, Universitat Salzburg, 1974. 137 pp.

Shakespeare's "debt to Daniel in *Antony and Cleopatra* has been much larger than anyone has so far seen fit to recognize." Leavenworth suggests that "while Shakespeare only occasionally attempted to improve upon the thought content of his borrowing from Daniel, he managed to charge all of them with the electrifying immediacy of his own poetic gift."

1208 Morrison, Mary. "Some Aspects of the Treatment of the Theme of *Antony and Cleopatra* in Tragedies of the Sixteenth Century." *Journal of European Studies* (University of East Anglia) 4 (1974): 113-25.

Morrison discusses the trend of sixteenth-century tragedies of Antony and Cleopatra in terms of their characterization, the attitude to history, and treatment of historical characters which later influenced Shakespeare.

1209 Shaw, John. "'In Every Corner of the Stage': *Antony and Cleopatra*, IV.iii." *Shakespeare Studies* 7 (1974): 227-32.

When Shakespeare changes his sources from Bacchus leaving Antony for Caesar's camp to Hercules leaving the earth, he dramatizes departure of strength and virtue, indicating the death of Antony and the end of greatness on earth. This change may have been suggested by *Revelation* and by a Durer illustration. This is one of the few examples in Shakespeare where literary and pictorial sources provided inspiration for an idea of staging.

1210 Fiskin, A.M.I. "*Antony and Cleopatra*: Tangled Skeins of Love and Power." *University of Denver Quarterly* 10 (1975): 93-105.

Arguing that North's Plutarch is "the primary source" *for Antony and Cleopatra*, Fiskin analyzes its minor motifs, Shakespeare's picture of great men in history, and the ennoblement of the lovers.

1211 Watson, G. "The Death of Cleopatra." *Notes and Queries* ns 25 (1978): 409-14.

In creating this scene, Shakespeare may have drawn on Galen as well as on Plutarch and probably on Paul of Aegina.

1212 Tobin, J.J.M. "Apuleius and Antony and Cleopatra, Once More." *Studia Neophilologica* 51 (1979): 225-28.

Besides Isis, some of the elements from *The Golden Asse* help in interpretation of *Antony and Cleopatra* and illuminate the reference to "terrene moon" (3.13.153).

1213 Watson, Gilbert. "The Death of Cleopatra." *Notes and Queries* ns 25 (1978): 409-14; 26 (1979): 133-37.

After discussing the historical circumstances of Cleopatra's death, Watson argues that Galen's *Theriake* may be one of Shakespeare's sources.

1214 Dronke, Peter. "Shakespeare and Joseph of Exeter." *Notes and Queries* ns 27 (1980): 172-74.

In Enobarbus's barge speech, Shakespeare may be indebted to a passage in the late-twelfth-century Trojan epic by Joseph of Exeter, which had been printed seven times between 1541 and 1608.

1215 Kennedy, William J. "Audience and Rhetorical Strategies in Jodelle, Shakespeare, and Lohenstein." *Assays: Critical Approaches to Medieval and Renaissance Texts* 1 (1981): 99-116.

Kennedy argues that "a complex pattern of interaction among tradition, text, and audiences in these plays [about Cleopatra] has significance for literary history, and it makes a comparison of their unequal dramatic results worthwhile." He proposes that "the structural roots of Jodelle's play lie in French courtly literature and early academic classicism of the mid-sixteenth century, Shakespeare's in the popular conventions of late Elizabethan theater, and Lohenstein's in German academic, courtly, and bourgeois culture in the second half of the seventeenth century." Shakespeare's spectators were expected to "the mercurial qualities" which "find their concrete textual analogy in the play's mercurial language. Rhymes, puns, assonances, and other verbal repetitions abound." Shakespeare "appeals to a wider group. Its common denominator is not class or rank but intelligence and sensitivity."

1216 Bhattacharya, Jogesh Chandra. "Subject-Matter in Art." *Journal of the Department of English* (Calcutta University) 17.1 (1981-82): 28-39.

Examples from *Antony and Cleopatra* and *Macbeth* and their comparison with their sources in Plutarch's *Lives* and in

Raphael Holinshed's *Chronicles* show how Shakespeare the artist converted available materials to his or her own purposes.

1217 Bowers, John M. "'I Am Marble-Constant': Cleopatra's Monumental End." *Huntington Library Quarterly* 46 (1983): 283-97.

Shakespeare seems to have been influenced in the invented suicide scenes in *Antony and Cleopatra* by his observations of funerary imagery like chantry-chapels and the personified figure of Death.

1218 Weis, René J.A. "*Caesar's Revenge*: A Neglected Elizabethan Source of *Antony and Cleopatra*." *Jahrbuch der deutschen Shakespeare-Gesellschaft West* 1983: 178-185.

A recognition of *Caesar's Revenge* as a source would help in understanding Shakespeare's writing methods and the moral ambiguities of the play.

1219 Bono, Barbara J. *Literary Transvaluation: From Vergilian Epic to Shakespearean Tragicomedy.* Berkeley and London: U of California P, 1984, pp. 140-224.

Transvaluation is "an artistic act of historical self-consciousness that at once acknowledges the perceived values of the antecedent text and transforms them to serve the uses of the present." Shakespeare's play is a transvaluation of Virgil's *Aeneid.*

1220 Tobin, J.J.M. *Shakespeare's Favorite Novel: A Study of* The Golden Asse *As Primary Source*. Lanham, MD: UP of America, 1984. xxviii, 189 pp.

After studying the influence of *The Golden Ass* on this play, Tobin concludes that "in its sources the tragedy is not so much Roman as Milesian."

1221 Baumbach, Lydia. "Shakespeare and the Classics." *Acta Classica* 28 (1985): 77-86.

Baumbach analyses "Shakespeare's debt to and use of his classical source for the Roman plays, North's Plutarch." She also underlines the "importance of Shakespeare in moulding our ideas about the Roman world'; his plays "will help to keep alive a knowledge of and interest in Classical Studies."

1222 Britton, Elizabeth L. "The Dido-Aeneas Story from Vergil to Dryden." *Dissertation Abstracts International* 45 (1985): 3642A (Virginia).

The chapters on *Antony and Cleopatra* and Dryden's *All for Love* examine the opposing interpretations of the Dido-Aeneas and Antony-Cleopatra stories.

1223 Simard, Rodney. "Source and *Antony and Cleopatra*: Shakespeare's Adaptation of Plutarch's Octavia." *Shakespeare Jahrbuch* (Weimar) 122 (1986): 65-74.

Shakespeare's "adaptation of Plutarch's Octavia is only one example of the subtlety with which he alters the theme and structure of *Antony and Cleopatra*."

1224 Dawson, R. MacG. "But Why Enobarbus?" *Notes and Queries* ns 34 (1987): 216-17.

Shakespeare "deliberately altered the name of Domitius to Enobarbus as 'a master-leaver and a fugitive' from the time he made his first appearance."

1225 Ronan, Clifford J. "*Caesar's Revenge* and the Roman Thoughts in *Antony and Cleopatra*." *Shakespeare Studies* 19 (1987): 171-82.

Shakespeare "had cast an eye on *Revenge* when he wrote or polished *Antony and Cleopatra*." "In language very similar to that in Revenge," Ronan argues, "Shakespeare not only refers to unpeopling Egypt but also to at least three other items appropriate to the recreation of an ancient Mediterranean world: (1) the royal tears of a victorious Triumvir over his dead rival; (2) the concept of imperialism as legalized land piracy; and (3) the way Egyptian mirth contrasts with busy, sober Roman thought."

1226 Steppat, Michael. "Shakespeare's Response to Dramatic Tradition in *Antony and Cleopatra*." *Shakespeare: Text, Language, Criticism: Essays in Honour of Marvin Spevack*. Ed. Bernhard Fabian and Kurt Tetzeli von Rosador. Hildesheim: Olms, 1987, pp. 254-79.

The Countess of Pembroke's translation of Garnier's *Marc Antoine* influenced Shakespeare's characterization of Antony and Samuel Daniel's *Tragedy of Cleopatra* influenced that of Cleopatra.

1227 Pelling, C.R.B., ed. *Plutarch: Life of Antony*. Cambridge Greek and Latin Classics. Cambridge: Cambridge UP, 1988. 338 pp.

This is the Greek text of Plutarch. In his introduction, Pelling emphasizes that Plutarch's "own leading themes and ideas" can be found in Shakespeare's play.

1228 Miles, Gary B. "How Roman Are Shakespeare's 'Romans'?" *Shakespeare Quarterly* 40 (1989): 257-83.

The historicity of Shakespeare's Roman plays must be assessed "with some effort to situate the terms of ancient discourse within the sociopolitical context according to which Romans structured and interpreted their lives." By shifting emphasis from the outer to the inner man, Shakespeare enriched his ancient sources and elaborated a theme in which they had little interest. It also means that Shakespeare did not understand "why his Roman subjects identified public performance and personal worth as persistently and as completely as they did"; Shakespeare also did not appreciate "the distinctive interplay between social expectation and political expediency that defined the terms on which Roman aristocrats acted out their lives."

1229 Elam, Keir. "Here is my Space: La teatralizzazione della storia in *Antony and Cleopatra*." *Antony and Cleopatra dal testo alla scena*. Ed. Mariangela Tempera. Bologna: Cooperative Libraria Universitaria Editrice, 1990, pp. 49-65.

This is a study of Shakespeare's treatment of historical sources in *Antony and Cleopatra*.

1230 Higgins, Anne. "Shakespeare's Saint Cleopatra." *Dalhousie Review* 70.1 (1990-91): 5-19.

Higgins proposes the medieval life of Saint Christina as found in the *South English Legendary* as a source for the tone of martyrdom and transcendence felt in Cleopatra's death scene in Act 5, Scene 2.

1231 Erickson, Glenn W. "Neoplatonic 'High Order' in *Antony and Cleopatra*." *Cauda Pavonis: Studies in Hermeticism* 11.2 (1992): 1-11.

An analysis of neoplatonic imagery involving astrology and Tarot cards shows that Shakespeare drew these allusions from North's Plutarch.

1232 Miller, Anthony. "The Metamorphic Tragedy of *Antony and Cleopatra*." *Sydney Studies in English* 18 (1992-93): 29-47.

Shakespeare's style and thematic concern with metamorphosis may have been influenced by Ovid's *Metamorphoses*.

1233 King, Laura S. "Sacred Eroticism, Rapturous Anguish: Christianity's Penitent Prostitutes and the Vexation of Allegory, 1370-1608." *Dissertation Abstracts International* 54 (1993-94): 3747A (California-Berkeley).

The Homelia de Maria Magdalena and the Digby *Mary Magdalene* influenced Chaucer and Shakespeare's *Antony and Cleopatra* and *Pericles*.

Textual Studies

1234 Ingleby, Clement M. *Shakespeare Hermeneutics, or The Still Lion, Being an Essay towards the Restoration of Shakespeare's Text.* 1875. Reprint. New York: Haskell House, 1971.

Ingleby justifies the use of conjecture in emending four passages from this play.

1235 Pollard, Alfred W. *Shakespeare Folios and Quartos: A Study in the Bibliography of Shakespeare's Plays 1594-1685.* London: Methuen, 1909. 175 pp.

This play was entered in the Stationers' Register on 20 May 1608 by Edward Blount, "one of the chief promoters of the Folio of 1623," but it was never printed until 1623. This entry may "have been of the nature of 'blocking' entries rather than inspired with any intention of early publication."

1236 Kellner, Leon. *Restoring Shakespeare: A Critical Analysis of the Misreadings in Shakespeare.* 1925. Reprint. New York: Biblo, 1969. 216 pp.

By examining the misprints and other features of printing, Kellner propses eighteen emendations to passages in this play. For example, in 1.2.25, he would change "a forenoon" to "one after one."

1237 Willoughby, Edwin E. *The Printing of the First Folio of Shakespeare.* Oxford: Oxford UP, 1932. xiii, 70 pp.

On the basis of his spelling of certain words, Willoughby believes that the Folio text of this play was set by Compositor

B. He describes the work as "moderately careful but not meticulous."

1238 Greg, W. W. *The Editorial Problem in Shakespeare: A Survey of the Foundations of the Text*. Oxford: Clarendon P, 1942. lv, 210 pp.

This playtext "is a producer's copy not a prompter's."

1239 Maxwell, J.C. "Shakespeare's Manuscript of *Antony and Cleopatra.*" *Notes and Queries* 196 (1951): 337.

Maxwell provides two illustrations to support his theory that the play had been printed from Shakespeare's manuscript.

1240 Greg, W.W. *The Shakespeare First Folio: Its Bibliographical and Textual History*. Oxford: Clarendon P, 1955. 496 pp.

In his comments on this play, Greg suggests that it "was printed from Shakespeare's foul papers."

1241 Sisson, C.J. "*Antony and Cleopatra.*" *New Readings in Shakespeare*. 2 vols. Cambridge: Cambridge UP, 1956, II, 259-76.

Sisson discusses the justification for various emendations and proposes his own readings for this text.

1242 Walker, Alice. "Principles of Annotation: Some Suggestions for Editors of Shakespeare." *Studies in Bibliography* 9 (1957): 95-105.

Walker points out two fallacies in editorial theory in the twentieth century in Shakespeare studies. First, "the assumption that fuller knowledge about transmission would establish which readings were right and which were wrong." Second, "palaeography would serve the main tool in emendation." Then she stresses that editors need "the traditional literary tools like historical study of Shakespeare's language."

1243 Galloway, David. "'I am dying, Egypt, dying'" Folio Repetition and the Editors." *Notes and Queries* 203 (1958): 330-35.

Galloway argues that "the folio is sole authority for *Antony and Cleopatra* and the case for its corruption in the First Monument Scene rests not on bibliographical evidence or critiical acumen but on two 'repetitions' merely because they are repetitions."

1244 Holmes, Martin. *Shakespeare's Public: The Touchstone of His Genius*. London: John Murray, 1960. 237 pp.

Holmes argues that Shakespeare took the description of Cleopatra's barge "not from any published work but from gossip and tradition because it was true." The Royal Barge of England was well known, and so was Sir John Melville's memoirs of Queen Elizabeth and Mary Queen of Scots in manuscript.

1245 Lloyd, Michael. "Plutarch's Daemons in Shakespeare." *Notes and Queries* ns 7 (1960): 324-27.

Shakespeare appears to have been familiar with Plutarch's theories of daemons or spirits, angels or geniuses.

1246 Hinman, Charlton. *The Printing and Proof-reading of the First Folio of Shakespeare*. 2 vols. Oxford: Oxford UP, 1963.

Hinman asserts that Compositor B set all of *Antony and Cleopatra* in the Folio.

1247 Nosworthy, J.M. *Shakespeare's Occasional Plays: Their Origin and Transmission*. New York: Barnes & Noble, 1965. 238 pp.

When Shakespeare adapted his plays for special occasions, "the author would have made his own revisions." Shakespeare "wrote *Macbeth*, including the disputed I.ii, at the time when he was already assembling his principal material for *Antony and Cleopatra*, so that the composition of the two tragedies must have been practically simultaneous."

1248 Howard-Hill, T.H., ed. *The Tragedie of Antony and Cleopatra.* Oxford Shakespeare Concordances. Oxford: Clarendon P; New York: Oxford U P, 1972. 351 pp.

This is a concordance to text of First Folio.

1249 Mitchell, Dennis S. "Shakespeare's *Antony and Cleopatra* II.ii.811-813." *Explicator* 35 (1976): 22-24.

Although editors have emended the punctuation in this passage, the Folio punctuation is correct in the larger imagistic context of the rivalry and metaphorical identity of Antony and Caesar.

1250 Bowers, Fredson. "Establishing Shakespeare's Text: Notes on Short Lines and the Problem of Verse Division." *Studies in Bibliography* 33 (1980): 74-130.

After pointing out difficulties with the "conventional editorial arrangement in Shakespearean mixed scenes of verse and prose," Bowers pleads that it has "to be more finely tuned since it is probable that too many prose speakers have been assigned random part-lines of verse."

1251 Bertram, Paul Benjamin. *White Spaces in Shakespeare: The Development of the Modern Text.* Cleveland: Bellflower P, Case Western Reserve U, 1981. 86 pp.

Bertram asserts that the lineation in the Folio is "swarming with vital clues to pauses and emphasis."

1252 Kimura, Teruhira. "Observations upon Some Textual and Annotatory Problems in *Antony and Cleopatra.*" *Shakespeare Studies* (Tokyo) 20 (1981-82): 91-107.

Not seen.

1253 Swander, Home. "Menas and the Editors: A Folio Script Unscripted." *Shakespeare Quarterly* 36 (1985): 165-87.

Most editors wrongly assign to Menas the lines that the Folio gives to Menecrates. This editorial handling of Menas "reverberates throughout the script, and weakens it, transforming it at critical points into a literary text: at these points and in this sense, the Editorial Text is, precisely, the Folio Script unscripted." These editorial interventions "arise from an unwarranted extension of the editor's task and in the service of a discipline that is defined by literary instead of theatrical considerations and knowledge."

1254 Sigurdson, Paul A. "To Weet or Not to Weet." *Shakespeare Newsletter* 36 (1986): 52.

Sigurdson proposes one emendation for *Antony and Cleopatra*, 1.1.38-39: changing "weet" to "eat."

1255 Proudfoot, Richard. "Two Notes on Shakespeare's Text." *KM 80: A Birthday Album for Kenneth Muir, Tuesday, 5 May 1987*. Liverpool: Liverpool UP, n.d, pp. 19-20.

Not seen.

1256 Spevack, Marvin. "On the Copy for *Antony and Cleopatra*." *'Fanned and winnowed opinions': Shakespearean Essays Presented to Harold Jenkins*. Ed. John W. Mahon and Thomas A. Pendleton. London: Methuen, 1987, pp. 202-215.

Spevack argues that editors cannot find "conclusive proof" for the copy underlying the Folio text, "and in all likelihood it will never exist." The copy "was Shakespeare's foul papers, or his fair papers, or a prompt copy, or a producer's copy—in Shakespeare's autograph or in a scribal hand, as the case may be."

1257 Spevack, Marvin. "The Editor as Philologist." *Text: Transactions of the Society for Textual Scholarship* 3 (1987): 91-106.

Spevack brings out certain weaknesses in J. Dover Wilson's arguments about the text of this play and stresses that editing should be "a rendition of it on its own terms."

1258 Spevack, Marvin. "On the Copy for *Antony and Cleopatra*." *"Fanned and Winnowed Opinions": Shakespearean Essays Presented to Harold Jenkins*. Ed. John W. Mahon and Thomas A. Pendleton. London and New York: Methuen, 1987, pp. 202-15.

Discussing the nature of orthographic evidence and pointing to weaknesses in John Dover Wilson's argument that Shakespeare's manuscript was the copy, Spevack stresses the inconclusiveness of evidence for deciding the type of copy from which *Antony and Cleopatra* was printed in the Folio.

1259 Wells, Stanley, and Gary Taylor, with John Jowett and William Montgomery. "*Antony and Cleopatra.*" *Shakespeare: A Textual Companion*. Oxford: Clarendon P, 1987, pp. 549-55.

Prepared as part of the editorial work for the complete Oxford Shakespeare, this is a detailed account of the Folio text. The general introduction "attempts both to define and defend: to explain and justify the decisions of the editors of the 1986 Oxford University Press Text of Shakespeare's *Complete Works*, and also, more generally, to describe the materials upon which all editors of Shakespeare must base their decisions." It summarizes the modern opinion on textual problems. *Antony and Cleopatra* was printed first in the First Folio "by Compositors B and E." The manuscript "appears to have been in a more finished condition than most of Shakespeare's foul papers, but shows no signs of originating in a prompt-book." There is no scene-act division in the Folio text; "to the standard division we add a scene reference at 4.7.4/2192, so 4.7.4 onwards becomes 4.8/Sc. 33 in our edition, and 4.8-15 become 4.9-

16/Sc. 34-41." The editors provide textual notes on pp. 549-53, incidentals on p. 553, and Folio stage directions on pp. 554-55.

1260 Sternberg, Paul R. "A Curious Press-Variant in Folio *Antony and Cleopatra*." *Library* 6th Series 12 (1990): 132.

Sternberg suggests that the uncorrected state of *Antony and Cleopatra*, II.vii.132, is "heere a," not "heare a," as is usually recorded, and he explains the implications of the correction for compositor studies of F.

1261 Delery, Clayton J. "The Subject Presumed to Know: Implied Authority and Editorial Apparatus." *Text: Transactions of the Society for Textual Scholarship* 5 (1991): 63-80.

Editors of Shakespeare and other writers "can transform themselves into the Subject Presumed to Know," because their "particular authority is often unquestioned by the reader who is more interested in product than in process." "By concealing textual castration, by concealing the absence of authority in a particular edition, editors and publishers can imply that there is a great deal more there than actually exists."

1262 Mueller, Martin. "Plutarch's 'Life of Brutus' and the Play of Its Repetitions in Shakespearean Drama." *Renaissance Drama* ns 22 (1991): 47-93.

Plutarch's portrayals of Brutus and Portia influenced *Antony and Cleopatra* and other plays, especially Shakespeare's variations on it in treating "civilization and its discontents."

1263 Little, Geoffrey. "The Womanning of Cleopatra's Barge." *Sydney Studies in English* 17 (1991-92): 43-45.

North's translation of Plutarch and nautical terminology help in clearing up the textual problems of *Antony and Cleopatra* 2.2.206-11.

1264 Kinghorn, A. M. "'All Joy O' the Worm' or, Death by Asp or Asps Unknown in Act V of *Antony and Cleopatra*." *English Studies* (Netherlands) 75 (1994): 104-09.

Shakespeare's handling of Cleopatra's death scene can be compared with that of his classical sources.

1265 Orgel, Stephen. "Acting Scripts, Performing Texts." *Crisis in Editing*. Ed. Randall McLeod. New York: AMS, 1994, pp. 252-94.

Seventeenth-century promptbooks of *Antony and Cleopatra* and other plays show the tension between text and script in Shakespeare's day and help in considering the relations between texts that have come down to the twentieth century and what Shakespeare's audience saw. The instability of the text licenses the editorial tradition that would control such instability.

1266 Bowers, Rick. "'Good night, sir': *Antony and Cleopatra* 2.3.8." *English Language Notes* 32.1 (1995): 8-11.

The First Folio reading is correct when it assigns 2.3.8 to Antony.

Bibliographies

1267 Jaggard, William. *William Shakespeare: A Dictionary of Every Known Issue of the Writings of Our National Poet and of Recorded Opinion Thereon in the English Language.* Stratford-on-Avon: Shakespeare P, 1911. 729 pp.

Jaggard's objective is to compile "an encyclopaedia of Shakespearean information and stage history." His list includes about 36,000 items. Editions of *Antony and Cleopatra* to 1909 can be found on pp. 282-85. There are cross references to books and articles. Most of the items are not annotated.

1268 Ebisch, Walther, and Levin L. Schücking. *A Shakespeare Bibliography.* Oxford: Clarendon P, 1931. 294 pp.

This bibliography brings together items about Shakespeare's life and work, beginning with the seventeenth century through to 1929. Entries are listed under these categories: Text, Literary Genesis, Art of Characterization, Subsequent History of the Play. Most of the entries are not annotated. It has items specially dealing with *Antony and Cleopatra* on pp. 250-51, most of them in German.

1269 Ebisch, Walther, and Levin L. Schücking. *Supplement for the Years 1930-1935 to A Shakespeare Bibliography.* Oxford: Clarendon P, 1937. 104 pp.

This supplement contains one item dealing with *Antony and Cleopatra.* listed under the category of Literary Genesis.

1270 Fucilla, J.G. "Shakespeare in Italian Criticism." *Philological Quarterly* 20 (1941): 559-72.

This is a supplement to the bibliographies compiled by Ebisch and Schücking.

1271 Guttman, Selma. *The Foreign Sources of Shakespeare's Works: An Annotated Bibliography of the Commentary Written this Subject between 1904 and 1940 together with Lists of Certain Translations Available to Shakespeare*. Morningside Heights, N.Y.: King's Crown P, 1947. 168 pp.

This index makes references to studies specifically concerned with *Antony and Cleopatra*.

1272 Smith, Gordon Ross. *A Classified Shakespeare Bibliography 1936-1958*. University Park: Pennsylvania State UP, 1963. 784 pp.

In the section devoted to Antony and Cleopatra (items B9380-B9505), there are 126 items. The categories are Texts, Literary Genesis and Analogues, Use of Language, General Criticism of the Play, Characterization, and Subsequent History of the Play.

1273 *Shakespeare: A Bibliography of Russian Translations and Literature on Shakespeare in Russian: 1748-1962*. All-Union State Library of Foreign Literature. Moscow: Publishing House "Kniga," 1964. 711 pp. In Russian.

This is "a bibliography of Shakespeare's writings, literary criticism of his works, reviews of their stage performances and other relevant materials that have been published in the Russian language in the USSR from 1748 to 1962."

1274 Berman, Ronald. "*Antony and Cleopatra*." *A Reader's Guide to Shakespeare's Plays*. Chicago: Scott, Foresman, 1965, pp. 117-21.

This is in part a discursive bibliography. The general headings are Text, Editions, Sources, Criticism, and Staging.

The last two categories are treated discursively. The 1973 edition is updated and slightly revised.

1275 Folsom, Michael B. *Shakespeare: A Marxist Bibliography.* New York: American Institute for Marxist Studies, 1965. 9 pp.

This brief bibliograpphy lists Shakespeare criticism and scholarship in English by Marxist critics.

1276 Velz, John. *Shakespeare and the Classical Tradition: A Critical Guide to Commentary, 1660-1960.* Minnepolis: U of Minnesota P; London: Oxford UP, 1968. 459 pp.

In this annotated bibliography, Velz tries "to summarize and appraise as broad a base of criticism and scholarship as feasible without losing sight of classical culture as a focal point." Over a hundred items deal with *Antony and Cleopatra.*

1277 Payne, Waveney R. N. *A Shakespeare Bibliography.* London: The Library Association, 1969. 93 pp.

This volume contains 576 items, nearly all of them books. Annotations are very brief, often only a sentence. Payne lists only three entries under criticism of this play.

1278 Wells, Stanley. *Shakespeare: A Reading Guide.* London: Oxford UP, 1970. 44 pp.

Wells lists, without annotations, editions and critical works on this play in the section on tragedies.

1279 *A Shakespeare Bibliography: The Catalogue of the Birmingham Shakespeare Library.* 7 vols. London: Mansell, 1971.

This is a catalog of the holdings which include individual editions and translations of this play.

1280 Stone, Lilly C., Chief Cataloger. *Folger Shakespeare Library: Catalog of the Shakespeare Collection*. Volume 2. Boston: G. K. Hall, 1972.

This catalog lists separate editions of *Antony and Cleopatra*, translations, and scholarly and critical studies on pp. 214-220.

1281 *Shakespeare and Shakespeariana*. 3 volumes. Tokyo: Meisei University Library, 1973, 1986, 1993.

This is a catalogue of over 16,000 titles acquired by the university library over a twenty-five-year period. Many of the items are related to *Antony and Cleopatra*.

1282 Spencer, T.J.B. "*Julius Caesar* and *Antony and Cleopatra*." *Shakespeare: Select Bibliographical Guides*. Ed. Stanley Wells. New York and London: Oxford UP, 1973, pp. 203-15.

The works cited in this bibliography fall under the categories of Shakespeare and Plutarch, general criticism, texts, and criticism of this play, and each category is the subject of a critical essay which points out the strengths and shortcomings of the works cited.

1283 Greenberg, Bette, and Albert Rothenberg. "William Shakespeare (1564-1616) Medico-Psychological and Psychoanalytic Studies on His Life and Works: A Bibliography." *International Review of Psycho-Analysis* 1 (1974): 245-56.

This is a listing of items without annotations.

1284 McManaway, James G., and Jeanne Addison Roberts. *A Selective Bibliography of Shakespeare: Editions, Textual Studies, Commentary*. Charlottesville: U P of Virginia for Folger Shakespeare Library, 1975. 316 pp.

This volume lists, without comment, 46 items concerned with *Antony and Cleopatra* (pp. 60-63).

1285 Jacobs, Henry E., and Claudia D. Johnson. *An Annotated Bibliography of Shakespearean Burlesques, Parodies, and Travesties*. New York: Garland, 1976. 202 pp.

This bibliography lists five items related to this play by F.C. Burnand, Charles Selby, and Christopher Ward and three scenes by R.W. Criswell.

1286 McLean, Andrew M. *Shakespeare: Annotated Bibliography and Media Guide for Teachers*. Urbana, IL: National Council of Teachers of English, 1980. 277 pp.

This bibliography is divided into six categories: teaching Shakespeare in public school; teaching Shakespeare in college; teaching Shakespeare as performance; teaching Shakespeare with other authors; Shakespeare in feature films and on television; guide to media for teaching Shakespeare(audio visual materials, records and feature films). The items are not numbered or indexed and only minimally annotated. There are items dealing with *Antony and Cleopatra*.

1287 Bevington, David. *Shakespeare*. Goldentree Bibliographies. Arlington Heights, Ill.: AHM Publishing Corporation, 1978. 259 pp.

The entries on this play (2109-2214) are presented under categories of General Studies and Character Studies, with cross references to other studies.

1288 Willbern, David. "William Shakespeare: A Bibliography of Psychoanalytic and Psychological Criticism, 1964-1975." *International Review of Psycho-Analysis* 5 (1978): 361-372. Enlarged and reprinted in *Representing Shakespeare: New Psychoanalytic Essays*. Ed. Murray M. Schwartz and Coppélia Kahn. Baltimore: Johns Hopkins UP, 1980, pp. 264-88.

This is a listing of items without annotations.

1289 McRoberts, J. Paul. *Shakespeare and the Medieval Tradition: An Annotated Bibliography*. New York: Garland, 1985. 256 pp.

This bibliography covers the years 1900-1980, with 933 items, some of them dealing with *Antony and Cleopatra.*

1290 Champion, Larry S. *The Essential Shakespeare: An Annotated Bibliography of Major Modern Studies.* Boston: G.K. Hall, 1986. 463 pp.

The section devoted to *Antony and Cleopatra* (pp. 286-97) lists items 980-82 under Editions, items 983-1020 under Criticism, and item 1021 under Stage History. Each entry is annotated.

1291 Bergeron, David M. *Shakespeare: A Study and Research Guide.* New York: St. Martin's P, 1975. 145 pp. Bergeron, David M, and Geraldo U. De Sousa. "Tragedies." *Shakespeare: A Study and Research Guide*. Revised 2nd ed. Lawrence: UP of Kansas, 1987, pp. 87-112.

This is an updated version of Bergeron's 1975 guide. The section on tragedies gives a number of useful studies from Bradley to 1985, with comments.

1292 Ross, Harris. *Film as Literature, Literature as Film: An Introduction to and Bibliography of Film's Relationship to Literature*. Bibliographies and Indexes in World Literature, No. 10. New York: Greenwood P, 1987. 346 pp.

This bibliography contains only one item related to *Antony and Cleopatra*.

1293 Weis, René J.A. "*Julius Caesar* and *Antony and Cleopatra*." *Shakespeare. A Bibliographical Guide*. Revised ed. Ed. Stanley Wells. Oxford: Clarendon P, 1990.

The works cited in this revised version of the 1973 bibliography fall under the categories of Texts and Criticism.

Editions and critical works related to *Antony and Cleopatra* are listed on pp. 292-95.

1294 Kolin, Philp C. *Shakespeare and Feminist Criticism: An Annotated Bibliography and Commentary*. Garland Reference Library of the Humanities 1345. New York: Garland, 1991. 420 pp.

There are 29 items dealing with *Antony and Cleopatra*.

1295 Sajdak, Bruce T., ed. *Shakespeare Index: An Annotated Bibliography of Critical Articles on the Plays 1959-1983*. 2 vols. Millwood, NY: Kraus International Publications, 1992.

The first volume contains a citations and author index; the second volume gives character, scene and subject indexes.

1296 Bergeron, David M. *Shakespeare: A Study and Research Guide*. 3rd. ed. Lawrence: U of Kansas P, 1995. 235 pp.

This revised guide contains a considerable number of new books surveyed under the categories: The Subject in Context, A Guide to the Resources, and The Research Paper.

Editions

1297 Clark, William George, and William Aldis Wright, eds. *The Works of William Shakespeare.* The Globe Edition. London: Macmillan, 1864. 1079 pp.

This is a one-volume edition of the Cambridge Edition, without notes. There is a glossary on pp. 1059-1179. The text of the Globe Editon was accepted as authoritative by many subsequent editors and has become a standard for line numbering.

1298 Clark, William George, John Glover, and Willism Aldis Wright, eds. *The Works of William Shakespeare.* Cambridge Edition. 9 vols. Cambridge, 1863-1866. Revised edition, 1891-1895.

Antony and Cleopatra is in volume 9 (1866), with notes.

1299 Craig, J.W., ed. *Works.* Oxford Shakespeare. London: Oxford UP, 1891.

The text of this play appears on pp. 968-1002. There is a glossary at the back.

1300 Deighton, Kenneth, ed. *Antony and Cleopatra.* Deighton's Grey Cover Shakespeare. London: Macmillan, 1891. xxviii, 230 pp.

In his introduction, Deighton discusses the sources of the play and provides an outline of the plot and an analysis of characters. There are notes in the back and an index to notes.

1301 Rolfe, W.J. Intro. *Antony and Cleopatra.* Seventeen illustrations by Paul Avril. New York: Duprat, 1891. xxii, 196 pp.

Glossary and notes are placed at the back. When Rolfe compares the play's poetry with the source in prose, "the latter appears only as the dry bones which the mighty magician has transformed into a living thing of beauty and a joy forever."

1302 Case, R.H., ed. *The Tragedy of Antony and Cleopatra*. The Works of Shakespeare. Indianapolis: Bobbs-Merrill, 1906; London: Methuen, 1906. lx, 211 pp.

In his introduction, Case discusses the date and text of this play, places it in the context of Shakespeare's development, and compares it with other treatments of the same subject. He reprints extracts from the 1579 edition of North's Plutarch. Notes are at the bottom of each page.

1303 Chambers, E.K., ed. *Antony and Cleopatra*. Red Letter Shakespeare. London: 1907.

Not seen.

1304 Furness, Horace Howard, ed. *The Tragedie of Anthonie, And Cleopatra*. A New Variorum Edition. Philadelphia: J.B. Lippincott, 1907. xx, 614 pp.

The Folio text of *Antony and Cleopatra* is accompanied by extensive notes and glosses. The complete text of Dryden's adaptation appears also. The source of the plot is discussed too.

1305 Rolfe, William J., ed. *Tragedy of Antony and Cleopatra*. New York: American Book Co., 1909. 295 pp.

In his introduction, the editor discusses the history of the play and the historical sources of the plot and provides general comments on the tragedy. Notes are placed at the end. In the appendices is a commentary on other plays on the same subject, a time-analysis of the play, and a list of characters. There is an "index of words and phrases explained."

1306 Bayfield, Matthew Albert. *A Study of Shakespeare's Versification . . . Including a Revised Text of Antony and Cleopatra.* Cambridge: Cambridge UP, 1920. 518 pp.

Bayfield seeks to "give an intelligible and consistent account of the structure and characteristic features of the dramatic verse, the essential principles of which appear to have been wholly misconceived hitherto, and secondly to show that there are many thousands of lives of it that are given in modern texts not as their author intended to be delivered, but clipped and trimmed to a featureless uniformity that he would have abhorred."

In this play, Shakespeare "embodies in its utmost perfect that ideal of dramatic verse at which he had long been aiming; more than from any other play one receives the impression of an art completely mastered." Shakespeare's "sureness of touch and the ease, one might say the nonchalance, with which the thing is done are so marvellous that one is reminded of the bewildering performance of a Japanese juggler, while the result is such as no one would have believed possible unless it had been achieved."

Bayfield suggests that "unless one assumes dictation on a large scale, it is difficult to account for the frequent misdivision of the lines in the verse, and the appearance of verse as prose and of prose printed in irregular lines as though it were verse." Bayfield suggests that his "revised text" will "enable readers to judge of the cumulative effect of the proposed changes."

1307 Canby, Henry Seidel, ed. *Antony and Cleopatra.* Yale Shakespeare. New Haven: Yale UP, 1921. 155 pp.

This edition contains the text of the play (1-133),Notes (133-42), and appendices on the source, history, and text of the play and suggestions for collateral reading. There is an index of words glossed.

1308 Hillebrand, Harold N., ed. *Antony and Cleopatra*. Heath's Arden Shakespeare. Boston: Heath, 1926.

Not seen.

1309 Wilson, John Dover. Introduction. *Antony and Cleopatra . . . A Facsimile of the First Folio Text*. London: Faber & Gwyer, 1928.

Wilson that "there is very little wrong with the text of *Antony and Cleopatra* beyond one or two omissions." He also provides a list of modern readings.

1310 Boas, Guy, ed. *Antony and Cleopatra*. The Scholar's Library. London: Macmillan; New York: St. Martin's P, 1935.

Not seen.

1311 Ridley, M.R., ed. *Antony and Cleopatra*. New Temple Shakespeare. London: Dent; New York: Dutton, 1935. 181 pp.

The editor deals with the text and date of composition, source, duration of action, and criticism of the play. Notes and glossary are at the back.

1312 Kittredge. George Lyman, ed. *The Works of William Shakespeare*. Boston: Ginn, 1936. 1561 pp.

There are no notes in this edition. A glossary for all plays appears on pp. 1529-61.

1313 Harrison, G.B., ed. *Antony and Cleopatra*. Penguin Shakespeare. London: Penguin Books, 1937. 154 pp.

Harrison provides a brief introduction on Shakespeare's life, Elizathan theatre, and the play. The notes and glossary are at the back. Harrison follows the Folio text closely and has kept the original arrangement and punctuation "except where they seemed definitely wrong."

1314 Parrott, Thomas Marc, ed. *Shakespeare: Twenty-three Plays and the Sonnets*. New York: Scribners, 1938. 1116 pp. Revised ed. 1953.

This edition reprints the Nonesuch text. There is no introduction. Modern English glosses appear in the margins.

1315 *The Complete Works of William Shakespeare*. The New Nonesuch Shakespeare. 4 volumes. London: Nonesuch Press, 1939.

This edition prints the Nonesuch text edited by Herbert Farjeon in 1929. There is no introduction, and modern English glosses appear in the margins.

1316 Farjeon, Herbert, ed. *Antony and Cleopatra. The Text of the First Folio edited and amended where Obscure by Herbert Farjeon*. Color Illustrations by Gordon Craig. New York: Limited Editions Club, 1939.

This edition does not have any notes or glosses.

1317 *The Complete Works of William Shakespeare*. Art-Type Edition. New York: Books, 1940. 1300 pp.

This volume includes the Temple notes, a brief biography and a glossary.

1318 Personnel of the Work Project Administration. *Facsimile Production of First Folio 1623: Twelfth Night, Macbeth, Anthony and Cleopatra*. San Francisco: California State Library, 1940.

The text of *Antony and Cleopatra* appears on pp. 340-368 on one side of each sheet.

1319 *Shakespeare's First Folio of 1623*. Boston: Graphic Service, 1940.

This positive microfilm copy includes notes by William Dana Orcutt.

1320 Kittredge, George Lyman, ed. *Antony and Cleopatra.* Boston: Ginn, 1941. xii, 218 pp.

The text of the play is from Kittredge's edition of Shakespeare's *Works*. The introduction deals especially with Antony as an "expression of Greek doctrine of *até*, infatuation." Textual notes and glossarial notes are at the back.

1321 *The Complete Works of William Shakespeare.* Forum Book Edition. Cleveland: World Syndicate Publishing Co., 1942. 1173 pp.

This edition has the Temple notes, a brief biography and unsigned introductions.

1322 *Tragedies of Shakespeare.* New York: Modern Library, 1943. 1266 pp.

The text of the play appears on pp. 883-984. There is no introduction. Notes are found on pp. 1178-81, glossary on pp. 1209-66.

1323 Parrott, Thomas Marc, ed. *Shakespeare: Twenty-three Plays and the Sonnets*. Published for the US Armed Forces Institute, War Dept. Educational Manual, EM 130. N.p.: Scribner's, 1944.

This is a reprint of item 1314.

1324 Harbage, Alfred, ed. *The Viking Portable Shakespeare.* New York: Viking, 1944. 792 pp.

Harbage has included excerpts from the play.

1325 Cady, Frank W., and Van H. Hartmell, eds. "*Antony and Cleopatra.*" *Shakespeare Arranged for Modern Reading*. Garden City, NY: Doubleday, 1946, pp. 1045-65. Reprint. Greenwich, CT: Fawcett, 1963.

Shakespeare's text is placed between prose summaries. The editors' purpose is to enable the reader "to get at the famous lines and passages which have gained the immortality of quotation" without having "to wade through extensive tracts of minor lines."

1326 Kittredge, George Lyman, ed. *Sixteen Plays of Shakespeare.* Boston: Ginn, 1946. 1541 pp.

The introduction to the play is found on pp. 1313-16, the text of the play on pp. 1317-60, notes on pp. 1361-1403, textual notes on pp. 1461-63, and glossary on pp. 1537-41.

1327 Entry deleted.

1328 Harrison, G. B., ed. *Shakespeare: Major Plays and the Sonnets.* New York: Harcourt, Brace, 1948. 1090 pp.

The introduction to the play is on pp. 863-66, the text on pp. 867-908. Notes are at bottom of page. Harrison provides a general introduction which deals with these topics: The Universality of Shakespeare; Records of the Life of Shakespeare; Shakespeare's England; Elizabethan Drama; The Elizabethan Playhouse; The Study of the Text; The Development of Shakespear's Art; Shakespeare and the Critics; Reading List.

1329 Spencer, Theodore. *The Tragedy of Antony and Cleopatra.* Crofts Classics. New York: Appleton-Century-Crofts, 1948. xii, 115 pp.

In his introduction, Spencer discusses dating, sources, and the play. He suggests that, in this play, Shakespeare's stagecraft "is at its boldest and most successful." Glossorial notes are at the bottom of each page, and there is one-page bibliography.

1330 Campbell, Oscar James, ed. *The Living Shakespeare: Twenty-Two Plays and the Sonnets*. New York: Macmillan, 1949. 1239 pp.

In his general introduction (pp. 1-75), Campbell discusses Shakespeare's youth, professional career, London, pre-Shakespearean drama, Shakespeare development, stage, company and text and provides a chronological table. In his introduction to the play (pp. 979-84), he argues that the play's "structure is that of an old-fashioned episodic chronicle play, which, while displaying a colorful page of the past, presents the tragedy of a great man's disastrous slavery to passion. The spirit of the work, however, is that of romance, creating an atmosphere intoxicating to all the senses, one which drowns all impulses to considered action in delicious languor and sensuous indulgence." The text of the play appears on pp. 985-1037, with notes at bottom of page.

1331 Wilson, John Dover, ed. *Antony and Cleopatra*. Cambridge Shakespeare. London: 1950. xlvii, 262 pp.

Wilson has provided an introduction and C.B. Young the stage history. Notes and glossary are at the back. There is a discussion of the copy for the text of 1623, which is "of unimpeachable authority; being set up to all appearances direct from the author's manuscript." Shakespeare "cannot have completed and produced it much later than about the middle of 1607." Wilson argues that "if Antony's supreme virtue is magnanimity, hers is vitality. And because she, 'all fire and air', is also the genius of the play, vitality is its true theme; vitality as glorified in them both, and in the form which Shakespeare most admired: 'the nobleness of life', the strength and majesty of human nature, its instincts of generosity, graciousness and large-heartedness; its gaiety of spirit, warmth of blood, 'infinite variety' of mood."

1332 Alexander, Peter, ed. *William Shakespeare: The Complete Works*. Tudor Edition. London: Collins, 1951. 1376 pp.

Alexander does not provide an introduction or notes. A glossary for the complete works is on pp. 1352-76.

1333 Craig, Hardin, ed. *The Complete Works of Shakespeare*.Chicago: Scott, Foresman, 1951. 1337 pp.

Craig discusses the play and gives stage history briefly. Notes and glosses are at the foot of the page.

1334 Harrison, G.B. *The Complete Works*. New York: Harcourt, Brace, 1952. 1666 pp.

The first eight sections of the general introduction are taken from the 1948 edition of the major plays and sonnets. Section 9 deals with Shakespeare scholarship and criticism from 1900 to 1950. The introduction to the play is identical with that of the 1948 edition and is found on pp. 1219-22 and the text of the play on pp. 1223-64. Notes are at bottom of pages. "The Order of the Garter" is an addition to the Appendices. An expanded reading list appears on pp. 1661-66.

1335 Olivier, Sir Laurence. Introduction. *The Tragedy of Antony and Cleopatra*. London: Folio Society, 1952. 134 pp.

This text is based on the New Temple Shakespeare, edited by M.R. Ridley. Glossary and an historical note are at the back.

1336 *The Complete Works of William Shakespeare*. 4 volumes. London: Nonesuch Press, 1953.

The text of this play appears in III, 941-1037. The modern readings are given in marginal notes.

1337 Henshaw, T. *Antony and Cleopatra*. London: Ginn, 1953. xc, 250 pp.

Not seen.

1338 Sisson, Charles Jasper, ed. *William Shakespeare: The Complete Works*. London: Odhams Press, 1953. 1376 pp.

Sisson provides a brief introduction to the play, but no notes. A glossary for all plays is on pp. 1345-76.

1339 Kökeritz, Helge, and Chalres T. Prouty, eds. *Mr. William Shakespeares Comedies, Histories, & Tragedies*. New Haven: Yale UP, 1954. 889 pp.

In this reduced facsimile of the First Folio, the text of *Antony and Cleopatra* is found on pp. 830-858.

1340 Ridley, M. R., ed. *Antony and Cleopatra*. The Arden Shakespeare. London: Methuen; Cambridge, MA: Harvard UP, 1954. xlix, 278 pp.

Based on R.H. Case's edition of 1906, Ridley reprints large sections of Case's material. He gives Case's discussion of date and sources, a comparison with great tragedies, the representation of Antony and Cleopatra, especially their morality and their motives for action, and discussion of plays on Antony and Cleopatra. Ridley summarizes three critical accounts (1909, 1944, 1950) and reprints previously published (1936) pages of his own criticism. Ridley's treatment of mislineation and punctuation appears in appendices.

1341 *The Works of Shakespeare*. Players Illustrated Edition. 3 volumes. Chicago: Spencer Press, 1955.

The tragedies are in Volume II. There is a glossary for all the plays.

1342 Phialas, Peter G., ed. *The Tragedy of Antony and Cleopatra.* New Yale Shakespeare. New Haven: Yale UP, 1955. 171 pp.

This edition contains the text of the play (1-137) and notes (138-57). In the three appendices is found a discussion of date and text and sources and a reading list. The editor argues for the strong probability that "this text was set up from a fair copy of Shakespeare's manuscript before its excessive length had been trimmed for stage performance." This text also follows the Folio lineation. This edition "dispenses with the traditional act and scene division which in other editions mark the action of the play," but it notes the act and scene divisions at the top of each page.

1343 *Complete Works of William Shakespeare.* Classics Club College Edition. Princeton, NJ: D. Van Nostrand Co., 1956. 1312 pp.

Not seen.

1344 Munro, John, ed. *The London Shakespeare.* Introduction. G.W.G. Wickham. 6 volumes. London: Eyre and Spottiswoode, 1957; New York: Simon and Schuster, 1958.

The introduction to the play is on VI, 1207-15 and the text on VI, 1216-1365. Notes are at bottom of page. The editor identifies three names in the play: the East represented by Egypt and lands beyond versus the West represented by Rome; the strife in the Triumvirate who divided and governed the world; the love and tragedy of Antony and Cleopatra.

1345 Alexander, Peter, ed. *William Shakespeare, The Comedies, The Histories, The Tragedies.* Preface by Tyrone Guthrie and illustrations by Edward Ardizzone. 3 vols. New York: Heritage Press, 1958.

Not seen.

1346 *The Complete Works of William Shakespeare Comprising His Plays and Poems*. Preface by Donald Wolfit. Introduction and glossary by Bretislav Hodek. New York: Spring Books, 1958. 1081 pp.

This is a reprint of the Collins Tudor Edition text. There is a brief introduction but no notes or glossary.

1347 Craig, Hardin, ed. *Shakespeare: A Historical and Critical Study with Annotated Texts of Twenty-one Plays*. Chicago: Scott, Foresman, 1958. 1194 pp.

This is a revised version of the 1931 edition. Craig provides a general introduction (pp. 1-76), which deals with topics like the Middle Ages and the Renaissance, life in England in Shakespeare's time, and Shakespeare's English. He discusses the play's publication and date, sources, Cleopatra, and stage history on pp. 724-27 and stresses that it was "hastily written" and "lacks general plan. After the middle of the play, Shakespeare more or less puts Plutarch on the stage." The text of the play is on pp. 935-88, with notes at bottom of page, and textual variants on p. 1159.

1348 Kittredge, George Lyman, ed. *The Kittredge-Players Edition of the Complete Works of William Shakespeare*. Chicago: Spencer P, 1958. 1561 pp.

This edition reprints Kittredge's inroduction from his 1936 edition.

1349 Oldendorf, H.J., and H. Arguile, eds. *Antony and Cleopatra*. Cape Town: Maskew Miler, 1958. 223 pp.

Not seen.

1350 Oyama, Toshiko, ed. *Antony and Cleopatra.* Tokyo: Shinozaki-Shorin, 1958. xvii, 393 pp.

The editor supplies introduction and notes in Japanese. There is a bibliography and glossary.

1351 Rylands, George. Introduction. *The Tragedies.* Wood engravings by Agnes Miller Parker. New York: Heritage P, 1959.

This text is based on that of Collins Tudor Shakespeare, ed. Peter Alexander. The text of the play is on III, 970-1074.

1352 Grabhorn, Mary, illustrator. *The Tragedies of Anthonie and Cleopatra.* San Francisco: Grabhorn P, 1960. 112 pp.

This is a reproduction of the First Folio text.

1353 Mack, Maynard, ed. *Antony and Cleopatra.* The Pelican Shakespeare. Harmondsworth: Penguin Books, 1960. Revised 1970. 159 pp.

Alfred Harbage supplies "Shakespeare and His Stage" and "The Texts of the Plays." Annotations are at bottom of page.

1354 Wright, Louis B., and Virginia A. LaMar, eds. *Antony and Cleopatra.* The Folger Library General Reader's Shakespeare. New York: Washington Square Press, 1961. xl, 144 pp.

The introduction to this edition discusses Shakespeare and his age and work under categories like stage history, the text, the author, the publication of his plays, and the Shakespearean theatre, followed by references for further reading. The text appears on odd pages, the notes on even.

1355 Houghton, R.E.C., ed. *Antony and Cleopatra.* New Clarendon Shakespeare. Oxford: Clarendon P, 1962. 256 pp.

In his introduction, the editor discusses date and style of the play, imagery, Shakespeare's sources and his use of them, the play and Roman history, the text, and the play's plot. He provides a commentary at the back, following by select literary criticism, and an appendix of extracts from North's *Plutarch.* Notes appear at bottom of pages.

1356 Ichikawa, Sanki, and Tukuji Mine, eds. *Antony and Cleopatra.* Tokyo: Keukyusha, 1963. xxxi, 282 pp.

Introduction and notes are in Japanese.

1357 Wright, Louis B., and Virginia A. LaMar, eds. *The Play's the Thing: Seventeen of Shakespeare's Greatest Dramas.* New York: Harper & Row, 1963. 781 pp.

Not seen.

1358 *The Complete Works of William Shakespeare.* The Abbey Library Edition. London: Murray Sales and Serivce, 1964. 2000 pp.

There is a foreword by Dame Sybil Thorndike, but no introductions or notes.

1359 Everett, Barbara, ed. *Antony and Cleopatra.* The Signet Classic Shakespeare. New York: New American Library; London: New English Library, 1964. 276 pp.

This edition considers the play's genre and provides a political-historical reading, based in Plutarch and accepting the play's own game metaphors. It has sound notes but no theatrical observations. There are a number of excerpts from A.C. Bradley, John F. Danby and Janet Adelman. Samuel Schoenbaum provides a stage and screen history.

1360 Vandiver, Edward P. "*The Tragedy of Antony and Cleopatra.*" *Highlights of Shakespeare's Plays: With Explanation, Summary, Comment and Emphasis on Famous Quotations.* Great Neck, NY: Barron's Educational Books, 1964, pp. 310-24. Revised and expanded ed. Woodbury, NY: Barron's Educational Series, 1976, pp. 328-44.

Vandiver provides "the most famous and the most interresting selections," with prose summaries of omitted scenes.

1361 Shattuck, Charles H. *The Shakespeare Promptbooks: A Descriptive Catalogue.* Urbana: U of Illinois P, 1965. 553 pp.

Shattuck has catalogued "*marked copies* of Shakespeare used in English-language, profesional theatre productions from the 1620's to 1961." For *Antony and Cleopatra* there are forty-seven items listed and described on pp. 33-42. The dates range from 1759 to 1960.

1362 Campbell, Oscar James, Alfred Rothschild, and Stuart Vaughan, eds. *Antony and Cleopatra.* New York: Bantam Books, 1966.

Not seen.

1363 Hinman, Charlton, ed. *The Norton Facsimile: The First Folio of Shakespeare.* New York: W. W. Norton, 1968. xxvii, 928 pp.

This facsimile edition reproduces the most fully corrected state of the First Folio according to a collation of copies at the Folger Shakespeare Library. The text of *Antony and Cleopatra* is found on pp. 340-68 (Folio pages) and 848-876 of this volume.

1364 Gianakaris, C.J., ed. *Antony and Cleopatra.* The Blackfriars Shakespeare. Dubuque, Iowa: Wm. C. Brown, 1969. xvi, 89 pp.

The editor's introduction deals with Shakspeare's life and times and discusses the play. Notes are at bottom of page. The editor argues that Shakespeare "poses the opposing moral views, taking great care niether to acquit Antony and Cleopatra nor to vilify them; they are what they are, and self-destruction is their final choice to escape their predicaments."

1365 Harbage, Alfred, gen. ed. *William Shakespeare: The Complete Works*. The Complete Pelican Shakespeare. Baltimore: Penguin, 1969. 1481 pp.

Maynard Mack's introduction is that of the separate Pelican edition of 1960. The text of the play appears on pp. 1173-1211, with notes and glosses at the foot.

1366 Walter, J.H., ed. *Antony and Cleopatra*. The Players' Shakespeare. London: Heinemann, 1969. 311 pp.

Not seen.

1367 Skillan, George, ed. *Antony and Cleopatra*. French's Acting Edition. London: Samuel French, 1970. xvii, 282 pp.

This edition provides a property plot, a note on lighting and the costumes, and Ivor Brown's foreword. Annotations appear in a separate column on each page. There are extensive commentaries on each scene and the movements of characters. The editor's objective is "to enable the young students of Shakespeare to realize the constructional principles that go to the making of his plays, the necessary formula and then the the process of interpretation that reveals their worth."

1368 Ingledew, John, ed. *Antony and Cleopatra*. Swan Shakespeare. London: Longman, 1971.

Ingledew emphasizes Shakespeare's ambiguity in the delineation of the principal characters and the audience response. He discusses language and verse and language difficulties. There are critical excerpts from Samuel Johnson to O.J. Campbell. A headnote introduces each scene. The glossorial notes are given at the top of the facing verso.

1369 Ribner, Irving and George Lyman Kittredge, eds. *The Complete Works of William Shakespeare*. Revised edition. Waltham, MA: Ginn, 1971. 1743 pp.

Ribner provides a new introduction to the play (pp. 1324-26), with brief discussions of text, literary tradition, dramatic tradition, Rome versus Egypt, Octavius Caesar, Mark Antony and Cleopatra. The text of *Antony and Cleopatra* appears on pp. 1327-74, with notes and glosses on rectos. Ribner stays close to Kittredge's text, removing some emendations and adding a few generally accepted ones. He records his deviations from Kittredge's text, and he gives Kittredge's readings in a note when he disagrees with him.

1370 Slater, Ann, ed. *Antony and Cleopatra*. Shakespeare Workshop. London: Ginn, 1971. 101 pp.

This text is based on the First Folio.

1371 Barnet, Sylvan, gen. ed. *The Complete Signet Classic Shakespeare*. New York: Harcourt Brace Jovanovich, 1972. 1776 pp.

The text of *Antony and Cleopatra* appears on pp. 1269-1311. Barbara Everett's introduction (pp. 1262-68) is identical to that of the single-volume edition. Brief notes on the sources and text are on pp. 1267-68. Notes are at the bottom of the pages. In his general introduction, Barnet covers these topics:

Shakespeare's life; the Shakespeare canon; Shakespeare's theater and actors; the dramatic background; style and structure; Shakespeare's English; the intellectual background; Shakespeare's comedies, history plays, and tragedies; nondramatic works; the texts of Shakespeare.

1372 Craig, Hardin, and David Bevington, eds. *The Complete Works of Shakespeare*. Revised edition. Glenview, IL: Scott, Foresman, 1973. 1447 pp.

The General Introduction (pp. 1-68) contains sections on life in Shakespeare's England, the drama before Shakespeare, London theatres and dramatic companies, the order of Shakespeare's plays, criticism of the plays, editions and editors, Shakespeare's English, and doubtful and lost plays. The text of *Antony and Cleopatra* appears on pp. 1073-1108, with notes and glosses at the foot. The Editor discusses the place of this play in the canon on p. 1319, sources on pp. 1374-48, stage history on pp. 1354-61, textual notes on pp. 1418-19, suggestions for reading and research on pp. 1362-87, and a glossary on pp. 1388-93.

1373 Evans, G. Blakemore, textual ed. *The Riverside Shakespeare*. Boston: Houghton Mifflin, 1974. 1902 pp.

The text of *Antony and Cleopatra* is on pp. 1347-86, with notes and glosses at the foot and textual notes on pp. 1387-91. In his introduction to the play (pp. 1343-46), Frank Kermode stresses that "Shakespeare's presentation of Antony choosing between Roman virtue and the voluptuous banquets of the East contained hints that would enable some of his auditors to relate it to the famous story; and since Voluptas was often given the iconographical attributes of Venus, Cleopatra, so often compared to that goddess, fills the role exactly." Antony's "will" refers to "the pleasures of the senses, represented not merely as a voluptuary's weakness, the soft beds of the east, but as a divine fertility like that of the Nile; it is the richness of the world of Isis before the death of Osiris and the birth of the Empire under temperate Caesar."

1374 Lesberg, Sandy, ed. *The Works of William Shakespeare.* The Peebles Classic Library. New York and London: Peebles P, 1975.

Not seen.

1375 Seltzer, Isadore, illus. *The Tragedy of Antony and Cleopatra.* Design by Daniel Haberman. Illustrations by Isadore Seltzer. New York: Royal Composing Room, 1976. 250 pp.

This is the text of the play without any scholarly apparatus.

1376 Jones, Emrys, ed. *Antony and Cleopatra.* The New Penguin Shakespeare. Harmondsworth: Penguin, 1977. 299 pp.

In his introduction, Jones provides an analysis of, and critical extrapolation from, the first scene; a source study; comments on structure, design, and form; analyses of the principals; and, a brief discussion of the nearly infinite verbal styles. Jones emphasizes the play's ambiguity, its refusal to evaluate the central characters.

1377 Halstead, William Perdue. *Shakespeare as Spoken: A Collation of 5000 Acting Editions and Promptbooks of Shakespeare.* Vol. 12. Ann Arbor: University Microfilms International, 1979.

Antony and Cleopatra is found in this volume on pp. 911-43. The Globe text is printed on the odd-numbered pages, the variants on the even. The collations are based on printed acting editions and promptbooks listed in William Jaggard's bibliography and Charles H. Shattuck's *Shakespeare Promptbooks.*

1378 Rowse, A.L., ed. "*Antony and Cleopatra.*" *The Annotated Shakespeare.* New York: Clarkson N. Potter, 1978, III, 466-539.

This edition has notes and glosses in the margins. It reproduces illustrations and photographs on nearly every page. In his introduction, Rowse suggests that "the play has not the dramatic intensity of the other high tragedies: its action is more dispersed and various, and its interest is almost as much political as it is amorous."

1379 Bevington, David, ed. *The Complete Works of Shakespeare.* Third ed. Glenview, IL: Scott, Foresman, 1980. 1745 pp.

Bevington has revised somewhat the General Introduction. His introduction to *Antony and Cleopatra* (pp. 1284-86) is unchanged. The text of *Antony and Cleopatra* is found on pp. 1287-1331. An appendix on Shakespeare in performance (pp. 1658-67) refers to a few productions of *Antony and Cleopatra.*

1380 Wilders, John, Introd. *Antony and Cleopatra.* Ed. Peter Alexander for the BBC-TV/Time-Life Series. Notes on the Production by Henry Fenwick, Notes on the Text by David Snodin, and Glossary by Graham May. London: British Broadcasting Corporation, 1981. 185 pp.

Not seen.

1381 Halstead, William P. *Statistical History of Acting Editions of Shakespeare: Supplement to* Shakespeare As Spoken. Vol. 13. Washington, DC: UP of America, 1983. 618 pp.

In this work Halstead analyses the relationships between the promptbooks listed on p. 93. In Part I, he lists and discusses editors (some of them actors and theater managers) of the promptbooks and printed texts. In Part II (pp. 84-121), he takes the plays in alphabetical order, lists the famous actors who have played prominent roles in each, and discusses each promptbook, specifying cuts and additions and tracing the relations between the various versions. Finally he goes through each play scene by scene, identifying lines cut.

1382 *Plays and Sonnets of William Shakespeare.* 7 volumes. Franklin Center, PA: Franklin Library, 1978-83.

Not seen.

1383 McKeith, Jan, and Richard Adams, eds. *Antony and Cleopatra.* Macmillan Students' Shakespeare. London: Macmillan, 1984. 289 pp.

The introduction touches on topics like the quicksands of criticism, friends, Romans and a rural fellow, the varying tide, the fleeting moon, the paradoxical nature of growth, greatness, the structural reflections of *high pyramides*. The notes appear on odd pages facing the text on even pages.

1384 Riemer, A.P., ed. *The Tragedy of Anthony and Cleopatra.* Challis Shakespeare. Sydney: Sydney UP; Ashford: HB Sales, 1985. 184 pp.

Riemer discusses the date and sources and the nature of the play in his introduction. His notes are at the bottom of the page; there are also chrological tables and a glossary of proper names. This edition "follows the Folio practice of treating short lines as independent units: should such unities combine with others to form a pentametric beat, the ear will alert the reader to this; elsewhere, the suppleness and complexity of Shakespeare's verse will impose itself on the 'inner ear'—artful irregularity was, after all, a most cherished artistic tool during the Renaissance."

1385 Rowse, A.L., ed. *Antony and Cleopatra.* Modern Text with Introduction. Contemporary Shakespeare Series. Lanham, MD: University Presses of America, 1986. 152 pp.

Rowse's motto is: "Let the text be freed of superfluous difficulties, remove obstacles to let it speak for itself, while adhering conservatively to every line." He provides a short introduction but no annotations.

1386 Wells, Stanley, and Gary Taylor, eds. *William Shakespeare: The Complete Works*. The Oxford Shakespeare. Oxford: Clarendon P, 1986. xlvii, 1432 pp.

This edition provides Wells's general introduction (xiii-xxxvii), a chronology of contemporary allusions to Shakespeare, introductions to individual plays, and a glossary (pp. 1415-30). The text of the play is on pp. 1128-66. There are no notes.

1387 Wells, Stanley, and Gary Taylor, eds. *William Shakespeare: The Complete Works*. Original-Spelling Edition. Oxford: Clarendon P, 1986. lxiii, 1456 pp.

This edition shares with the previously available modernized-spelling volume Wells's general introduction, a chronology of contemporary allusions to Shakespeare, introductions to individual plays, and a glossary. Vivian Salmon provides an essay on Shakespeare's language.

1388 Bevington, David, ed; David Scott Kastan, James Hammersmith, and Robert Kean Turner, associate eds. *Antony and Cleopatra*. Bantam Classic. New York: Bantam Books, 1988. xxxvi, 186 pp.

This edition provides a "newly edited text and substantially revised, edited, and amplified notes, introductions, and other materials."

1389 Everett, Barbara, ed. *The Tragedy of Antony and Cleopatra*. Revised ed. Signet Classic Shakespeare. New York: New American Library, 1988. 297 pp.

This is a reprint of the 1964 edition, along with additional selections from criticism, a stage history by S. Schoenbaum, and a new preface and updated selective bibliography by Sylvan Barnett.

1390 Andrews, John F., ed. *Julius Caesar* and *Antony and Cleopatra*. Foreword. Tony Randall. Guild Shakespeare. Garden City: Doubleday Book and Music Clubs, 1989.

The text of this play is on pp. 223-543, with annotations on even pages facing the text on odd pages.

1391 Bevington, David, ed. *Antony and Cleopatra*. The New Cambridge Shakespeare. Cambridge: Cambridge UP, 1990. 274 pp.

Bevington discusses the play's date and sources, evaluates secondary scholarship on the sources, leaning away from topical interpretations and towards an understanding of the contradictory classical and modern readings. He deals with the contrarieties of critical response and the ironic gap between word and deed. The editor analyses genre and structure and the interaction of verbal and stage imagery. He provides a lengthy stage history, ample and scholarly textual notes, headnotes to each scene concerning location, sources and staging problems, and relevant secondary scholarship.

1392 Spevack, Marvin, ed. *Antony and Cleopatra*. Michael Steppart, and Marga Munkelt, associate eds. New Variorum Edition of Shakespeare. New York: Modern Language Association, 1990. xxxvi, 885 pp.

This is a modified diplomatic reprint of the F text accompanied by textual notes recording departures from F in editions from 1632 through 1989 and explanatory notes that explicate language and summarize the discussions of earlier editors and commentators. It includes several appendixes: emendations of accidentals and conjectural emendations; textual matters; date of composition; sources influences, and analogues; criticism, with separate sections for genre, themes, technique, and characters; staging and stage history; and, a bibliography.

1393 Tilak, Raghukul, ed. *Antony and Cleopatra*. Rajhans English Literature Series. 3rd. ed. Meerut: Rajhans Prakashan Mandir, 1990. 395 pp.

This edition includes the text and a paraphrase on facing pages, life of Shakespeare, Elizabethan theatre and audience, treatment of history, historical background, questions and answers, and suggested readings.

1394 Tucker, Patrick, and Michael Holden, eds. *The Tragedie of Anthonie, and Cleopatra*. Shakespeare's Globe Acting Editions. London: M.H. Publications, 1990. N.p.

This reprints the F text in an "acting" edition consisting of a plot, the prompt script with exits and entrances, a part script for each role, and textual and explanatory notes. The editors try to approximate the text as it would have been used by Elizabethan actors.

1395 Bevington, David M., ed. *The Complete Works of Shakespeare*. 4th edition. New York: HarperCollins, 1992. cvi, 1648 pp.

Bevington provides a general introduction (pp. i-cvi) and an introduction to the play (pp. 1293-96). The text of the play appears on pp. 1296-1344, with notes and glosses at bottom of page. There is a discussion of sources (pp. A-50-51), Shakespeare in performance, textual notes (pp. A-120-21), bibliography (pp. A-96-97), and glossary (pp. A-125-30).

1396 McKieth, Ian, and Richard Adams, eds. *Antony and Cleopatra*. Macmillan Shakespeare. Walton-on-THames, England: Nelson, 1992. 289 pp.

This is a reprint of an annotated student edition, with an introduction, published in 1984.

1397 Andrews, John F., ed. *Antony and Cleopatra*. Foreword. Tony Randall. Everyman Shakespeare. London: Everyman-Dent; Rutland, VT: Tuttle, 1993. liii, 365 pp.

Andrews presents a chronology of Shakespeare's life and times, perspectives on the play, a plot summary, and suggestions for further reading. The annotations are on even pages facing the text of odd pages.

1398 Tony Tanner, intro. *Tragedies.* Vol. 2. Everyman's Library. New York: Knopf, 1993. cxxxv, 770 pp.

Barbara Everett has edited the play for this edition (II, 353-499). In his introduction, Tanner argues that in this play "the poetry of excess leads to the unbounded, unboundaried, spaces of infinity. Saving leads to earthly empire, squandering opens an avenue of Eternity. All air and fire—and poetry. Bounty over plus."

1399 Berry, Mary, and Michael Clamp, eds. *Antony and Cleopatra.* Cambridge School Shakespeare. Cambridge: Cambridge UP, 1994. 252 pp.

This is an annotated student edition, with questions for study on pages facing the text. It includes a discussion of characters, politics, language, and stage history.

1400 Chopra, D.K., ed. *Antony and Cleopatra.* Narain's Series. Agra, India: Lakshmi Narain Agarwarl, 1994? 360 pp.

This edition gives a general introduction, text with paraphrse, summary of scenes, character sketches, explanatory notes, and questions and answers about the play.

1401 Jones, Emrys. "*Antony and Cleopatra.*" *Three Roman Plays.* Penguin Classics. New York: Penguin Books, 1994. 672 pp.

This collection includes Emrys Jones's New Penguin Shakespeare edition of the play.

1402 Neill, Michael, ed. *Anthony and Cleopatra.* Oxford Shakespeare. Oxford: Clarendon P, 1994. World's Classics. Oxford: Oxford UP, 1994. 388 pp.

Based on the First Folio, this critical edition supplies an introduction which discusses the reception, sources, date of composition, publishing history, stage history, textual problems, and such critical topics as anticlimax, identity, Enobarbus as choric fool, paradox, and gender.

1403 Turner, John, ed. *The Tragedie of Anthonie, and Cleopatra.* Shakespearean Originals: First Editions. New York: Prentice-Hall/Harvester Wheatsheaf, 1995. 178 pp.

The editor's intention "is to make the original Folio text available in all its openness as a play script whose possibilities are as various as theatrical performance may make them." In his introduction, Turner argues that, "in describing the competitiveness of the life of honour," Shakespeare focuses "upon the instability of its alliances, the unpredictability of its military encounters and, more generally, upon the mutability of all earthly fortunes." He is "depicting the endemic instability of a dying culture and the determined efforts of Caesar to bring about a new order, centralised and stabilised under his own imperial power."

1404 Wilders, John, ed. *Antony and Cleopatra.* Arden Shakespeare: Third Series. London and New York: Routledge, 1995. xviii, 331 pp.

This is a critical edition based on the First Folio, with an introduction which deals with Jacobean productions, unity, structure, moral judgment, genre, language and style, sources, date of composition, and textual problems, and stage history.

1405 Greenblatt, Stephen, gen. ed. *The Norton Shakespeare. Based on the Oxford Edition.* New York and London: Norton, 1997. 3420 pp.

The text of *Antony and Cleopatra* appears on pp. 2628-2708, with notes at foot of page. In his introduction to the play pp. (2619-27), Walter Cohen argues that the play's interpretation "depends on the relationship one sees between the ending and the partly incompatible material that has preceded it." Greenblatt's general introduction (pp. 1-76), deals with "Shakespeare's World," "The Playing Field," "Shakespeare's Life and Art," and "The Dream of the Master Text." Andrew Gurr discusses the Shakespearean stage (pp. 3281-3301)

Translations

Albanian

1406 Noli, Fran S., trans. Tirana: N. Sh. e B., 1957. Earliest edition listed: 1926.

Arabic

1407 Ibrahim, Muhammad ‘Awad, trans. *Antuni wa Kliyubatra*. Egypt, Dar al Ma’ahrif, 1960.

Armenian

1408 Dashtento, Khachick, trans. “*Antony and Cleopatra*.” *Selected Works*. Yerevan: Armenian State Publishing House, 1955, III, 185-293.

Bilorussian

1409 Gauruk, Iuryi, trans. *Antony and Cleopatra*. Minsk: Mastatskaia Literature, 1982. 197 pp.

Bengali

1410 Guha, Asok, trans. *Yyantani end Kliyopatra*. Calcutta: Biswas, 1908. 108 pp. *Antony and Cleopatra* for children.

Bulgarian

1411 Petrov, Aleri, trans. “*Antony and Cleopatra*.” *The Tragedies*. Vol. 2. Sofia: Narodna Kultura, 1973.

1412 Rainov, B., trans. *Antonii i Kleopatra*. Varna, 1987.

Catalan

1413 Sagarra, Joseph M., trans. *Antoni i Cleopatra*. Pubs. de' l'Institute del Teatre. Collecio Popular de Teatre Classic Universal 5. Barcelona: Editorial Brugeuera, 1980. 158 pp.

Chinese

1414 Chow Mei Fond, trans. "*Antony and Cleopatra*." *Complete Works*. Vol. 29. Shanghai, 1929.

1415 "*Antony and Celopatra*." Hsiang-Kang: Ta kuang ch'u pan she, 1974.

Croatian

1416 Stefanovic, S., trans. *Antonije i Kleopatra*. Belgrade, 1933.

1417 Nedic, B., and V. Zivojinovic, trans. *Antonije i Kleopatra*. Beograd: Prosveta, 1953. xiii, 3308. Printed in Cyrillic.

Czech

1418 Saudek, E.A., trans. *Antonius a Kleopatra*. *Divadlo* (Praha) April, May 1961, No. 4, 1-17; No. 5, 1-24.

1419 Saudek, E.A., trans. *Antonius a Kleopatra*. Shakespeare. *Tragedie II*. Praha: SNKLK, 1963. 682 pp.

Danish

1420 Lombolt, E., trans. *Antonius og Cleopatra*. Aarhaus: University, 1967.

1421 Slok, Johannes, Trans. *Antonius og Cleopatra*. Copenhagen: Berlingske Forlag, 1972. 213 pp. "Noter," 122-182; "Kommentar," 188-213.

Dutch

1422 Koster, E.B., trans. *Antonius en Cleopatra.* Rotterdam, 1904. 158 pp.

1423 Courteaux, Willy, trans. *Antonius en Cleopatra.* Klassicke Galerij, 152. Amsterdam: Wereld-Bibl., 1962. 143 pp.

Esperanto

1424 Andrew, S.A., trans. *Antonio kaj Kleopatra.* Rickmansworth: Esperanto Publishing Co., 1947. 96 pp.

French

1425 Boistel, J. B. R. *Antoine et Cléopâtre.* Paris, 1743.

1426 [La Place, Pierre Antoine de, trans.] *Le Theatre Anglois.* Vol. III. London, 1746.

1427 Le Tourneru, [Pierre Prime Felicien], trans. *Shakespeare: Traduit de l'Anglois.* Vol. VI. Paris: L'Auteur, Merigot & Valade, 1779.

1428 Guizot, F., and A. Pichot, trans. *L'Oeuvres completes de Shakespeare, Traduites de l'Anglais par LeTourneur.* New ed. Vol III. Paris: Ladvocat, 1821.

1429 Hugo, François-Victor, trans. *Oeuvres completes de W. Shakespeare.* 2nd ed. Vol. VII. Paris: Pagnerre, 1868.

1430 Montégut, Emile, trans. *Antoine et Cléopâtre. Oeuvres complete de Shakespeare.* 2nd ed. Paris: Hachette, 1878.

1431 Lambin, Georges, trans. *Antony and Cléopâtre.*Paris: Societe les belles lettres, 1926. English and French on opposite pages.

1432 Gide, André, and Jean Louis Barrault, trans. *Theatre complet.* Vol. 8. Neuchatel Ides et Clindes, 1947.

1433 Lambin, J., trans. *Antoine et Cléopâtre*. Coll. Shakespeare. Paris: Belles Lettres, 1957. 274.

German

1434 Benda, Johann W. O., trans. *Shakespeare's dramatische Werke*. Vol IX. Leipzig: Goschen, 1825.

1435 Tieck, Ludwig, and August Wilhelm von Schlegel, trans. *Shakespeare's dramatische Werke*. Vol. V. Berlin: Reimer, 1831.

1436 Moltke, Max, trans. *Antonius und Kleopatra. William Shakespeare's sammtliche Werke*. Vol. I. Leipzig: Cavael, [1868].

1437 Schmidt, A. *Antonius und Cleopatra*. Deutsche Shakespeare-Gesellschaft. Berlin, 1870.

1438 Bodenstedt, Friedrich, trans. *William Shakespeare's Dramatische Werke*. 2nd ed. Vol VII. Leipzig: Brockhaus, 1873.

1439 Alfieri, V. *Antonio et Cleopatra*. Bohn's Editions. London, 1876.

1440 Koch, Max, trans. *Antonius und Kleopatra. Shakespeare's dramatische Werke*. Trans. A. W. Schlegel et al. Vol. IX. Stuttgart: Cotta & Kroner, 1882.

1441 Keller, Wolfgang, trans. *Antonius und Kleopatra*. Berlin: Bong, 1912.

1442 Imelmann, Rudolf, trans. *Antonius und Cleopatra*. Leipzig: Insel, 1923.

1443 Schlagel, A. W., and L. Tieck, trans. *Shakespeare: Antonius und Cleopatra, Englisch und Deutsch*. Rowholts Klassiker 15. Hamburg: Rowohlt, 1962. 202 pp.

1444 Baudissin, Wolf Graf, trans., revised by Alfred Gunther. *Antonius und Kleopatra*. Reclams UB 39. Stuttgart: Reclam, 1964.

1445 Fried, Erich, trans. *Antonius und Kleopatra*. Berlin, 1970.

1446 Hagberg, Carl August, trans. *Antonius och Kleopatra*. Revised and with an Introduction and Notes by Sven Collbert. Lund: Liber, 1975.

1447 Schamp, Dieter. *Die Tragodie von Antonius und Cleopatra*. Fischerhude Theatertexte 1. Fischerhude: Verlag Atelier im Bauerrnhaus, 1978. 138 pp.

1448 Swaczynna, Wolfgang, trans. *Die Tragodie von Antonius und Kleopatra. The Tragedie of Anthonie and Cleopatra*. Barenreiter Schauspiel. Kassel: Johannes Stauda, 1985. 214 pp.

1449 Daphinoff, Dimiter, trans. and ed. *Antony and Cleopatra/Antonius und Kleopatra: Englisch-deutsche Studienausgabe*. Englisch-deutsche Studienausgabe der Dramen Shakespeares. Tubingen and Basel: Franke, 1995. 455 pp.

Greek

1450 Damiralis, Michael, trans. *Antony and Cleopatra*. *Parnassos* 5 (1881): 913-1000. Reprint 1882, 1912, 1928, 1957.

1451 Rotas, Vasil, trans. *Antonios kai Cleopatra*. Athens: Icaros, 1957. 152 pp.

1452 Protaios, Georgia, and Stathes Protaios, trans. *Antonios kai Cleopatra*. Athens: Daremas, 1963.

Hebrew

1453 Grossman, Reuben, trans. *The Tragedy of Antony and Cleopatra*. Tel-Aviv: Dvir, 1947. 205 pp.

1454 Liebes, J.G., trans. *Antony and Cleopatra.* Tel-Aviv, 1952.

1455 Banli, Hillel, trans. *Antonius u-cleopatra.* Tel Aviv: Newman, 1952.

1456 Alterman, Nathan, trans. *Yulius Kessar. Anthony u-Cleopatra.* Tel Aviv: Ha'kibbutz Ha'meuhad, 1982. 342 pp.

1457 Alterman, Nathan, trans. *Antonius u-cleopatra.* Tel Aviv: Ha-kibbutz ha-meu'had, [1987]. 317 pp.

Hungarian

1458 Sandor, Forditotta Heversi, trans. *Antonius es Cleopatra.* Budapest: R. Lampel, n. d. 126 pp.

1459 Vas, Istvan, trans. *Antonius es Kleopatra.* Budapest: Europa, 1960. 160 pp.

Italian

1460 Zanco, Aurelio, trans. *Antonio e Cleopatra.* Florence: Sansoni, 1931.

1461 Gambino, Ercole Angelonii, trans. *Antonio e Cleopatra.* Annibale Pastore, ed. *Shakespeare degli Italiani.* Torino: Societa Editrice Torinese, 1950. lxxx, 687.

1462 Lodovici, Cesare Vico, trans. *Antonio e Cleopatra.* Piccola Biblioteca Scientifico-letteraria, 47. [Turin:] Einaudi, 1952. 160 pp.

1463 Zanco, Aurelio, trns. *Antonio e Cleopatra.* Revised text. Biblioteca Sansoniana Straniera, No. 70. Florence: Sansoni, 1956. xxviii, 101.

1464 Obertello, Alfredo, ed. *La Tragedia di Antonio e Cleopatra.* Rome, 1957.

1465 Rusconi, Carlo, trans. "*Antonio e Cleopatra.*" *Il Teatro di Shakespeare*. Vol. III. Rome: Astra, 1957.

1466 Baldini, Gabrielo, trans. *Antonio e Cleopatra*. Bibl. univ. Rizzoli 1899. Milano: Rizzoli, 1962. 151 pp.

1467 Lodovici, Cesare Vico, trans. *Antonio e Cleopatra*. Collezione di Teatro 17. Torino: g. Einaudi, 1963. 118 pp.

1468 Traina, Cino, trans. *Antonio et Cleopatra*. Roma: Editori Associati, 1963. 141 pp.

1469 Obertello, Alfredo, ed. "*Antonoio e Cleopatra.*" *Teatro inglese*. Teatro di tutto il mondo. Vol. I. [1964] 614 pp.

1470 Qasimodo, Salvatore, trans. *Antonio e Cleopatra*. English and Italian Parallel Texts. Milan: Arnoldo Mondadori Editore, 1966. 507 pp.

1471 Chinol, Elio, trans. *Antonio e Cleopatra*. Edizione integrale bilingue. Milano: Mursia, 1985. 271 pp.

1472 Lombardo, Agostino, trans. "*Antonio e Cleopatra*, Atto quarto, atto quinto." Mariangela Tempera, ed. *Antony and Cleopatra dal testo alla scena*. Bologna: Cooperative Libraria Universitaria Editrice, 1990, pp. 9-48.

Japanese

1473 Tsubouchi Shoyo, trans. *Antony and Cleopatra*. Waseda UP, 1915.

1474 Tsubouchi Shoyo, trans. *Antony and Cleopatra*. Revised ed. Chuo Koron Sha, 1935.

1475 Akira Honda, trans. *Antony and Cleopatra*. Tokyo: Iwanami Shoten, 1958. 1194 pp.

1476 Uzu, Jiro, trans. *Antony and Cleopatra*. Shakespeare II, World Literature Series. Tokyo: Chikuma Shoho, 1965.

Latvian

1477 Rainis, J. trans. *Antonijus un Kleopatra*. St. Petersburg, 1913 [?]. 127 pp.

Malayalam

1478 Panikar, Ayappa, trans. *Antony and Cleopatra*. N.p, n.d.

Marathi

1479 Brve, Ananta Vamana, adaptor. *Antony and Cleopatra*. N.p., 1906. 147 pp.

Norwegian

1480 Eckhoff, Lorentz, trans. *Antonius og Kleopatra*. Oslo: H. Aschehong, 1962. 231 pp.

Polish

1481 Brandstaetter, Prgelozyla R., trans. *Antoniuz i Kleopatra*. Warsaw: Panstwowy Instytut Wydawn., 1958. 227 pp.

1482 Drozdowski, Bohdan, trans. *Antoniusz i Kleopatra*. Warsaw: Panstwowy Inst. Wydawniczy, 1983. 196 pp.

1483 Slomczynski, Maciej, trans. *Tragedia Antoniusza i Kleopatry*. Krakow: Wydawnictwo Literackie, 1987. 240 pp.

Portuguese

1484 Valadas, Nuno, trans. *Antonio et Cleopatra*. Coleccao Classicos 25. Lisboa: Editorial Presenca, 1970. 247 pp.

1485 Nunes, Carlos Alberto, trans. *Antonio e Cleopatra, Julio Cesar*. Tragedia. Edicoes de Ouro, Colecao Universidade. Rio de Janeiro: Editora Tecnoprint, 1978. 276 pp.

1486 Medeiros, Cunha, Francisco Calros de Almeida, and Oscar Mendes, trans. *Antonio e Cleopatra. Obra Completa*. Nova Versao. 3 vols. Rio de Janeiro: Editora Nova Aguilar, S.A., 1988. I: 790-872.

1487 O'Shea, Jose Roberto, trans. *Antony and Cleopatra: Bilingual Edition*. Sao Paulo: Editora Siciliano, 1997.

Romanian

1488 Ghica, S.I., trans. *Antoniu si Cleopatra*. Bucurest: Gutenberg, 1893. 134 pp.

1489 Stern, A., trans. *Antoniu si Cleopatra*. Bucharest: Socee, 1922.

1490 *Antoniu si Cleopatra*. Bucharest: Fundatia pentru literature si arta, 1945.

1491 Vianu, Tudor, trans. *Antoniu si Cleopatra*. Bucharest: ESPLA (State Publishing House for Literature and the Arts), 1951.

1492 Vianu, Tudor, trans. *Antoniu si Cleopatra*. Vol. 9. In Shakespeare. *Opere*. 11 vols. Bucharest: ESPLS, 1961.

Russian

1493 Donskoy, M., trans. *Antony and Cleopatra. The Collected Works of Shakespeare*. Anikst, Alexander, and A. A. Smirnov, eds. Vol. 7. Moscow: Iskusstvo, 1960.

1494 Chau, Simon S. C. "The Nature and Limitation of Shakespeare Translation." *New Asia Academy Collected Works of Shakespeare* 1 (1978): 239-250.

Serbian

1495 Simic, Zivojin, and Sima Pandurovic, trans. *Antonije i Kleopatra. Celovkuppna dela* (Complete Works). Vol. I. Cetinje: Narodna kujiga, 1975. 1572.

Sinhalese

1496 Stephen Silva, S.D., trans. *Antony and Cleopatra.* Colombo, 1926.

Slovak

1497 Rozner, Jan, and Zora Jesenska, trans. *Antony and Cleopatra.* Bratislava: Tatran, 1968.

Spanish

1498 Via, L., J.O. Marti, and S. Vilaregut, trans. *Antoni i Cleopatra.* Barcelona, 1899.

1499 Marin, L. Astrana, trans. *Antoni i Cleopatra.* Madrid, 1930.

1500 Marin, L. Astrana, trans. *Antoni i Cleopatra.* Bueno Aires, 1944.

1501 Maria de Sagarra, Josep, trans. *Coriole. Juli Cesar. Antoni i Cleopatra.* Barcelona: Alpha, 1958. 352 pp.

1502 Zozaya Ariztia, Maria Pilar, ed. Tito *Andronico, Antonio y Cleopatra, Coriolanio y Cimbelino, de William Shakespeare.* Barcelona: Planeta, 1983.

Swedish

1503 Thomander, J.S. *Antonius och Cleopatra.* Stockholm, 1825. 246 pp.

1504 Hallaström, Per. *Antonius och Cleopatra*. Stockholm, 1926. 119 pp.

Turkish

1505 Cevdet, Abdullah, trans. *Antonius ile Kleopatra*. Istanbul: Matbaa-i ictihad istikbal, 1921.

1506 Korkut, Saffet, trans. *Antonius ile Kleopatra*. Ankara: Maarif Matbaasi, 1944. xvi, 161.

1507 Sami, S., trans. *Antonius ile Kleopatra*. Istanbul: Hilmi, 1946.

Urdu

1508 Rahman, Munibul, trans. *Antony and Cleopatra*. Delhi: Maktaba Jamia, 1979. 136 pp.

Ukrainian

1509 Kulisha, P.A., trans. *Antonu i Kleopatra*. U L'vovi: Nankoue T-vo im Shevchenka, 1901.

Stage History

1510 Davies, Thomas. *Dramatic Miscellanies*. 2 vols. 1783. Reprint. New York: AMS, 1973.

Davies comments on David Garrick's revival, altered by Edward Capell, "with all the advantages of new scenes, habits, and other decorations proper to the play."

1511 Hazlitt, William. "A View of the English Stage or A Series of Dramatic Criticisms: *Antony and Cleopatra* [Nov. 16, 1813]." *The Complete Works*. Ed. P. P. Howe. Centenary Edition. 21 vols. London: Dent, 1930, V, 190-92.

Reviewing a performance at Covent Garden, Hazlitt stressed that this play "is every where full of that pervading comprehensive power, by which the poet seemed to identify himself with time and nature. The pomp and voluptuous charms of Cleopatra are displayed in all their force and lustre, as well as the effeminate grandeur of the soul of Mark Antony."

1512 Archer, William. "'Antony and Cleopatra' in Manchester." *The Theatrical World of 1897*. London: Walter Scott, 1898, pp. 66-72.

Archer discusses the 1897 production of the play in Manchester, with Louis Calvert as Antony Janet Achurch as Cleopatra. Calvert's Antony "is rugged, forcible, and effective. It lacks elevation, and is not very strong in diction; but it has plenty of impetuosity and vitality." Achurch "seemed to me quite at her best in the last act, where she gave a haggard nobility to the figure of the dying Queen that was original and memorable.

1513 Macready, William Charles. *Diaries, 1833-1851*. Ed. William Toynbee. 2 vols. New York: G. P. Putnam's, 1912.

In his private journals, Macready comments on his roles in the play, the way he prepared his roles, and his sense of elation or dissatisfaction.

1514 Winter, William. "*Antony and Cleopatra*." *Shakespeare on the Stage*. Third Series. New York: Moffat, Yard, 1916, pp. 431-67.

Winter provides an account of porudctions of this play in British and American theatres from Garrick's version of 1759 to Julia Marlowe and Edward Hugh Sothern in 1908.

1515 Odell, George C. D. *Shakespeare from Batterton to Irving*. 2 vols. New York: Scribner's, 1920. Reprint. New York: Benjamin Blom, 1963.

Odell discusses many of the outstanding productions of *Antony and Cleopatra* from the Restoration to the early twentieth century. It briefly refers to its adaptations as melodrama and other forms. It mentions costumes and scenery and some of the prominent actors like Garrick, Kemble, F.R. Benson and Lillie Langtry.

1516 Darlington, W.A. "*Antony and Cleopatra* at Stratford." *Through the Fourth Wall*. London: Chapman & Hall, 1922, pp. 70-74.

Darlington praises Dorothy Green's Cleopatra as "really quite out of the common" and Edmund Willard's Antony as "a good, honest, manly piece of work."

1517 Rhodes, R. Crompton. *The Stagery of Shakespeare*. Birmingham: Cornish Brothers, 1922. 102 pp.

Rhodes suggests that in this play "the balcony became the monument into which the Queen of Egypt locked herself from Caesar." He is also "convinced that the death of Antony was not originally played in the balcony."

1518 Stone, George Winchester, Jr. "Garrick's Presentation of *Antony and Cleopatra.*" *Review of English Studies* 13 (1937): 20-38.

Stone gives David Garrick "the credit for first staging the play, after Shakespeare's time, and for presenting in it unadulterated Shakespeare to an age which was all too used to viewing 'improved' versions of his works." He considers Garrick and Capell's cuts as "judicious" and believes that Garrick succeeded in providing a superior acting version of the play.

1519 Farjeon, Herbert. "*Antony and Cleopatra.*" *The Shakespearean Scene: Dramatic Criticisms.* London: Hutchinson, 1940, pp. 170-77.

Farjeon reprints his reviews of three London production by Andrew Leigh (1925), Harcourt Williams (1930), and Theodore Komisarjevsky (1936).

1520 Crosse, Gordon. *Fifty Years of Shakespearean Playgoing.* London: A. R. Mowbray, 1941. 159 pp.

Crosse evaluates various productions by directors like Beerbohm Tree, Harcourt Williams, and M. Komisarjivsky.

1521 Atkinson, Brooks. "Antony and Cleopatra." *Times* (New York) 27 November 1947: 49.

This is a review of Guthrie McClintic's production in New York, in which Katharine Cornell did not show much passion and Godfrey Tearle succeed better as a soldier than as a lover.

1522 Atkinson, Brooks. "Egyptian Siren." *Times* (New York) 7 December 1947: II, 1.

Atkinson reiterates his earlier view that McClintic's production "skims lightly over the surface of the play."

1523 Brown, John Mason. "O Eastern Star!" *Saturday Review* 20 December 1947: 22-25.

"Visually, a more beautiful production of Shakespeare has not been made in our time than this 'Antony and Cleopatra'." As for Cornell herself, she has never given a more enchanting performance than she does as Antony's Egyptian dish." "Vocally and in her person, she captures nearly all of the changing moods of this chameleon who happened to be a monarch."

1524 Berger, Eric. "Curtain Goes Up." *Senior Scholastic* 52.11 (19 April 1948): 13-14.

Berger describes the rehearsals of the play under the direction of Guthrie McClintic.

1525 Rylands, George. "Elizabethan Drama in the West End." *Shakespeare Survey* 1 (1948): 103-105.

The setting for this production "was so pretentious and uncomfortable that the tragedy never had a chance, from the great processional opening which was muddled away to nothing until the hauling up of the hero with pulleys and a fishing-net on to the platform surmounting what appeared to be an air-raid shelter or an elevator with sliding doors." Its stage "was so cluttered with permanent solids that the essential contrast of the juxtaposed scenes in Rome and Alexandria was quite lost."

1526 Byrne, Muriel St. Clare. "Fifty Years of Shakespearian Production: 1898-1948." *Shakespeare Survey* 2 (1949): 1-20.

Byrne discusses the productions of Beerbohm Tree, Glen Byam Shaw, and Harcourt Williams.

1527 Gilder, Rosamond. "Shakespeare in New York: 1947-48." *Shakespeare Survey* 2 (1949): 130-31.

Katherine Cornell's production "accentuated what one might call the political aspects of the play" and "the theme of power politics, of the battle for supremacy in the Mediterranean basin." Cornell's interpretation was "particularly happy in the gayer, kindlier scenes between Cleopatra and her handmaids and rose to truly noble heights in the majestic closing passages." Godfrey Tearle's Antony was "a lusty, vigorous fellow whose character had already begun to deteriorate through unrestrained self-indulgence and self-conceit."

1528 Williams, Harcourt. *Old Vic Saga*. London: Winchester, 1949. 240 pp.

Williams described how his company treated this play as "a rapid sequence of events almost kaleidoscopic in effect." For costumes, they "went to the pictures of Paul Veronese and Tiepolo." John Gielgud and Dorothy Green played the principal roles.

1529 Atkinson, Brooks. "'Antony and Cleopatra' Put on by the Oliviers as the Second of Their Twin Bill." *Times* (New York) 21 December 1951: 22.

Atkinson suggests that "Laurence Olivier as the reckless Antony and Vivien Leigh as the royal Cleopatra are perfectly matched in a production that conveys the richness, fire and majesty of Shakespeare."

1530 Atkinson, Brooks. "Olivier and Leigh." *Times* (New York) 30 December 1951: II, 1.

In *Antony and Cleopatra*, "fully in command not only of the parts but of the romantic tragedy as a whole, the Oliviers sweep through it with force and beauty; and they are ably abetted by several other first-rate actors who understand the dramatic values of what they are playing."

1531 Smith, Warren. "Evidence of Scaffolding on Shakespeare's Stage." *Review of English Studies* ns 2 (1951): 22-29.

Smith argues for the use of dais of the state or a scaffolding on stage which would solve the enigma of Cleopatra's monument.

1532 Venezky, Alice S. *Pageantry on the Shakespearean Stage*. New York: Twayne, 1951. 242 pp.

When they saw the play, "surely Shakespeare's audience was reminded not so much of Roman history as of English pageanty along the Thames." Cleopatra's "final tribute employs elements of the pageant to recall Antony's greatness and magnificence."

1533 Venezky, Alice. "Current Shakespearean Productions in England and France." *Shakespeare Quarterly* 2 (1951): 335-42.

This production uses the revolving stage "to maintain continuous action as the scene moves from Egypt to Rome and back again." Laurence Olivier and Vivien Leigh "stress the physical affection and the humanity of the royal pair, rather than their nobility."

1534 Worsley, T.C. "The World Well Lost." *New Statesman* 19 May 1951: 559-60.

This was a successful production even if Vivien Leigh "lacked the requisite classical stature and sensuality to play Cleopatra." Worsley praises Olivier's Antony as "exactly right to the last hair," and commends the use of the revolving stage which made it easy to shift scenes from Rome to Egypt.

1535 Brown, John Mason. "A Queen's Story." *Saturday Review* 35 (12 January 1952): 24-27.

Vivien Leigh "succeeds in matching the ever-changing moods and meeting the heavy demands of Shakespeare's heroine." Antony's Julius in Shaw's *n* "is as wise as his Antony is abandoned, as intellectual as the latter is physical, and both of them are men to whom authority comes easily."

1536 Kerr, Walter. "Cleopatra and Friend." *Commonweal* 11 January 1952: 349.

In reviewing Shakespeare and Shaw's *Caesar and Cleopatra*, Kerr commends Oliver's strong Antony over his tired Caesar, and notes that Leigh could not bring together the two dramatists' very different versions of Cleopatra; she missed some of each but succeeded in creating "a single, believable, and commanding person."

1537 "Antony and Cleopatra." *Times* (London) 29 April 1953: 8.

This reviewer describes Michael Redgrave as "a superb Antony" and compares Peggy Ashcroft's Cleopatra with "an exquisite miniature of a passionate yet calculating monarch." It was "nearer to perfection than any in living memory.

1538 Barker, Felix. "Traditions at the St. James's, 1948-53." *The Oliviers: A Biography*. New York: Lippincott, 1953, pp. 334-60.

Barker summarizes the approaches of the Oliviers to the two roles and explains the challenges offered by Antony's contradictory moods and Cleopatra's "infinite variety."

1539 Atkinson, Brooks. "Stratford-upon-Avon." *Times* (New York) 10 May 1953: II, 1

Atkinson feels that "Mr. Redgrave and Miss Ashcroft have not set fire to 'Antony and Cleopatra" as Laurence Olivier and Vivien Leigh did." The Stratford production "has less of the sensuality of the text. The moderate climate of England has overwhelmed the sultry recklessness of the Middle East."

1540 Brown, Ivor. *The Shakespeare Memorial Theatre, 1951-523: A Photographic Record*. London: Max Reinhardt, 1953. 18 pp.

Brown comments on Glen Byam Shaw's 1953 production and provides photographs.

1541 Fleming, Peter. "Antony and Cleopatra." *Spectator* 8 May 1953: 571.

This reviewer lavishly praises Redgrave and Ashcroft in this play.

1542 Hobson, Harold. "'Richard III' and 'Antony and Cleopatra' at Stratford." *Christian Science Monitor* 16 May 1953: 10A.

Ashcroft's Cleopatra "does not attempt to dominate Antony by fleshly allure, but by strength of will and shrewishness of tongue."

1543 Kemp, T.C., and J.C. Trewin. *The Stratford Festival: A History of the Shakespeare Memorial Theatre*. Birmingham: Cornish Brothers, 1953. 295 pp.

This is a brief discussion of the revivals by Frank Benson in 1898 and 1912 and by W. Bridges-Adams in 1921 and 1931.

1544 Keown, Eric. "Antony and Cleopatra." *Punch* 13 May 1953: 586-87.

Redgrave has gained in depth in his portrayal of Antony and Ashcroft has become more sensual in her Cleopatra.

1545 Leech, Clifford. "Stratford 1953." *Shakespeare Quarterly* 4 (1953): 461-66.

Antony and Cleopatra was presented on a simple set of "a flight of steps, two slender pillars and a cyclorama for almost the whole" of the play. Michael Redgrave "was an impressive figure, too, and yet not afraid to bring out Antony's successive humiliations. Peggy Ashcroft, "moving outside her normal range, had a firm grasp of the early scenes where Cleopatra enjoys her power and is tortured when she knows its limits." The two of them "could not fully become the Egyptian dish and its greedy devourer."

1546 Rees, Joan. "An Elizabethan Eyewitness of *Antony and Cleopatra*." *Shakespeare Survey* 6 (1953): 91-93.

A passage in the 1607 version of Daniel's *Cleopatra* is a reminiscence of an actual performance of Shakespeare's play.

1547 Rylands, George. "Festival Shakespeare in the West End." *Shakespeare Survey* 6 (1953): 140-146.

"Who will forget Vivien Leigh, robed and crowned in the habiliments of an Egyptian goddess, beauty on a monument smiling extremity out of act?" Laurence Olivier "sacrificed Antony to Cleopatra and 'for his ordinary paid his heart'." This was "a splendid and delightful" production "for variety and pace, for colour and vitality."

1548 Trewin, J.C. "Nile and Seine." *Illustrated London News* 16 May 1953: 798.

Trewin compares Redgrave and Ashcroft with the best in memory. One of the commendable features of the direction was "its speed."

1549 Walker, Roy. "*Antony and Cleopatra*." *Times Literary Supplement* 29 May 1953: 349.

Walker discusses the staging of the lifting up of the dying Antony into the monument.

1550 Holmes, Martin. "A Regency Cleopatra." *Theatre Notebook* 8 (1954): 46-47.

Holmes examines two prints showing costumes worn in an 1813-1814 production of *Antony and Cleopatra* at Covent Garden, with reproductions.

1551 Kemp, T.C. "Acting Shakespeare: Modern Tendencies in Playing and Production." *Shakespeare Survey* 7 (1954): 121-127.

In Glen Byam Shaw's 1953 production, Alexandria was "a pillared open space with steps to varying levels, a place of free air and wide sky under which Peggy Ashcroft established Cleopatra's domination beyond all questioning." Cleopatra was "a mature woman who knew exactly what she was doing and exalted quietly in every moment of it." Michael Redgrave "suggested the shagginess, the sensuality, the incipient coarseness of the man who is running to seed."

1552 Maulnier, Thierry. "De Shakespare a Jean Genet." *La Revue de Paris*, February 1954, pp. 1338-41.

This is a review of a performance of *Antony and Cleopatra* in Paris by the Memorial Theatre Company.

1553 Saunders, J.W. "Vaulting the Rails." *Shakespeare Survey* 7 (1954): 69-81.

In the Monument Scene, Saunders proposes that "the platform itself, as proper and desirable, could have served as the main stage, the op of the monument, and the lower level could have been represented—why not?— by the yard."

1554 Findlater, Richard. "Shylock, Lear, and Antony (1953)." *Michael Redgrave: Actor*. London: William Heinemann, 1956, pp. 118-32.

Findlater evaluates Redgrave's Antony as definitive and considers his physical appearance, voice, and gestures most suitable for the noble role.

1555 Smith, Irwin. "'Gates' on Shakespeare's Stage." *Shakespeare Quarterly* 7 (1956): 157-76.

Smith's intention is "to examine gate scenes in several plays, to suggest that temporary property gates were needed and that their construction was practicable, and thus to create the presumption that they existed as equipment available for use in any scene to which they were appropriate." The opening of the gates would reveal Cleopatra's monument, the interior of Corioles, and Juliet's tomb.

1556 Anon. "*Antony and Cleopatra.*" *Theatre World* April 1957: 13-17.

These are photoographs of the Old Vic production.

1557 Anon. "Shakespeare's Plays on Soviet Stages." *USSR* 13 (1957): 56.

Photographs of Soviet productions of *Antony and Cleopatra*, *Hamlet*, and *Lear*.

1558 Barnes, T.R. "Cold Vic." *Journal of Education* (London) 39 (1957): 260.

Reviews of *Antony and Cleopatra* and *Macbeth* at the Old Vic.

1559 Bridges-Adams, William. *The Irresistible Theatre*. London: Secker & Warburg, 1957. 446 pp.

This study contains a brief discussion of the problems in producing *Antony and Cleopatra*.

1560 Byrne, Muriel St. Clare. "The Shakespeare Season." *Shakespeare Quarterly* 8 (1957): 461-92.

Robert Helpmann's production "had swiftness and dignity and was admirably lucid." The costumes were striking: "Rome in purples, dull, darkish blues and greys, with a bright blue and some good green tones for the Pompey scenes: Egypt in delicate fawns, set off with greys and black and white, with Cleopatra in deep red, rich blues and greens, white and gold, and Antony a magnificent figure in scarlet and gold." Keith Mitchell was a splendid Antony. Margaret Whiting had "contrast and variety of mood, light and shade in the voice, great expressivness in the eyes and animation in the countenance."

1561 Clarke, Mary. "*Antony and Cleopatra*." *Shakespeare at the Old Vic 1956-57*. London: Hamish Hamilton, 1957. 111 pp.

This is a comprehensive account of Robert Helpmann's 1957 revival and a survey of critical responses. The play was revived uner the Old Vic Five Year First Folio Plan in the fourth season.

1562 Hogan, Charles Beecher. *Shakespeare in the Theatre, 1701-1800: A Record of Performances in London, 1751-1800*. Oxford: Clarendon P, 1957. 798 pp.

Hogan records Garrick's 1759 production, with a cast list and a summary of cuts in the text.

1563 Hosley, Richard. "Shakespeare's Use of a Gallery over the Stage." *Shakespeare Survey* 10 (1957): 77-89.

Shakespeare's company used the gallery to which Antony was raised over the stage." Once up, Antony would "sit in the front opening of the gallery or one of its boxes, clustered about by Cleopatra, Charmian, and Iras;" Cleopatra would "perhaps 'swoon' against the parapet of the gallery after Antony's death;" Diomedes and the Guard would watch these actions "from the stage below."

1564 Ropollo, Joseph Patrick. "American Premieres of Two Shakespearean Plays in New Orleans." *Tulane Studies in English* 7 (1957): 125-32. Reprinted in *Shakespeare in the South: Essays on Performance*. Ed. Philip C. Kolin. Jackson: UP of Mississippi, 1983, pp. 112-27.

This play was first performed in the United States in New Orleans on March 8, 1838, at the St. Charles Theatre, with Ellen Tree as Cleopatra and William Hiled as Antony. A local reviewer pronounced Ellen Tree's Cleopatra as "perfect."

1565 Helpmann, Robert. "Antony and Cleopatra." *Times* (London) 6 March 1957: 14.

One of the chief features of this production is "to give purposefulness, speed and shape to a play which is apt to make a sprawling impression." Keith Michell's Antony "is inclined a little to overdo his scenes of amorous dalliance, but that may be because of his anxiety to make it perfectly plain that it is the spirit of fascination that binds these twain, not the spirit of love." Margaret Whiting "hardly tries to create an impression of seductiveness; but she partly succeeds in suggesting a strength of personality which gives plausibility to the queen's weaving of endless snares to retain her power over Antony."

1566 Trewin, J.C. "[Robert 's production of *Antony and Cleopatra]*" *Illustrated London News* 16 March 1957: 438.

This is a positive evaluation of Robert Helpmann's Old Vic production, but Trewin did not like the doubling of minor roles and the "discovery" of the principals on stage at the opening.

1567 Gelb, Arthur. "Antony and Cleopatra." *Times* (New York) 14 January 1959: 28.

This concert version of the play, with music by David Amram, pulsated "with excitement. Even before a line is spoken, the off-stage music, the stark, raked platform, the stylized black and while of the actors' costumes subtly relieved by a jewel or scrap of richly colored velvet, portends high drama." Colleen Dewhurst's Cleopatra "is voluptuous, fiery, viperish and regal." George C. Scott's Antony "summons some fine and convincing passion" only in the final scene. Then "he forgets the tricks of tongue clicking and facial twitching that are distressing in the early scenes and gives full reign to the agony of the noble and defeated Antony."

1568 Hewes, Henry. "Head-Shaking and Shakespeare." *Saturday Review* 31 January 1959: 24-25.

Joseph Papp failed even though he had George C. Scott and Colleen Dewhurst to work with.

1569 Funke, Lewis. "Antony and Cleopatra." *Times* (New York) 1 August 1960: 19.

The American Shakespeare Festival production, under Jack Laundau's direction, "sparkles more than it splutters, and its defects are outshone by its virtues." Katharine Hepburn's Cleopatra "is a Queen of the Nile who is one of the great coquettes of history, a woman of passion and temperament, a woman who has attributes of a queen and yet deep within her the mark of the strumpet." Robert Ryan is "a robust Antony" who "has the attributes of a man who would succumb to the wiles of Cleopatra." It is "not a memorable" but "an honorable" production.

1570 Hewes, Henry. "The Duchess of Tiber." *Saturday Review* 20 August 1960: 33.

Katherine Hepburn made an intelligent and energetic Cleopatra in Jack Landau's production in Connecticut, but Robert Ryan did not succeed as Antony.

1571 McGlinchee, Claire. "Stratford, Connecticut, Shakespare Festival, 1960." *Shakespeare Quarterly* 11 (1960): 469-72.

In her Cleopatra, Katharine Hepburn "has improved in voice and manner," and did her best in the death scenes. Ryan showed little of "the poet's conception of Antony as a supreme example of 'greatness fallen'. His Antony was consistently a man with a hangover."

1572 Perkin, Robert L. "Shakespeare in the Rockies III." *Shakespeare Quarterly* 11 (1960): 460-65.

Antony and Cleopatra had "sweep, viogr, boldness, and a Cleopatra (Molly Riley) who became the infinite woman incarnate" George Wall's Antony, however, "was too grand in manner, with too much head flinging, cape swirling, bentknee posturing and a swooping, gliding stride when Antony should walk firmly as a third pillar of the world."

1573 Saunders, J. W. "Staging at the Globe, 1599-1613." *Shakespeare Quarterly* 11 (1960): 402-425. Reprinted in *The Seventeenth-Century Stage.* Ed. G.E. Bentley. Patterns of Literary Criticism 6. Chicago: U of Chicago, 1968, pp. 235-66.

Instead of being done at an "upper level in the Tiring-House," the text indicates that the "Monument" scene should be presented on "an elevated acting area accessible from below on two sides." The two levels "here can only be represented by the Platform and the Yard."

1574 "Shakespearean Productions in the National Theatre (Hungary)" (in Russian). *Innostranneja literatura* 3 (1960): 275.

This is an account of the productions of *Antony and Cleopatra* and other plays.

1575 Trewin, J.C. *Benson and the Bensonians.* London: Barrie & Rockliff, 1960. 302 pp.

Trewin comments briefly on Frank Benson's 1898 revival with Constance Benson as Cleopatra and the 1912 one with Dorothy Green.

1576 Adams, John Cranford. *The Globe Playhouse: Its Design and Equipment.* 2nd ed. New York: Barnes & Noble, 1961. 435 pp.

Shakespeare's text is helpful in solving staging problems. For example, the Folio text of *Antony and Cleopatra* "is sparing of its stage directions, but the dialogue and inescapable inferences enable us to reconstruct what took place." Adams suggests that, in doing the Monument scene, Shakespeare's company used "a rope lowered from a windlass concealed in the huts."

1577 Burnim, Kalman. *David Garrick Director*. Pittsburgh: U of Pittsburgh P, 1961. 234 pp.

After five months of preparation, Garrick staged "a splendid" *Antony and Cleopatra* on January 3, 1759. The manager-actor never recouped his costs for the production closed after only six performances. The Roman characters "were presented with something akin to appropriate dress."

1578 Trewin, J.C. "Heard at Court." *Illustrated London News* 25 February 1961: 322.

This is a review of Birmingham rep's *Antony and Cleopatra*.

1579 Tynan, Kenneth. *Curtains*. New York: Athenaeum, 1961. 495 pp.

Tynan reprints here his reviews of the 1951 and 1953 revivals of this play.

1580 Weiner, Albert B. "Elizabethan Interior and Aloft Scenes: A Speculative Essay." *Theatre Survey* 2 (1961): 15-34.

Agreeing with C. Walter Hodges, Weiner suggests that the Globe Theatre had a semi-portable pavilion, with a flat, solid roof, strong enough to support a number of actors, where the Monument Scene might have been performed.

1581 Davies, Lawrence E. "Margaret Webster Battles Weather at Berkeley." *Times* (New York) 14 September 1963: 12.

Webster directed the play in open-air Hearst Greek Theatre with a cast of 80, "none of whom were professional, and who could not hold dress rehearsals in the daytime." Webster explained that "we are running an educational theater and one of the things we have to do is to educate."

1582 Funke, Lewis. "The Theater: 'Antony and Cleopatra'." *Times* (New York) 21 June 1963: 33.

This is a rather mixed appraisal of Joseph Papp's 1963 staging with Colleen Dewhurst. Papp "has a tendency toward surplus foolery and even over-broad playing." Dewhurst's efforts "to convey Cleopatra's 'infinite variety' carried her into gauche moments."

1583 Griffin, Alice. "The New York Shakespeare Festival, 1963." *Shakespeare Quarterly* 14 (1963): 441-43.

The New York Shakespeare Festival in Central Park "seemed to seek audience approval by playing Shakespeare 'down', by adding display where it failed to achieve drama, by reducing great characters like Antony and Cleopatra to television serial size, and by substituting physical farce when the actor was inadequate for his role." Michael Higgins's "proasaic, puzzled Antony was hardly a triple pillar of the world." Colleen Dewhurst, "the regal" Cleopatra, "achieved a larger-than-life impression," with "her feline figure, quicksilver shifts in mood and control in the emotional scenes."

1584 Hewes, Henry. "Shakesapeare in Central Park; Stage Seen on Small Screen." *Saturday Review* 6 July 1963: 17.

This is "an easygoing, friendly performance of the play in which the historical figures seem unremote and unextraordinary." Michael Higgins's Antony "seems less the great warrior or the great lover, than he does a world-weary official guiltily suffering through a consciously self-destructive relationship with a woman." Colleen Dewhurst's Cleopatra "appears to be playing a compulsive game with Antony in which every tiny victory temporarily reassures her of her ability to possess men." Though entertaining, "the tragedy remains dormant until the final scenes, when Antony's last stand against the odds gives off a brief spark."

1585 Linthicum, M. Channing. *Costume in the Drama of Shakespeare and His Contemporaries*. 1936. Reprint. New York: Russell & Russell, 1963. 307 pp.

This is a brief survey of sixteenth and early seventeenth-century colours, their production, symbolism and periods of fashion; a discussion of costume textiles and garments; the earliest date of their use in England; and a definition of each of these colours, textiles, garments, with illustrative quotations from drama and contemporary accounts. A number of passages is cited from this play.

1586 Prosser, Eleanor. "Shakespeare at Ashland and San Diego." *Shakespeare Quarterly* 14 (1963): 445-54.

Antony and Cleopatra at San Diego was a failure because it stressed "the animal sensuality of the lovers." Antony (Louis Edmonds) was "an aging playbody" and Cleopatra (Jacqueline Brookes) "an erratic wanton."

1587 Beckerman, Bernard. *Shakespeare at the Globe*. New York: Macmillan, 1964. 254 pp.

Antony and Cleopatra is one of the fifteen Shakespearean productions at the Globe. Beckerman discusses the repertory, the dramaturgy, the stage, and the acting of this and other plays.

1588 Davies, Robertson. *Shakespeare's Boy Actors*. 1939. Reprint. New York: Russell & Russell, 1964. 208 pp.

Cleopatra's role is "well within the technical emotional scope of a boy actor of sixteen or seventeen. In presenting Cleopatra the boy actor would show her primarily as a queen with a queen's dignity."

1589 Hosley, Richard. "The Staging of the Monument Scenes in *Antony and Cleopatra*." *Library Chronicle* (University of Pennsylvania) 30 (1964): 62-71.

Hosley argues that the monument scenes Antony may "have been carried on stage, and heaved aloft, in a seated position, for it would have been fully in accord with Elizabethan technique if the Soldiers carried Antony on stage in a chair."

1590 Jamieson, Michael. "Shakespeare's Celibate Stage: The Problem of Accommodation to the Boy Actress in *As You Like It*, *Antony and Cleopatra*, and *The Winter's Tale*." Duthie, G. I., ed. *Papers, Mainly Shakespearian*. Aberdeen U Studies 147. Edinburgh: Oliver and Boyd for the U of Aberdeen, 1964, pp. 21-39. Reprinted in *The Seventeenth-Century Stage*. Ed. G.E. Bentley. Patterns of Literary Criticism 6. Chicago: U of Chicago P, 1968, pp. 70-93.

Shakespeare "used devices of imagery and rhetoric in an essentially dramatic way, seizing on every suggestion he found in Plutarch, to make Cleopatra playable on the Jacobean stage, but, in accommodating himself to the boy-actress, he did not sacrifice a single emotional effect."

1591 Knight, G. Wilson. *Shakespearian Productions*. 3rd ed. London: Faber, 1964. 4th expanded ed. London: Routledge & Kegan Paul, 1968. 323 pp.

Knight stresses that in productions of Antony and Cleopatra and other plays, "it is the business of the Shakespearian stage to explore the interpenetration of human affairs and spiritual." He finds it unsatisfactory that "our productions should remain content with verbal accuracy and an intellectual response; rather they should enlist every legitimate resource of eye and ear and action to awake the imagination and thence expand our consciousness beyond the terms of twentieth-century belief."

1592 Shedd, Robert G. "The Great Lakes Shakespeare Festival, 1964: *Henry VI*—and *Hamlet* too!" *Shakespeare Quarterly* 15 (1964): 423-26.

This production was disappointing because Eve Collyer and David Tress "were not used to working with this company, perhaps because of an unmistakable disparity in their ages, and perhaps because they have been differently trained." They could not rise up to the demands of the leading roles. They gave "a very regal Cleopata a la Dame Edith Evans, and an Antony in the muscle-flexing and bombastic tradition—an Egypt and an Antony who seemed acutely uncomfortable together."

1593 Trewin, J.C. *Shakespeare on the English Stage 1900-1964. A Survey of Productions*. London: Barrie and Rockliff, 1964. 328 pp.

This survey of Shakespearean performances in Britain since 1900 comments on Tree (His Majesty, 1906); Holloway and Evans (Old Vic, 1925); Gielgud and Green (Old Vic, 1930; Isham and Massingham (Stratford, 1931); Lawson and Newcombe (Old Vic, 1934); Emerton and Lacey (Stratford, 1935); Wolfit and Leontovich (New, 1936); Eustrel and Luce (Stratford, 1945); Tearle and Evans (Piccadilly, 1946); Oliver and Leigh (St. James, 1951); Redgrave and Ashcroft (Stratford and Princes, 1953); Michell and Whiting (Old Vic, 1957).

1594 Watkins, Ronald. *On Producing Shakespeare*. 2nd ed. New York: Benjamin Blom, 1965. 335 pp.

Watkins refers to a number of scenes from this play in his discussion of producing Shakespeare.

1595 Edinborough, Arnold. "Stratford, Ontario—1967." *Shakespeare Quarterly* 18 (1967): 399-403.

Having no liking for or empathy with monarchy, Langham turned Zoe Caldwell's Cleopatra into "a hot little Egyptian bitch" and Christopher Plummer's Antony into "an aging Roman rake." Plummer "never convinced us that he was the emperor of half the world." Caldwell did not make the audience feel that "to kiss her hand was to break through a barrier of imperial protocol; it was merely a preciously sensual achievement."

1596 Hewes, Henry. "Rare Spirits." *Saturday Review* 19 August 1967: 22.

This production "is a sophisticated affair pursued as a merry release from the world's sobriety." Plummer's Antony "is an all-appreciative audience for Miss Caldwell's skylarking Cleopatra as she launches into a hilarious imitation of Caesar's imperiousness." This one is "a fascinating attempt by two remarkable actors to truly explore the inner natures of history's most famous couple."

1597 Kerr, Walter. "*Antony and Cleopatra.*" *Times* (New York) 17 September 1967: II, 1.

A special feature of Langham's production, "with Christopher Plummer shaking his bewildered head as Antony and Zoe Caldwell curling her lip in mock surprise as Cleopatra, lies in its constant underscoring of the proposition that gestures are only gestures and not one of them is trustworthy. They are acting for one another, sometimes sportively, sometimes strategically, sometimes to hurt." Michael Langham's direction "helps accent the play-with-a-play sense by bumping tableaux into one another, head-long." He "is all speed and abruptness."

1598 Smith, Irwin. "Their Exits and Reentrances." *Shakespeare Quarterly* 18 (1967): 7-16.

When there were no intermissions, a character which was to appear in two consecutive scenes, left one ten lines before the end and entered the next ten lines after the start. This "served the practical theatrical purpose of providing time for an actor cross from one side of the stage to the other behind the scenes, or to go from one unit to another of the multiple stage, in preparation for the scene to follow." Cleopatra's exit at 4.12.39 and her entry at 4.13 are examples of this convention.

1599 Styan, J.L. *Shakespeare's Stagecraft*. Cambridge: Cambridge UP, 1967. 244 pp.

In this "introduction to Shakespeare's visual and aural stagecraft," Styan illustrates his points with discussions of twenty-three scenes from *Antony and Cleopatra*.

1600 Sullivan, Dan. "Vital 'Antony and Cleopatra'." *Times* (New York) 2 August 1967: 25.

Christopher Plummer and Zoe Caldwell possessed "the bold movement and the vigorous (but never controlled) gesture that can give Shakespeare's words the extra dimension of dance." Antony was "a sensitive man simultaneously betrayed and rewarded by his lust." Caldwell "plays the role more for our understanding than for our sympathy." She "can curse like a sailor and curl up like a kitten and—probably—cook." She was "a queen transfigured by death almost into a goddess."

1601 Langham, Michael. "*Antony and Cleopatra*: Pre-Production Notes." *The Stratford Scene 1958-1968*. Ed. Peter Raby. Toronto: Clarke, Irwin, 1968, pp. 78-84

This play "is as much a view of history in the making as it is a love—or lust—story. The fortunes of a country are commonly determined not so much by the needs of the people as by the rivalry of one General or politicians with another, the sexual frustration of an Emperor, the dyspepsia of a President." The play can be easily made "pageant-like on the stage. We must avoid that, and focus all possible attention on the leading characters. We must keep it all simple and strong so that each of the thousand impressions—and the play *is* a series of impressions—is clearly etched."

1602 Norton, Elliot. "*Antony and Cleopatra*." *The Stratford Scene 1958-1968*. Ed. Peter Raby. Toronto: Clarke, Irwin, 1968, pp. 85-87.

"God created Zoe Caldwell to play Cleopatra," announces Norton. Caldwell "has an astonishing voice. She can purr like a lioness, his like an adder or, when anger shakes her Cleopatra, bellow out the words with the power of a boat whistle." Caldwell "was extraordinary in the final scenes, from the moment of decision when she told Charmian and Iras that she understood Caesar's true intentions. She died grandly; she prepared for death in the same way. On a makeshift throne, in rich robes, decked with the kind of jewellery that suited this queen, she was now most certainly 'regal'." As Antony, Christopher Plummer "had his greatest success towards the end, after the Roman leader understands finally what has happened, that he is defeated. After Antony's final defeat, Mr. Plummer dropped his light theatricality, his jauntiness, his boyishness, to enter into the spirit of the character, as a great man who has lost his greatness and is now prepared to expiate."

1603 Barnes, Clive. "Theater: Chichester Packing Them In." *Times* (New York) 30 August 1969: 10.

Barnes writes in praise of Peter Dews's direction in the 1969 Chichhester Festival production. John Clements did not have much energy, but Margaret Leighton gave one of the best Cleopatras. Leighton's "is a performance full of light, shade and meaning, moving from the willful and spirited, to its conclusion, where Cleopatra is lost in a solitary and marbled death." John Clements "is an Antony that supports his Cleopatra rather than matches her, yet it is a performance of consistent honesty and, particularly at the end, occasional grandeur."

1604 Brown, John Russell. *Shakespeare's Plays in Performance.* New York: St. Martin's P, 1969. 244 pp.

Brown argues that "at the end of *Antony and Cleopatra* there are many words, but here physical enactment is a continual accompaniment, modifying and extending the verbal impression given to the audience."

1605 Dawson, Helen. "*Antony and Cleopatra*." *Plays and Players,* September 1969: 22.

Robert Helmpann's revival was a failure in spite of a few flashes of "spamodic dignity."

1606 Saner, Reginald. "*Antony and Cleopatra*: How Pompey's Honor Struck a Contemporary." *Shakespeare Quarterly* 20 (1969): 117-20.

The writer of an anonymous pamphlet, *Bloudy Murther* (written in 1614), recalled a performance of *Antony and Cleopatra* in his reference to Pompey.

1607 Speaight, Robert W. "Shakespeare in Britain." *Shakespeare Quarterly* 20 (1969): 435-41.

The setting at the Chichester Festival production was simple: "a central platform, with an opening underneath, and a staircase on either side." Sir John Clements as Antony and Margaret Leighton as Cleopatra were "seen as something more than a pair of lovers besotted by sensuality; they were seen practically as man and wife, and mutually indispensable as man and wife are supposed to be." This Cleopatra was "submissive to a man whom she knew to be impossible but irresistible none the less."

1608 Sprague, A.C., and J.C. Trewin. *Shakespeare's Plays Today. Some Customs and Conventions of the Stage*. Columbia: U of South Carolina P, 1970. 147 pp.

Assessing the work of different directors of this and other plays, Sprague and Trewin conclude that "the best director must always be the man who abjures the programme note, keeps to the text, watches its orchestration—the 'march of music' said Shaw—and sees that his invention never minimizes the master in whose service he works."

1609 Wardle, Irving. "Noble but Less than Heroic." *Times* (London) 24 July 1969: 7.

Margaret Leighton and John Clements could not reflect the sensuality and passion of the lovers, even though they captured the nobility and stature of Cleopatra and Antony.

1610 Allen, Shirley S. "Phelps and Shakespeare: Manager." *Samuel Phelps and Sadler's Wells Theatre.* Middletown, CT: Wesleyan UP, 1971, pp. 200-51.

Allen assesses this "as one of the most important productions of a theatrical generation" and "one of the most satisfying." She "notes specific departures from Shakespeare's text, examines the historical emphasis on scenery and costume, and summarizes contemporary critical reaction to the performances of Phelps and Glyn."

1611 Brown, Ivor. *Shakespeare and the Actors.* New York: Coward-McCann, 1971. 208 pp.

This play "is a notable example of speech that is aflame with desire while the action is left to the imagination."

1612 Findlater, Richard. *The Player Kings.* New York: Stein & Day, 1971. 288 pp.

Findlater comments briefly on the Laurence Olivier/Vivien Leigh production.

1613 Horobetz, Lynn K. "Shakespeare at the Old Globe, 1971." *Shakespeare Quarterly* 22 (1971): 385-87.

"There was no fire and air" in the Globe's production in San Diego. The actors "were either half naked or weighted down with bulk." They exhibited passion in three ways: "heavy breathing, clenched fists, or sinking slowly to the knees." M. Learned as Cleopatra "was in love with an an idealized hero, but more in love with the idea of her own dramatic death." This performance "remained a woodenly overstaged pageant which never touched the heart."

1614 Payne, Rhoda. "Shakespeare on Stage: A Study in the Criticism and Production of Five Plays." *Dissertation Abstracts* 32 (1971): 1682A (Case Western Reserve).

This is a critical examination and catalogue of books, essays and articles about the productions of *Antony and Cleopatra* and four other plays.

1615 Seltzer, Daniel. "The Actors and Staging." *A New Companion to Shakespeare Studies*. Ed. Kenneth Muir and S. Schoenbaum. Cambridge: Cambridge UP, 1971, pp. 35-54.

Seltzer briefly discusses this play in his analysis of the actors and staging in Shakespeare's time.

1616 Sprague, A.C. "Shakespeare's Plays on the English Stage." *A New Companion to Shakespeare Studies*. Ed. Kenneth Muir and S. Schoenbaum. Cambridge: Cambridge UP, 1971, pp. 199-210.

Sprague briefly alludes to this play in his account of the stage history of Shakespeare's works.

1617 Barnes, Clive. "Theater: Roman Plays." *Times* (New York) 1 September 1972: L 19.

Barnes praises Trevor Nunn's Roman cycle and the acting of Janet Suzman and Richard Johnson.

1618 Billington, Michael. "*Antony and Cleopatra* in Stratford." *Guardian Weekly* 16 August 1972: 8.

This "production is built around a stark contrast of civilisations. Rome, predictably, is a place of brazen trumpets, cold calculation and white knees; Egypt, on the other hand, is a whirl of voluptuous opulence in which people move drowsily under billowing Felliniesque canopies and in which even Antony seeks escape from a royal hooker in a seductive hookah. But more important, by giving due weight to the Roman scenes Mr. Nunn evokes the sordid world of political intrigue from which Antony seeks refuge." The director tries "to communicate the authentic Shakespearean vision: the fact that hero and heroine are simultaneously ageing libertine and decaying queen and great lovers who through passion triumph over death." On the whole, "it's a fleet, intelligent production giving us both the politics and the poetry."

1619 Harley, Graham D. "The 1972 Season at Stratford, Connecticut." *Shakespeare Quarterly* 23 (1972): 395-97.

Harley found this to be an extremely disappointing production. Salome Jens as Cleopatra "was outclassed by the part—apparently having not the slightest notion of how to speak verse, or indeed how to speak at all." Paul Hecht's Antony "trod a devious and ultimately futile path to his last mismanaged deed, and when a huge Roman banner descended in front of Cleopatra's monument to hide his dead body, it seemed the final ignominy: all that magnificent human potential blotted out by a blank national emblem."

1620 Hurren, Kenneth. "Two on the Nile." *Spectator* 19 August 1972: 291-92.

Hurren stresses the visual splendor of this production. "The way in which Cleopatra's court is kitted out might well have excited the envy of the late Tutankhamun (even the platoon of flabby, shave-heaved eunuchs appear to have small fortunes in gold and lapis lazuli hung about their necks) and the backcloths and stage-setting properties, though minimal (a canopy here, a bed there, a few artistically scattered lounging cushions), are stunningly picturesque." Janet Suzman "seems to understand well enough that she is playing a woman for whose specific favours in bed a man threw away a third of an empire. She does not, nevertheless, suggest such a woman." Richard Johnson's Antony "is too much in decline, and he misses that residual greatness that might have carried them both to the heights of tragic passion."

1621 Lambert, J.W. "Stratford-on-Avon's Notable 'Antony'." *Christian Science Monitor* 31 August 1972: 8.

Trevor Nunn constantly reminds the audience that "the sexual enslavement of the aging Mark Antony to Cleopatra was a factor in that very shaping of the western world for which the Romans are remembered." Richard Johnson's "is the grizzled portrait of a man all too well aware of his own self-destruction." Janet Suzman's Cleopatra "puts less emphasis upon sultry sensuality, more, with her helmet of black hair and clear, strong features, upon the waywardness of a beautiful and intelligent woman strangely at the mercy of impatient caprice."

1622 Lewsen, Charles. "*Antony and Cleopatra*: Stratford-on-Avon." *Times* (London) 16 August 1972: 13.

In this "play about two people whose love has wide-reaching political repercussions, Mr. Nunn has staged the encounters of the lovers as highly conscious public performances." Richard Johnson portrays Antony's fall "in the broadest brush strokes; the successive steps towards tragedy are not clearly particularized." Janet Suzman "presents Cleopatra's caprice with immense relish and wit." She "moves from rhetoric to naturalistic aside with perfect ease; her sense of vocal detail is matched in simple physical effect when, looking at Octavius's proffered hand, she clearly compares it in her mind with the hand of Antony."

1623 Murphy, J.L. "The Colorado Shakespeare Festival." *Shakespeare Quarterly* 23 (1972): 402-04.

The Colorado Shakespeare Festival presented "a successful visual embodiment of a verbal and intellectual theme in the play." Egypt "is earth and fire, Rome water and air. This cosmology and its psychological correspondences are woven throughout the lines of Shakespeare's text." The set design was gorgeous: "With flame colours and warm brown earth colors pervasive on the Egyptian side, the aquamarine blue, white, and silver of the Roman world dramatized, not merely suggested, what the words and action of the difficult text was putting before us on the playing areas." Scott Porter, as Antony, and his wife, Mary Ed Porter, as Cleopatra, turned in "commanding performances."

1624 Nightingale, Benedict. "Decline and Growth." *New Statesman* 25 August 1972: 265.

Nightingale emphasizes that "the vast white beehive of the Stratford stage has rarely been used to finer visual effect, whether it be setting off the garish pomp of the Egyptian court, with its beaked priests and shiny, brown eunuchs, or reflecting the puritanism of Rome, all starched togas and clean, humourless faces." Trevor Nunn's Antony and Cleopatra "seem attractive, exuberant and irresponsible, overgrown adolescents who must learn the danger of self-indulgent play: a conception which, to say no more, gives those playing the parts the opportunity to change and develop as the evening proceeds." Richard Johnson's Antony, "mellow, fruity and relaxed at first, acquires a thicker speech and an unsteadier gait in the face of shame, though, even he's capable of defying the fates with a marvellous shout of rage or conviviality." Janet Suzman "is a girl in the process of becoming a queen, or, perhaps, the Shaw Cleopatra becoming the Shakespeare Cleopatra."

1625 Rostron, David. "F.R. Benson's Early Productions of Shakespeare's Roman Plays at Stratford." *Theatre Notebook* 25 (1971-72): 46-54.

Critical reception of Benson's late nineteenth-century productions of *Antony and Cleopatra* and other plays.

1626 Speaight, Robert. "Shakespeare in Britain—The Stratford Season." *Shakespeare Quarterly* 23 (1972): 384-87.

Trevor Nunn's "was the best production I have ever seen," because "the texture of the production matched with extraordinary fidelity the texture of the play." Janet Suzman in the role of Cleopatra "enchants the eye and ear, and satisfies the mind." She "is naturally royal without being affectedly regal." Richard Johnson's Antony "had a careless grandeur and irresistible largesse." He "was simply the *homme moyen sensuel*, but raised through intensity of feeling and sublimity of speech a Matterhorn's height above mediocrity."

1627 Tierney, Margaret. "*Antony and Cleopatra*." *Plays and Players* October 1972: 42-43.

In the opening tableau of this production, "Egypt dominates, subjugating the great Roman to the point where Antony is prepared to parade in Egyptian get-up, in which he looks slightly ridiculous." There is a saying that "people love as they are. Antony, the generous man, loves generously, forgiving her time and again. Cleopatra, the selfish greedy woman, loves selfishly and greedily." Janet Suzman's Cleopatra is "not a sensuous wanton, but a cunning political animal who schemes for the world and loses it through being too clever by half." Richard Johnson's "grey-maned old lion is magnificent in his decline—a greathearted 'old ruffian', more likeable in the setting of his sun than he ever was in the pride of his triumph."

1628 Young, B.A. "*Antony and Cleopatra*." *Financial Times* 16 August 1972: 3.

This production opens with a brief pageant which displays Cleopatra's character. "There is a procession of richly clad courtiers, soldiers, musicians and eunuchs, and in the middle of them are Cleopatra and Antony, playing at majesty." Antony and Cleopatra "are utterly frivolous and careless of their responsibilities." Janet Suzman exhibits "the sudden changes of temper, the intrinsic dignity and the childish dishonesty, the majesty and the trivialities." Richard John's Antony "shouts his way through the part, though he usually makes me feel that the shouts are justifiable." "If an affair between two spoilt, selfish people can be called romance, it does justice to this too; and tragedy is tellingly handled at the end."

1629 Billington, Michael. "Romans at the Aldwych." *Guardian* 24 October 1973: 12.

This is a positive review of Trevor Nunn's Roman cycle, which praises especially Janet Suzman's "skittish, teasing, sexy" Cleopatra.

1630 Crick, Bernard. "The Politics of Rome." *Times Higher Education Supplement* 21 December 1973: 11.

Trever Nunn's production "was made transcendentally splendid by the quite incredible team playing which is the hallmark of the Royal Shakespeare Company." Every small part "was given its full value and the play emancipated from the stars in all sorts of good ways, ways which reveal thoughts of Shakespeare too often lost." Much of the play "is about the rival claims of politics *and* love, not about the neglect of politics for love."

1631 de Jongh, Nicholas. "*Antony and Cleopatra*." *Plays and Players,* October 1973: 56-57.

Vanessa Redgrave and Julian Glover's were a failure under Tony Richardson's direction.

1632 Hobson, Harold. "Powerful Corruption." *Sunday Times* (London) 12 August 1973: 33.

Hobson applauds the "life, provocation, and excitement" in Toby Robertson's revival.

1633 Ippolito, Gerald Joseph. "Death Scenes in English Drama 1585-1610." Unpublished Ph.D. thesis, U of Birmingham, 1973.

The details of the stage action in this play's death scene "seem consistent with what happens in North's translation of

Plutarch, as Hosley suggests, which provides specific information to how Antony killed himself; of how he was borne to Cleopatra's monument (not in a chair as Hosley argues) but 'in his men's arms to the entry of the monument'; and the manner in which he was raised to Cleopatra's level."

1634 Peter, John. "Cohesion in the Roman Plays." *Times Educational Supplement* 2 November 1973: 94.

Peter considers Trevor Nunn's revival as "an achievement of the first magnitude."

1635 Speaight, Robert. *Shakespeare on the Stage: An Illustrated History of Shakespearian Performance.* London: Collins, 1973. 304 pp.

Speaight discusses productions of Phelps, Beerbohm Tree, John Gielgud, Peggy Ashcroft, and Laurence Oivier and Vivien Leigh; he also refers to some of the performances of the play in France, Russia and Austria.

1636 Thompson, Peter. "The Royal Shakespeare Season 1972 Reviewed." *Shakespeare Survey* 26 (1973): 139-50.

In this production, "the billowing canopy and coloured light of the opening mime promised the visual which followed." Richard Johnson as Antony used "physical posture to imply moral schism." In Rome, "he stood straight, and spoke decisively"; in Egypt, he "was slightly stooped, self-consciously ageing, the vacillating Antony divided against himself." Janet Suzman "was gloriously dressed, witty, graceful and sexually alert," but "she was also frivolous and evidently superficial." The Monument "was so genuinely a fortress, so visibly impregnable, that its capture by the Roman soldiers achieved the status of a major event." In its aftermath Cleopatra "could prepare herself for a deliberate and stately death."

1637 Trewin, J.C. "Plain and Coloured." *Illustrated London News* October 1973: 103.

Trewin recommends favourably Toby Robertson's design, direction and pace but criticizes his handling of such minor scenes as the emissary of Antony's schoolmaster and the Seleucus episode.

1638 Wardle, Irving. "The Romans: Aldwych." *Times* (London) 25 October 1973: 11.

Trevor Nunn's focus on Antony as a great man was "full of power and insight." The Roman series was a great theatrical achievement.

1639 Jackson, Russell Bennett. "Antony and Cleopatra." "Pictorial Shakespeare, 1880-1890: A Study of Major London Productions." 2 vols. Ph.D. thesis, U of Birmingham, 1975.

Jackson discusses productions of this play in his analysis.

1640 Salgado, Gamini. *Eyewitnesses of Shakespeare. First Hand Accounts of Performances 1590-1890*. London: Chatto & Windus for Sussex UP, 1975. 360 pp.

Salgado cites excerpts from Thomas Davies, *Illustrated London News* (27 October 1849), *Punch* (6 December 1890), and William Archer (20 March 1897).

1641 Smith, Warren D. *Shakespeare's Playhouse. A Handbook.* Hanover, NH: UP of New England for U of Rhode Island, 1975. 119 pp.

Smith proposes that there was a dais of the state or some other piece of scaffolding on the Globe stage.

1642 Barnes, Clive. "Stage: 'Cleopatra' and 'Ernest' in Canada." *Times* (New York) 12 June 1976: 12.

Barnes looks favourably upon Robin Phillips's direction which stressed Keith Baxter's Antony and Maggie Smith's Cleopatra as victims of destiny.

1643 Pettigrew, John. "Stratford 1976." *Journal of Canadian Studies* 9.4 (November 1976): 33-48.

Pettigrew reviews this revival in the context of the entire season and finds fault with the sets, costumes, and acting in Robin Phillips's production and labels it "the weakest of the season."

1644 Chaillet, Ned. "Traverse Plays Antony and Cleopatra." *Times* (London) 26 August 1977: 9.

Alec McCowen and Dorothy Tutin did not have the necessary presence and stature for the principal roles in Toby Robertson's production.

1645 Jackson, Berners W. "Stratford Festival Canada." *Shakespeare Quarterly* 28 (1977): 197-206.

Keith Baxter and Maggie Smith as the principals "were invincible egotists, dazzling performers on the world's stage to whom their times had given star-rating." Smith presented Cleopatra "as a great actress, a quicksilver creature, elusive and unpredictable—an accomplished enchantress whose stock-in-trade was infinite variety." Baxter's Antony was "a ruffled bear—his attempted magnanimity increasingly distempered by exasperation, his sincerity questioned, his anger mocked—finally taking his departure, mollified but uneasy." Shakespeare's words, "set to that lucid music, held the audience spellbound, conditioned the mind and the emotions irresistibly, so that Cleopatra's final remarks were, without a touch of sentimentality, powerfully moving."

1646 Lamb, Margaret A. "Shakespeare's *Antony and Cleopatra* on the English Stage." *Dissertation Abstracts International* 37 (1977): 5444A (NYU).

See item 1669.

1647 Berkowitz, Gerald M. "Antony and Cleopatra." *Educational Theatre Journal* 30 (1978): 113-14.

This revival by Toby Robertson's Prospect Theatre Company did not have a heroic Antony in Alec McCowen nor a passionate Cleopatra in Dorothy Tutin.

1648 Blumenthal, Eileen. "Toils of Grace." *Village Voice* 27 November 1978: 111-12.

Brook's skill in directing Shakespeare "lies in how he penetrates to the center of a play and then expresses its essential spirt in contemporary images." In this production, Brook "does not so much transpose the play's sensibility to our times (no need to) as pare away the quasi-Roman, quasi-Elizabethan, quasi-how-you're-supposed-to-do-Shakespeare trappings that usually obscure it. Characterizations are freed of ceremonial pomp and presented in clear, bold terms; the staging is concentrated and spare." "With short-cropped hair and simple-elegant, flowing dresses and caftans," Glenda Jackson "commands the stage as if it were her own magnetic field; even at rest, she has vitality brimming in her limbs, her facial muscles, her eyes." Alan Howard is disappointing because he does not convey "any sense of overwhelming passion: we do not see what Cleopatra activates in him, the wild juices into which she taps."

1649 David, Richard. *Shakespeare in the Theatre*. Cambridge: Cambridge UP, 1978. 263 pp.

David analyzes the 1972 and 1973 productions of the play and gives a cast list for Stratford-upon-Avon in 1972.

1650 Elsom, John "An Indulgent Affair." *Listener* 19 October 1978: 571-72.

In Peter Brook's "elegant" production, Glenda Jackson presents Cleopatra "as a determined woman (rather than sly and vacillating), as mannish, with short-cropped hair (rather than conventionally sexy) and as an ironic observe of male emotions (rather than a queen with a courtesan's skills." Alan Howard's Antony "is not a brave warrior gone wrong, but an overgrown boy, bragging and playing with himself, under the cold eyes of a sexual nurse." Elsom feels that Brook's interpretation "doesn't work" because it "is so much against the bias of the text that it is hard to understand why the characters behave as they do." Antony and Cleopatra "ceases to be about how an empire was thrown away for love, but about how dependency breeds dependency, until the whole structure of interlocking needs collapses into weak suicides and lazy treacheries."

1651 Goldberg, Hennryk, and Rainer Kerndl. "Shakespeare Phantasievoll inszeniert: Hohe Darstellungs-kultur des TNP aus Frankreich." *Neuws Deutschland* 14-15 October 1978: 11.

This is a review of productions of *Antony and Cleopatra* and *Pericles* by the Theatre National Populaire at the 22nd Berlin Festival.

1652 Higgins, John. "An Interview with Peter Brook." *Times* (London) 18 October 1978: 11.

Brook's aim is to correct the misunderstanding that Antony and Cleopatra "is a spectacular play"; it "has been smothered by images superimposed by the Victorian era and by the cinema." In this play, "everything concerns personal relationships; people, including those with famous names are introduced in closeup as in, say, *Holocaust*." Cleopatra "in the flesh has nothing to do with the Cleopatra Enobarbus describes. Shakespeare was not covering her in mystery." Antony is not "a tired man." He "dies having lived well by his own lights, but never having achieved a higher level of existence. That is left to Cleopatra."

1653 Kroll, Jack. "Oh, To Be in England." *Newsweek* 27 November 1978: 65-66, 69.

Brook's "is a small, intimate personal play set within a vast, public one." "Outside, history heaves and retches like some sick monster, while within the charmed circle Antony and Cleopatra want nothing more than to live their passion with the sophisticated resources of those who have total power." Howard's Antony "is strong and eloquent, but we don't smell the obsession that melts his imperial manhood." Glenda Jackson "is too controlled to be the iridescent wanton that enslaved the greatest of world leaders."

1654 Levin, Bernard. *Sunday Times* (London) 15 October 1978: 35.

Peter Brook, the director, stresses that Antony and Cleopatra are "a pair of narcissists three-quarters in love with easeful death because they cannot take life seriously—because, presumably, they cannot believe that it is real." Glenda Jackson's "edged, disembodied voice delivers even the catalogue of her forthcoming humiliations as Caesar's captive in tones of amused indifference." Alan Howard wants to break away from Cleopatra, but he "has no serious intention of doing so, any more than Miss Jackson really believes that there is nothing left remarkable beneath the visiting moon merely because Antony is dead."

1655 Treglown, Jeremy. "*Antony and Cleopatra*." *Plays and Players,* December 1978: 18.

Peter Brook makes the Rome/Egypt contrast "far subtler than in most readings." Jonathan Pryce's Octavius "is a pacific, almost priestlike figure, a serious but by no means flinty embodiment of his divine imperial role." Roman senators "are similarly restrained and kindly seeming." Cleopatra and her women are " both volatile and almost eerily suave." Alan

Howard "comes over as too young as Antony, though the production goes out of its way to emphasize his age."

1656 Trewin, J.C. "*Antony and Cleopatra.*" *Going to Shakespeare.* London: Allen & Unwin, 1978, pp. 221-27.

Trewin assesses Birmingham Repertory's 1961 production and comments on Theodore Komisarjevsky, Vivien Leigh and Peggy Ashcroft.

1657 Trewin, J.C. "The High Noises." *Illustrated London News* December 1978: 121.

Trewin upholds Peter Brook's production "as faithful as possible" to a difficult play which challenged the spectators' imaginative powers.

1658 Wardle, Irving. "*Antony and Cleopatra.*" *Times* (London) 11 October 1978: 9.

Peter Brook, the director, believes that Shakespeare "gives you more from moment to moment than any other dramatist. And in this case, Brook goes out of his way to point up all the things that do not conform to the myth of a world well lost." Alan Howard's Antony and Glenda Jackson's Cleopatra "make a stupendous and utterly unmoving pair. They are plainly victims of a *folie a deux* and the production shows in merciless detail the price they pay for it." Antony's situation "is a terrible mess: and in showing it to be precisely that, with Mr. Howard finally stumbling towards the monument in an unbelievable daze, the production deliberately forfeits any aspirations to the heroic." In the final scene, "the clown with the asp is for once a real red-nosed comedian, who delays her grand departure from the world with a series of false exits."

1659 Watters, Tamie. 'Brook Continues His Shakespearean Surprises." *Christian Science Moniotr* 17 November 1978: 27.

Brook gives "a literal reading of the text in which the facts stound as boldly as a pyramide against an Egyptian sky." Alan Howard's "somewhat effete, blond-bearded Antony is intentionally absurd in his doggish devotion to Miss Jackson's Cleopatra (looking like an imperious Egyptian cat with ears protruding though her short hair)." Glenda Jackson "summons up a serpent with a ripple of her supple body, an Eastern goddess with a stylized gesture, and the Sphinx with a headdress."

1660 Eder, Richard. "A Lucid 'Antony and Cleopatra' from Peter Brook." *Times* (New York) 19 August 1979: D3.

Eder praises Brook for not letting his artistic energey "obscure or distract from the dramatic and poetic lines of the play. Almost invairably it is used to clarify them, to preserve them, to nudge things back in balance whenever the force of a particular performer with a particular line provides a momentary blinding distraction." Glenda Jackson's "slender, graceful neck, and small, close-cropped head allow her a snake-like series of motions as she dazzles Antony, but the physical suggestion is more of a useful domestic gartersnake than a serpent of the Nile." Alan Howrard's Antony "is a remarkable portrait of a virile hero in decay. He is beefy and with a slight suggestion of the swollen; yet his force and charm are continually coming to the surface."

1661 Kennedy, Dennis. "*Antony and Cleopatra*." *Theatre Journal* 31 (1979): 420-23.

Peter Brook's production was not satisfactory. "The reading of the play was not clear, the visual aspects conflicted again and again with the acting, the music was pedestrian, and the youth of the principal performers resulted in a sense of confinement rather than liberation." As Antony, Alan Howard "seemed lost, unheroic and undefined." Glenda Jackson's Cleopatra "was intelligent and vivacious but strangely asexual."

1662 Lask, Thomas. "An 'Antony' in Spanish and English." *Times* (New York) 2 February 1979: C25.

Estelle Parsons's production "alternates slices of the play in English with slices in Spanish in a translation by Luis Astrana Marin." Parsons seemed "to rely on the same business for the different scenes: much hand-clasping, frequent embracing and too much raising of voices." Kathleen Gaffney in her Cleopatra "emphasized the volatile, self-centered, capricious, histrionic sides of the queen in a performance that was both enchanting and visually attractive." Francisco Prado's Antony "was more effective as the debauched, sybaritic Roman than as a master of a third of the world."

1663 Obraztsoova, A. "R. Planchon's 'Political Extravaganza'." *Problems of Style and Genre in Theatrical Art: A Collection of Papers*. Moscow: Moscow State Theatrical Institute, Leningrad State Institute of Theatre, Music, and Cinema, 1979, pp. 44-55. In Russian.

This is a discussion of R. Planchon's production of *Antony and Cleopatra*.

1664 Stodder, Joseph H., and Lillian Wilds. "Shakespeare in Southern California." *Shakespare Quarterly* 30 (1979): 232-45.

At the Globe House, Los Angeles, the diriector stressed "racial contrast in casting." Eugenia Wright "was excellent in her projection of the spectrum of emotions and moods characterizing Shakespeare's heroine." Tom Lancaster as Antony "offered a well-attuned complement" to her Cleopatra.

1665 Trewin, J.C. "Shakespeare in Britain." *Shakespeare Quarterly* 30 (1979): 151-58.

Peter Brook "sees the play as a web of personal, intimate relationships." His was "an expository production: a director concerned with the words, not with experimental reeling and writhing and fainting in coils." Alan Howard and Glenda Jackson's partnership "fitted precisely into Brook's astringent, unromanticized version of the play: one that did hold the sound and the sense and permitted Alan Howard to explore the verse in those strange, thrusting tones."

1666 Berthelsen, Alice Ann Boggs. "The Globe of the Great Southwest." *Shakespeare Quarterly* 31 (1980): 248.

Antony and Cleopatra at Odessa, Texas, in 1979 was "a fast-paced, uncut version" and done "as a bright episode of ancient history," Karen Kee Campbell's Cleopatra "conveyed, at once, a strength and a vulnerability." John McKinney portrayed Antony "with a quasi-contemplative snobbery that resulted in a shallow, self-serving war hero, wooing the seductress with poker-faced stiffness and brittle prose."

1667 Cook, Judith. "'A lass unparallel'd': Cleopatra." *Women in Shakespeare*. London: Harrap, 1980, pp. 131-41.

Cook has interviewed Peggy Ashcroft, Barbara Jefford, Glenda Jackson and Janet Suzman about their roles as Cleopatra. She concludes that "getting her [Cleopatra] right is a formidable task, and what makes it fascinating is how different actresses see that rightness—sometimes in utterly opposite ways."

1668 Holmberg, Arthur. "Estelle Parsons's *Antony and Cleopatra*." *Shakespeare Quarterly* 31 (1980): 195-97.

Estelle Parsons, directing this play at The Internet Theatre, New York, "startled, provoked, and angered the audience into a new perception" of it. She used ethnic differences in speech, gesture, and movement to show the clash between two cultures so that "the white Egyptians represented a graceful and ancient aristocracy—well groomed, elegantly poised, and doomed." The Romans, "upstarts from the West, lacked finesse and polish." Kathleen Gaffney who played Cleopatra, "was a stunning cross between Rita Hayworth and Susan Hayward, and the icon of a celluloid love goddess was carried out in her wardrobe, inspired by the clumsy glamour of Hollywood in the Forties." Francisco Prado as Antony "was a darkly handsome and super macho man of men." Parsons "emphasized the farcical and brutal elements in the script, and the evening never flagged for want of visual stimulation or directorial energy."

1669 Lamb. Margaret. *Antony and Cleopatra on the English Stage.* Rutherford, Madison, Teaneck: Fairleigh Dickinson UP, 1980. 241 pp.

Based on her dissertation, Lamb's is a comprehensive analysis of productions from the earliest to Peter Brook's 1978 revival in England. She draws on contemporary reviews and personal accounts to compare and evaluate various performances. This play's stage history "illustrates the progress of Anglo-Saxon critics' long losing battle to make Shakespeare Christian as well as classical." Famous actors like Macready and Tree " were reported to be disappointing as the lover Antony, more convincing as the warrior stricken with remorse at his neglect of duty."

1670 Mullin, Michael. *Theatre at Stratford-upon-Avon: A Catalogue-Index to Productions of the Shakespeare Memorial/Royal Shakespeare Theatre 1879-1978.* 2 vols. Westport, CT: Greenwood P, 1980. xxxvi, 1038 pp.

Mullin lists productions of his plays for 1898, 1912, 1921, 1924, 1927, 1931, 1935, 1945, 1953, 1954, 1972, 1973. Each entry identifies the director, designer, light designer, actors, and reviews. There is a calendar of productions.

1671 Shibata, Toshihiko. "Shakespeare in Tokyo." *Shakespeare Quarterly* 31 (1980): 403-04.

This is a review of 1979 productions of *As You Like It* and *Antony and Cleopatra,* with full rosters of cast and production personnel for each production. Koreya Senda, the director, adds quite a bit of his own to the play. For example, he gives three new scenes to Cleopatra. One, she is "being lavishly dressed with the help of her waiting women for the supposed audience given to Herod." Two, she practises sword play and archery. Three, she schemes to get a larger share of the region

Antony had conquered. Antony's "bungling suicide and Cleopatra's hauling him up invited laughter." This production had been spoiled by excessive "touching up."

1672 Vasadze, A. Nemirovitch-Danchenko in Tbilisi." *Literaturnaya Gauzia* (Tbilisi 6 (1980): 173-95. In Russian.

These are reminiscences of V.I. Nemirovitch-Danchenko's talks during his stay in Tbilisi in 1941 when his *Antony and Cleopatra* production was being discussed.

1673 Warren, Roger. "Shakespeare at Stratford and the National Theatre, 1979." *Shakespeare Survey* 33 (1980): 169-80.

The stage for this production was designed as "an intimate area enclosed by a semi-circle of glass panels providing a number of exits to the outside world." During the Monument Scene, "a square red curtain was lowered behind Cleopatra, and then lowered further to become the floor of the monument: as there were no levels, the dying Antony was simply dragged to her along the floor, wrapped in her women's scarves." Alan Howard "had the scale and vocal range for Antony," but "seemed to be demonstrating rather than embodying the character." Similarly, Glenda Jackson "gave a coolly accurate, objective demonstration of Cleopatra's infinite variety, one mood meticulously established before giving place to the next."

1674 Babula, William. "*Antony and Cleopatra.*" *Shakespeare in Production, 1935-1978. A Selective Catalogue*. New York: Garland, 1981, pp. 11-20.

Babula provides synopses of major reviews of twenty-one productions of the play from 1935 to 1978.

1675 Hallin, T. "Jonathan Miller on the Shakespeare Plays." *Shakespeare Quarterly* 32 (1981): 132-45.

For Miller, *Antony and Cleopatra* "is really about Queen Elizabeth and Leicester" and "a disguised satire on the politics of

Elizabethan England plus an overt treatment of certain classical themes as seen through the eyes of a late sixteenth-century Gentleman." Antony suffers from "accidia" or "advanced laziness." Antony "sees himself as pulled down, not merely by this woman, but by the life she represents, the life of languidness, and of too much food, and too much drinking, and getting up too late, and going to bed too late."

1676 Mazer, Cary M. *Shakespeare Refashioned. Elizabethan Plays on Edwardian Stages*. Theater and Dramatic Studies, No. 5. UMI Research P, 1981. 267 pp.

This study briefly discusses productions of *Antony and Cleopatra* by Oscar Asche and Beerbohm Tree.

1677 Adler, Doris. "The Unlacing of Cleopatra." *Theatre Journal* 34 (1982): 451-66.

On the basis of a comparative analysis of performances by Helen Faucit, Mrs. Siddons, Isabella Glyn, Mrs. Cora Potter, Sarah Bernhardt, Lilie Langtry and Fannie Davenport, Adler suggests that "the nature and attributes of Cleopatra are associated in the communal mind or imagination with a particular physical configuration and a particular mode of dress. An audience in a particular time knows how Cleopatra must look and accepts only those realized images that match that knowledge." Hence a successful rendering of Cleopatra is a "mysterious and irrational act of discovering what the audience knows must be there, but only recognizes when it appears."

1678 Beauman, Sally. *The Royal Shakespeare Company: A History of Ten Decades*. Oxford: Oxford UP, 1982. 388 pp.

Beauman comments briefly on the productions of Byam Shaw, Trevor Nunn and Peter Brook.

1679 Burrows, Jill. "Soldierly Authority." *Times Educational Supplement* 22 October 1982: 25.

Michael Gambon captured Antony's soldierly stature and Helen Mirren gave signs of dementia in her death scene, in Adrian Noble's production.

1680 Radin, Victoria. "Sex-kitten Shows Her Claws." *Observer* (London) 17 October 1982: 34.

While praising Michael Gambon and Helen Mirren, Radin criticizes the revival for an inarticulate delivery of verse. Cleopatra's scarves worked as reminder of "the killer instinct that lurks in obsessive sexual love."

1681 Wells, Stanley. "Simplicity and Spontaneity." *Times Literary Supplement* 29 October 1982: 1191.

Wells prefers Adrian Noble's liberation of the play from spectacle and commends its focus on personal relationships.

1682 Gordon, Giles. "Song and Dance." *Spectator* 23 April 1983: 30.

Gordon thinks little of Helen Mirren's "tired eroticism" and Michael Gambon's Antony in the early part of Adrian Noble's production.

1683 Hall, Peter. *Peter Hall's Diaries: The Story of a Dramatic Battle.* Ed. John Goodwin. London: Hamish Hamilton, 1983. xiii, 507 pp.

Hall comments briefly on the productions of this play that he directed.

1684 Jackson, Russell. "Antony and Cleopatra." *Cahiers Elisabéthains* 24 (October 1983): 108-09.

Helen Mirren delineated a "willful, sexy, commanding" Cleopatra against Michael Gambon's "aging *roue*" of an Antony under Adrian Noble's direction.

1685 Mulryne, J.R. "*Antony and Cleopatra*: Penny Plain or Tuppence Coloured." Soc. Fr. Shakespeare Actes du Congres 1982. *Ou Texte a la scene: Langages du theatre*. Ed. Marie-Thérèse Jones-Davies. Paris: Touzot, 1983, pp. 93-109.

In trying to discover how "the force and coherence" of *Antony and Cleopatra* can be represented on stage, Mulryne analyzes the contrast between the visual opulence of Trevor Nunn's Royal Shakespeare Company production of 1972 with the starkness of Peter Brook's 1978 production at Stratford. He concludes that they do not completely capture "many of the essential energies of the text."

1686 Redgrave, Michael. *In My Mind's I: An Actor's Autobiography.* New York: Viking, 1983.

For this actor, Antony was "a part that calls on all the strength you have and tests out every weakness."

1687 Scott, Michael. *Antony and Cleopatra: Text and Performance.* London: Macmillan; Atlantic Highlands, NJ: Humanities P, 1983. 80 pp.

In Part I, Scott provides a critical introduction to the play. Part II focuses on its productions of Benthall/Olivier (1951), Nunn (1972), Miller (1980), Peter Brook (1978), and Adrian Noble (1982). Scott argues that the focus of a production "depends on the conception of the lovers: Olivier's tragic fall was understandable in the context of Leigh's quiet beauty; Johnson's aging pragmatist complemented Suzman's sensual politician; Howard's despair discovered a strength in Jackson's calm; Blakely's weary dissolute found refuge in Lapotaire's need for fulfilment." The play "is something of an enigma. It can accommodate contrasting interpretations, but as yet it seems to have foiled the modern directors' attempt to encompass in one production its 'infinite variety'."

1688 Thomson, Peter. *Shakespeare's Theatre*. London: Routledge, 1983. 190 pp.

There are a number of references to this play in Thomson's study.

1689 Warren, Roger. "Shakespeare in England, 1982-83." *Shakespeare Quarterly* 34 (1983): 334-60.

In the Nottingham Playhouse production of 1982, Kate O'Mara, an actress of a limited range, "had to suggest Cleopatra's variety by alternating between wry statement, often accompanied by a twisted smile, and violent tantrums." Ian McCulloch's "was a relaxed, expansive Antony, whose shattered confidence after the disaster at Actium was vividly conveyed in his re-entry, slow and heavy, and in the uncharacteristic self-display of his claim that he 'ended' Brutus and Cassius at Philippi."

At The Other Place in Stratford-upon-Avon, Michael Gambon in defeat "used the abrupt, clipped, almost unhinged style." Helen Mirren's Cleopatra "was much more heartfelt than her Antony, and it was she who finally achieved tragic style."

1690 Fleck, S. Agnes. "Terence Knapp's Shakespearean Productions in Tokyo." *Shakespeare Translation* 10 (1984): 49-62.

This is an assessment of Gekidan Kumo's production of *Antony and Cleopatra* and *Macbeth* in 1969. These plays "had been staged as they would have been staged in the West and played in imitation of Western productions." The uncut translation of *Antony and Cleopatra* by Fukuda ran for five hours.

1691 Heales, Robyn, and Dennis Bartholmeusz. "Shakespeare in Sydney and Australia." *Shakespeare Quarterly* 35 (1984): 479-84.

Antony and Cleopatra at the Playbox Theatre, Melbourne, broke up into "brilliant fragments, some of which were uniquely statisfying. The sets were " abstract in the post Brechtian style, with no attempt at illusion, no attempt to be anything but themselves." They consisted of three mobile platforms on wheels, and they were like battering rams in the battle scenes.

1692 Burrows, Jill. "Ignore the Obvious." *Times Educational Supplement* 13 April 1984: 26.

This is a review of the 1982 Theatre Co. production of the play at the University of Essex, 1984. It casts a male Cleopatra against a male Antony. Cross-casting "does away with that lazy romantic identification theatrical love stories invite: we can observe the eroticism without being vicariously flattered by it."

1693 Hill, Errol. *Shakespeare in Sable. A History of Black Shakespearean Actors*. Amherst: U of Massachusetts P, 1984. 217.

Henrietta Vincent Davis played Cleopatra on the American boards in the late nineteenth century. Earle Hyman acted as Alexas in the 1950, and Ellen Holly portrayed Iras in 1963 in the New York Shakespeare Festival production.

1694 Jackson, Russell. "The Triumph of *Antony and Cleopatra*." Deutsche Shakespeare-Gesellschaft West. *Jahrbuch 1984*: 128-48.

Jackson explains the various intentions and figurative uses of triumph scenes and their appeal to the audiences in several productions.

1695 Male, David A. *Antony and Cleopatra*. Shakespeare on Stage Series. Cambridge: Cambridge UP, 1984. 36 pp.

Male examines different aspects of producing this play:—actors, designer, director—and the role of the audience and the critics. He discusses the structure of the play and analyzes a number of performances, illustrating his points with photographs.

1696 Roche, S. Wallace. "A La Langtry." *Theatre Notebook* 38 (1984): 122-31.

Roche has discovered W. Sapte, Jr.'s *Mdlle Cleopatra*, produced in 1891 as *Antony and Cleopatra*; it is a travesty of Lilie Langry's performance in the play in 1890.

1697 Shrimpton, Nicholas. "Shakespeare Performances in Stratford-upon-Avon and London." *Shakespeare Survey* 37 (1984): 163-173.

"A bare stage and platform were the only set" in Adrien Noble's production at The Other Place, "though audiences hungry for spectacle could content themselves with the sight of Helen Mirren's sumptuous and scarcely concealed physique." Michael Gambon's Antony "was an ageing man from a passionate race, still hungry for passion and aware that time was running out." "More tender than imperious, most impressive when was most intimate," Helen Mirren "gave remarkable depth to the final acts. In mourning for Antony she contrived an extraordinary ruin of her beauty—squatting on a grubby blanket, dressed in black with her hair scraped back and ash and dirt on her face."

1698 Booth, Stephen. "The Shakespearean Actor as Kamikaze Pilot." *Shakespeare Quarterly* 36 (1985): 553-70.

The audiences always feel disappointed in the actors playing the title roles of Antony and Cleopatra, Brutus in *Julius Caesar*, and Prince Hal in *1 Henry IV*. "We can believe ourselves capable of imagining a being who invites judgment by the standards of ordinary men and is also beyond the range of such standards because, and I think only because, the role of Antony—the role of Antony as we assume it to be, not the role of Antony as it is in fact written—is beyond the range of any actor who plays him." This "apparent incapacity is the means by which Shakespeare truly presents us with the only kind of impossible creature that is truly impossible—one that remains impossible."

1699 Gewirtz, Arthur. "*Antony and Cleopatra* in Shanghai." *Shakespeare Quarterly* 36 (1985): 237-38.

Hu Wei Min, who directed the Shanghai Youth Theatre Production in 1984, stylized it in the tradition of classical Chinese opera: "Charmian declined swan-like into death. Antony stood to deliver his death speech; at his final words two supernumeraries suddenly materialized to catch him as he fell backwards. Posturing, pirouetting, hanging onto scenery disfigured the production throughout." Jia Huang "offered a larger-than-life Antony, a Roman among the Romans, an Egyptians among the Egyptians, unable to forget Rome in Egypt, powerless to forget Egypt in Rome." Li Yuan, "actually 23, lent her Cleopatra plenty of energy but nothing of queenliness, guile, or ripeness—and certainly not Cleopatra's infinite variety."

1700 Mullin, Michael. "Colorado Shakespeare Festival 1985." *Shakespeare Quarterly* 36 (1985): 470-72.

Antony's "passion for Cleopatra," wrote Libby Appel, the director, in her program notes, "is the deep intoxication of middle age when death has become a reality, when life is urged to yield up quickly its utmost treasures of delight." Guided by this insight, the direcotr sent Antony "on the downhill slide, drunken, as besotted with Cleopatra and Egypt as any beach boy in his fifties could be with Acapulco."

1701 Stringfellow, Carolyne Ellison. "Shakespeare and Dryden in the Nineteenth Century: John Phillip Kemble's Pastiche of *Antony and Cleopatra*." *Postscript: Publications of the Philological Association of the Carolinas* 2 (1985): 49-56.

Stringfellow considers omissions, transpositions, reworkings of characters, and other changes in Kemble's sorry efforts to combine *Antony and Cleopatra* and Dryden's *All for Love*.

1702 Warren, Roger. "Shakespeare at Stratford-upon-Avon." *Shakespeare Quarterly* 36 (1985): 79-87.

In Robin Phillips's production of the play at Chichester Festival, Diana Rigg "suggested Cleopatra's variety by her flexible delivery, ranging during a single speech from a warmly eloquent 'Eternity was on our lips' to a snarled description of Antony as 'the greatest *liar*'." Denis Quilley's Antony "smiled in knowing recognition of her games." These moments "promised a subtle probing of the relationship that never materialized." This Antony "remained to the end merely a noble hero led astray.

1703 Berry, Ralph. "The Imperial Theme." *Shakespeare and the Victorian Stage*. Ed. Richard Foulkes. Cambridge: Cambridge UP, 1986, pp. 153-60.

There is a brief discussion of Tree's *Antony and Cleopatra* "located in the *Zeitgeist*," which was a "Roman-oriental spectacle.

1704 Cooper, Roberta Krensky. *The American Shakespeare Theatre: Stratford, 1955-1985*. Folger Books. Washington, DC: Folger Shakespeare Library, 1986. 353 pp.

Cooper evaluates the productions of this play in 1960 and 1972 by the American Shakespeare Theatre.

1705 Leiter, Samuel L., ed. *Shakespeare Around the Globe: A Guide to Notable Postwar Revivals*. New York: Greenwood P, 1986, pp. 17-38.

This is a review of thirteen professional productions of *Antony and Cleopatra* from 1946 to 1982. Leiter describes and provides names of the principal players and others who had major responsibility in each production. The British have dominated postwar stagings, followed by Americans and Canadians. Since World War II, the play has also been done in France, Italy, Sweden, Austria, Norway, Germany, Soviet Union, Yugoslavia, Hungary, and Japan. A section headed "Sources" (pp. 36-38) gives a list of the reviews from which the commentaries have been compiled. Additional revivals appear on p. 851 and a geographical breakdown of productions on pp. 875-84.

1706 Olivier, Laurence. "*Antony and Cleopatra*." *On Acting*. New York: Simon and Schuster, 1986, pp. 334-60.

Olivier gives his memories of the experience of delineating Shakespeare and Shaw in 1951. He looks upon Antony as "an absolute twerp," and he also notes that Leigh's was "the best Cleopatra ever."

1707 Peter, John. "For Disservices Rendered." *Sunday Times* (London) 1 June 1986: 49.

Vanessa Redgrave's conception of Cleopatra as "a middle-aged punk tomboy" in Toby Robertson's attempt to suggest a boy actor does not reflect Shakespeare's text.

1708 Van Der Merwe, Pieter. "Sketches for Scenery by Clarkson Stanfield: New Finds, 1980-84." *Theatre Notebook* 40.1 (1986): 22-29.

This article provides previously unknown sketches and watercolours for *Antony and Cleopatra* and *The Merchant of Venice*.

1709 Wardle, Irving. "Grandeur in a Mocking Grimace." *Times* (London) 28 May 1986: 19.

Wardle admires Vanessa Redgrave's "vain, arrogant, androgynous" Cleopatra.

1710 Warren, Roger. "Shakespeare in Britain, 1985." *Shakespeare Quarterly* 37 (1986): 114-20.

At the Chichester Festival, Daphne Dare's "transparent scenes and flimsy white Arab-style costumes gave a clinical, almost antiseptic feel to the Egyptian court, removing any hint of hedonistic luxury, and failing to suggest any contrast with Rome. This deprived the principals of any real context." Diana Rigg "suggested Cleopatra's variety by her flexible delivery," and Denis Quilley's "genial, expansive Antony had her measure: he smiled in knowing recognition of her games."

1711 Everett, Barbara. "On a Sumptuous Scale." *Times Literary Supplement* 24 April 1987: 439.

Peter Hall's "is a Renaissance, even a 'Veronese,' *Antony and Cleopatra*, which translates the scenic into the picturesque." Everett did not find Peter Hall's production very satisfactory. Anthony Hopkins's Antony "has a grizzled charm and mildness which make his farewell to his servants extremely touching; he communicates less, however, of the world-leader's rage and generosity, his courage and lechery, above all of his dangerous edge, the power to alarm." Judi Dench "never quite (even when punching messengers) gets what is terrible and beautiful in Cleopatra: the repose of her effortless sense of power." Dench and Hopkins "are, in the end, just too nice, too sympathatic; neither finally achieves exceptionality, that extraordinary human authority which lifts the play into tragedy." Hall's production, "though impressive up to a point, is strangely humourless in a manner not explained by the simple fact of its genre (the superb Galley Scene falls flat, for the first time in my experience)."

1712 Gardiner, Lyn. "The Challenge of Cleopatra." *Drama* 164 (1987): 21-23.

Judi Dench discusses the acting challenges in her career and talks especially about her delineation of Cleopatra under Peter Hall's direction.

1713 "How Mark Antony Lost His Toga." *Sunday Times* (London) 5 April 1987: 52.

This is a brief report about Alison Chitty's costumes and sets for Peter Hall's 1987 revival at National Theatre, which had been influenced by the Renaissance paintings of Veronese and Mantegna.

1714 James, John. "Duty and Desire." *Times Educational Supplement* 1 May 1987: 33.

Peter Hall's "is the very model of English Shakespearean production at its best." "Trusting the text, allowing the verse to exert its magic, Hall paces the action perfectly clearly, distinguishing between Rome's cold virtue and the heady langour of the East." Judi Dench impressed the house "as maddeningly sexy, mercurial in mood, commanding and bantering by turns, dangerously restless and raptly still."

1715 Langton, Robert Gore. "A Pair So Famous." *Plays and Players,* April 1987: 5-7.

Langton gives a summary of his conversations with Peter Hall and Alison Chitty six weeks before the opening of *Anotny and Cleopatra* at the National Theatre. Hall considers this play "the most comprehensive, universal, all embracing of the tragedies. It's a deeply human play about the political and personal consequences of unbridled passion."

1716 Peter, John. "Renaissance of the Golden Stage." *Sunday Times* (London) 12 April 1987: 55.

The Peter Hall production "is the British theatre at its spellbinding and magnificent best." Hopkins's Antony "is a restless prowler, suggesting one of those successful men to whom tension and ambition is more important than achievement." Judi Dench's Cleopatra is "both mature and volatile: she has a constant lust for life, like an animal which is both simple and incomprehensible." Hopkins and Dench "speak this soaring, voluptuous, difficult text with that finest of techniques which is based on artistic intelligence and true human feeling: two massive but golden performances from a golden age."

1717 Ratcliffe, Michael. "Triumph in Death on the Nile." *Observer* (London) 12 April 1987: 18.

In Peter Hall's production, Judi Dench "is scornful and sassy, blessed with terrific energy, temper and wit." She "has kept her Antony not by any received notions of female beauty but by sexuality and intelligence combined, and by her irresistible, dark-throated, broken laugh. She paints the words with warm, bright colours." Hopkins "makes Antony an affectionate, exhausted and introspective old lion, spoken with fine sense of elegy but frankly a bit short on the sex and the fun."

1718 Ray, Robin. "Rome 1, Egypt 1: National Theatre on Winning Forum." *Punch* 22 April 1987: 49-51.

Under Peter Hall's direction, "a brooding restlessness is at the core of" Dench's and Hopkins's "interpretations, a physical unquiet born of frustration and despair; his movement is abstracted—a substitute for decisive thought; hers the prowling of a feline, dreading the certainty of being caged."

1719 Rissik, Andrew. "*Antony and Cleopatra*." *Plays and Players,* June 1987: 14-15.

Finding Peter Hall's production "fitfully impressive," Rissik describes Anthony Hopkins's Antony as "a grizzled old dog of a man, at ease with the plain, masculine custom of the army, but bewildered by women and watchfully tense in their company." Judi Dench "has clearly never loved this man, but her voice is solemn and husky, full of dust and sunlight, and in her head she can hear the grand language of eternity." In Hall's production, "the tragedy always seems inevitable, and he allows it to acquire a drawn-out Wagnerian luxuriance, and at the end the verse rings with dark, celebratory splendour."

1720 Shattuck, Charles H. *Shakespeare on the American Stage. Vol. 2: From Booth and Barrett to Sothern* and *Marlowe*. Washington, DC: Folger Shakespeare Library, 1987. 339 pp.

Shattuck discusses the performances of Rose Eytinge (1877), Cora Potter 1889), Sothern and Julia Marlowe (1995), and Helena Modjeska (1898) in this play and productions of Anglin, Tree and Ames.

1721 Wardle, Irving. "Electrifying Detail and Tragic Exhilaration." *Times* (London) 11 April 1987: 14.

According to this reviewer, "for the first time in living memory, the English stage has two actors capable of doing full justice to the roles of Antony and Cleopatra." Judi Dench's "restless prowling and incessant jerks of the head reflect her inner caprice, instantly cancelled orders, and emotional somersaults that ensure that she always has the whip hand." Hopkins "is the passive partner, allowing himself to be seduced because he believes himself invulnerable."

1722 Wolf, Matt. "Return of the National." *American Theatre* 4.6 (September 1987): 38-39.

The Hopkins and Dench team "amply fulfills the assertive grandeur of the text." The actors present their "public and private selves—joint witnesses to an empire in upheaval, who save their great upheavals for their own passionate affair." Antony and Cleopatra's primary concerns "are their mutually exalted perceptions of one another; this is a play about the ideal, not the actual, and each partner's willingness to deify the other is borne out with an emotional bravura that bursts through their stolid corporeality."

1723 Billington, Michael. "Infinite Variety." *Peggy Ashcroft*. London: John Murray, 1988, pp. 125-50.

Ashcroft's "success lay in starting with a clear concept: in this case a very clear physical idea of the character." She "triumphed over her own temperamental and physical limitations to become the Cleopatra of her generation."

1724 Dessen, Alan C. "Exploring the Script: Shakespearean Pay-offs in 1987." *Shakespeare Quarterly* 39 (1988): 217-26.

Sir Peter Hall emphasized "the Elizabethan flow of the scenes, whereby entering figures appeared and began to speak while exiting figures were still in view." In this way, "scene beginnings often commented meaningfully (or ironically) upon scene endings so as to produce a larger counterpoint than I have ever before seen realized so effectively on stage."

1725 Nyberg, Lennart. *The Shakespearean Ideal: Shakespeare Production and the Modern Theatre in Britain*. Uppsala: Almqvist & Wiksell, 1988. 144 pp.

There are references to Antony and Cleopatra in this "attempt to show the interrelationship between modern drama and theatre and the production of Shakespearean drama in the 1960s and 1970s."

1726 Thomson, Leslie. "*Antony and Cleopatra*, Act 4, Scene 16: 'A heavy sight'." *Shakespare Survey* 41 (1989): 77-90.

Shakespeare intended the "dying Antony to be raised to Cleopatra in her monument." This awkward physical action underscores Cleopatra's "power to pull Antony to her, both physically and emotionally" and serves as a key organizing principle of language and structure.

1727 Wells, Stanley. "Shakespeare Performances in London and Stratford-upon-Avon 1986-1987." *Shakespeare Survey* 41 (1989): 159-82.

For Peter Hall's production at the Royal National Theatre, Alison Chitty "designed a great, bronzed, crescent-shaped structure that could define a manageable acting area, but was capable also of rearranging itself to suggest changes of location, and of retreating altogether when the full stage was needed." Anthony Hopkins "was more convincingly the 'old ruffian' than the noble warrior." Judi Dench "brought greatness to the production in a feat of classical acting by which she extended herself into every aspect of the role, from the sordid to the sublime, while never losing the sense of a unifying self that could encompass Cleopatra's 'infinite variety'."

1728 Caretti, Laura. "Recitare Cleopatra." Mariangela Tempera, ed. *Antony and Cleopatra dal testo alla scena.* Bologna: Cooperative Libraria Universitaria Editrice, 1990, pp. 143-64.

This is a survey of actresses in the role of Cleopatra, including Elizabeth Younge, Isabella Glyn, Lillie Langtry, Sarah Bernhardt, Eleonora Duse, Peggy Ashcroft, Janet Suzman, Glenda Jackson, and Valeria Moriconi.

1729 Flint, Kate. "Significant Otherness: Sex, Silence, and Cleopatra." *Critical Essays on Antony and Cleopatra.* Ed. Linda Cookson and Bryan Loughrey. Longman Literature Guides. Harlow, Essex: Longman, 1990, pp. 9-17.

Flint examines the stage history of the play to understand how renderings of Cleopatra's sexuality reflect the gender assumptions and sexual stereotyping of the day.

1730 Hirst, David L. "My Other Elements: Adattamento di Antony and Cleopatra." *Antony and Cleopatra dal testo alla scena.* Ed. Mariangela Tempera. Bologna: Cooperative Libraria Universitaria Editrice, 1990, pp. 133-41.

Hirst, the director, discusses has adaptation of *Antony and Cleopatra* as *My Other Elements*, produced by the University of Birmingham Drama Department at Ferrara in 1987.

1731 McRae, John. "'A strumpet and her fool' ruolo e recita: Note per una regia di Antony and Cleopatra." Mariangela Tempera, ed. *Antony and Cleopatra dal testo alla scena.* Bologna: Cooperative Libraria Universitaria Editrice, 1990, pp. 125-32.

These are director's notes for a production of *Antony and Cleopatra* at Teatro Abelian, Bari.

1732 Williams, Simon. *Shakespeare on the German Stage: 1586-1914*. Vol. 1. Cambridge: Cambridge UP, 1990. 245 pp.

This play was first performed in Germany in Bierbach in 1769 and again in 1852 at Dresden court theatre. Heinrich Laube "drastically reduced" the script to twelve scenes and twenty-three characters.

1733 Hoyle, Martin. "*Antony and Cleopatra.*" *Times* (London) 18 May 1991: 21.

For her production in Liverpool, Yvonne Brewster, the director, "the play has been pruned, characters amalgamated and even unsexed." There is "no feeling of a love that defies society and politics hurtling towards inexorable doom. Nor does the central pair convey magnificent thoroughbreds galloping towards the slaughterhouse, masters of the world who throw it all away." Dona Croll's Cleopatra "excels in the queen's frivolity and petulance." Jeffery Kissoon "makes a battered, romantic warrior of Antony, occasional physical stiffness balanced by a varied vocal palette."

1734 Knustan, Roslyn Lander. *The Repertory of Shakespeare's Company 1594-1613*. Fayetteville: U of Arkansas P, 1991. 252 pp.

This study locates the play in the repertory of Shakespeare's company.

1735 Lowen, Tirzah. *Peter Hall Directs Antony and Cleopatra*. With photographs by John Haynes. Methuen Drama Series. London: Methuen, 1990; New York: Limelight Editions, 1991. 176 pp.

This is an analysis of Peter Hall's 1987 production of the play at the National Theatre. Lowen introduces readers to the actors and production personnel, publicity and publication staff, and technicians involved in the production. She also explores such issues of interpretation as the speaking of Shakespeare's verse and the relationship between rehearsal and performance, and provides background materials. Lowen describes how the play took shape through thirteen weeks of rehearsals.

1736 Teague, Frances N. *Shakespeare's Speaking Properties.* Lewisburg: Bucknell UP, 1991. 222 pp.

Teague argues that the early texts of this and other plays, "both quarto and folio, are as close as a modern student can get to the actual performances of Shakespeare's company; they are, therefore, the place that one must go to learn of the properties for each play." She cites Act 5 as "a particularly useful instance of the way that properties operate as characterizing devices." In 1.5.39-47, Alexas brings Cleopatra a pearl from Antony, which is "a powerful symbol of passion."

1737 Williams, Raymond. "*Antony and Cleopatra.*" *Drama in Performance.* New ed. Milton Keynes and Philadelphia: Open UP, 1991, pp. 53-80.

Originally published in 1954 and revised in 1968, this new edition has an introduction and a bibliography by Graham Holderness. In "locating dramatic texts in the conditions and conventions of their original performance and reading them to disclose their performance potentialities," Williams devotes a chapter to *Antony and Cleopatra.* There is a brief description of the Globe Theatre, a synopsis of scenes, and comments on some of the scenes.

1738 Coursen, H.R. "The RSC, Nunn-Schofield *Antony and Cleopatra*: Freeing the Script." *Shakespearean Performance As Interpretation.* Newark: U of Delaware P, 1992; London: Associated University Presses, 1992, pp. 190-95.

This production "incorporates all of the things that television can do well. The 'varying shores of the world' are not reached for here, but they are not missed, so harmonious are the individual performers."

1739 Crowl, Samuel. *Shakespeare Observed: Studies in Performance on Stage and Screen*. Athens: Ohio UP, 1992. 195 pp.

In his analysis of some of the major developments in Shakespearean production since 1960, Crowl gives a detailed account of Peter Hall's staging of *Antony and Cleopatra* in 1987 (pp. 93-100) and refers once to Charlton Heston's 1972 film and once to Trevor Nunn's television adaptation.

1740 Edelman, Charles. *Brawl Ridiculous: Swordfighting in Shakespeare's Plays*. The Revels Plays Companion Library. Manchester: Manchester UP, 1995. 218 pp.

While discussing Shakespeare's "achievement in transforming the playhouse's traditional connection with swordfighting into a versatile and important poetic elements within the great poetry of his plays," Edelman uses a number of examples from this play.

1741 King, T.J. *Casting Shakespeare's Plays*. Cambridge: Cambridge UP, 1992. 284 pp.

Based on evidence in playhouse documents and other sources, this study describes the casting requirements of *Antony and Cleopatra*. Twelve men can play nineteen principal male roles and four boys four principal female roles. Thirteen men can do thirty-seven small speaking roles and forty-six mutes; three boys can play twelve mutes.

1742 Munkelt, Marge. "Restoring Shakespeare's *Antony and Cleopatra* on the Nineteenth-Century Stage: Samuel Phelps and Isabella Glyn." *Theatre History Studies* 12 (1992): 1-12.

After a careful examination of different promptbooks, Munkelt concludes that Samuel Phelps's is "the first text of the play since the eighteenth century to use Shakespeare's words only." He cut it without adding any words of his own. Isabella Glyn, the Cleopatra against Phelps's Antony in 1849, "continues restoring the play on Phelps's line in her own text used for public readings in New York in the 1870s."

1743 Nightingale, Benedict. "A Cleopatra of Infinite Variety." *Times* (London) 7 November 1992: Weekend 16.

Clare Higgins "is an intelligent Cleopatra—note her deliberately inscrutable handling of Caesar's smug envoy—but it is intensity and volatility of feeling that mainly mark her." Richard Johnson's Antony "looks a bit as if he's been sleeping off a 10-hour drinking bout in a ditch. Yet it is undeniably a magnifico who has coarsened." In this Antony, "there is authority behind the sweaty hair, facial stubble and thick, marinated growl. There is also plenty of detail inside the besotted sugar daddy he sometimes resembles."

1744 Williamson, Sandra L., ed. "*Antony and Cleopatra.*" *Shakespearean Criticism*. Vol. 17. Detroit and London: Gale, 1992, pp. 1-123.

This volume of stage history contains a history of the productions of this play, reviews and retrospective accounts, comparisons and reviews, staging issues, and further reading. The excerpts from reviews and books cover these eight productions: 1759, 1849, 1951, 1953, 1967, 1972, 1978, 1987.

1745 Makaryk, Irena R. "Woman Scorned: *Antony and Cleopatra* at Moscow's Vakhtanzou Theatre." *Foreign Shakespeare*. Ed. Dennis Kennedy. Cambridge: Cambridge UP, 1993, pp. 178-94.

Makaryk explains "the consequences for the place of woman in such a totalizing view of theatre and criticism by examining the reviews of Eugenii Simonov's 1971 production of *Antony and Cleopatra*." These reviews "suggest the ease with which classics like Shakespeare may be assimilated into official ideologies when a totalizing view of the work is presented."

1746 Holland, Peter. "Shakespeare Performances in England, 1992." *Shakespeare Survey* 46 (1994): 159-89.

In the Royal Shakespeare Company's 1992 production, Richard Johnson's Antony "is not attractive, even in an elderly grizzled way," and this unbalances it so much that the actor "could do nothing to project a reason for Cleopatra's facination with him to match his justifiable obsession with her." In the last scenes, there was "a sense of cavernous desolation in the monument, here played out on the stage-floor since the raising of Antony by ropes attached to his stretcher had surprising effect of lowering Cleopatra's group in the monument down to stage level."

1747 Miles, Keith. "*Antony and Cleopatra* in Performance." *English Review* 4, 4 (1994): 2-5.

This play has been so infrequently performed on the British stage because it has been undervalued and because of misconception of the technical difficulties in staging.

1748 Mullin, Michael. *Theatre at Stratford-upon-Avon, First Supplement. A Catalogue-Index to Productions of the Royal Shakespeare Company, 1979-1993*. Bibliographies and Indexes in the Performing Arts, No. 17. Westport, CT: Greenwood P, 1994. xxvi, 320 pp.

Mullin lists productions of this play for 1979, 1982, 1983, 1992, and 1993; he also gives information about the reviews of each production.

1749 Nightingale, Benedict. "The asp did it, but who cares?" *Times* (London) 18 August 1994: 30.

At the Edinburgh Festival, Gert Voss and Eva Mattes, as Antony and Cleopatra, "exchange the odd strong word and even an occasional slap," but "their acquaintance has not progressed to the point where it is producing electricity either sexual or emotional." Voss is "a mild, undemonstrative chap, happiest with his whisky and his fag, and barely ruffled by the defeat of his entire fleet. Mattes "lolls about in a glittery cress, acting spoiled, shallow, manipulative and nothing much more."

1750 Coursen, H.R. *Reading Shakespeare on Stage*. Newark: U of Delaware P, 1995. 298 pp.

The objective of this study is "to encourage informed response to production, and to suggest how an individual's reaction to a production can find a voice." Coursen argues that "the vastness of the script places *Antony and Cleopatra* near the top of the list of difficult plays to produce, but the gross cross-cultural leaps and the soaring verse found a home on the Olivier stage" at the National Theatre in Peter Hall's production of 1987. Coursen summarizes critical response by suggesting that "this production had been the exploration of the script that we expect of Peter Hall, an experience of a play we do not understand until we see it performed, an experience that proved that we understand the play only through experience."

1751 Dunbar, Monique. "Cleopatra or Hamlet? Sarah between Sardou and Shakespeare." *Shakespeare Yearbook* 5 (1995): 233-61.

Bernhardt's Cleopatra in her collaboration with Victorien Sardou on *Cléopâtre* was heavily influenced by *Antony and Cleopatra.*

1752 Mullin, Michael. "*Antony and Cleopatra*, Stratford-upon-Avon, 1953." *Shakespeare Worldwide* 14-15 (1995): 267-86.

Mullin examines the inception and staging of Glen Byam Shaw's 1953-54 production.

1753 Nightingale, Benedict. "Redgrave Loses her Deposit." *Times* (London) 6 June 1995: 40.

Vanessa Redgrave, who both directs and performs Cleopatra, tries, in her own words, to "highlight the contemporary resonance of this powerful political drama, elucidating the personal tragedies within an occupied land."

Hence, this Alexandria "has clearly not recovered from the burning of its famous library, let alone its strafing by planes during the Suez crisis, and Imperial Rome is about as welcoming a place as Belsen." The sexual attraction between Paul Butler's Antony and Redgrave "is not great, even after she has changed her English deb's dress for a black outfit that inexplicably leaves her looking like Mary Queen of Scots." Redgrave "is variously harsh and strident, gentle and tender, mischievous and manipulative." And "a beaming American Antony wanders through the chaos like Santa Claus on Prozac."

1754 Zeiger, E. James. "Taming the Monster: Solving Five Essential Problems in *Antony and Cleopatra*." *On-Stage Studies* 18 (1995): 102-12.

Zeiger explains how Jack Clay, in his *Antony and Cleopatra*, deals with the size of the script and casting requirements, stylistic approaches to scenic and costume requirements, the Act 2 bacchanal, the battle scenes, and the hoisting of Antony into Cleopatra's monument.

1755 Bate, Jonathan, and Russell Jackson, eds. *Shakespeare: An Illustrated Stage History*. Oxford: Oxford UP, 1996. 253 pp.

The contributors to this volume in honor of Stanley W. Wells "draw on many kinds of evidence—from archaeology to political polemic to painting—in order to demonstrate how the history of Shakespeare on the stage has always been bound up with wider histories and broader cultural cannges." There are numerous references to *Antony and Cleopatra* in their historical context, but Judi Dench is the only one who gives a few details about her role as Cleopatra in 1987 in a Royal National Theatre production directed by Sir Peter Hall.

Major Productions

1756 1759
Drury Lane, London
Director, David Garrick
Principal Cast, David Garrick, Mary Ann Yates

1757 1813
Covent Garden, London
Director, J. P. Kemble
Principal Cast, Charles M. Young, Helen Faucit

1758 1833
Drury Lane, London
Director, William Charles Macready
Principal Cast, William Charles Macready, Louisa Anne Phillips

1759 1849
Sadler's Wells, London
Director, Samuel Phelps
Principal Cast, Samuel Phelps, Isabella Glyn

1760 1855
Standard, London
Director, John Douglass
Principal Cast, Henry Marston, Isabella Glyn

1761 1866
Prince's, Manchester
Director, Charles Calvert
Principal Cast, Charles Calvert, Adelaide Calvert

1762 1867
Princess's, London
Director, George J. Vining
Principal Cast, Henry Loraine, Isabella Glyn

1763 1873
Drury Lane, London
Director, Frederick B. Chatterton
Principal Cast, James Anderson, Ellin Wallis

1764 1890
Royal Princess's, London
Director, Lewis Wingfield
Principal Cast, Charles Coghlan, Lilie Langtry

1765 1897
Queen's, Manchester
Director, Louis Calvert
Principal Cast, Louis Calvert, Janet Achurch

1766 1898
Festival, Stratford-upon-Avon
Director, Frank Benson
Principal Cast, Frank Benson, Constance Benson

1767 1900
Lyceum, London
Director, Frank Benson
Principal Cast, Frank Benson, Constance Benson

1768 1906
His Majesty's, London
Director, Beerbohm Tree
Principal Cast, Beerbohm Tree, Constance Collier

1769 1912
Festival, Stratford-upon-Avon
Director, Frank Benson
Principal Cast, Frank Benson, Dorothy Green

1770 1921
Oxford University Dramatic Society, Oxford
Director, William Bridges-Adams
Principal Cast, C.B. Ramage, Cathleen Nesbitt

1771 1921
Festival, Stratford-upon-Avon
Director, William Bridges-Adams
Principal Cast, Edmund Willard, Dorothy Green

1772 1922
Old Vic, London
Director, Robert Atkins
Principal Cast, Wilfrid Walter, Esther Waterhouse

1773 1924
Festival, Stratford-upon-Avon
Director, William Bridges-Adams
Principal Cast, Baliol Holloway, Dorothy Green

1774 1925
Old Vic, London
Director, Andrew Leigh
Principal Cast, Baliol Holloway, Edith Evans

1775 1927
Cinema, Stratford-upon-Avon
Director, William Bridges-Adams
Principal Cast, Wilfrid Walter, Dorothy Green

1776 1930
Old Vic, London
Director, Harcourt Williams
Principal Cast, John Gielgud, Dorothy Green

1777 1931
Cinema, Stratford-upon-Avon
Director, William Bridges-Adams
Principal Cast, Gyles Isham, Dorothy Massingham

1778 1934
Old Vic, London
Director, Henry Cass
Principal Cast, Wilfrid Lawson, Mary Newcombe

1779 1935
Festival, Stratford-upon-Avon
Director, Iden Payne
Principal Cast, Roy Emerton, Catherine Lacey

1780 1936
New, London
Director, Theodore Komisarjevsky
Principal Cast, Donald Wolfit, Eugenie Leontovich

1781 1945
Festival, Stratford-upon-Avon
Director, Robert Atkins
Principal Cast, Anthony Eustrel, Claire Luce

1782 1946
Piccadilly, London
Director, Glen Byam Shaw
Principal Cast, Godfrey Tearle, Edith Evans

1783 1946
Martin Beck Theatre, New York
Director, Guthrie McClintic
Principal Cast, Godfrey Tearle, Katharine Cornell

1784 1951
St. James's, London; Ziegfeld Theatre, New York
Director, Michael Benthall
Principal Cast, Laurence Olivier, Vivien Leigh

1785 1953
Festival, Stratford-upon-Avon
Director, Glen Byam Shaw
Principal Cast, Michael Redgrave, Peggy Ashcroft

1786 1957
Old Vic, London
Director, Robert Hselpmann
Principal Cast, Keith Mitchell, Margaret Whiting

1787 1959
New York Shakespeare Festival
Director, Joseph Papp
Principal Cast, George C. Scott, Colleen Dewhurst

1788 1960
American Shakespeare Theatre, Stratford, Connecticut
Director, Jack Landau
Principal Cast, Robert Ryan, Katharine Hepburn

1789 1961
Birmingham Repertory, Birmingham
Director, Bernard Hepton
Principal Cast, Tony Steedman, Elizabeth Sprigg

1790 1963
Central Park, New York
Director, Joseph Papp
Principal Cast, Michael Higgins, Colleen Dewhurst

1791 1965
National Youth Theatre, Scala
Director, Michael Croft
Principal Cast, John Nightingale, Helen Mirren

1792 1965
Oxford Playhouse, Oxford
Director, Frank Hauser
Principal Cast, John Turner, Barbara Jefford

1793 1967
Stratford Shakespeare Festival, Stratford, Ontario
Director, Michael Langham
Principal Cast, Christopher Plummer, Zoe Caldwell

1794 1969
Festival, Chichester, England
Director, Peter Dews
Principal Cast, John Clements, Margaret Leighton

1795 1972
Festival, Stratford-upon-Avon
Director, Trevor Nunn
Principal Cast, Richard Johnson, Janet Suzman

1796 1972
American Theatre Company, Stratford, Connecticut
Director, Michael Kahn
Principal Cast, Paul Hecht, Salome Jens

1797 1973
Bankside Globe, London
Director, Tony Richardson
Principal Cast, Julian Glover, Vanessa Redgrave

1798 1976
Stratford Shakespeare Festival, Stratford, Ontario
Director, Robin Phillips
Principal Cast, Keith Baxter, Maggie Smith

1799 1976
Young Vic, London
Director, Frank Dunlop
Principal Cast, Michael Graham Cox, Delphine Seyrig

1800 1977
Prospect Theatre at Old Vic, London
Director, Toby Robertson
Principal Cast, Alec McCowen, Dorothy Tutin

1801 1978
Festival, Stratford-upon-Avon
Director, Peter Brook
Principal Cast, Alan Howard, Glenda Jackson

1802 1979
Interart Theatre, New York
Diresctor, Estelle Parsons
Principal Cast, Francisco Prado, Kathleen Gaffney

1803 1981
Alliance Theatre Company, Atlanta
Director, Fred Chappell
Principal Cast, Edward J. Moore, Jane Alexander

1804 1981
Mermaid Theatre, London
Directors, Bernard Miles and Ron Pemmber
Principal Cast, Timothy Dalton, Carmen Du Sautoy

1805 1982
Nottingham Playhouse
Principal Cast, Ian McCullock, Kate O'Mara

1806 1983
Young Vic, London
Director, Kenneth Hackk
Principal Cast, Keith Baxter, Judy Parfitt

1807 1983
The Other Place, Stratford-upon-Avon; The Pit, Barbican, London
Director, Adrian Noble
Principal Cast, Michael Gambon, Helen Mirren

1808 1985
Chichester Festival Theatre
Director, Robin Phillips
Principal Cast, Dennis Quilley, Diana Rigg

1809 1986
Theatre Clwyd, Wales; Haymarket, London
Director, Toby Robertson
Principal Cast, Timothy Dalton, Vanessa Redgrave

1810 1987
Olivier Stage, National Theatre, London
Director, Peter Hall
Principal Cast, Anthony Hopkins, Judy Dench

1811 1987
Contact Theatre, Manchester
Director, Brigid Larmour
Principal Cast, Wyllie Longmore, Clare Dow

1812 1991
Festival Theatre, Stratford-upon-Avon1991
Royal Shakespeare Company
Director, John Caird
Principal Cast Richard Johnson, Clare Higgins

1813 1993
Festival Theatre
Stratford Shakespeare Festival, Stratford, Ontario
Director, Richard Monette
Principal Cast, Leon Pownall, Goldie Semple

Films

1814 Ball, Robert H. *Shakespeare on Silent Film: A Strange Eventful History*. London: Allen and Unwin, 1968. 403 pp.

Ball analyzes four silent films of this play: Vitagraph, 1908; Pathé, 1913; Cines, 1913; Universal, 1924. Vitagraph advertised its version as a "stupendous production, a fine picture of Roman pride and Eastern magnificence, elaborately staged, superbly acted. Pathé described its work as "a massive and glittering production showing the barbaric splendor of the Great Queen's court." Cines claims to have done an "enormous amount of research, planning, and construction to obtain historical accuracy." The Universal film was "an 'hysterical history' comedy."

1815 *Explorations in Shakespeare: A Series*. Eleven parts. 23 min. each, color. Producer: NBC-TV, 1969.

"*Antony and Cleopatra*: The World Well Lost" examines the conflict between Antony's roles, his duty as a statesman and his obligation as Cleopatra's lover.

1816 Kermode, Frank. "Shakespeare in the Movies." *New York Review of Books* 18 (4 May 1972): 18-21. Reprinted in *Film Theory: Introductory Readings*. Ed. Gerald Mast and Marshall Cohen. New York: Oxford UP, 1974, pp. 322-32.

Charlton Heston's movie is "a work of no imagination. During the negotiations for Antony's marriage to Octavia two gladiators thump one another in the arena below." Heston "is a conscientious Antony, large, generous, cruel, and so on, but inexpressive and clumsy with verse." Hildegarde Neil's Cleopatra "has neither presence (when she speaks of her majesty, as she often does, we take it as a kind of in-joke) nor sexuality."

1817 Morris, Peter. *Shakespeare on Film.* Ottawa: Canadian Film Institute, 1972.

In a brief note on p. 15, Morris evaluates the Parthian Production movie which stressed the scenes between Antony and Cleopatra.

1818 Morris, Peter. "Shakespeare on Film." *Films in Review* 24 (1973): 132-63.

Morris suggests that the "freedom of the unlocalized Shakespeare stage and the unrestricted sense of movement seem in some ways to foreshadow the cinema." In his index of films for 1929-51, he discusses Parthian Productions' black-and-white 33-minute film, in which Pauline Letts and Robert Speaight played the leading roles. This is a condensed version in which "the political sub-plots and part of Enobarbus are almost entirely omitted and many of the major speeches are cut. A narrator explains some of the time and place translations." The production "in general lacks poetic feeling, the acting is stilted and many of the speeches are inaudible."

1819 Parker, Barry M. *The Folger Shakespeare Filmography.* Washington, DC: Folger Books, 1979. 64 pp.

This is a list of sound films only, and it includes adaptations, dance and musical versions, and instructional and abridged versions.

1820 Foreman, Walter C. "Cleopatras, Passengers, and Cities of Women." *Purdue University Seventh Annual Conference on Film, March 24-26, 1983, West Lafayette, Indiana.* West Lafayette: Depatment of English, Purdue University, 1983, pp. 219-25.

The stress on mutability in *Antony and Cleopatra* provides a context for this discussion of Michelangelo

Antonioni's emphasis on shifting shapes and images in his films.

1821 Holderness, Graham, and Christopher McCullough, compilers. "Shakespeare on the Screen: A Selective Filmography." *Shakespeare Survey* 39 (1986): 13-37.

This is a listing of three versions of *Antony and Cleopatra* for the silent screen (1908-1910), two speaking versions (1951-1972), and three versions filmed for television (1963-1981). Each entry includes the names of the producer, director, designer, the principal players and, where applicable, the name of the distributor or the archive where the film is stored.

1822 Flesch, William. "Proximity and Power: Shakespearean and Cinematic Space." *Theatre Journal* 39 (1987): 277-93.

Flesch argues that Shakespeare is "antitheatrical" because "his plays tend towards the dislocation of the presence in representation." Antony and Cleopatra "stage the opposition between presence and proximity as the opposition between Rome and Alexandria. But proximity is not available to staging, to the theatrics of presence. In addition to staging an opposition, Antony and Cleopatra imagines and images proximity, adumbrates film (anticipates cinematic shadows)." The interaction between the two lovers is "spectral" "as though Shakespeare were describing the powerless mode of love as necessarily alien to presence."

1823 Willson, Robert F., Jr. "Shakespeare and Hollywood: Two film Cliches." *Journal of Popular Film and Television* 15 (1987): 83-84.

Willson criticizes cliches in film, especially in connection with the filming of *Antony and Cleopatra*. For example, Octavius Caesar "foreshadows the typical movie Western hero-lawman who must sacrifice personal happiness for the cause of justice."

1824 Collick, John. *Shakespeare, Cinema and Society*. Manchester: Manchester UP, 1989. 208 pp.

Collick suggests that "the boom in Shakespeare film was sparked off by the American company Vitagraph," which made *Antony and Cleopatra* and other films in 1908. They ran between ten and twenty minutes, and "the acting and set were increasingly used to evoke the illusion of a staged performance."

1825 Nicolai, Rina. "Cleopatra. Cinecitta, 1963." *Antony and Cleopatra dal testo alla scena*. Ed. Mariangela Tempera. Bologna: Cooperative Libraria Universitaria Editrice, 1990, pp. 109-24.

This is an analysis of the structure and treatment of sources in Joseph L. Mankiewicz's 1963 film, *Cleopatra*.

1826 Carra, Lawrence, director. *Antony and Cleopatra*. Video cassettes by Crest Video Marketing, 1992. 183 minutes.

This is a video release of a film made for Bard Productions.

1827 Crowl, Samuel. "A World Elsewhere: the Roman Plays on Film and Television." *Shakespeare and the Moving Image. The Plays on Film and Television*. Ed. Anthony Davies and Stantley Wells. Cambridge: Cambridge UP, 1994, pp. 146-62.

This is an analysis of Charlton Heston's movie (1972) and the television productions by Trevor Nunn (1974), Jonathan Miller (1980), and Lawrence Carra Bard version (1985). This play's "geographical, political, and emotional expanse and excess would seem to make it a natural candidate for effective treatment on film. By the same token, its vastness would seem to be confined by television's limitations." But, "paradoxically, the three television versions we have of the play are all superior to Charlton Heston's film which seeks to translate the play into the sweep of a Hollywood epic and like Heston's Antony becomes quite unravelled in the process." Trevor Nunn's Egypt "is golden and languorous; less a place than a state of mind." Richard

Johnson's Antony "is a large, generous, bear-like man who is by turns delighted, perplexed, and ultimately baffled by Suzman's Cleopatra."

Jonathan Miller's version "is formal, even chaste—Antony and Cleopatra rarely touch and never kiss, even when the text tells them to do so, until Antony's dying moments—inspired by the depiction of the classical world in Renaissance paintings." Jane Lapotaire's "sharp, pale, extremely ironic Cleopatra, with a strand of pearls tight at her neck and exquisite matching earrings, might have steeped right out of a Bronzino portrait." Colin Blakely's Antony is "straightforward and hearty."

Lawrence Carra's production "has the virtue, for a novice audience, of being a less complicated reading of the play than Miller's, and it allows Lynn Redgrave (Cleopatra) and Timothy Dalton (Antony) to give full rein to the play's passionate moments."

Heston's film "not only fails, visually and verbally, to capture the dynamics of Shakespeare's play but also fails to create an interesting epic inspired by a Shakespearian source."

Music

1828 Naylor, Edward W. *Shakespeare and Music*. London: Dent, 1931. Reprint. New York: Da Capo P & Benjamin Blom, 1965. 212 pp.

In 4.3.12 of this play, hautboys supply the supposed ominous "music in the air."

1829 Wilson, Christopher. "*Antony and Cleopatra*." *Shakespeare and Music*. London: "The Stage" Office, 1922. Reprint. New York: Da Capo P, 1977, pp. 1-7.

Wilson provides details of the music composed about and related to this play by composers Like Sir Henry Biship, KH. Graun, Augusta Enna, Rodolphe Kreutzu, Hector Berlioz, Havergal Biran, Ethel Smyth, Schubert, Michael Balling, Thomas Chilcot, Frances Alletson.

1830 Noble, Richmond. *Shakespeare's Use of Song with the Text of the Principal Songs*. London: Oxford UP, 1923. 160 pp.

Noble proposes that the model for the song, "Come thou monarch of the vine" in this play, is the Pentecostal Hymn of the Christian Church.

1831 Sternfeld, F. W. *Music in Shakespearean Tragedy*. London: Routledge & Kegan Paul, 1963. 334 pp.

Sternfield suggests that "for Cleopatra's barge the description is reduced to amorous flures, and Antony's downfall is augured by shrill oboes."

1832 Schonberg, Harold C. "Onstage, It Was 'Antony and Cleopatra'." *Times* (New York) 17 September 1966: 18.

Schonberg suggests that "almost everything about the evening, artistically speaking, failed in total impact." Barber's score "is something of a hybrid—neither fully traditional nor fully modern; skillfully put together but lacking ardor and eloquence; big in sound but stingy with arresting melodic idea." Franco Zeffrelli filled up the stage with Cleopatra's barge which h"floated on a silver Nile, oars moving in unison. There was a camel. There were goats and horses. Far in the distance a wee Egyptian fleet set out to fight the Romans."

1833 Seng, Peter J. "*Antony and Cleopatra*." *The Vocal Songs in the Plays of Shakespeare. A Critical History*. Cambridge, MA: Harvard UP, 1967, pp. 211-13.

Seng provides the text of the song from this play, general critical commentary, textual notes, and information about music for the song. The music and song give "a sense of uninhibited drunken revel."

1834 Harbage, Alfred, ed. *Shakespeare's Songs. Illustrated with the Original Musical Settings*. Philadelphia: Macrae Smith, 1970. 96 pp.

Harbage supplies a text of the song and its music and suggests that "the four lines are sung by page and the rest by the drunken guests as they dance in a ring on Pompey's barge."

1835 Long, John H. "*Antony and Cleopatra*." *Shakespeare's Use of Music: The Histories and Tragedies*. Gainesville: U of Florida P, 1971, pp. 201-18.

Long concludes that the music in this play "originates from two distinct sources, Plutarch and Shakespeare." Shakespeare "used the music suggested by Plutarch to enrich the characterization of Antony, but he supplied the military signals which provide ironic comments and speed the action of the play."

Shakespeare's original additions are such technical devices as trumpet calls, flourishes, alarums, and other military signals which "serve purely dramatic purposes."

1836 Neuse, Richard. "A Cabaret Version of *Antony and Cleopatra*." *Shakespeare Quarterly* 31 (1980): 186-7.

This Rhode Island Shakespeare Theater production of *Antony and Cleopatra* "exchanged Rome and Alexandria for the Berlin of Brecht and Isherwood." It was "Cabaret-inspired: a pianist, his back turned to the audience, sat onstage, and occasionally played throughout the proceedings; Octavius Caesar and his entourage, in double-breasted business suits, looked vaguely like Capone-era gangsters; and Cleopatra's attendants seemed ready to do the Charleston at any moment." Instead of using the whole script, the company presents "a series of *allusions* to that original, so that at least a part of the audience experience consists in recalling the larger context to which theatrical performance alludes."

1837 Bartell, Gerald, and Sybil Robinson, narrators. *Antony and Cleopatra and Coriolanus*. Shakespeare Digest Series, 1981. 60 minutes.

This is an aduio cassette made by Classic Theatre.

1838 Brissenden, Alan. *Shakespeare and the Dance.* Atlantic Heights, NJ: Humanities P, 1981. 145 pp.

In 2.7 of this play, "meaning of the dance and its accompanying song is in powerful ironic counterpoint to the vast grandeur of the cosmic imagery which gives so much to the tone of the play."

1839 Hunt, Christopher. "*Antony and Cleopatra*: Samuel Barber." *Opera Quarterly* 3 (1985): 92-94.

This is a review of a recording of Barber's opera (New World Records, NW 322/323/324).

1840 Jolly, James Lester, Jr. "American Operas based on the Plays of William Shakespeare 1648-1978." *Dissertation Abstracts International* 47 (1985): 107A (LSU&A&M).

Jolly discusses Louise Gruenberg and Samuel Barber who have based their operas on *Antony and Cleopatra.*

1841 Reed, John. *The Schubert Song Companion.* With Prose Translation by Norma Deane and Cellia Larner. Manchester: Manchester UP, 1985. 510 pp.

Reed gives background and historical information on Schubert's songs from Shakespeare; one of them is *Trinklied* from *Antony and Cleopatra.*

1842 Rylands, George, director. *Antony and Cleopatra.* Performed by the Marlowe Dramatic Society. Audio cassettes by Audio Partners, 1985. 183 minutes.

This is a cassette release of the early 1960s audio production.

1843 Schmidgall, Gary. "Barber's 'Pair So Famous'." *Shakespeare and Opera.* New York: Oxford UP, 1990, pp. 298-305.

This is an account of the difficulties of composing an opera based on this play, the disasterous opening night of Barber's Antony and Cleopatra at the Metropolitan Opera House on 16 September 1966, and Barber's subsequent revisions. Barber's opera, "even in its final form, offers a few, mostly lamentable object lessons in the difficulties of 'reading' a Shakepearean script musically."

1844 Heyman, Barbara B. "A New Opera House: *Antony and Cleopatra.*" *Saumel Barber: The Composer and His Music.* New York and Oxford: Oxford UP, 1992, pp. 428-60.

This "study of the progress of Antony and Cleopatra, from the forging of the libretto to its production, points to the wide chasm between Barber's and Zeffrelli's concepts of the opera as a major factor in the overwhelming failure in 1966. Fair appraisal of the music was not completely resolved until the opera was revised with the help of Menotti in 1975." Heyman provides a detailed narrative of the composition, production, reception, revision, and subsequent performances of this opera.

1845 Neighbarger, Randy L. *An Outward Show: Music for Shakespeare on the London Stage, 1660-1830*. Contributions to the Study of Music and Dance, No. 27. Westport, CT: Greenwood P, 1992. 318 pp.

The only Shakespearean text "known to have been set by Handel are a few lines from *Antony and Cleopatra,* incorporated into *Alexander Bulas* by librettist Thomas Morell."

1846 Solomon, Jon. "The Spectacle of Samuel Barber's *Antony and Cleopatra*." *Opera and the Golden West*. Ed. John L. DiGaetani and Josef P. Serefman. Rutherford, NJ: Fairleigh Dickinson UP, 1994, pp. 244-54.

Solomon tries to explain why "two of the most memorable artistic disappointments of the last thirty years—Joseph L. Mankiewicz's film *Cleopatra* (1963) and Samuel Barber's opera *Antony and Cleopatra* (1966)—both portrayed the same heroine." He suggests that "audiences in the 1960s were no longer allured by historical romance and felt the grandeur to be excessive." It may have been "the distance from America or their luxuriant lifestyles." The producers "made serious miscalculations as to what the critics and public would find acceptable or artistically excessive."

Television

1847 The Spread of the Eagle: Part 7, "The Serpent", part 8, "The Alliance," Part 9 "The Monument". Great Britain 1963. TV, b/w. BBC. Producer/director Peter Dews; designer: Clifford Hatts. 35 mm.

Keith Michell played Antony and Mary Morris was Cleopatra for this series.

1848 *Antony and Cleopatra*. RSC/Audio-Visual productions, 1974.

Directed by Trevor Nunn, the principal roles were played by Janet Suzman and Richard Johnson.

1849 Coursen, H.R. "Trevor Nunn's TV *Antony and Cleopatra*." *Maine Times* April 1975. Reprinted in *Shakespeare on Television*. Ed. J.C. Bulman and H.R. Coursen. Hanover, NH: UP of New England, 1988, p. 247.

This is the first time this play has been made for film or TV audiences. Nunn "allowed Antony and Cleopatra to grow, as they do in the play, through a series of ebbings and flowings, until Suzman convinces us that she is both the serpent of Old Nile and a woman, rising on her arias to reunion with her Antony." Richard Johnson as Antony was "only semiconvincing most of the way."

1850 *Antony and Cleopatra*.. BBC 1981. 171-minute color videotape.

Directed by Jonathan Miller, this is a part of the BBC Shakespeare series, principal roles by Colin Blakely and Jane Lapotaire.

1851 Lower, Charles B. "The Shakespeare Plays on TV: Antony and Cleopatra." *Shakespeare on Film Newsletter* 6 (1982): 2, 7.

This is an analysis of Jonathan Miller's production of the play for the BBC-TV.

1852 Bulman, J.C., and H.R. Coursen, eds. *Shakespeare on Television*. Hanover, NH: UP of New England, 1988. 324 pp.

This anthology reprints excerpts from several reviews of the Trevor Nunn and Jonathan Miller productions of the play for TV and Robert Speaight's review of Trevor Nunn's play with Janet Suzman and Richard Johnson.

1853 Coursen, H.R. "The BBC-TV *Antony and Cleopatra*: Far More Harm Than Good." *Shakespeare on Television*. Ed. J.C. Bulman and H.R. Coursen. Hanover, NH: UP of New England, 1988, pp. 272-73.

Coursen characterizes Miller's approach "all wrong" in this production: "Instead of an imaginative entrance to the production, we are subjected to opinion, a quasi-ideational format, delivered, literally, off-the-cuff, a revelation of directorial intention that defeats whatever dramatic intentions the production might reveal." Some of the problems here are "bad casting, obvious under-rehearsal, or the director's unwillingness to seek the tensions and conflicts of the play and its every scene." Coursen adds that "Miller's defense against what Shakespeare understood is to filter the play to us via Veronese, thereby rendering the play static, passionless, undramatic, and frozen in a time that Shakespeare should be allowed to transcend."

1854 David, Richard. "Shakespeare in Miniature: The BBC *Antony and Cleopatra*." *Shakespeare on Television*. Ed. J.C. Bulman and H.R. Coursen. Hanover, NH: UP of New England, 1988, pp. 139-144.

Jonathan Miller presented the play "with concentration and consistency." The play's "action all took place within enclosed spaces, mostly in small interiors ingeniously diversified by means of a minimum of decor, perhaps a single, drape, red or purple, in the background combining, in Venetian richness, with a clear yellow or viridian costume in the foreground." David feels that "the necessary miniaturisation for TV must be more damaging to *Antony and Cleopatra* than to any other play in the canon."

1855 Willis, Susan. *The BBC Shakespeare Plays: Making the Televised Canon.* Chapel Hill: U of North Carolina P, 1991. 362 pp.

Willis presents "a history of the BBC's production of Shakespeare's entire dramatic canon for television, a discussion of the producers and major directors who shaped the series, and a consideration of the technical elements of television that distinguish these productions from stage to film." Jonathan Miller, the producer, experimented "not only with a painterly look but also with a wooden platform as set and interpretive casting." He treated this a as "a tale of two prominent, self-indulgent figures who were past their prime." Colin Blakely's Antony "becomes the warrior who has fought for years, accentuating the contrast with young Octavius coming into his prime as Antony leaves his." Jane Lapotaire "brought to Cleopatra a fire without the standard sex goddess qualities, which Miller sought to avoid." Willis concludes that "producing the plays for television does not deny their theatrical power nor vie with it; rather it pays tribute to it."

Teaching Aids

1856 *Antony and Cleopatra*: Politics, Myth and Theater/*Coriolanus*: Politics and Tragedy. Distributor: Audio Learning.

These are lectures by J. Goode and T. Eagleton.

1857 "*Antony and Cleopatra*." Argo-ZPR.

This record by the Marlowe Society features the voices of J.R. Johnson and Irene Worth.

1858 *Antony and Cleopatra*. Caedmon-SRS. Record.

1859 Scenes from *Antony and Cleopatra*. Caedmon. A. Quayle and P. Brown.

1860 *Cleopatra*.

The reader for this recording is C. Luce.

1861 John Barrymore Reads Shakespeare. Phonodisc. Produced by Audio Rarities. Distributed by Dauntless International. 1 s., 12 in., 33 1/3 rpm.

1862 *Shakespearean Tragedy*. Filmstrip. Produced and distributed by Films for the Humanities, Inc 15 min. sound filmstrips.

1863 *The Works of Shakespeare*. Filmstrip. Distributed by Merit Audio Visual.

1864 *Scenes from the Tragedies*. Phonodisc. Distributed by Listening Library.

1865 *Shakespeare for Actors*. Phonodisc. Distributed by Listening Library.

1866 "Antony and Cleopatra." Shakespeare Living Library. Eleven parts. 30 min. each.

The second part deals with *A Midsummer Night's Dream* and *Antony and Cleopatra*.

1867 *Antony and Cleopatra*. 34 min., b/w. 1952

A British repertory company performs a number of scenes for the benefit of students.

1868 "Antony and Cleopatra." 15 min., b/w. 1957.

Produced by Charles Deane, the Old Vic Repertory Company presents the quarrel between Caesar and Antony (III.xiii).

1869 *Antony and Cleopatra*. [Audiocassette] New York: Caedmon: for the Shakespeare Recording Society, 1963.

1870 "Cleopatra." 34 min., col. 1965.

Rex Harrison shows how Shakespeare created one of his most complex characters. It includes readings from the play.

1871 "Antony and Cleopatra." "Approach to Shakespeare: A Series." 60 minutes.

This is a discussion of the play between A.R. Humphreys and R.A. Foakes and includes readings of key scenes.

1872 *Antony and Cleopatra*. [Videocassette]. 1980.

1873 *Approach to Shakespeare: A Series*. Phonotape. Produced and distributed by BFA Educational Media, 1982.

1874 Lower, Charles B. "The Shakespeare Plays on TV: *Antony and Cleopatra*." *Shakespeare on Film Newsletter* 6, 2 (1982): 2, 7.

This is an anlytical review of Jonathan Miller's production of the play for the BBC-TV/Time-Life series.

1875 *Antony and Cleopatra*. Videorecording. Los Angeles: Century Home Video, 1983.

1876 Gardner, Mary. "Teaching Antony and Cleopatra (A Personal Impression)." *Occasional Papers and Reviews, Shakespeare Society of Southern Africa* 2, 2 (1987): 11-12.

Not seen.

1877 Thomas, Peter. "An A Level Approach to *Antony and Cleopatra*." *Shakespeare and Schools Newsletter* (Cambridge Institute of Education) 2 (Spring 1987): 9.

Not seen.

1878 *The Roman Tragedies*. Directed by Noel Hardy. London: Inner London Educational Authority, 1988.

1879 *The Roman Tragedies*. Videorecording. Director: David Whitworth. Princeton: Films for the Humanities & Sciences, 1991.

1880 *Antony and Cleopatra*. Videorecording. Director: Jon Scoffield. Rennaissance Clessics. [U.K.}: Polygrama Video, 1992. Cast: Richard Johnson, Janet Suzman, Corin Redgrave, Patrick Stewart.

Adaptations and Synopses

1881 May, Thomas. *The Tragedie of Cleopatra Queen of Aegypt.* 1626.

1882 Sedley, Sir C. *Antony and Cleopatra.* London, 1677. Reprint. London: Cornmarket P, 1969.

This is "an exceedingly poor version of the story in rhyming verse."

1883 Dryden, John. *All for Love.* 1678. *Four Tragedies.* Edited by L.A. Beaurline and Fredson Bowers. Chicago and London: U of Chicago P, 1967, pp. 190-280.

This play dominated the stage to mid-nineteenth century either by itself or mixed with parts of Shakespeare's play.

1884 Capell, Edward, and David Garrick. *Antony and Cleopatra. . .* fitted for the Stage by abridging only. . . at the Theatre-Royal in Drury Lane, by his Majesty's Servants. London: J. & R. Tonson, 1758. Facsimile reprint. London: Cornmarket Press, 1969.

This is the text of the play adapted by Edward Capell for Garrick for a production in 1759.

1885 Brooke, Henry. *Antony and Cleopatra.* 1778. *Cornmarket Adaptations of Shakespeare's Plays.* Ed. H. Neville Davies. London: Cornmarket, 1970.

This adaptation contains only "one third, or perhaps one half" of Shakespeare's play.

1886 [Kemble, John Philip, ed.] *Tragedy of Antony and Cleopatra*; with Alterations and with Additions from Dryden; as Now perform'd at the Theatre-Royal, Covent-Garden. London: J. Barker, 1813.

Kemble adapted this text for his revival of the play on 15 November 1813.

1887 *Tragedy of Antony and Cleopatra*, arranged and adapted for Representation by Andrew Halliday. London: Tinsley Brothers, 1873.

This is Halliday's adaptation for Chatterton's 1873 production. In his preface, Halliday argued that "surely it is better to have a little of Shakespeare than none at all."

1888 "*Antony and Cleopatra*." *Senior Scholastic* 52, 11 (19 April 1948): 15-18.

This is a condensed version of the whole play.

1889 Chute, Marchette. "*Antony and Cleopatra*." *Tales from Shakespeare*. Cleveland: World Publishing Co., 1956, pp. 227-38.

Chute retells the story of the play.

1890 Yamazaki, Junko. "Adaptations of Shakespeare's Plays in the Restoration: The Structure of *All for Love*." *Ningen-bunka Kenkyu Nenpo* (Ochanomizu Women's University) 4 (1980): 187-99. In Japanese.

Not seen.

1891 Novak, Maximillian E. "Criticism, Adaptation, Politics, and the Shakespearean Model of Dryden' s *All for Love*." Roseann Runte, ed. *Studies in Eighteenth-Century Culture VII*. Madison: U of Wisconsin P for the American Society for Eighteenth-Century Studies, 1978, pp. 375-87.

This is an analysis of Dryden's adaptation in comparison with Shakespeare's play.

1892 Burnand, Sir Francis Cowley. "Antony and Cleopatra; or History and Her-story in a Modern Nilo-metre (1866)." *Nineteenth-Century Shakespeare Burlesques.* Selected by Stanley Wells. 5 vols. Wilmington, DE: Michael Glazier, 1978, IV, 141-91.

This is the only burlesque of the play in this collection.

1893 Morris, Margery. *Two Roman Stories from Shakespeare. Simplified and Retold.* Illustrations by Campbell Kennedy. Collins English Library, level 2. London: Collins, 1979. 48 pp.

Antony and Cleopatra is one of the plays re-told here.

1894 Garfield, Leon. "Antony and Cleopatra." *Shakespeare Stories II.* Illustrations by Michael Foreman. New York: Houghton Mifflin, 1995, pp. 67-100.

Garfield tells the story of the play for juveniles.

1895 Zacchi, Romana. "Dryden alla cordte di Cleopatra." *Antony and Cleopatra dal testo alla scena.* Ed. Mariangela Tempera. Bologna: Cooperative Libraria Universitaria Editrice, 1990, pp. 67-79.

Zacchi discusses Dryden's play as an adaptation of Shakespeare's tragedy.

Additional Entries

1896 Cibber, Colley. *Caesar in Egypt: A Tragedy*. London: J. Watts, 1736.

1897 Landor, W.S. *Antony and Octavius: Scenes for the Study*. London: Bradbury & Evans, 1856. 101 pp.

1898 Wilson, John Dover, ed. *Antony and Cleopatra*. Cambridge Pocket Shakespeare. Cambridge: Cambridge UP, 1959. 141 pp.

This edition gives the New Shakespeare text and glossary with corrections.

1899 Gardner, Stanley, ed. *Antony and Cleopatra*. London English Literature Series. London: U of London P, 1963. 224 pp.

Gardner provides a critical commentary on the play, the text with notes at bottom of pages, and three appendices on Shakespeare's philosophy of love, North's Plutarch, and the staging of the Monument scenes.

1900 Lindheim, Bogislav von. "Problems and Limits of Textual Emendation." *Festschrift für Walter Hübner*. Ed. Dieter Riesner and Helmut Gneuss. Berlin: Erich Schmidt Verlag, 1964, pp. 3-15.

Lindheim suggests that "a corrupt reading should never be considered in isolation; it should always be judged within a wider context." In his analysis of *Antony and Cleopatra*, 5.2.2-8, he proposes that Warburton's emendation of "dung" to "dug" "cannot stand the test of a closer and more careful examination of the facts."

1901 Campbell, O.J., and Edward G. Quinn, eds. *The Reader's Encyclopedia of Shakespeare*. New York: Thomas Y. Crowell, 1966. 1014 pp.

Campbell and Quinn provide "all the essential information available about every feature of Shakespeare's life and works." The entry on *Antony and Cleopatra* deals with the text, sources, criticism, stage history, and a bibliography and excerpts from selected criticism.

1902 *Antony and Cleopatra*. Aldus Shakespeare. Reader's Digest Books. New York: Funk and Wagnalls Paperback, 1967. liii, 189 pp.

This reprint gives notes at bottom of pages and a glossary at the back. Israel Gollancz discusses such matters as date, source of plot, and duration action. Henry Norman Hudson provides a critical introduction. There is a synopsis of the play J. Ellis Burdick and excerpts from Davies, Boas, Hallam, Skottowe and Bathurst.

1903 Wellwarth, George E., ed. "Antony and Cleopatra." *Themes of Drama: An Anthology*. New York: Thomas Y. Crowell, 1973, pp. 249-332.

Wellwarth uses this play to illustrate the theme of love. Notes art at bottom of pages.

1904 Sanders, Wilbur, and Howard Jacobson. "*Antony and Cleopatra*: Gentle Madam, No." *Shakespeare's Magnanimity, Four Tragic Heroes, Their Friends, and Families*. New York: Oxford UP, 1978, pp. 95-135.

In this and other plays about absolutist and self-absorbed men like Antony, Shakespeare emphasizes the need for "lenient accommodations to a middling world." These heroes display their moral values by engaging themselves with the world and the realities of human nature. For Jacobson, who has written the chapter on *Antony and Cleopatra*, Antony's story reveals his "purpose melted in the warm human glow, an unmanning, in the name of melancholy affectionateness, relentless and contagious." But Shakespeare suggests that "Cleopatra's way" is "delightful and even, in the cheerfullest possible way, inspiring." Cleopatra "is under no more illusion about the realities that were her past than she is about those that circumscribe her present. She is under no illusion, but in the natural buoyancy of her spirits, knowing neither cynicism nor dejection, she plumps for one."

1905 Shakespeare, William. *Antony and Cleopatra.* Designed and produced by Ronald King, with notes and an introductory essay, "The Elusive Absolute," by Keith Please. Guildford, England: Circle P Publications, 1979. xi, 59 pp.

This "is a limited edition of three hundred books with five hors commerce copies, forty artist's proofs, and ten marked Cricle Press, held for presentation; all the books signed by the artist."

1906 Whallon, William. *Problem and Spectacle: Studies in the Oresteia.* Heidelberg: Carl Winter, 1980. 159 pp.

Arguing that "the male-as-female conventions led Shakespeare and Aeschylus to depictions of algolagnia," Whallon believes that "Clytemnestra and Cleopatra answer to each as sadism and masochism do" and that "both Clytemnestra and Cleopatra find sexual pleasure in pain, the one in scourging, the other in being scourged." Clytemnestra "is of a stronger will than Agamemnon and Aegisthus; Cleopatra has drained Antony of his masculinity. Neither is simply womanish, and neither should sound so, or otherwise seem so."

1907 Tennenhouse, Leonard. *Power on Display: The Politics of Shakespeare's Genre.* New York and London: Methuen, 1986. 206 pp.

Interpreting Antony and Cleopatra as a post-Elizabethan play, Tennenhouse argues that the Jacobeans broke the bond between political and sexual desire. Women under James I did not provide "a legitimate means for access to membership in the corporate body." Hence the author considers this play as "Shakespeare's elegy for the signs and symbols which legitimized power. Of these, the single most important figure was that of the desiring and desired woman, her body her valued for its ornamental surface, her feet deeply rooted in the ground."

1908 Birch, Beverly. "Antony and Cleopatra." *Shakespeare's Stories: Histories.* Illustrated by Robin Green. New York: Peter Bedrick Books, 1988, pp. 102-26.

Birch retells the story of the play.

1909 *American Arias for Sopranos; A Diverse Selection of Arias from American Composers.* New York: G. Schirmer, 1990. 111 pp.

This collection includes Samuel Barber's "Give Me Some Music" from *Antony and Cleopatra.*

1910 Marra, Giulio. "Antony and Cleopatra: Storia e Storia." *Il Tragico e il Comico: Aspetti e saggi Shakespeariani.* Biblioteca di Cultura 430. Rome: Bulzoni Editore, 1991, pp. 311-35.

Not seen.

1911 Thompson, Ann, Thomas L. Berger, A.R. Braunmuller, Philip Edwards, and Lois Potter. "*Antony and Cleopatra.*" *Which Shakespeare: A User's Guide to Editions.* Milton Keynes and Philadelphia: Open UP, 1992, 32-36

This is a comparative assessment of the merits and limitations of eight editions of the play from John Dover Wilson's Cambridge to David Bevington's New Cambridge.

1912 Bloom, Allan D. "*Antony and Cleopatra.*" *Love and Friendship.* New York: Simon & Schuster, 1993, pp. 297-325.

Shakespeare "shows us the end of antiquity in the person of Antony, and he paints a picture, warts and all, that nevertheless is intended to fill us with sympathy, admiration, and perhaps even nostalgia, if this is a sentiment in which Shakespeare indulges himself." Antony's "erotic passions" are "the source of his capacity to apprehend a human satisfaction manifestly greater than that of being the world's sole ruler." The real "meaning of eros" in Antony and Cleopatra's lives lies in this: "Generation after generation they are renascent on a stage on this earth, and thus Shakespeare pricks our heart with longing, not for a lost world, but for something that is always accessible to man as man. This is really a triumph."

1913 Charney, Maurice. "*Antony and Cleopatra*." *All of Shakespeare*. New York: Columbia UP, 1993, pp. 289-98.

Charney has "conceived" this book "as a play-by-play and poem-by-poem commentary on Shakespeare's works" and seeks to "call the reader's attention to lines and passages not noticed before and to interrelations among plays." Shakespeare "wanted us to think that there is no way of separating the histrionic from the real: there is only a single reality in *Antony and Cleopatra* composed of many contradictory parts."

1914 Gillies, John. *Shakespeare and the Geography of Difference*. Cambridge: Cambridge UP, 1994. 255 pp.

Antony encounters the exotic "in the course of an outward or literally 'exorbitant' adventure beyond the geographical and moral confines of the Roman world." Antony is "master of an insidiously 'Asiatic' rhetorical style, admirer of Alexander, proponent of a subversively 'cosmopolitan' model of empire as against the hallowed Romanocentric model, spurner of his Roman wife and Roman mores, lover of a foreign queen, and finally leader of invading hordes from the East." For these reasons, "the 'historical' Antonius is a case-study in 'exorbitance'; the classic example of a conqueror who 'went too far'."

1915 Belsey, Catherine. "Cleopatra's Seduction." *Alternative Shakespeares 2*. Ed. Terence Hawkes. London and New York: Routledge, 1996, pp. 38-62.

Plutarch's Cleopatra "seduces Antony by her conversational skills, by participating equally with him in all his favourite diversions, and in the end by eliciting his pity." In Shakespeare's rendering, however, "Cleopatra is shown consistently exploiting the lack which is the cause of desire: 'she makes hungry/Where she most satisfies' (2.2.247-48); and she does it by promising what she frequently, but not predictably, fails to deliver, by being in consistently *elsewhere*."

1916 Blayney, Peter W.M., ed. *The Norton Facsimile: The First Folio of Shakespeare*. 2nd ed. New York: W. W. Norton, 1996. xxxvii, 928 pp.

Blayney's "Introduction to the Second Edition" (xxvii-xxxvii) updates and corrects Hinman's original introduction. It is divided into five major parts: The First Folio and Its Publisher; The Players and Their Manuscripts; The Proofreading; The Printing; Compositor Attributions. Blayney offers revised views of the London book trade, of play-manuscripts, and of the Folio's printing and proofreading. The new introduction ends with a table identifying Folio compositors and their work. The text of *Antony and Cleopatra* is found on pp. 340-68 (Folio pages) and 848-876 of this volume.

1917 Dusinberre, Juliet. "Squeaking Cleopatra: Gender and Performance in *Antony and Cleopatra*." *Shakespeare, Theory, and Performance*. Ed. James C. Bulman. London and New York: Routledge, 1996, pp. 46-67.

Dusinberre argues that "Shakespeare's highlighting of the boy's part in *Antony and Cleopatra* creates a drama which constantly comments on its own status as theatrical performance." The spectators "are implicated in its dissolution of gender boundaries, each individual challenged by the representations of sexuality on stage, and never allowed by the dramatist to submerge that sense of separation into a comfortable group consciousness." The playwright himself "engaged in a dialogue not only with inherited narratives, but with the political world, in which performance also, for James as for Elizabeth, encompassed the triumvirate of military, sexual, and theatrical action."

1918 Hiscock, Andrew. *Authority and Desire: Cries of Interpretation in Shakespeare and Racine*. New York: Peter Lang, 1996. 318 pp.

According to Hiscock, this play focuses "on the vulnerability and subjugation of the protagonists as they attempt to forestall the decline of passion and compassion in a world given over to statecraft." He suggests that "the colonising forces of Caesar re-interpret the empire as an arena of surveillance and containment; his regimentation of cultural life inevitably diminishes the rich multifariousness of the Eastern Empire, but it also makes restraint and organization available to a chaotic world."

1919 Holderness, Graham, Bryan Loughrey, and Andrew Murphy, eds. *Shakespeare: The Roman Plays*. Longman Critical Readers. London and New York: Longman, 1996. 200 pp.

This anthology of criticism contains excerpts from books by Leonard Tennenhouse, Janet Adelman, and Jonathan Dollimore.

1920 Loomba, Ania. "Shakespeare and Cultural Difference." *Alternative Shakespeares 2*. Ed. Terence Hawkes. London and New York: Routledge, 1996, pp. 164-91.

Loomba argues that, "like Othello, Shakespeare's Cleopatra is framed by a discourse of non-European devilry and libidinousness." This play "participates in recurrent contemporary debates on disorderly women, and it reveals the interaction of such debates with colonial ideologies by showing a feminized Egypt in a sexualized struggle for power against a masculine imperial Rome."

1921 Kahn, Coppélia. "Antony's Wound." *Roman Shakespeare: Warriors, Wounds, and Women*. Feminist Readings of Shakespeare. London and New York: Routledge, 1997, pp. 110-43.

Kahn argues that "in dramatizing the story of Antony and Cleopatra, Shakespeare fell heir to a legacy of representation on which the Latin curriculum and the *studia humanitatis* of the Renaissance were founded, a legacy organized by and centering on the mythic construction of Octavius Caesar as the destined victor in a prolonged power struggle who instituted the *pax romana* that ushered in the Christian era." Virgil believes that gods had ordained the victory of Octavius; "we can see it as exemplifying a pattern of agonistic rivalry already familiar in both Roman history and Shakespeare's Roman works." Octavius Caesar and Antony's "contest for master is at least as important in Shakespeare's play as the love story." In these two figures, "Shakespeare dramatizes the homosocial bonding that is Rome's hallmark. On an ideological level, this rivalry not only guides the sword that, however awkwardly, gives Antony the 'bungled' wound that sends him to a hero's death; it also guides his life."

1922 Wells, Stanley, ed. *Shakespeare in the Theatre. An Anthology of Criticism*. Oxford: Clarendon P, 1997. 338 pp.

In his anthology of theatre criticism, Wells has included Michael Billington's 1987 review of *Antony and Cleopatra*, directed by Peter Hall. For Billington, it is "not only the most intelligently spoken Shakespeare I have heard in years but it also contains two performances from Judi Dench and Anthony Hopkins that, in their comprehensive humanity, rank with Ashcroft and Redgrave at Stratford many moons ago." Hall's production "is about two middle-aged people—carnal, deceitful, often sad—seeking in love a reality greater than themselves."

Index

Listings refer to entry number, rather than page number.

About the author:

After receiving his Ph.D. in English from Syracuse University, Yashdip S. Bains has taught at universities in Canada, India, and the United States. In addition to numerous articles in scholarly journals, he has written two books on the authenticity of Shakespeare's first Quartos and one on English Canadian Theatre. Bains is an adjunct professor of English and Comparative Literature at the University of Cincinnati.